The Christology of John Owen

Richard W. Daniels

REFORMATION HERITAGE BOOKS
Grand Rapids, Michigan

Copyright © 2004
Reformation Heritage Books
2965 Leonard St., NE, Grand Rapids, Michigan 49525
Phone: 616-977-0599 / Fax: 616-285-3246
e-mail: orders@heritagebooks.org
website: www.heritagebooks.org

ISBN #1-892777-37-1

All rights reserved. Printed in the United States of America.

For additional Reformed literature, request a free book list from the above addresses.

Join all the glorious names
Of wisdom, love and pow'r,
That mortals ever knew,
That angels ever bore:
All are too mean to speak His worth
Too mean to set my Saviour forth.

Great Prophet of my God,
My tongue would bless Thy name:
By Thee the joyful news
Of our salvation came:
The joyful news of sins forgiv'n
Of hell subdued, and peace with heav'n.

Jesus, my great High Priest,
Offer'd His blood and died;
My guilty conscience seeks
No sacrifice beside:
His pow'rful blood did once atone
And now it pleads before the throne.

My dear Almighty Lord
My Conqueror and my King!
Thy matchless power and love,
Thy saving grace, I sing:
Thine is the power—oh, may I sit
In willing bonds beneath Thy feet.

Then let my soul arise,
And tread the tempter down;
My Captain leads me forth
To conquest and a crown.
The feeblest saint shall win the day,
Though death and hell obstruct the way.
—Isaac Watts

Acknowledgments

This work was originally published at the conclusion of a prolonged course of study at Westminster Theological Seminary in Philadelphia. I suppose it is understood that such a course of study will be challenging to say the least, but with the added complication of a severely debilitating disease suffered by my partner in this "pilgrimage below" we would have been quite overwhelmed if he who brings his children into the wilderness had not been pleased to carry us through it "on eagle's wings." With praise and thanksgiving to God for his abundant mercies, I would like to acknowledge my profound indebtedness to the instruments of his grace to myself and my wife, who had such a part in the completion of this project.

First and foremost I would like to thank my parents, who committed themselves at considerable sacrifice to undertake for our financial needs, and who have done everything in their power to encourage and support us. For a lifetime of favors far too numerous to mention here, the present work is affectionately dedicated to Cloyce and Theresa Daniels.

It would be impossible to recall all the benefits we have received from the brothers and sisters of Chelten Baptist Church. To the office-bearers, the members of the Glennside/Abington group, the "Fifties" Sunday School class, and many other special friends who upheld us with prayers and gifts and labors of love, we also say thank you.

Of the many valuable professors at Westminster Theological Seminary I would like to express my special gratitude to Dr. D. Clair Davis, my dissertation advisor, and Dr. Sinclair B. Ferguson. Without Dr. Davis' encouragement, I would not have enrolled in the doctoral program at all. His kindness and insight were a continuing source of support and stimulation during my studies. Dr. Davis first stimulated my interest in the problem of Puritan Christology in his course in English Puritanism. Dr. Ferguson confirmed my thinking that a study of the Christology of John Owen would be valuable, and afterwards gave considerable guidance in my research and writing. His expert editorial comments and meticulous proofreading of the dissertation are most appreciated, as is his friendship to us. I am also grateful for the advice of Dr. Richard A. Muller, who read and approved the dissertation for the degree.

A few years later the dissertation was read by my esteemed friend and colleague in the New England Reformed Fellowship, Dr. Douglas Vickers, who lovingly scolded me for not endeavoring to get it published. His advice for revising the work and encouragement in getting it published is also greatly appreciated. A great blessing to me also has been the friendship of Rev. David Green, moderator of the New England Reformed Fellowship, and Reformed Congregational Fellowship. A true "Owenian," David has been a great encouragement in my life and ministry, and in the publication of this work. I wish to thank Dr. Joel Beeke of Reformation Heritage Books for agreeing to publish the work and for his editorial direction. Dr. Beeke's expertise in Owen and in the current state of studies in the Post-reformation era renders his approval of the work especially encouraging. Finally, I would like to acknowledge the great help of my wife and best friend, Sandy, who has returned many deprivations with many more prayers for me and for this work.

Some changes have been made in the text, the most substantial of these being the addition of the chapter on "The Christ-centered Church." This had been intended for the original, but was not completed in time. Other additions include the section on "The Free Offer of the

Acknowledgments

Gospel," and more footnotes referring to Christological works by Owen's contemporaries. Seventeenth-century spellings have been retained in quoted portions throughout the work.

I pray that this book will encourage someone to "take up and read" Owen for themselves, and so be blessed as I have been in learning from one who had looked so earnestly at the face of Jesus Christ.

Richard W. Daniels
Wanchese, North Carolina

Table of Contents

Acknowledgements

Chapter
1. Introduction 1
2. "Who Do Men Say That I Am?" 22
3. "Who Do You Say That I Am?" 49
4. "Flesh and Blood Has Not
   Revealed it unto You" 76
5. The Doctrine of the Trinity 94
6. Owen's Proof of the Deity of Christ 117
7. God's Eternal Counsels 147
8. Creation and Providence 178
9. *Cur Deus Homo:* The Manifestation of the
   Glory of God 194
10. "Beginning with Moses" 230
11. "God was Manifested in the Flesh" 262
12. "He Ascended into Heaven" 309
13. "A Priest Forever" 329
14. "He Who Speaks from Heaven" 385
15. "Thy Throne, O God" 422
16. A Christ-Centered Church 450
17. "To Live is Christ" 481
18. Conclusion 516

Works cited 524
Bibliography 531

CHAPTER

1

Introduction

There are three reasons why the modern reader might question the usefulness or even the legitimacy of a book length study of the Christology of a seventeenth-century English Puritan. First, there is the question of fact: did English Puritanism even have a Christology, and if so, did it advance Christology beyond that inherited from sixteenth century Reformed theology? Second, there is the question of orthodoxy: if the Puritans had an interest in Christology, it was fatally flawed, a strange amalgam of the Bible, Aristotelian metaphysics, Roman law, and late medieval covenantalism. Like the Chalcedonian Christology of antiquity, it bore no resemblance to the Jesus pictured in the gospels. Even granting the truthfulness of the Chalcedonian formula, Christological developments associated with "Reformed Scholasticism" have been disputed from the sixteenth century to the present. Third, there is the question of relevance: assuming the existence and orthodoxy of a Puritan Christology, of what value is it to the modern Christian? These are important questions, to which we now turn.

The Need for a Puritan Christology
In spite of a renewal of interest in English Puritanism in the last half of the twentieth century, there remains a se-

vere deficiency of studies in Puritan Christology. While a number of significant studies exist on the Christologies of the Fathers and Doctors of the church, of the Reformers and of a number of modern theologians, no study has yet been published on the Christology of any major figure in English Puritanism. To some extent this may be due to Marshall Knappen's assertion in his influential study, *Tudor Puritanism*, that under the mighty influence of John Calvin the Puritans showed a "surprising lack of christological thought" and that the person of Christ "figures very little in their literature" (Knappen 1939, 376). Perry Miller likewise minimized the role of Christ for the Puritans (Miller 1939, 45).

This view of English Puritan thought is exemplified by John Eusden's remarks in his introduction to *William Ames' Marrow of Theology*. Referring to Luther and the seventeenth-century English Puritans, Eusden says,

> Perhaps the greatest contrast occurs, at least where one reads Ames, in concepts about the person and work of Christ. The Christo-centrism of Martin Luther is not shared by most English Puritans. Christ for them was a necessary part of the divine-human drama, but they did not feel a deep, confessional attraction towards him as a divine person.... The Puritans did not walk on the Lutheran *via cruces* [way of the cross]; or if they did they traveled hurriedly and often without imagination. The incarnation for the Puritans was not a mystery in which man should lose himself; it was to be explained and placed before man as an article of faith. (Eusden 1968, 20)

With regard to the incarnation Eusden alleges that Luther "chose to present the incarnation more simply, yet more profoundly, as the offering of divine love before which sinful men stood in awe and in thanksgiving," suggesting that the Puritans, by contrast, assumed a confident posture claiming to "know all about the incarnation." He also contrasts the Puritans' emphasis upon the ascension and exaltation of Christ with "divine participation in a humble life, the agony of the cross, or the role of suffering in redemption" (Eusden 1968, 21). The present work will demonstrate that, with respect to one of the most eminent Puritans, these remarks simply do not fit.

More recent studies have made a little progress toward reversing this misunderstanding of the importance of Christ in Puritanism.[1] The year after the publication of Eusden's work on William Ames, Bert Affleck Jr. argued the existence of Christocentricity in the theology of one of the most influential of English Puritans, Richard Sibbes. Affleck points out that Sibbes' "doctrine of God demands a Christocentric explication," that his "pneumatology requires a Christological base," that his "soteriology assumes a Christological reference," and finally that "ecclesiology also, in Sibbes' thought, is Christology" (Affleck, Jr. 1969, 25-26). Affleck understandably renounces any claim to emphasize the centrality of Christology in all Puritans, confining his comments to Sibbes. However, we would ask, given the great influence of Sibbes may we not expect to see his Christocentrism reflected in a good portion of his scholars?

A study of Puritan piety by Jonathan Won has emphasized the great significance of the doctrine of the believer's union and communion with Christ. While noting differences with Calvin in terms of the comparative emphasis given to the doctrines of union versus communion, Won shows that the English Puritans he studied retained many of the themes of Calvin's thought. The differences lay in their greater stress upon communion with Christ, and upon his humanity. The Puritans "capitalized on the humanness of Christ in order to bring Christ close to believers as one who had shared the same miseries and struggles in his incarnate life." "Their devotion was...oriented to touch people's lives where they hurt" (Won 1989, 351-54).

The present study deals with the Christology of one of the very foremost of the English Puritans, John Owen. Yet, even in the case of Owen we find that, as with many other studies of Puritan theology, Christology has been given an emphasis behind that given to the Holy Spirit. For instance, Godfrey N. Vose, in a very helpful study of Owen, says,

> Puritan Christology has sometimes been underestimated. Owen spends considerable theological effort in detailed expositions of the Person and work of Christ and an enquiry into his doctrine at this point may well serve to qualify Knappen's judgment that the "Puritans did not possess a high Christology." (1963, 315)

Nevertheless, Vose says that the doctrine of the Holy Spirit "undoubtedly has first place" in emphasis in Owen's theological system.

> Does this mean that Christology is relegated to the background in Owen's thought? Not at all. Owen would insist that the Holy Spirit is also to be recognized properly as 'the Spirit of Christ'; that it is the work of the Spirit to testify of Christ and to glorify him. But because it is the Holy Spirit who brings home to the reader the truth and authority of Scripture, who empowers the church, who makes good the covenant in regenerating and sanctifying the individual according to its terms, therefore his Person and work must be understood as the hinge of the New Testament, the divine means by which the believer is led into all truth. (1963, 315)

Vose says of Owen, that "over-shadowing all his other interests and studies," the doctrine of the Holy Spirit "was his theological concern, and this is why he deserves to be called the Protestant theologian of the Holy Spirit" (1963,

314). Whether Owen deserves to be called the Protestant theologian of the Holy Spirit is not the question here, but whether this concern overshadowed all his other interests and studies.

Dewey Wallace, in "The Life and Thought of John Owen to 1660," has accurately pointed out the "Christocentric cast" in Owen's thought, observing that Owen "never allowed his theological work to begin or end with any other point than the central point of Christian piety itself, the sense of the grace of Christ." Wallace rightly observes concerning Owen:

> ...the Christocentric emphasis which we have seen important in his discussion of the nature of God comes clearly to the fore. In all his discussions of the work of Christ we see that his main concern is that Christ's work may become central in any discussion of God's grace or man's piety. (Wallace 1965, 276)

Interestingly, Wallace attributes Owen's Christocentric cast to his doctrine of limited atonement (1965, 336), a doctrine that is usually, but wrongly, identified with a departure from Christocentrism. One criticism of this excellent presentation of Owen may be directed at Wallace's assertion that Owen's life work was a reaction to the Arminian controversy, a much too narrow and negative motivation for Owen's extensive labors.

Owen demonstrates a remarkable balance in his theological interests. He is thoroughly Trinitarian in his thinking, convinced that the Triune God has chosen to deal with man by way of a mediator. Whether the action is directed from God to us or from us to God, Christ is the focus.[2] True Trinitarian thinking, it would seem, must be Christocentric, and Christocentric thinking, Trinitarian. Owen's emphasis upon the Holy Spirit, as great as that was, was primarily for what the Spirit accomplishes: the restoration and transformation of fallen men through the knowledge of God in Christ. This is the "hinge" of Owenian thought, as Owen believed it was the sum and substance of all biblical religion.

Modern Trends in Christology
Rejection of the Christocentric-Trinitarian Paradigm
At this point, the modern student of current trends in Christological thought might be assuring himself of what he suspected already, that a study of Owenian Christology would be an exercise better suited for the antiquarian than the modern seeker of spiritual reality. These concerns and the reasons for them are well summarized by Paul W. Newman in his work, *A Spirit Christology*.[3] Voicing the objections of a growing number of writers representing a general trend in modern non-evangelical Christology, Newman makes an extended plea for a "paradigm shift in Christian theology."

According to Newman, there was a "shift in paradigm in the early centuries of Christian tradition...from theocentricity to christocentricity" (Newman 1987, 5). This Christocentric Trinitarian paradigm is presently "in crisis," because recent biblical studies, theological insights and cultural sensitivity demand that orthodox Christology, and the Christocentric and redemptive theology associated with it, be seen as aberrations and departures from pristine Christian teaching. In other words, Newman is arguing for a second "paradigm shift"—a complete abandonment of Trinitarian thinking together with the doctrine of redemption founded on belief in the Triune God and the incarnation. To these arguments, to related issues not raised by Newman, and to the reasons we believe a study of Owen concerning them is helpful, we now turn.

One argument advanced for the abandonment of the traditional paradigm is the challenge to the traditional belief in salvation history. This challenge arises from the belief that the Old Testament Scriptures have a meaning independent from those later Christian interpretations that saw Christ in the Old Testament, and from the belief that the practice of regarding the Hebrew Scriptures as the "Old" Testament which is authenticated and completed by the Christian Scriptures is "difficult to justify" (Newman 1987, 5-6). However, Owen endeavored to show that when they are allowed to speak for themselves, these Scriptures unmistakably promise, and with ever increasing clarity describe, a coming Messiah who provided a central theme for rabbinical commentary of the sacred volume and, more importantly, the foundation for the faith of the Old Testament people. The Christocentric interpretation of the Hebrew Scriptures, far from diminishing their significance invests them with a significance, a unity, a purpose, and an authority which is difficult or impossible to be preserved for them otherwise. Owen demonstrates that, assuming the Hebrew Scriptures to be the Word of God, the practice of regarding them as the Old Testament needing completion by the New is not only well justified, but actually indicated in the Old Testament itself (as well as numerous New Testament references). Owen never held, however, that they needed to be "authenticated" by the new, as they were always "self-authenticating," like every true revelation from God (4:8-9, 73-82).

Secondly, it is argued that the New Testament authors and Jesus himself were thoroughly monotheistic and theocentric—a theocentricity "not easily reconciled with the views of Jesus that were developed in classical christology" (Newman 1987, 7). This supposed conflict between monotheism / theocentricism on the one hand, and Trinitarianism / Christo-centricism on the other, is an ancient one, revived in the sixteenth century, and receiving Owen's critical examination and biblical reply.

A third reason given is the "unbiblical" character of

incarnational Christology: "The crux of the matter is whether or not the New Testament contains the idea of a personal divine being who was pre-existent to Jesus, who in the Incarnation is identified as Jesus and who is subsequently post-existent as the risen Christ" (Newman 1987, 7). This is indeed the "crux of the matter." It is at just this point that Owen can be of help. The seventeenth century witnessed many who argued that incarnational theology was unbiblical. For the most part, the arguments raised in the seventeenth century are not materially different from those employed ever since, and the rejoinders from their orthodox opponents were often more painstakingly argued than those heard in the modern debate.

Fourth, it is alleged that classical orthodoxy is motivated by the desire to prevent reductions in the church's faith. "It seems to be a commonly accepted tradition to regard any variation from classical orthodoxy as 'reductions' although, in fact, they may include meanings and emphases which are missing or reduced in emphasis in the classical formulas themselves" (Newman 1987, 8). The question is, do the classical formulas actually result in the loss of anything genuinely enriching, or do they rather preserve that in the Christian faith that provides it with, in the words of Paul, "unsearchable riches"? Again, the modern critic has put his finger on an important issue, but perhaps the raising of this objection is more the outcome of a failure in the church to make those unreachable riches known, than it is due to the classical formulas. This, at any rate, was Owen's fear: that the church was becoming impoverished through the failure of its pastors to preach, and of "ordinary Christians" to take pains to understand, the doctrine of the person and work of Christ.

Fifth, salvation is reduced to a "single event." The doctrine of the incarnation arose in connection with the doctrines of creation and fall. Since these two doctrines are "no longer tenable," it would seem the idea of a once-for-all act of God in the incarnation and atonement must be scrapped as well (Newman 1987, 10). This objection raises at least two problems. First, it is quite inappropriate to label the saving work of Christ a "single event," at least in terms of its Reformed expression. More important, however, is the significance of the creation and fall. Whether these doctrines are "tenable" is a question of biblical authority; how they relate to the doctrine of the incarnation and atonement is a question of hermeneutics and theological method. In the current Christological debate the question of presuppositions constitutes a limiting factor, as far as any real resolution is concerned. Owen was keenly aware of the ultimate importance of the question of theological presuppositions for the seventeenth-century debate, and therefore labored to demonstrate the authority of Scripture.

A sixth charge is that classical Christology is docetic. The heart of this objection is the alleged difficulty in accounting for Jesus' humanness given the Chalcedonian principle of his impersonality (*anhypostasia*).[4] A. N. S. Lane has accused Chalcedon of failing to maintain "a practical belief in Christ as fully human" by denying the human limitations of Christ (Lane 1982, 269). The Chalcedonian formula allegedly suffers the problem of "incoherence." As Newman argues,

> How he could be a real human being and still be the Second Person of the Holy Trinity raises the problem of incoherence. The British authors of *The Myth of God Incarnate* and its sequels have addressed this question with particular intensity. They have asked if the idea of a real human being who is also really God is not the same class of incoherent ideas as square-circles. They have suggested that the idea of incarnation is valuable as a metaphor for the way in which God is present but insist that the idea of Incarnation, with a capital "I" meaning God become the human being Jesus, is incoherent because

"speaking of God being a part of his own creation or a part of that creation being God...does seem...to involve a logical self-contradiction. (Newman 1987, 15-16 [quoting Wiles 1979, 6])

Such an objection, however, ignores the concept of "mystery," a concept logically arising from scriptural teaching concerning the incomprehensibility of God and the creaturely limitations of human knowledge (Bavinck 1951, 13). Begging the question, it unwarrantably dismisses the biblical evidence for the incarnation, while misrepresenting the doctrine itself. By painting it in such simplistic and self-contradictory terms, it distorts the doctrine as seriously, if not as crassly, as did medieval portraits of a three-headed trinity. Owen can help us in all of these respects.

Seventh, Chalcedon is accused of being "ontological," as opposed to the "functional" New Testament. A. N. S. Lane says "this criticism depends for its force on the assumption that New Testament Christology is purely functional and not at all ontological. But this is not so" (Lane 1982, 263-64; cf. Fuller, 1965, 247-50). As we will see, one of Owen's strengths is his intense interest in the relation of the ontological and the economic in Christology. However, Lane also points to the Greek concept of Divine immutability as exerting an unscriptural influence upon Chalcedon. The resultant doctrine of an impassible Son united with a suffering man he rejects as "unashamedly" but unscripturally dualistic (Lane 1982, 265-68).[5]

Another objection is the soteriological crisis "arising from the traditional logic of forgiveness." It is argued that the "Latin" doctrine of the atonement by sacrifice and satisfaction is "a departure from Hebrew thinking about expiation and salvation" (Newman 1987, 17). Hebrew thinking and Jesus' own teaching, it is claimed, emphasized forgiveness upon repentance, without satisfaction for sin. Consequently, "If the logical necessity for a fully divine sacrifice to be made in order to expiate sin were relinquished, the christological debate about the deity of Christ might lead to a different conclusion" (Newman 1987, 18). Again, there is nothing in this objection that was not raised by the Socinians of the seventeenth century. If John Owen is correct, the doctrine of satisfaction will not be so easily dismissed, nor will man's situation as scripturally defined be so simply alleviated.

Newman raises other problems that, no doubt, need addressing. What he denominates a helpful "paradigm shift," however, is remarkably similar to what John Owen identified as an endeavor to "destroy the foundations" of the Christian religion. While the authors of *The Myth of God Incarnate* deny any desire to go back to the "old liberalism," there is very little that is new in their objections to classical Christology. The reader may not agree that these objections constitute, in Owen's words, "long-since-exploded sophisms, inconsequent consequences, weak objections, fully, soundly answered many a day since," but if Owen's work demonstrates that these premises are invalid, that Chalcedonian Christology is what it intends to be (namely, the minimal rather than the exhaustive description of the incomprehensible mystery of the person of the God-man described in the pages of Holy Scripture), that it is possible to go "beyond Chalcedon" without going against it, and that a Trinitarian Christocentric theology is both scripturally sound and satisfying to man's deepest religious needs, we will be forced to ask ourselves whether Christian theology needs to adopt a new paradigm or to return to the earnest, prayerful investigation and proclamation of Christ's unsearchable riches.

Rejection of "Reformed Orthodoxy"
There is a "second front" against the Christology of Puritanism, however: those who place some value upon the Christology of Chalcedon but oppose the particular emphases and doctrines characteristic of seventeenth-century

Calvinism. Along this second front there are three principal forces: first, neo-orthodox opposition to orthodoxy's loss of Christocentrism; second, the opposition of Arminians, modern "Amyraldians," and others to Puritanism's "covenant theology," with its "limited atonement"; and third, other opponents of the "satisfaction" theory of the atonement.

Neo-orthodoxy's grievance with orthodoxy is interesting because of its own concern for Christocentricity. Two areas in particular where Neo-orthodoxy finds fault with orthodoxy in its failure to be Christocentric are its doctrine of revelation, in which the Bible is allegedly substituted for Christ, and in its doctrine of redemption, in which Christ is said to be lost in an absolute decree. We see a neo-orthodox cast, for example, in Bert Affleck's approval of Sibbes' Christocentricity. When Dr. Affleck says Sibbes' doctrine of Scripture is Christocentric, he does so because in his view Sibbes distinguished "between the Christocentric Word and the scriptural Word" (Affleck, Jr. 1969, 168). The Christocentric Word of God is the gospel; the Scriptures are a "mode" of the Word. When Protestant orthodoxy equated the Scriptures with the Word of God, they departed from the Christocentric doctrine of revelation taught by the Reformers, and "led us down a path to a theology to be learned and debated but not compelling enough to be lived" (Affleck, Jr. 1969, 168). In his valuable *Post-Reformation Reformed Dogmatics*, Richard A. Muller has argued, against neo-orthodoxy, that orthodoxy's doctrine of revelation "is essentially christocentric in its implications—and it clearly shows that the Protestant orthodox of the sixteenth and seventeenth centuries are not the purveyors of a rationalistic approach to theological system" (Muller 2003, 406). Muller had argued this point in an earlier article in which John Owen appears as an example of an orthodox theologian who follows "very closely the doctrine of Calvin in relating Christ, the Logos, the essential Word, to the Word of God written" (Muller 1983, 313-16.). Muller says the orthodox "with few exceptions, demonstrate a far richer conception of the meaning of the Word of God than one would expect" from the critique made by Emil Brunner (Muller 1983, 318).

The second doctrine over which the neo-orthodox contend with seventeenth century orthodoxy is the place of Christ in the decree of election. It is argued by J. K. S. Reid, for instance, that while Calvin began to introduce the idea of Christ as having a crucial role in election, later Calvinism lost this idea, rather than developing it. Referring to Calvin's remarks that "Christ represents himself as the author of election," Reid says,

> This is indeed a remarkable statement, and had it attained in Calvinism the place of importance to which its character entitles it, there is little question that much of the controversy over Predestination would have been avoided. But in fact, it only appears once in the *Institutes*, the flicker of a flame which promises light, but whose promise is never fulfilled. (1948, 8-9)

In failing to develop these seminal ideas of Calvin, orthodoxy failed to "achieve for Christ a secure and effective part in the design and preparation of the decree of election" (1948, 10, 16). Reid's painful conclusion to his evaluation of orthodoxy is that

> As one passes in review the various roles assigned to Christ in election, it is difficult not to despair. In every one, the function of Christ is to carry out something already fixed and definitive. At one end of the scale, Christ is merely the exhibitor of a decision already made in an eternity in which He has Himself been, even if existent, at least inoperative. At the other end, His role is to give effect to a decree in whose formation He has apparently had no hand. It is the *haereditas damnosa* [ruinous inheri-

tance] taken over from Calvin himself: no less here than there, decree is prior to grace. (1948, 16)

Interestingly, he points to Melanchthon's phrase, "*hoc est Christum cognoscere, beneficia eius cognoscere*" ["this is to know Christ, to know His benefits"], and laments that Calvinism worked out the doctrine of predestination "without the corrective influence of Melanchthon's principle" (1948, 166). Whatever may be true of continental Calvinism (and it would be difficult to argue that Heidelberg theology supports Reid's judgment at this point), Reid's criticism simply does not apply to John Owen, as the present work will show (see Muller 1986, 11, 33-34).

Another form of opposition to the Christology of seventeenth-century Calvinism is particularly aimed at its doctrines of the work of Christ and the covenant of grace. Modern followers of the Dutch theologian Jacobus Arminius, for instance, view Calvinism as a limitation of the gospel, and the Calvinistic doctrine of the atonement as a "logical consequence" of the doctrine of absolute predestination rather than the Bible's own teaching on the subject (Pinnock 1975, 12). Many modern students of theology express a high regard for the teachings of John Calvin, but point to "Calvinism" in its seventeenth century expression as representing a serious departure from his theology. The doctrine of "limited atonement" is one of the areas in which this departure occurs, with tremendous repercussions in the area of faith and assurance (Armstrong 1969, 130-60; Kendall 1979, 210-13). Like the Amyraldians of the seventeenth century, many Christians are desirous of a "middle ground" between Calvinism and Arminianism in the teaching of "hypothetical universalism" where the sovereignty and grace of God are exalted but the alleged difficulties attached to the doctrine of "limited atonement" are eliminated (Pinnock 1989, passim). The Christological issues at the heart of this controversy receive an in-depth analysis by John Owen.

Still another form of opposition asserts that the Protestant doctrine of the atonement, as a work of penal substitution, is at best one possible motif or image among other equally or more important ones. The advocate of this position may be a confessed Trinitarian, but opposes the doctrine that the atonement is a substitutionary expiation and propitiation for sin. One who represents this type of thinking is John Driver in his work *Understanding the Atonement*. In this work, Driver argues that the Bible employs a "plurality of images" in its description of the work of Christ. "The apostolic community" he argues, allowed all of these images,

> to stand in a complementary relationship rather than attempting to reduce them to a single theory or dogmatic statement. The value of any one of these images depends on allowing it to remain in relationship to all the rest. Insofar as they have been held together, they have communicated powerfully the meaning of the death and resurrection of Christ. (Driver 1986, 18-19)

Among the various images and motifs Driver expounds are the "conflict victory liberation motif," the "vicarious suffering motif," various "archetypal images" including "representative man, pioneer, forerunner, and first born," the motifs of martyr, sacrifice, redemption purchase, expiation and the wrath of God, reconciliation, justification, and the adoption-family image (Driver 1986, 19-28). When Driver maintains that these images exist in a "complementary relationship," must be "held together," and must not be reduced to a single dogmatic statement, he is arguing for a multi-faceted but not for a systematic understanding of the atonement. Consequently, while they may be held together to contribute to the understanding of the work of Christ, they are not held together to contribute to the mutual understanding of each other.

It is a mistake, however, to view the Protestant doctrine of the atonement as consisting only of the motif of sacrifice and satisfaction. If it has seemed such, it is for two reasons: first, the doctrine of satisfaction has a certain priority in a systematic understanding of the work of Christ; secondly, this priority has made it a "rock of offense," and a point of contention. The Puritans, for all their conflict with the Socinians of their day over this issue, cannot be convicted of confining the work of Christ to that of making a propitiation for sin. In particular, we will see Owen holding together the many wonderful aspects of the Savior's work in an organic and not merely a mechanical way, and doing so with remarkable consistency, skill, and imagination.

A Practical Study
"It is all well and good to be orthodox, but the modern Christian isn't really interested in the hair-splitting 'ivory tower' speculations of 'dry as dust' Puritans." The modern Christian may yet inquire how a study of a Puritan's Christology could be of any "practical" value. There is a substantial academic reason for stressing the *practical* value of the study of John Owen. The Puritans never failed to stress, to make explicit, the experiential and practical dimensions implicit in Calvin's definition of man's highest wisdom as the knowledge of God and of himself (*Institutes*, I. 1. i.). William Ames, for example, defined theology as the "doctrine of living unto God" (Ames 1629, 77-78), while Owen, more closely resembling Calvin, to Calvin's two-part definition of true wisdom added "skill to walk with God" (2:80). It was such a conviction of the necessity of the practice of the Christian life that led to the characteristic "plain style" of the Puritan sermon. In the typical Puritan sermon, following the discovery and assertion of the theological doctrine contained in the text, came the "use" or application of the doctrine to the hearer. Yet, there was a danger in the em-

phasis upon "practical divinity"; practice might take precedence over divinity until divinity (i.e., doctrine) became unimportant. People might forget the principle that, as Owen said, "Gospel truth is the only root where on gospel holiness will grow" (7:188). There is reason to believe that this transformation was taking place within the churches of seventeenth-century English dissent, as John Owen was painfully aware. What is true of the practical emphasis in Puritan theology in general is especially true of Owenian Christology. The strong practical emphasis in Owen's Christology is not an interesting sidelight, but one of its distinguishing characteristics. In a deliberate attempt to build his theological edifice upon Christ, Owen firmly secures his practical divinity upon the foundation of Christology, and shows that Christ's person is the center for Christian ethics. In so doing, Owen secures his Puritan practice from dislodging the theological foundation upon which it was built.

How will it benefit us practically? First, it will answer many of our questions about Christ. Owen was a genius with an encyclopedic knowledge of the Scriptures and of the great theological systems available in his day, to which were added amazing logical prowess and deep spiritual devotion. Andrew Thompson said that Owen "makes you feel when he has reached the end of his subject, that he has also exhausted it" (1:xxxviii). While Owen would be the first to confess that he had but scanned the shoreline of this great ocean of the knowledge of God to be obtained from the Scriptures, nevertheless his ability to address and elucidate many of the issues still under discussion should be very profitable to us. Secondly, this study will illustrate Owen's manner of edifying the Christian through the exposition of the "unsearchable riches of Christ." In particular, we will see how Owen put into practice his conviction that the mysteries of the gospel, far from being doctrines to be confessed but having no great impact upon the Christian life, are actually the most important for him to know and believe, as constituting the true center for all of his faith and life.

The Plan of this Book

One of the great difficulties in the exposition of so prolific an author as Owen is that of clearly presenting the data gathered from his many works without distorting his thought by lifting his words out of their contexts and forcing them onto a foreign grid (i.e., that of the interpreter). The present work builds upon a grid which, for the most part, was suggested by Owen himself, namely, the outline of a catechism prepared by him in 1645, with modifications suggested by the outlines of his major Christological works entitled *Christologia* (1679), and *Meditations and Discourses on the Glory of Christ, in his Person, Office, and Grace* (1684). The only major departure from this is in the placing of the study of Christ's offices of Prophet, Priest, and King after the doctrine of the two states. This saves needless repetition and enables us more easily to observe the significance of the person of Christ to those offices, and their role in redemptive history.

The second chapter will provide the reader with an overview of seventeenth-century developments that created the background for Owen's Christological labors. With this as a backdrop, chapter 3 will present a historical and partly thematic overview of Owen's Christological works. After this introductory survey, our study will follow the pattern presented in his catechism. We begin with a study of prolegomena, where we will find the presuppositions and methodology of Owen's theology. Following Owen's example, we turn next to the study of the Trinity, where we will note the great, pervasive, significance of the doctrine of the Trinity for Owen's theology. From a general study of the doctrine of the Trinity, we will consider more carefully Owen's proof of the Deity of Christ. After addressing the doctrine of God, we follow Owen in turning our attention to the works of God, which he divides into internal works, such as the decree (chapter 7), and external works, such as creation and providence (chapter 8). Owen's exposition of these doctrines is remarkable for its profound, rarely equaled Christocentricity. Chapter 9 explores Owen's answer to the question, why did God the Son become incarnate. It is only as we understand the answer to this question, which focuses upon the work that Christ came to do, that we can understand the doctrine of Christ's person.

From a systematic study of the objectives of Christ's incarnation, we turn in chapter 10 to examine Owen's interpretation of the Old Testament revelation of the coming Messiah. This naturally leads to the culmination of this Messianic hope in the manifestation of God in the flesh. In chapter 11 we will examine carefully Owen's doctrine of the incarnation and its significance upon the earthly life of Jesus. Our examination of Owen's teaching of the "two states" of Christ concludes with a look at the Mediator's glorious exaltation. At this point, we turn to consider the work of Christ in much greater detail through the study of Owen's doctrine of Christ's three-fold mediatorial office of Prophet, Priest, and King (chapters 13-15). Such a study of Owen's doctrine of the person and work of Christ cannot be completed without observing his application of Christology to ecclesiology and the Christian life (chapters 16 and 17).

Finally, one bibliographical point needs to be emphasized. All references to the *Works of John Owen* in this book are to the standard 1850 William H. Gould edition in 24 volumes, as reprinted by The Banner of Truth (volumes 1-16) and Baker Book House (volumes 18-24). Readers using the seven-volume set of Owen's *Hebrews* commentary should remember that its volumes 1-7 correspond to volumes 18-24 of the standard edition. Volume 17, containing Owen's *Latin* works, is very rare. Its English contents have been published in volume 16 of the Banner of Truth edition, which is cited in this text. Its Latin contents have been translated by Stephen P. Westcott in *Biblical Theology* (Pittsburgh: Soli Deo Gloria Publications, 1994). Current electronic editions of Owen's works omit volume 17, which means that their volumes 17-23 correspond to volumes 18-24 in the standard edition. Therefore, anyone wishing to find Owen quotations on an electronic edition should subtract 1 from numbers greater than 17 cited in this text, and then use the program's "search" capability to locate the correct page.

---

[1] This was true when first written in 1990. Although we know of no major work devoted to the Christology of any single Puritan theologian, Richard A. Muller's work on *The Trinity of God* (volume 4 of his *Post-Reformation Reformed Dogmatics*) leaves no room to doubt the importance of Christology to Puritanism. See Muller 2003, 4:83-332.

[2] Cf. Richard Sibbes: "God shines in the face of Christ, and as he comes down and makes himself known to us in his Son, so we must go up to him in his Son..." (Sibbes 1862-64, 7:346).

[3] Newman's *Spirit Christology* is quoted here for two reasons: first, it is a modern text which neatly summarizes the most recent literature from a non-orthodox perspective; second, his case against orthodoxy, combined with his proposed alternative, provides a striking parallel to the opposition made against orthodoxy in the time of John Owen. For a more detailed analysis of classical Christology and its modern critics, see Donald Macleod's *The Person of Christ* (Macleod, 1998).

[4] "**anhypostasis** (ἀνυπόστασις): *impersonality*, or (more precisely) *non-self-subsistence*; a term applied to the human nature of Christ insofar as it has no subsistence or person in and of itself but rather subsists in the person of the Word for the sake of the incarnation" (Muller 1985, 35).

[5] "Protestant orthodoxy provided, in the seventeenth century, a pattern of definition of the divine immutability representative of traditional Western theism and typical of the doctrine against which modern criticism has been directed"; and they did so on the basis of the scriptural witness to "an ethical, moral, intentional and volitional changelessness in God" (Muller 1983a, 25-26). With regard to the incarnation, Muller notes the Protestant use of traditional ortho-

doxy argues cogently that the scriptural idea of the incarnation is one of the "*assumptio carnis* [assumption of the flesh] rather than... a divine becoming" (1983a, 33-36). Furthermore, he shows that the seventeenth century orthodox theologians made a "basis for piety and reverent worship" out of the "relation...between the immutability of God's transcendent being and the constancy of his purpose, the steadfastness of his love, the faithfulness of his promises" (1983a, 38-39).

CHAPTER

2

"Who Do Men Say That I Am?"

The aim of the present chapter is to acquaint the reader with the seventeenth-century climate in Christological thought which provided the setting of Owen's labors. Owen identifies several opponents to the foundation of the church, the person of Jesus Christ. He explicitly refers to "Papists," Arminians, Socinians, and Quakers; and alludes to others who undermine the church's faith either by asserting the sufficiency of a natural theology, or by emphasizing the exemplary role of Jesus Christ to the practical neglect of his role as propitiatory substitute to the extent that a true incarnation of God the Son is rendered unnecessary. In an era when the idea of "mystery" in religion was under fire, and the "reasonableness of Christianity" was its greatest virtue, Owen saw that trends (even in evangelical preaching) toward a rational apologetic and a morality based upon natural law were dangerous to the defense of the truth, to vital piety, and ultimately to the Christian religion.

Perhaps the simplest way of understanding the struggle is to view it as the continuation of a conflict between late-medieval rationalism and mysticism on the one hand, versus Bible-based Christological developments of the Lutheran and Reformed wings of the Protestant Reformation on the other. When this approach is taken, it

"Who Do Men Say That I Am?"   23

becomes easier to take into account, and to distinguish between, the tremendously complex and interrelated forces at work upon and within the English Reformed Church. The Puritans were heirs to a threefold legacy from the Renaissance and Reformation, consisting of 1) rational, 2) mystical, and 3) biblical elements. The Lutheran and Reformed movements, despite the demonstrated influence of Renaissance humanism and late-medieval mysticism, may be distinguished from these by an insistence upon the primacy of divine scriptural revelation. When reason was in conflict with revelation the orthodox watchword was "Let God be true and every man a liar." This difference is clearly seen in the conflict between Luther and Erasmus over the doctrine of predestination. Much closer to our subject are the disputes between Calvin and the Italian antitrinitarians, Blandrata, Gentile, and Alciati.

There is a clear difference between the Reformers, who are determined to submit their understandings to the Scriptures, and "Erasmian" Humanists who reject the Reformers' interpretations of Scripture when these conflicted with the Renaissance philosophy of man. The setting of theological debate in the age of the Renaissance meant the necessity of establishing the correct estimation of reason's role. Put briefly, the answer given by reformed orthodoxy was that reason "had an instrumental function within the bounds of faith, and not a magisterial function" (Muller 2003, 141).

It is important to emphasize this with regard to Puritan studies. In his excellent study, *The Authority of the Bible and the Rise of the Modern World*, Henning Graf-Reventlow asserts:

> The real driving force of Puritan activity, its criticism of the church and the demand for reform which it addressed towards that church, was not so much Calvinistic theology as exemplified in the doctrine

of predestination. Rather, these zealots were motivated by the humanistic call *ad fontes* [to the sources].... In particular, the emergence of ethics as their central concern shows that the Puritans continued the concerns of Humanism. The legacy of Erasmus proves to be stronger than the legacy of the Reformation. (1985, 97)

Such a comment assumes that Puritan ethics are based upon Erasmian rather than Reformed principles. Graf-Reventlow has correctly identified a movement within the non-conformist churches towards this emphasis upon ethics. Whether any sort of ethical emphasis whatsoever constitutes a departure from the Reformation (as if Reformed theology did not necessarily include ethical content), and whether the participants in a movement towards Erasmianism and away from Calvinism may any longer even be considered as "Puritans," are two different but necessary questions. The position assumed in the present work is that both must be answered in the negative. From its outset and throughout the Puritan age, Reformed theology emphasized union with Christ and the covenantal character of God's relationship with his people—two doctrines which called for the highest ethical standards of behavior. Presbyterian, Congregational, and Baptist Puritan confessional statements demonstrate the same underlying convictions with respect to the place of the law of God and good works. The readiness of leading Puritans to label as "Arminianizing" or as "Socinianizing" any ethical teaching which neglected the importance of justification by imputed righteousness, or which emphasized the sufficiency of natural revelation, means we can accept Graf-Reventlow's observation as true for a growing number within the "Puritan movement" only in the most general sense of the term. It is definitely not true for the "Puritanism" represented by the divines of the Westminster, Savoy, and the First and Second London Baptist confessions.

There is no reason to assume, with Graf-Reventlow, that a concern shared by Puritans and non-Puritan Renaissance humanists diminishes the significance of this difference. On the other hand, it illustrates the blurring of the lines that has made "Puritanism" a term so difficult to define. Furthermore, the consistent application of this principle was an ideal not always attained. Nevertheless, the supremacy of Scripture was a fundamental conviction of the Puritans.

The same may be seen with respect to the influence of mysticism. Luther was deeply indebted to the mysticism of Eckhart and Tauler. However, it is noteworthy that his reformation theology is very much a rejection of this theology at one of its most important points: the doctrine of the divine spark in the soul (*synderesis*).[1] Afterwards, in disputes with "enthusiasts" of various sorts, the mystical priority on experience over the written word became a fundamental source of conflict between Protestant and Radical Reformers. In seventeenth-century Puritanism there is an intense interest in spiritual experience; however, the Puritans insisted that all experience be "tried by the word" of Scripture.

The Reformers and their successors were faced with the task of duly employing the gifts of God for the exposition of his word, a word of grace to sinners, a word bringing about the knowledge, even the experience of the living God, while avoiding (to use a favorite image) the Scylla of mysticism and the Charybdis of rationalism. The Puritans endeavored to steer a middle course, not so much by splitting the difference between two extremes, but by endeavoring to preach "the whole counsel of God," avoiding the errors embraced by the rationalists who saw them as "enthusiasts" or the mystics who looked on them as "prisoners of the dead letter."

Arminianism and the Development of Rational Theology in England

Arminius' Conflict with Reformed Christology

The development of Christological thought in seventeenth-century England was radically influenced by the rise of Arminianism. This was for three reasons. First, Arminianism had its own Christology, which was quite different from that of the Reformed. The soteriological difference between Calvinism and Arminianism had a Christological foundation not always observed in subsequent discussions of the conflict, but lying at its heart nevertheless. Secondly, by its opposition of the Reformed doctrine of the work of Christ, Arminianism significantly stimulated its development. Warfield observes that the doctrine of satisfaction "reached its complete development only at the hands of the so-called Protestant Scholastics of the seventeenth century," and mentions two treatises by Francis Turretin and John Owen as examples (Warfield 1950, 368). Turretin's *The Atonement of Christ* and Owen's *The Death of Death in the Death of Christ* were written in response to Arminianism and Amyraldianism. Thirdly, it encouraged an anti-Calvinistic and pro-Socinian mood in seventeenth-century England, through its emphasis upon a rational theology.

How did Arminius' Christology differ from that of the Reformed? First, Arminius emphatically denied the natural divinity (*autotheotes*) of the Son (Warfield 1956, 263). According to Richard A. Muller,

> In the context of developing Reformed theology, Arminius' doctrine represents a variant Christology that takes no cognizance of the centrality of Calvin's formulation of Christ as *autotheos* [God-in-himself] to Reformed soteriology. It bears more resemblance to Gentilis' formulation against Calvin than to Calvin's own formulation. This may account for the connection drawn by some Calvinists between Arminianism

and various anti-trinitarian heresies. Like Gentilis, Arminius argues that the Reformed doctrine of the Son's divinity violated the unity of God's essence by postulating three separate deities in the place of the persons of the Trinity. (1976, 407-408)

Describing the tremendous significance of this fact to subsequent Christological developments he says, "Whereas interpreters of Arminius have emphasized Arminius' stress on the Work of Christ, the primary variation relates to the doctrine of Christ's Person and the concept of self-existence (*aseity*). Once having altered the doctrine of the Person of Christ, Arminius could set forth a variant conception of the order of the decrees: the Christology determines the structure of the system" (1976, 409).

Arminius' subordinationism was carried further by his disciple and apologist Episcopius, who writes of the triune God:

> It is certain...that this divinity and the divine perfections are to be attributed to these three persons, not collaterally and coordinately, but subordinately.... This subordination...should be carefully attended to, because of its extremely great usefulness, since by it not only is there fundamentally overthrown the *tritheotes* [three-gods] which colateralism almost necessarily involves, but also the Father's glory is preserved to Him unimpaired. (quoted by Warfield 1956, 265)

For Episcopius, the "true subordination" of the Son to the Father meant that he could not be *autotheos*. That is, he refused to separate an ontological subordination from an economic one. Ritschl notes "the Arminian doctrine of God is fashioned after the model of the treatment given to it by the Socinian Crell, through Episcopius" (1872, 314n). As Warfield says, "The path thus opened by Episcopius was eagerly walked in by his successors. All that may be thought to be latent in Episcopius came to light in Curcellaeus" (1956, 265), whom Owen called a "middle man" with the Socinians (12:49). Another coming heavily under this influence was Dr. George Bull (Warfield 1956, 266-70).

Along with reversing the Reformed emphasis upon the Son's proper-deity (*autotheotes*), Arminius introduced a number of changes in the understanding of the Son's work. In his doctrine of the covenant of grace, Arminius does not regard the law as part of the covenant, but holds that "although the first covenant of works was nullified by the fall, the law exists as a path toward justification parallel to and distinct from faith" (Muller 1976, 404; cf. Owen 1852, 23:61). As Muller points out,

> In the context of Arminius' synergism this doctrine presents the possibility of a legalism far more pronounced than that of the doctrines of seventeenth century federalism. Separation of the law from the covenant of grace also implies, contrary to the position of Calvinists and federalists alike, that Christ is not eternally the Mediator but is effectively the Mediator only following the Incarnation in the execution of his threefold Office. (1976, 404)

Muller also observes, "The problem of the Arminian Christology extends to the interpretation of the two states and the *kenosis*," and to the place of Christ in the doctrine of election (1976, 414-17; cf. Muller 1988, 145-63).

Impact upon the Development of Rational Theology
In addition to the more specific doctrinal issues raised by Arminianism, there were several more general issues which had a great impact upon English thought. A number of writers have ably set out the significance of the rise of Arminianism in the seventeenth century for the rise of Socinianism and rationalism in the English churches.[2] As Tulloch says, "Arminianism was a great deal more than a dogmatic theory. It was also, or at least it rapidly became, a method of religious inquiry" (1874, 1:19). Tulloch de-

scribes this method of religious inquiry as a revival of the "rational side of the original Protestant movement," which is, no doubt, the way it was perceived by its adherents. Though Tulloch's description of the Arminian movement has been superseded by more recent studies, it still provides a good description of how seventeenth century Arminians viewed themselves and the issues.

In addition to the emphasis given to the power of reason in theological inquiry, the Arminians stressed the right of private judgment against the teaching authority of the church. Expressing the Arminian perspective upon the issue, Tulloch says, "The setting forth of so many symbols and forms of belief had hindered Christian inquiry, impeded Christian liberty, and opened the way to faction and schisms in the church." The authority of Scripture was allegedly thereby "more and more weakened, until at length it had fallen away and been transferred to these human formularies as more perfect" (1874, 1:24-25). Tulloch also notes the Arminian opposition to human creeds in favor of leaving the Word in its original form. Thus there was with them, as with the Socinians, a firmly anticreedal attitude, taken in support of the right of private judgment and in opposition to confessional and church authority.[3] One particular development attributed by Tulloch to the controversy was the distinction between fundamental doctrines, a distinction that he called the "most significant and solvent of all the rational principles enunciated by Arminianism" (1874, 1:34). However, Tulloch failed to observe that the Reformed orthodox also distinguished between fundamental and non-fundamental doctrines (cf. Muller 2003, 406-30). The crucial question becomes, what those fundamental doctrines are.

Progress
The leaven of the "Arminian" method had been working within the English church long before the outbreak of the

controversy, which, along with Puritan demands to advance the Reformation, seemed to furnish the heat that made it rise. Thus, the Arminian controversy was quickly intertwined with the struggle over ritual and church order, and soon, the opponents of Puritan polity were challenging their theological system as well. As an alternative, they advanced Arminianism under the leadership of Archbishop Laud. In a nutshell, for a number of reasons including but not limited to the Arminian struggle, the English church became increasingly divided. By 1660, "Calvinism" as it was associated with the political power, had passed its peak: the Restoration of Charles II meant that all the political forces in the nation added their pressure to the various influences which were distinctly anti-Calvinist. G. R. Cragg says the theology of the Restoration was Arminian in the sense that the characteristic feature of Arminianism is its conditionalness, and moderateness is the mark of its method. He adds,

> The way in which Arminianism had become a political issue had tended to dilute its theological distinctiveness, and as the Restoration period progressed, the results were increasingly apparent. There was no longer any deep concern with the doctrine of grace; men emphasized the beneficial example which Christ had left us, not the atoning work he had wrought on our behalf.... English Arminianism lost its distinctive note as it merged imperceptibly with Latitudinarianism and Rationalism. (Cragg 1950, 29-30)

Cambridge Platonism

One of the catalysts in this change was the very influential group of men known as the "Cambridge Platonists." Most of the group was educated at Emmanuel College, retaining a superficial affinity to the Puritanism once taught there but encouraging its transformation from a biblical to a humanistic religion. This transformation was accomplished by men of exemplary reputation for learning, piety, and humanitarian affection through the appeal to "reason." Benjamin Whichcote, legitimately called the founder of the school, often described reason as "the candle of the Lord." To follow reason, he taught, is to follow God. As F. J. Powicke points out, theirs was not mere rationalism: "Nothing is the true improvement of our rational faculties but the exercise of the several virtues of sobriety, modesty, gentleness, humility, obedience to God and charity to men" (1926, 47). In the Cambridge Platonists, we have a seventeenth-century translation of Renaissance Platonism into English thought (Roberts 1968, 33).[4]

Basil Willey stressed the significance of the Cambridge Platonists in that they employed "seventeenth century criteria of the Real towards the restatement of religious belief" (1949, 136). Ralph Cudworth's *Intellectual System of the Universe* is a perfect example of this practice. This platonic apology for Christianity succeeds only at the cost of the orthodox doctrine of the Trinity. Referring to the sermons of Whichcote and John Smith, Willey says:

> We find them here playing their part in the movement towards "enlightenment" by constantly substituting an entelechy, an idea, or a state of mind for one or other of the dramatic or pictorial representations of the traditional scheme. Take for instance, the doctrine of salvation. The popular conception of salvation was of course bound up with all the imagery, biblical and theological, associated with the Fall and the Atonement. The Platonists were opposed to many of the implications of the Fall doctrine, in particular the customary depreciation of human nature and human Reason by orthodox divines. (1949, 136)

Willey's remarks illustrate well the latitudinarian and anti-trinitarian tendency of Cambridge Platonism:

> The aim of Whichcote and Smith in their preaching was to call men off from dogmas and barren speculation, and to urge them to fix upon the "Real"; ... They reject no article of the Faith, but they shift the emphasis of exhortation, affirming values where orthodoxy affirmed facts. (1949, 138; cf. Jones, 1914, 305-19)

Like the Arminians referred to above, they were ardently opposed to what they perceived to be dogmatism. "The whole trend of their teaching was directed in subtle ways against the foundations of the prevailing theology. It was an attack on Calvinism from within" (Cragg 1950, 39). Cragg points out the effect of this upon Calvinism in general and to some particular doctrines that are of interest to our study:

> This was a new form of criticism—criticism which ignored the polity of Calvinism but shook the whole system by questioning its basic conceptions. In effect the Cambridge Platonists turned from the familiar theological picture altogether. The old and oft repeated version of the sacrifice for sin had no place in their teaching, and they conceived of salvation as a form and spirit entirely different from the vivid pictorial imagery of the Calvinists....
>
> The Puritans had not only emphasized the importance of doctrine, but had dwelt with particular fondness on the mysteries of belief. The Cambridge Platonists never fell into the facile rationalism which repudiates mysteries simply because they are mysteries, but they deprecated so great a preoccupation with obscure and unintelligible doctrines. (1950, 40)

With regard to the Cambridge Platonists' account of the gospel, Willey says, "They tend, without ostensible change of creed, to substitute, for the second Person of the Trinity, or the Crucified Redeemer, the divine teacher whose life and words show God and man in that state of union at which all religion aims" (1949, 152). The person of Christ represents for Smith a "type of the union of the divine and human natures, and an earnest of what God would further do for believers." He says, "the whole business and undertaking of Christ is eminently available both to give relief and ease to our Minds and Hearts, and also to encourage us to Godliness or a Godlike righteousness" (Willey 1949, 153). Their emphasis was upon reformation rather than redemption (Lichtenstein, 186). Perhaps this is nowhere more in evidence than in Henry More's *Explanation of the Grand Mystery of Godliness*; a work showing little interest in the doctrine of Christ's person. Godliness is the key.

Socinianism
A detailed survey of the history of Socinianism in England is beyond our purpose,[5] but it is important to note that its rise was associated with the onset of Arminianism and Cambridge Platonism. While the Cambridge Platonists did not go so far as to affirm the specific doctrines of Socinianism, and even denied them, they nevertheless prepared the soil that received the Socinian seed. The same spirit of toleration and free inquiry, the same assumed antithesis between a rational interpretation of Scripture and the confessions of the creedal churches is present in both.

Socinianism *per se* was imported from Poland through Holland with the great assistance of the printed page. According to Earl Morse Wilbur,

> Soon after the middle of the seventeenth century more than three score Socinian books had been published in Holland,... They were in the main brief doctrinal discussions by Socinius, Smalcius, Schlichting and other champions of Socinian views,

> or were commentaries on New Testament writings made by Crellius or other Socinian scholars.... The authorities of the established church do not seem to have made any serious attempt to suppress these writings; for Archbishop Laud was much less concerned that members of the church should all agree in the details of their professed beliefs than that they should all worship in the forms officially adopted. Thus it came to pass that Socinian views were quietly diffused among not a few of the Episcopal party now dominating the national church. (1952, 185-86)

It seems this was the case until the more doctrinally zealous Presbyterian party gained the ascendancy in Parliament in the 1640's. In 1648, Parliament passed "An Ordinance for Punishing Blasphemies and Heresies." The ordinance was not only too late; it was not enforced, and the rise of Cromwellian Independency made it unlikely to be. As Wilbur says,

> It was fortunate for the Unitarian cause in England that this was so, for otherwise the first Englishman to avow Unitarian beliefs boldly and clearly, and to publish them fearlessly, undeterred by repeated imprisonments, must assuredly have fallen victim to the ordinance, which the guardians of orthodoxy were ready to invoke against him. (1952, 192)

The reference is to John Biddle.[6]

R. S. Franks summarized the basic character of Socinianism well as "the product of a union between the humanism of Erasmus and the logical criticism of the school of Duns Scotus, effected in a mind liberated by the Reformation from the authority of the church, but unsubjugated by Luther's new religious principle of justification by faith" (1962, 362). Since much of Owen's work is explicitly in response to Socinian opinions, we will not discuss them here.

Quakerism

A general survey of the origins and teachings of the Quakers during the seventeenth century would reveal several ways in which they might reasonably have been seen by Owen as undermining the foundation of the church in their opposition to the doctrine of the Person of Christ, as the following sampling typical of Quaker opinion demonstrates.

In 1660, Samuel Fisher, one of the chief Quaker apologists, published *Rusticos ad Academicos* [*An Ordinary Man to the Academicians*] against the works of four Puritan divines including Owen and Richard Baxter. The work contains the most learned attempt, from a Quaker perspective, to refute the Puritan doctrine of Scripture. This perspective taught that,

> the Light of Christ in the conscience and not the external text of the letter of Scripture is the only firm foundation of the church's faith, the only true touchstone of all doctrines, the only right rule of all saving belief and holy life, the infallible Spirit's infallible guidance of all that follow Him as their guide. (Braithwaite 1955, 289)

His basic argument ran like this: The canon of Scripture is arbitrarily chosen by men, its text is corrupt, its translations imperfect. An examination of the synoptic gospels (particularly the preface to Luke's gospel) shows that the evangelists are writing as witnesses to history, "not without an active concurrence of...rational faculties." For these reasons the Scriptures are an imperfect foundation for faith, while the Spirit's guidance within is infallible because it is immediate (Braithwaite 1955, 289-92). He mistakenly takes Owen's use of the language of "dictation" literally, rather than realizing that, as with Calvin, this refers to the equation of the words of Scripture with the words of God, rather than the actual method by which these words come to be used by the biblical writers.

From 1657 to 1659, Fisher wrote *The Great Mystery of the Great Whore*, a general rejoinder to the many anti-Quaker publications of the period. In a section against John Owen (his "chief antagonist" according to Braithwaite), he takes issue with Owen's *Catechism*. Against Owen's Protestant doctrine of Scripture, Fisher replies,

> There was truth learned before the Scriptures were written, and the Scriptures of truth are the words of God, which ends in Christ the Word; and there is no truth learned, but as the spirit doth lead into all truth, which comes from Christ the truth, which was before the Scripture was written: And the *spirit of truth leads into all truth of the Scripture*; and many has the Scriptures, but knows not Christ the Truth, but as the spirit leads them, and reveals them: and so he hath thrown out Christ and the spirit. (quoted in Braithwaite 1955, 300)

Fisher's critique of Owen and the doctrine Owen holds provides an unhappily accurate picture of the Quaker's misunderstanding of the Puritan doctrine of Christ and the Scriptures. Owen also will affirm that there was truth learned before the Scriptures were written, and that this truth was from the Spirit of Christ. He will emphasize the absolute necessity of the Holy Spirit for the belief in, and understanding of, the Scripture, which remains God's living voice. To say he has "thrown out Christ and the spirit" because he insists upon Scripture for the revelation of the mind and will of God is to misrepresent his doctrine of Christ, the Spirit, and the Scripture.

Against Owen's assertion that there is one God in three persons, Fisher makes the simplistic retort, "Where doth the Apostle tell us of three persons, but tells us of Father, Son, and holy Ghost; but thou, out of the Masse-book, and old common-prayer book, who are the mutterers about three persons" (Braithwaite 1955, 300).

Another Quaker publication typical of those which

aroused the alarm of the orthodox Puritans was *A Lamentation for the Scattered Tribes*, by Francis Howgill. Howgill argued that in their zeal to conform their practice to that of the primitive church, the pastors of the separated fellowships had become "ministers of the letter." They were teaching a religion grounded on the report of Christ dying at Jerusalem: the belief in this report they called "faith" (Braithwaite 1955, 96-97).[7] Thus, whereas the Puritans had always preached against a merely "historical" and consequently "dead" faith, Howgill and other Quakers were substituting a faith without a foundation in the historical gospel (cf. Owen 1852, 21:115-22).

In 1668, William Penn echoed Fisher's sentiments in a book entitled *The Sandy Foundation Shaken*, written against the Presbyterian Thomas Vincent. His purpose was to refute "those generally believed and applauded Doctrines of One God, subsisting in three distinct and separate Persons, the Impossibility of God's pardoning Sinners, without a plenary Satisfaction, and the justification of impure persons by an imputative Righteousness" (Penn 1825, 1:129). He denied the One Godhead subsisting in three distinct and separate persons saying,

> No one substance can have three distinct subsistences and preserve its own unity. For granting them the most favorable definitions, every subsistence will have its own substance so that three distinct manners of being, will require three distinct substances or beings; consequently three Gods. For if the infinite God-head subsists in three separate manners or forms, then is not any one of them a perfect and complete subsistence without the other two; so parts and something finite is in God. Or if infinite, then three distinct infinite subsistences; and what is this but to assert three Gods, since none is infinite but God? And on the contrary, there being an inseparable betwixt the substance and its subsistence, the unity of substance will not admit of a

trinity of incommunicable or distinct subsistences. (1825, 1:134)

Penn represents the most common type of attack upon the doctrine of the Trinity. The terms Trinitarians employ as imperfect expressions of an inexplicable mystery are subjected to severe analysis. As we will see, however, the unreasonable nature of the analysis is apparent to Owen, as it was to Calvin (*Institutes* I. 13. iii-vi).

Penn next appeals to the usual Scripture passages for the unity of God:

> If God as the Scriptures testify, hath never been declared or believed, but as the Holy One, then it will follow that God is not an Holy Three, nor doth subsist in three distinct and separate Holy Ones. Neither can this receive the least prejudice from the frequent but impertinent distinction, that he is one in substance, but three in persons or subsistences; since God was not declared or believed incompletely, or without his subsistence.... So that either the testimonies of the aforementioned Scriptures are to be believed concerning God, that he is entirely and completely, not abstractly and distinctly, the Holy One, or else their authority to be denied by these trinitarians. And on the contrary, if they pretend to credit those holy testimonies, they must necessarily conclude their kind of trinity a fiction. (1825, 1:136)

Penn attempts to refute the doctrine of the Trinity from "right reason," concluding his rebuttal with the accusation that the doctrine was "born above three hundred years after the ancient gospel was declared;... through the nice distinctions, and too daring curiosity of the bishop of Alexandria.... Thus it was conceived in ignorance, and brought forth and maintained by cruelty" (1825, 1:138).

Penn then turns against the "vulgar doctrine of satisfaction being dependent on the second person of the trinity" (1825, 1:139). His argument is almost identical to the Socinian assertion that the pardoning grace of God precludes the necessity of satisfaction and is antithetical to it. Consequently, Penn argues, "remission came by believing his testimony, and obeying his precepts, and not by a strict satisfaction" (1825, 1:140). Finally, in a typical Socinian manner, he argues against the doctrine of justification by imputed righteousness (1825, 1:141).

In an apology for *The Sandy Foundation Shaken*, Penn denied the charge of Socinianism (by taking refuge in Sabellianism). He nevertheless reveals his acquaintance with Socinian works and shows a high respect for Socinus (1825, 1:160). Against the charge of denying satisfaction he appeals to Dr. Stillingfleet's reply to Crellius in which the Anglican grants "the possibility of God's pardoning sins as debts, without such a rigid satisfaction, and the impossibility of Christ's so suffering for the world" (1825, 1:161). The two works just mentioned were acclaimed by Socinians who distributed Penn's writings and took up his defense.

The seventeenth-century's most eminent Quaker theologian was Robert Barclay. Often regarded as quite orthodox from the standpoint of a general evangelicalism, an examination of his work reveals that, despite his general acknowledgement of the Trinity, the incarnation, and Christ's sacrificial death, he maintains the preference for the "Inner Light" over the written word, and the inner Christ of sanctifying grace over Christ's alien righteousness made ours in justification.[8] The mystical character of Barclay's theology is clearly illustrated by Leif Eeg-Oloffson (1954).

For reasons quite different from Owen, Barclay believed in the necessity of Christ's deity for his role of giving the right knowledge of God. Christ dwells in man "through the Inner Light," "medially, as He is in that seed, which is in us; whereas he to wit, the eternal word" dwelt in "that holy man...immediately" (Barclay 1692, 334). Comparing Jesus to the rest of mankind, Barclay says, "The same that was in Him, is in us. There is no other difference than between the source and the stream, which are one in their nature" (Eeg-Oloffson 1954, 80-81). Barclay contrasts the knowledge coming through the inner light with that given through Scripture, church tradition, creation, and providence, saying "inward and immediate revelation is the sure and certain way to attain the true and saving knowledge of God" (Barclay 1692, 273). Those others give an intellectualistic, even an uncertain knowledge; this, a right one. "Everything outer in the psychological sense can only give an outer, wrong knowledge of God in the mystic sense" (Eeg-Oloffson 1954, 100).

With respect to the doctrine of justification he asserts that the mediation of Christ may be seen in two different ways: "Christ for us in His crucified body outside us," and "Christ in us," through the inner light. From the first, man gets a measure of the power, spirit, life and mercy, which were in Christ Jesus and, as God's free gift, can counteract, conquer and uproot the evil seed. As Eeg-Oloffson observes,

> The redemption, carried out by Christ on the Cross of Golgotha, has no necessary connection with the mystical justification in man. Every man can receive justification through Christ as the Inner Light, even if he has never got to know anything about the Cross of Golgotha. Christ's historic work of redemption does not denote anything absolutely new that has found its place in history, but is rather an exemplification in the outer, of that which has always been in the depths of the soul. (Eeg-Oloffson 1954, 105)

According to Barclay, the

> cause of our justification is the love of God manifested in the appearance of Jesus Christ in the flesh,

> who by his life, death, sufferings, and obedience made a way for our reconciliation, and became a sacrifice for the remission of sins, that are past, and purchased unto us this seed and grace, from which this birth arises, and in which Jesus Christ is inwardly received, formed and brought forth in us, in his own pure and holy image of righteousness; by which our souls live unto God, and are clothed with him, and have put him on. (Barclay 1692, 379)

Barclay's rejection of justification through faith alone (*sola fide*), then, naturally results from his doctrine of the Inner Light. Barclay rejects imputed righteousness, identifying the inner, real righteousness with sanctification: "God is reconciled with man after He has sanctified him and made him righteous in a psychological respect. . . . [not] brought about by man's moral efforts, but by Christ's indwelling in man" (Eeg-Oloffson 1954, 116).

The Quaker doctrine of the "Inner Light," even when accompanied by affirmations of belief in the Trinity, had major theological repercussions. It diminished the authority of the Bible on which the doctrine of the Trinity was based, several eminent Quakers explicitly attacked the doctrine of the Trinity. The Inner Light teaching encouraged a subjective standard of judgment for theological knowledge. While Luther had parted company with medieval mysticism because its doctrine of the divine spark (*synderesis*) ran contrary to his understanding of Scripture's teaching on radical depravity and the doctrine of justification by grace alone (*sola gratia*), Quakerism went in just the opposite direction: its mystical denial of radical depravity encouraged a moralistic denial of the Reformed doctrine of grace. While asserting belief in the historic Christ, the imputation of his righteousness was generally denied or, if asserted at all, made of little significance compared to the righteousness produced by the Christ within. Hence, they held a doctrine of justification closely resembling that of Trent. Paul Tillich has rightly observed the close relation between Mysticism and Rationalism in this period (Tillich 1967, 286, 315). We have seen this relation in the emphasis upon the "candle of the Lord" in the Cambridge Platonists, and now (from a very slightly different perspective) in the Quakers' very rationalistic opposition to the authority of the Scriptures and against the doctrine of the Trinity.

Latitudinarianism
While the Cambridge Platonists shared with the Puritans an interest in ecclesiastical reform, their nearer kinsmen theologically were to be found among the clergy of the Anglican establishment who came to be known as "Latitude men" or "Latitudinarians." The connections between them were quite strong: Roberts says most of the latitudinarians "were tutored by Smith, Cudworth or More, and doubtless listened to Whichcote preach in Trinity Church" (Roberts 1968, 226). One point of distinction is that while both stressed reason, the Latitudinarians lacked the mysticism of the Platonists (Roberts 1968, 227). Calling it the "dominant theological school of the new era," Cragg asserted that "more than any other it prepared the way for the characteristic outlooks and attitudes of the eighteenth century. At almost every point its assumptions stood in marked contrast to those of Calvinism" (Cragg 1950, 33-34). A brief survey of the opinions of several important Latitudinarians will illustrate why John Owen so lamented the loss of Christocentric preaching in the church of his day.

According to Bishop Edward Fowler, the gospel gives us the example of Christ's life, His declaration of pardon, and His proffers of grace to assist us in well doing. Fowler argues that God could have forgiven sin without the sacrifice of Christ but, "therefore was Christ set forth to be a propitiatary sacrifice for sin,... that it might be a cogent motive, and a most prevailing argument to sinners to forsake their sins" (Fowler 1791, 342). In his interpretation of Romans 8:3 ("For what the law could not do, in that it was weak through the flesh, God sending his own Son in the likeness of sinful flesh, and for sin, condemned sin in the flesh"), he says that Christ "by this means shewing how hateful it is to God, took a most powerful course to kill and destroy it." He concludes his argument by saying,

> In that Christ hath laid down his life at the appointment of God the Father for the purpose of making an atonement for sin, this gives all men unspeakably greater assurance of the pardon of true penitents than the bare consideration of the divine goodness could ever have done: and so by this means have we the greatest encouragement ourselves. (1791, 342)

On the other hand he argues that the death of the Savior "is in a special manner effectual" because "by virtue of the authority he is by this means invested and dignified with, and particularly as he is King of the church, hath he sent the Holy Ghost to sanctifie us, to excite us to all holy actions, and to assist us in the performance of them," adding that,

> whereas it is frequently affirmed in the holy Scriptures, that the end of Christ's death was also the forgiveness of our sins, and the reconciling of us to his Father, we are not so to understand those places, as if these blessings were absolutely thereby procured for us, or any otherwise than upon condition of our effectual believing, and yielding obedience to his Gospel.... Christ died to put us in a capacity of pardon; the actual removing of our guilt is not the necessary and immediate result of his death, but suspended till such time as the aforementioned conditions, by the help of his grace, are performed by us.

But moreover, it is in order to our being encouraged to sincere endeavors to forsake all sin, and to be universally obedient for the time to come, that our Saviour shed his blood for the pardon of it: this was intended in his death, as it is subservient to that purpose; the assurance of having all our sin forgiven upon our sincere reformation, being a necessary motive thereunto. (1791, 344)

Fowler's doctrine of the atonement, we see, was a mixture of Abelardian, Tridentine, and Arminian elements.

Fowler's comparison between Christianity and heathen religion clearly manifests a tendency in the direction of the principles espoused by the Deists:

FIRST, that the good principles that were by natural light dictated to them, and which reason rightly improved did persuade them to entertain as undoubtedly true, or might have done, are farther confirmed by divine revelation in the Gospel to us. As, that there is but one God: that he is an absolutely perfect Being, infinitely powerful, wise, just, merciful. That we owe our lives and all the comforts of them to him; that he is our sovereign Lord, to whom absolute subjection is indispensably due:...

SECONDLY, those good principles that the heathens by the greatest improvement of their religion could at best conclude very probable, are made undoubtedly certain by Revelation: As,

First, that of the immortality of our souls....

Secondly, the doctrine of rewards and punishments in the life to come (which is for substance the same as the former) according to our behavior in this life....

Thirdly, that men's sins shall be forgiven upon true repentance....

Fourthly, the doctrine of God's readiness to assist men by his special grace in their endeavors after virtue....

THIRDLY, we have other doctrines made known to us by the Gospel, which no man could ever without divine revelation in the least have dreamed of. (1791, 362-63)

As the one and ultimate end of Christ's coming was to turn us from our iniquities, the doctrine that justifying faith consists "in recumbance and reliance upon him," Fowler insists, "hath given infinite advantage to the dangerous error of Antinomianism. The imputation of Christ's righteousness means that God deals "with sincerely righteous persons, as if they were perfectly so, for the sake of Christ's righteousness" (1791, 392). As C. F. Allison makes clear, the fear of Antinomianism became a strong motive towards the modification of the doctrine of justification (1966, 194-97).

Regardless of the sources of his theology, Fowler is clearly expounding a Socinian understanding of Christ's offices. Christ has come principally as an ambassador of God, not as a priest to render a perfect substitutionary sacrifice for man's sins.

Archbishop Tillotson provides a good example of one type of preaching which Owen was particularly concerned with, namely, that of the confessionally orthodox preacher who neglected to communicate the necessary knowledge of Christ's person and work to his hearers. Tillotson said, "According to the terms of the Gospel, the great condition of our justification and acceptance with God is the real renovation of our hearts and lives" (quoted by Hunt, 1870, 101). Hunt describes Tillotson's preaching of the atonement by saying that although his doctrine is orthodox,

> he rarely makes it the subject of his sermons. Even then he does not so much preach it, as preach about it. The Puritans said that he did not preach Christ. He answered that he preached what Christ preached. He taught the necessity and the blessed-

ness of being righteous. He took his stand on the moral constitution of man. (1870, 102)

This is perfectly illustrated in Birch's *Life of Tillotson*: "When he left Keddington in Suffolk, the people universally complained that Jesus Christ had not been preached among them since Tillotson had been settled in the parish" (quoted by Hunt 1870, 102).

Tillotson's doctrine of heavenly reward for earthly virtue was hardly distinguishable from Lord Hurlbut's deistic moral philosophy. "Without rewards and punishments virtue would be a dry speculation, and men would give up the pursuit of religion" (Hunt 1870, 103.). "Revelation," says Tillotson, "was a republication of natural religion. In fact it was natural religion enforced by rewards" (Tillotson's *Works*, Vol. 5:53, 54; quoted by Hunt 1870, 105). As Hunt explains the significance of this for Tillotson, we see one of several areas where Owen will make a distinct break with a fellow non-conformist:

> But as the natural notions were certain, and as nothing could be received as revelation which contradicts them, it is evident that the old view of revelation was in danger of a change. This subject had been already discussed by Lord Herbert whose main principles were now adopted by all rational theologians, to whom they did not appear as subversive of Christianity, but rather, as Richard Baxter had said, of singular use in establishing it. (Hunt 1870, 105)

Another Latitudinarian who came into direct conflict with Owen was William Sherlock, whose work we will meet in the following chapter.

Conclusion

The preceding survey illustrates the general trend in the seventeenth century away from the Christology that had been espoused by the Reformed theologians of the sixteenth century. The seventeenth century witnessed the development of a rationalistic/mystical theological spirit inherited from the Renaissance that was directly antithetical to the Calvinistic understanding of Christ's person and work. The new Christology was not due to a better understanding of the scriptural data on the person and work of Christ. It was not better exegesis of the Scriptures, but dissatisfaction with Calvinism in general, with the politics of its advocates, etc. (cf. Bolam, et al, 1968, *passim*), which led to the rejection of its Christology.

Owen was well aware of the philosophical and theological pleas made by the participants in the movement just described. In his analysis, the root cause of this apostasy was an "evil heart of unbelief." As he summarizes it,

There are three things in the gospel and the profession of it about which unbelief is apt to act itself by this dislike; which if not obviated will prove a beginning of turning away from the whole: First, the purity and spirituality of its worship; secondly, The strictness and universality of its holiness or obedience; and thirdly, The grace and mystery of its doctrine. (21:114)

With particular application to the Quakers and Socinians, Owen adds, "Secret dislike of the principal mysteries of the gospel is the original and cause of most of the degeneracies, backslidings, and apostasies that are found amongst professors in these latter days" (21:115, 118, 122).

To such a generation of professors, including sincere believers in need of "establishment" and edification, John Owen argued the necessity and benefit of a genuine and vital knowledge of Christ. The following chapter will introduce the reader to the various ways he made his case.

---

[1] This idea was originally presented to me by Dr. Scott Hendrix in a course on "The Development of Luther's Theology," at Lutheran Theological Seminary, Philadelphia, Pa., in 1985. Cf. Ozment 1980, 239-44.

[2] See Cragg (1950), McLachlan (1951), Roberts (1968), Wallace (1965), and Wilbur (1952).

[3] See Wilbur (1952), McLachlan (1951), and Owen (12:10-53).

[4] The important differences between the Cambridge Platonists and the Puritans are clearly observable in the correspondence between Whichcote and Anthony Tuckney (Roberts 1968, 42-65; Jones 1914, 288-304).

[5] For contemporary accounts of the history of Socinianism see Francis Cheynell (1643), and Owen (12:12-53).

[6] It is a remarkable evidence of the fluidity of the term "Puritan," that Biddle is included among them in Benjamin Brook's *Lives of the Puritans* (Brook 1813, 3: 411-17.)

[7] E.g., Bunyan's rejoinder to Edward Burrough (Bunyan, 1853, 2:132-219)

[8] In his *Quakarisme the Pathway to Paganisme* (1678), John Brown of Wamphray lists over 330 "arrogant, erroneous, and blasphemous assertions" in Barclay's *Apology*.

CHAPTER

3

"Who Do You Say That I Am?"

In the present chapter, we will briefly survey those works of John Owen that deal with Christology. This should be valuable for several reasons. Owen never wrote a systematic theology such as Calvin's *Institutes*, or Ames' *Marrow*, or even Thomas Watson's *Body of Divinity*. We cannot turn to any single work of Owen in the hope of finding a comprehensive treatment of his theological system. While his treatise on the Holy Spirit provides a comprehensive view of his thoughts on the third person of the Trinity, none of his Christological treatises attempts to be similarly comprehensive. We can only guess at the reasons for this. It seems Owen was reluctant to undertake the task of writing a treatise when he felt the subject had been well done by others. When the current religious situation revealed that a doctrine was in need of additional clarification, demonstration, vindication, or application, Owen would rise to the occasion, as the following survey will illustrate. Whenever he finally undertook one of these tasks, he was exhaustive. As his biographer Andrew Thompson put it, "He leaves nothing to be added by one who shall follow in the same path, not even little gleanings at the corners of the field" (1:cix). One consequence of such a strategy is that when Owen has "exhausted" a subject in one treatise, the reader is given a good view of

Owen's position on that subject. Again, quoting Thompson, "There is no writer in whose opinions throughout life there is more of consistency and unity" (1:cix). Consequently, although Owen's fundamental convictions remained remarkably constant once they had been definitively stated (he often repeats, or refers the reader to another of his works), a variety of purposes subsequently elicited a variety of styles and applications. As a result, we are provided with the materials with which to examine his Christology from several angles, enabling us to see through the forms to the content of his Christology. The present chapter will examine these "forms" chronologically, pointing out important themes along the way, while the remainder of this work will focus on the content in detail.

"Whom We Preach"
In 1645, having already published his *Display of Arminianism*, and *The Duty of Pastors and People Distinguished*, Owen published two Catechisms (a "Greater" and "Lesser") which he titled the *Principles of the Doctrine of Christ*. These were written principally as instruments for the pastoral care of his flock in the parish of Fordham in Essex. That a man called to tend the flock of God in Puritan England would prepare a catechism is not surprising. That he should write it with such an emphasis upon the doctrine of Christ (though the phrase "doctrine of Christ" is often synonymous with the "doctrine taught by Christ," or "Christian doctrine") strongly suggests that, so early in his career and at so general and practical a level, Owen had a deep conviction of the importance of the "use of the person of Christ in religion" and the significance of the doctrine of Christ's person and work in theology. In the preface of the work, written about two years after assuming the pastorate, he says his intention in writing was "to hold out those necessary truths

wherein you have been in my preaching more fully instructed." "The Greater," he says, "will call to mind much of what hath been taught you in public, especially concerning the Person and Offices of Jesus Christ" (1:465).

The following year, very shortly following the end of the first civil war, Owen preached before Parliament a sermon entitled "A Vision of Unchangeable, Free Mercy," making a fervent plea for the settling of gospel preachers in neglected areas of Wales and England. Owen gives the following description of the man without the gospel "wanting" (i.e., lacking) Jesus Christ:

> Jesus Christ is all, and in all; and where he is wanting there can be no good. Hunger cannot truly be satisfied without manna, the bread of life, which is Jesus Christ;—and what shall a hungry man do that hath no bread? Thirst cannot be quenched without that water or living spring, which is Jesus Christ;—and what shall a thirsty soul do without water? A captive, as we are all, cannot be delivered without redemption, which is Jesus Christ; and what shall the prisoner do without his ransom? Fools, as we are all, cannot be instructed without wisdom, which is Jesus Christ;— without him we perish in our folly. All building without him is on the sand, which shall surely fall. All working without him is in the fire, where it will be consumed. All riches without him have wings, and will away.

Like the householder of Mathew 13:52, Owen "brings forth out of his treasure things new and old" in his endeavor to express the inexpressible:

> *"Mallem ruere cum Christo, quam regnare cum Caesare"* ["Better to come to ruin with Christ, than to reign with Caesar"], said Luther. A dungeon with Christ is a throne; and a throne without Christ, a hell. Nothing so ill, but Christ will compensate. The greatest evil in the world is sin, and the greatest sin was the first; and yet Gregory feared not to cry, "*O felix culpa,*

quae talem mervit redemptorem!"—"O happy fault, which found such a Redeemer!"

Then, building to a magnificent *crescendo*, with a Pauline outburst of praise:

> All mercies without Christ are bitter; and every cup is sweet that is seasoned but with a drop of his blood;—he truly is *"amor et deliciae humani generis,"*—the love and delight of the sons of men,—without whom they must perish eternally; "for there is no other name given unto them, whereby they may be saved, Acts iv. 12. He is the Way; men without him are Cains, wanderers, vagabonds:—he is the Truth; men without him are liars, like the devil, who was so of old:—he is the Life; without him men are dead, dead in trespasses and sins: he is the Light; without him men are in darkness, and go they know not whither:—he is the Vine; those that are not grafted in him are withered branches, prepared for the fire:—he is the Rock; men not built on him are carried away with a flood: he is Alpha and Omega, the first and the last, the author and the ender, the founder and the finisher of our salvation. He that hath not him, hath neither beginning of good, nor shall have end of misery. O blessed Jesus! how much better were it not to be, than to be without thee!—never to be born, than not to die in thee! A thousand hells come short of this, eternally to want Jesus Christ, as men do that want the gospel. (8:35-36)

Several features of Owen's thought may be observed in this quotation. First, Owen's back-to-back references to Luther and Gregory merely hint at the catholicity of his doctrine. While not ignorant of the diversity of Christological expression in past ages of the church, Owen is much more impressed by the unity of the church in its common faith, love, and experience of Christ (1:6-27; 13:129, 145; 15:77-81; 24:346).

Much more apparent in the foregoing quotation,

however, is Owen's own esteem of Christ. It is important to bear this in mind because Owen's reputation as a polemicist has obscured an important feature of his character as a Christian: while seldom expressed quite so ardently as here, it is clear from many places that Owen was captive to a deep and passionate love of Christ Jesus (1:3, 4, 149-69, 385; 2:40-78, 124-32, 136-40; 9:467-84). Such love constrained him, as he had been given the gifts, to labor in promoting that which he regarded as "the principal design" and "highest duty of them unto whom he is precious," which was "to hold the truth concerning him, (his person, spirit, grace, office, and authority,) and to abound in all duties of faith, love, trust, honour, and delight in him—so also to declare his excellency, to plead the cause of his glory, to vindicate his honour, and to witness him the only rest and reward of the souls of men, as they are called and have opportunity" (1:5).

That this concern motivated even his most polemical and scholastic works is observable in the preface to one of these, his *Diatriba de Justicia Divina, seu Justiciae Vindicatricis Vindiciae* [*Diatribe Concerning Divine Justice, or A Vindication of Vindicatory Justice*], where Owen explains why he resisted the temptation not to publish:

> Let but...the word of the cross have 'free course and be glorified;' let wretched sinners learn daily more and more of fellowship with Christ in his sufferings, of the necessity of satisfaction for sins by the blood of the Son of God, so that he who is 'white and ruddy, and the chiefest among ten thousand,' may appear so to them, 'yea altogether lovely,' till, being admitted into the chambers of the church's husband, they drink 'love that is better than wine,' and 'become willing people in the day of his power, and in the beauty of holiness;' and I shall very little regard being 'judged of man's judgment.' (10:489)

Finally, as the aim of the sermon was the settling of

gospel preachers in neglected areas of the kingdom (cf. 8:189), Owen indicates in these words the great subject of the gospel ministry: Christ and his benefits. It was, in the words of Paul, "to proclaim the unsearchable riches of Christ" (Eph. 3: 8). Expressed otherwise it was "the ministry of reconciliation," or "Christ and him crucified." These phrases are typical titles or organizing themes in a host of Puritan sermons and treatises.[1] More important than the titles, however, is the intensity with which many express their conviction of the necessity of preaching Christ: "No doctrine is more excellent, or necessary to be preached and studied, than Jesus Christ, and him crucified" (Flavel 1820, 34). Nor was it sufficient merely to "lecture" on the doctrine of Christ: "wherever there is a declaration of the excellencies of Christ, in his person, grace or office, it should be accompanied with an invitation and exhortation unto sinners to come unto him" (1:420).

"The Redeemer of God's Elect"
Two years later Owen published his *Salus Electorum, Sanguis Jesu; or The Death of Death in the Death of Christ*, an extensive, minutely detailed exegetical and systematic exposition of the doctrine of redemption, centering on the nature and extent of the atonement. This work, written to show that the doctrine of universal redemption is, in the words of J. I. Packer, "unscriptural and destructive of the gospel," deserves its reputation as a "classic" treatment of the Reformed doctrine of the atonement. The doctrine of the atonement will be considered in detail in chapter fourteen below, but a few words about this treatise are in order here.

The Death of Death is directed against "three variations on the theme of universal redemption" (Packer, 1959, 23). The first of these is that of classical Arminianism, the Arminianism condemned by the Synod of Dort and refuted by Owen in his *Display of Arminianism* (1642). The second variation was the theory of "hypothetical universalism" invented by Cameron and advanced by Amyraut of the Reformed Academy of Saumur (cf. Armstrong, 1969, 158-221). In 1643, Thomas Moore, a "lay theologian of East Anglia" published *The Universality of God's Free Grace*, a work in which all the principal scriptural texts pleaded in support of universal redemption find expression. Moore also raised several arguments still employed by Arminians. Moore's is the third variation.

In his preface to the *Death of Death*, Owen notes that "abler pens" had undertaken the refutation of these errors. Explaining his dissatisfaction with those works, and his intentions concerning his own, he says,

> they had all tied up themselves to some certain parts of the controversy, especially the removing of objections, neither compassing nor methodizing the whole; whereby I discerned that the nature of the things under debate,—namely, satisfaction, reconciliation, redemption, and the like,—was left exceedingly in the dark, and the strong foundation of the whole building not so much as once discovered. It was always upon my desires that some one would undertake the main, and unfold out of the word, from the bottom, the whole dispensation of the love of God to his elect in Jesus Christ, with the conveyance of it through the promises of the gospel, being in all the fruits thereof purchased and procured by the oblation and intercession of Jesus Christ; by which it could not but be made apparent what was the great design of the blessed Trinity in this great work of redemption, with how vain an attempt and fruitless endeavour it must needs be to extend it beyond the bounds and limits assigned unto it by the principal agents therein. That arguments also might be produced for the confirmation of the truth we assert, in opposition to the error opposed, and so the weak established and dissenters

> convinced, was much in my wishes. The doctrine of the satisfaction of Christ, his merit, and the reconciliation wrought thereby, understood aright by few, and of late oppugned by some, being so nearly related to the point of redemption, I desired also to have seen cleared, unfolded, vindicated, by some able pen. (10:155-56)

Other "able pens" not forthcoming, Owen set himself to the task.

The treatise, consequently, has two general objectives. The first is to provide a positive exposition of the doctrine of redemption (rather than simply to return one more volley in the exchange of arguments). This is the very strategy that has given the work its enduring quality. As J. I. Packer says, "Owen's work is a constructive, broad-based biblical analysis of the heart of the gospel," adding that,

> nobody has a right to dismiss the doctrine of the limitedness of atonement as a monstrosity of Calvinistic logic until he has refuted Owen's proof that it is part of the uniform biblical presentation of redemption, clearly taught in plain text after plain text. And nobody has done that yet. (Packer, 1959, 13)[2]

The salvation of man is expounded as an act of the triune God. The redemption of sinners, by their reconciliation, justification, sanctification, adoption, and glorification, is the "end" of the death of Christ, which the "Father and himself intended in it," and which was "effectually fulfilled and accomplished by it" (10:157). The doctrine of universal atonement, Owen demonstrates, depends upon the denial of these principles. As he explains,

> the masters of his opinion do see full well and easily, that if that be the end of the death of Christ which we have from the Scripture asserted, if those before recounted be the immediate fruits and products thereof, then one of these two things will necessarily follow:—that either, first, God and

> Christ failed of their end proposed, and did not accomplish that which they intended, the death of Christ being not a fitly-proportioned means for the attaining of that end (for any cause of failing cannot be assigned); which to assert seems to us blasphemously injurious to the wisdom, power, and perfection of God, as like-wise derogatory to the worth and value of the death of Christ;—or else, that all men, all the posterity of Adam, must be saved, purged, sanctified, and glorified; which surely they will not maintain, at least the Scripture and the woeful experience of millions will not allow. Wherefore, to cast a tolerable colour upon their persuasion, they must and do deny that God or his Son had any such absolute aim or end in the death... of Jesus Christ, or that any such thing was immediately procured and purchased by it. (10:159-60)

In this manner, Owen shifts the focus of the argument from a debate over words (e.g., "all," "world") to the more fundamental question of the Scripture's overall teaching concerning the attributes of God, the purpose of God in the atonement, and the nature and efficacy of that atonement.

After an explanation of the nature of ends and means, Owen proceeds to demonstrate the Trinitarian nature of redemption. The great agent in our salvation is the Triune God, with each of the divine persons acting distinctly in its accomplishment (10:163-79). Owen concludes this portion of his argument with an assertion that we will find to be a fundamental part of his understanding of the work of Christ:

> And thus have we discovered the blessed agents and undertakers in this work, their several actions and orderly concurrence unto the whole; which though they may be thus distinguished, yet they are not so divided but that every one must be ascribed to the whole nature, whereof each person is *"in solidum"* [entirely] partaker, and as they begin it, so

they will jointly carry along the application of it unto its ultimate issue and accomplishment. (10:179)

In the following section of the work Owen looks at the "means used by the fore-recounted agents in this work." He says, "Now, because the several actions of Father and Spirit were all exercised towards Christ, and terminated in him, as God and man, he only and his performances are to be considered as the means in this work, the several concurrences of both the other persons before mentioned being presupposed as necessarily antecedent or concomitant" (10:179). This is the first clear and specific assertion of Owen's Christocentric understanding of the work of redemption. Owen also introduces us here to his understanding of the mediator (10:179).

Next, Owen examines the ends of the death of Christ—namely, the manifestation of the glory of God's attributes, and the bringing of sinners unto God (10:201, 202). For the end of "bringing us unto God," Christ purchased both "the condition" (i.e., faith and "all fruits flowing from it in sanctification and universal holiness"), and "the thing promised upon that condition" (10:202), that is, full salvation. The connection is firmly established between the "impetration" or procurement of "the good things of God," and the "application" of those things to the sinner. What Christ has procured and the certainty of the application of that to the sinner are the questions at the heart of the dispute over the extent of the atonement.

The second of the general objectives in this treatise is the meticulous examination of arguments presented on various sides of the issue. Though, as pointed out earlier, Owen had shifted the focus away from the debate over words, it was still necessary to address the meanings of those Scriptures apparently supporting a universal redemption, and to respond to other arguments raised in its behalf. Perhaps the best measure of Owen's case is given by R. S. Franks, in his historical study, *The Work of*

Christ. Though expressing disagreement with Owen's doctrine, Franks says,

> One cannot close Owen's treatise without feeling admiration for its strong, nervous English, its forcible logic, and its deep religious feeling. McLeod Campbell has expressed the view that, if the idea of strict satisfaction be granted, Owen's logic in favour of the doctrine of particular redemption is unanswerable. If then the result be untenable, the inference is that the premise itself needs revision. (Franks, 1962, 471)

The premise Franks refers to is the doctrine of satisfaction to divine justice. However, as the following two works demonstrate, that premise is not easily dismissed.

In 1649, in an appendix to his *Aphorisms of Justification*, Richard Baxter criticized Owen's assertions made in *The Death of Death*, with regard to (among other points) the nature of the payment made by Christ for the sins of his elect. The importance of this question to Owen is evident from his assertion that,

> There have not been many things, in my whole inquiry after the mind of God in his word, which have more exercised my thoughts than the right ordering and distinct disposal of these whereof we treat. If the Lord hath discovered any thing unto me, or made out any thing by me, that may be for the benefit of any of his, I shall rejoice; it being always my desire that all things might fall out to the advantage of the gospel. (10:437)

In addition to replies to Baxter, Owen's *Of the Death of Christ, the Price He Paid, and the Purchase He Made* includes his judgments on the opinions of Bishop Davenant and Hugo Grotius. As Baxter had censured Owen's terminology and lack of scholastic precision, the *Death of Christ* is a more technically precise work than the former. More in the style of a scholastic reply, disputed points from the former treatise are meticulously examined. Among other problems addressed, Owen answers the old question raised in 1544 by antitrinitarians in the Grissons and later by Laelius Socinus to Calvin (Wilbur 1945, 99; Tedeschi 1965, 195): How is the freedom of pardon consistent with a doctrine of satisfaction?

After an Oxford scholar named Thomas Lushington published a translation of Crellius' *Commentary on the Epistle to the Hebrews* and a new Latin edition of the *Racovian Catechism*, the Oxford divines requested their vice-chancellor to refute the work of Crellius. Among other points, these works stimulated Owen to address a more fundamental question with regard to the satisfaction of divine justice: not what Christ is said to have paid, but in what sense, if any, may it be said that the satisfaction of divine justice was necessary at all. To this question, the Socinians had always responded in the negative, asserting Christ did not come to make a satisfaction to justice but to induce faith and repentance toward God, who freely forgives sinners upon their repentance. A number of Reformed theologians had also responded in the negative, but for a different reason: God had freely determined that his justice was to be satisfied by the sacrifice of Christ; to make the satisfaction of divine justice necessary was to impinge upon the sovereign freedom of God. It was instead, therefore, a matter of the divine economy.

In *The Death of Death*, Owen had asserted the same, but by 1653 he had changed his opinion. In the course of publicly defending the necessity of satisfaction against the Socinians, Vice-chancellor Owen made certain statements to which a number of the scholars expressed their disagreement. As Owen clarified his position and answered the objections of his opponents, he "was greatly encouraged in the conferences with these gentlemen to take a deeper view of the subject, and to examine it more closely, for the future benefit of mankind" (10:487). The outcome was his *Diatriba de Justicia Divina, seu Justiciae Vindicatricis Vindiciae* [*Diatribe about Divine Justice, or a Vindication of Vindicatory Justice*], in which Owen not only responded to the Socinians, but also delivered his judgment upon the opinions of William Twisse, Samuel Rutherford, and Gisbert Voetius (three titans of English, Scottish, and Dutch Reformed orthodoxy) concerning the absolute necessity of the atonement.

In 1653, under Cromwell's promise of toleration to all who profess the fundamentals of Christianity, John Biddle published *A Twofold Catechism*, to which the Council of State commissioned Owen to prepare a reply. Owen's answer, *Vindiciae Evangelicae* [Vindication of the Gospel] (1655), was his largest and most detailed strictly polemical treatise with regard to the doctrine of the Person of Christ (though not limited to that doctrine). The *Vindiciae* is a thorough, exegetical, point-by-point refutation of Socinian objections to Reformed theology as expressed in the Racovian catechism and, specifically, the catechism recently released by Biddle. In addition, Owen includes a critique of certain exegetical comments made by Hugo Grotius, which tended to support Socinianism. The *Vindiciae* is particularly valuable for several reasons. It provides Owen's most extensive exposition of the principal scriptural texts in support of the doctrine of the deity of Christ and his incarnation, as well as his criticism of the theological reasoning of the Socinians. In the preface, Owen provides a valuable resource in English for the history of antitrinitarianism, an analysis of the causes of antitrinitarianism and precautions to be taken in the refutation of the heresy.

"Mystic Sweet Communion"

The application of Christology to Christian piety is very evident in a 1657 work, *On Communion with God*. Although this work does not focus exclusively on the doctrine of Christ (written to provide the reader with an understanding of the communion which he is to experience with the persons of the Trinity considered distinctly), two-thirds of the work is devoted to the spiritual communion the believer has particularly with Jesus Christ.

An excellent description of the general character of this book was given in *The Biblical Repository* upon publication of Goold's edition of Owen's works. The unknown reviewer writes,

> No performance of Dr. Owen is more full of his peculiarities than that on *Communion*; none is likely to be more unpalatable to readers of wavering theology, and superficial experience. Its conclusions startle those who learnt from recent exegesis to treat the Song of Solomon as an expression of amatory warmth. But as some are found even now to prize the letters of Samuel Rutherford, the same class will not undervalue a writer who like Rutherford was equally at home in the niceties of scholastic distinction, the strategy of polemic defense, and the raptures of divine contemplation. The book appeared in 1657, after Owen's vice-chancellorship at Oxford, and was the summary of pulpit exercises, extending over some years of pastoral teaching. Our editor remarks with justice, that the term Communion, used in the title, denotes not merely the interchange of feeling between God in his gracious character and a soul in a gracious state, but the gracious relationship upon which this holy relationship is founded; which will account for the strong admixture of doctrine with the details of evangelical emotion.... Citations of classic and patristic Latin and Greek, and copious adduction of Hebrew originals, rabbinical glosses and sentences of school-doctors, stand side by side with fervid description of evangelical raptures, and the longing of divine affection. (*The Biblical Repository*, 1852, 170-71)

The blissful communion which Owen describes is

distinguishable from transcendental ecstasies in which the intellect is bypassed in a rush of emotion. The joy of the bride arises from her perception of the excellencies of the bridegroom. These are perceived as the Holy Spirit reveals them to her through the word. Hence, the subject of this sacred bliss is expounded with detailed attention upon such topics as Christ's wisdom and righteousness and grace. These are some of the things which the saints receive in communion with Christ.

This treatise elicited a belated response by William Sherlock entitled *A Discourse concerning the Knowledge of Jesus Christ, and on Union and Communion with Him* (1674). The previously quoted reviewer correctly observed that Sherlock "anticipates almost all the cavils of American new-divinity"; adding "we wish those who employ his spent missiles would give heed to the vigorous argument by which they are retorted" (*The Biblical Repository* 1852, 171). Sherlock's work touched off the "Communion Controversy" which, according to Goold, "soon embraced a wider range of topics, and points of more importance, than the merits of Owen's book" (2:276), namely, the doctrines of revelation and justification.[3]

In his *Vindication of the Preceding Discourse*, Owen says of Sherlock's work, "The first thing he quarrels about, is my asserting the necessity of acquaintance with the person of Christ; which expression he frequently makes use of afterward in a way of reproach" (2:286). This reflects Owen's conflict with the moralism of his time, which increasingly diminished the necessity of "acquaintance" with the person of Christ. The important thing for the moralists was knowing and obeying Christ's gospel, not loving Christ's person. This deistical tendency (for Christ's "gospel" was understood as equivalent to principles advanced by the Deists, the law of nature) was a constant alarm to Owen.

In response to Sherlock, Owen says,

> The crime, therefore, wherewith I am here charged, is my assertion that it is necessary that Christians should know Jesus Christ; which I have afterward increased, by affirming also that they ought to love him: for by Jesus Christ all the world of Christians intend the person of Christ; and the most of them, all of them,—the Socinians only excepted,—by his person, "the Word made flesh," or the Son of God incarnate, the mediator between God and man. (2:286)

Sherlock had drawn attention to the fact that "Christ" was used metonymically for the "gospel of Christ," to which Owen replies, "to conclude thence that Jesus Christ is not Jesus Christ, or that it is not the person of Christ that is firstly and properly intended by that name in the gospel, is a lewd and impious imagination; and we may as well make Christ to be only a light within us, as to be the doctrine of the gospel without us" (2:286). Sherlock's latitudinarian moralism, it would seem, was no more the knowledge of Christ than was Quaker mysticism.

Owen's admonition of Sherlock reflects an emphasis we find to be a principal concern of his as a pastor and theologian:

> I will mind this author of that, whereof if he be ignorant, he is unfit to be a teacher of others, and which if he deny, he is unworthy the name of a Christian,—namely, that by the knowledge of the person of Christ, the great mystery of God manifest in the flesh, as revealed and declared in the gospel, we are led into a clear and full understanding of many other mysteries of grace and truth; which are all centered in his person, and without which we can have no true nor sound understanding of them. I shall speak it yet again, that this author, if it be possible, may understand it; or, however, that he and his co-partners in design may know that I neither am nor ever will be ashamed of it:—that without the knowledge of the person of Christ, which is our ac-

quaintance with him (as we are commanded to acquaint ourselves with God) as he is the eternal Son of God incarnate, the mediator between God and man, with the mystery of the love, grace and truth of God therein, as revealed and declared in the Scripture, there is no true, useful, saving knowledge of the gospel to be attained. This being the substance of what is asserted in my discourse, I challenge this man, or any...to assert and maintain the contrary, if so be they are indeed armed with such a confidence as to impugn the foundations of Christianity. (2:288-89)

One interesting feature of the work is a lengthy quotation from Richard Hooker's *Laws of Ecclesiastical Polity*. From Hooker's exposition of the communion which the saints enjoy with Christ in the Lord's supper, Owen concluded that the doctrine of union and communion which he had himself taught was the very doctrine of the Church of England as expounded by Hooker and other leading Anglican divines, from which Sherlock and likeminded Latitudinarians had departed (2:280-85).

Owen's "Fundamentalism"

Within three years of the publication of *On Communion with God*, Owen would produce three treatises on the doctrine of revelation. The first, *Of the Divine Original, Authority, Self-Evidencing Light, and Power of the Scriptures*, along with a similar and more extensive work, *The Reason of Faith* (1677), constitute a Calvinistic apologetic for scriptural authority. In the words of Thomas Chalmers, the *Divine Original* proves "that the written Word itself possesses a self-evidencing light and power for manifesting its own divine original, superior to the testimony of eye-witnesses, or the evidence of miracles, or those supernatural gifts with which the first teachers of Christianity were endowed for accrediting their divine mission" (16:296). The second of the three treatises was a dissertation, which was delivered before the University of Oxford: *Pro Sacris Scripturis Adversus hujus Temporis Fanaticos* [In Behalf of Sacred Scripture against the Fanatics of These Times]. Among other things, *Pro Sacris Scripturis* addresses two matters related to Christology, revelation, and hermeneutics, which were raised by the Quakers: the meaning of the "Word of God" as that expression relates to Scripture, and the "Inner Light." Thirdly, in 1661 Owen wrote his *Theologoumena Pantodapa* [Theological Affirmations of All Sorts], a work which, according to Goold, was praised by Ryland as "an incomparable work, perhaps the very greatest of the kind ever written by a British divine" (17:2).[4] Theology is possible only for the regenerate, as it is a spiritual gift. As Goold describes it,

> Christ is the author of spiritual gifts; and the unction by which he imparts them to us is from the Holy Ghost.... The object of this knowledge is all truth pertaining to the kingdom of Christ; the mode of its communication is supernatural and by the Spirit; its foundation is laid in a spiritual understanding; its primary effect is conformity to the image of God in Christ (17:12-13).

The aim of the book again is to demonstrate the necessity of the Christian revelation as that unique and all-sufficient revelation of the mind and will of God to an apostate race.

It was in the interest of the foundation of Christianity that Owen published his *Christologia, or Declaration of the Glorious Mystery of the Person of Christ, God and man, with the infinite wisdom, love, and power of God in the constitution thereof. As also, of the grounds and reasons of his incarnation; the nature of his ministry in heaven; the present state of the church above thereon; and the use of his person in religion* (1679). The work opens by drawing attention to the Savior's question to his disciples of "their apprehensions concerning his person" which is found in the sixteenth chapter of Matthew. In his ensuing exposition of Matthew 16:18 ("upon this rock I will build my church, and the gates of hell shall not prevail against it"), Owen introduces a question not only at the heart of the Protestant cause, but of crucial importance to the Christian faith, namely, what is the foundation of the church, the "Rock" on which it is built? After arguing convincingly that the Roman papacy cannot be the foundation referred to, Owen announces that the text supports three great truths. First, "the person of Christ, the Son of the living God, as vested with his offices, whereunto he was called and anointed, is the foundation of the church, the rock whereon it is built." Owen says,

> The foundation of the church is twofold: (1.) Real; (2.) Doctrinal. And in both ways, Christ alone is the foundation. The real foundation of the church he is, by virtue of the mystical union of it unto him, with all the benefits whereof, and whereby, it is made partaker. For thence alone hath it spiritual life, grace, mercy, perfection, and glory:... And he is the doctrinal foundation of it, in that the faith or doctrine concerning him and his offices is that divine truth which in a peculiar manner animates and constitutes the church of the New Testament. (1:34)

So pervasive is this foundation (*fundamentum*) motif in Owen's Christology, and in the *Christologia* in particular, that it is necessary to consider it further.

As the previous quotation indicates, Owen viewed Christ as the foundation of the church in two ways: personal and doctrinal. The relation between these is very important, because the benefits of Christ as the real foundation are, in most respects and in an immeasurable degree, communicated to the church through the laying of him, and building upon him as the doctrinal foundation; that is, through "preaching Christ." Consequently, it is the "design of the Christian" to see that his life is built upon Christ. Furthermore, it is the design of the Christian preacher to lay that doctrinal foundation in the hearts of his hearers and to edify the church by duly building upon that foundation. This is the standard by which to judge all doctrine: "Whatever complies with the revelation hereof is true and genuine; what does not is various and strange" (24:428).[5]

Since the introduction of Heinrich Bullinger's *Exposition of the Apocalypse* and the publication of Foxe's *Book of Martyrs*, English Reformed theologians had viewed the history of the church in terms of the conflict between Christ and anti-Christ. Owen did likewise, but in the *Christologia* he points in particular to the way this conflict centered upon the doctrine of the person of Christ. Satan's design, therefore, having failed to destroy the "real" foundation of the church through his attacks upon Jesus Christ during his earthly life, has been to bring the church of Christ to ruin—first by persecution, and secondly, failing in that, by attacking the church at its doctrinal foundation through the introduction of Christological heresies. Of the study of these heresies Owen says,

> I esteem it useful, that the very ordinary sort of Christians should, at least in general, be acquainted with what hath passed in this great contest about the person of Christ, from the beginning. For there are two things relating thereunto wherein their faith is greatly concerned. First, there is evidence given therein unto the truth of those predictions of the Scripture, wherein this fatal apostasy from the truth, and opposition unto the Lord Christ are foretold: and, secondly, an eminent instance of his power and faithfulness, in the disappointment and conquest of the gates of hell in the management of this opposition. (1:9)

Owen's analysis of the ancient church's management of Christological heresy shows his own understanding of the proper course to be taken in the seventeenth century.

First, he emphasizes that the defense of the truth was undertaken by the "guides and rulers of the church" and that this was "by the Scripture...confirmed with apostolical tradition consonant thereunto" (1:9). "All true believers, in their several stations—by mutual watchfulness, preaching, or writing, according unto their calls and abilities—effectually used the outward means for the preservation and propagation of the faith of the church" (1:9). Owen emphasizes that this method was effectual, whereas the employment of "arts and arms of another kind" has never been. Whether this conviction is the cause or the effect of his views of toleration is difficult to determine, but there can be no doubt that Owen believed the preached word was the God-ordained and effectual means for the preservation of Christianity.

Second, although Owen uses and defends the use of extra-scriptural words in the exposition of the Trinity, he points to their introduction into the theological vocabulary of the church as giving "occasion...unto endless contentions about them" (1:10). One of Owen's principal criticisms was that

> the curious and serpentine wits of men, finding themselves by this means set at liberty to think and discourse of those mysteries of the blessed Trinity, and the person of Christ, without much regard unto plain divine testimonies, (in such ways wherein cunning and sophistry did much bear sway,) began to multiply such new, curious, and false notions about them,... as caused new disturbances, and those of large extent and long continuance. (1:11)

While holding to the classical doctrines of the Trinity and the incarnation, Owen is very critical of the unscriptural ways these were debated in the past, particularly by the schoolmen, who thereby encouraged the rise of antitrinitarianism (12:42).

Owen mentions several forms of ancient heresy,

which he applies to contemporary forms of opposition to the church's foundation. First, he mentions Gnosticism, "which introduced other doctrines and notions of divine things, absolutely exclusive of the person and mediation of Christ," adding,

> This was the first way that Satan attempted the faith of the church, viz., by substituting a perfecting light and knowledge in the room of the person of Christ. And, for aught I know, it may be one of the last ways whereby he will endeavour for the accomplishment of the same design. Nor had I made mention of these pernicious imaginations, which have laid rotting in oblivion for some many generations, but that some again endeavour to revive them, at least so far as they were advanced and directed against the faith and knowledge of the person of Christ. (1:38)

To this he adds his criticism of the specific Christological heresies.

Owen next identifies five general classes of opponents to the foundation of the church, the person of Christ. First, there are the Romanists, who in the place of Christ set up another head of the church, i.e., who undermine the foundation of the church by directing Christ's remarks concerning that foundation away from himself and toward Peter. Second, there are the Socinians who make a direct attack upon the foundation of the church. Third, some, such as the Quakers, deny the person of Christ in a practical way, by replacing the true Christ with an imaginary subjective Christ within. Owen appears to name two more classes of opponents to the person of Christ. Some reject the necessity of revelation, on the assumption that a religion based upon nature is sufficient. Here is a clearly deistical sentiment observed and requiring opposition sixteen years before the publication of *Christianity not Mysterious*. He points to others, generally orthodox, who we may suppose either fail to regard the righteousness of Christ as the formal cause of justification (see Allison 1966, passim), or who fail to communicate the practical centrality of Christ's person and work to their hearers. These place a great emphasis upon holy living, but undertake the preaching of holiness non-evangelically, so that Owen is forced to voice the lament of Augustine: "*sed nomen Jesu non erat ibi*" ["There were in it many things laudable and delectable, but the name of Jesus was not there"] (1:42).

Given his Puritan theology, one might expect that even the doctrine of the hypostatic union would receive an exposition that is scriptural in its origin and practical in its application. This is exactly the case. It may come as a surprise that in the *Christologia* the hypostatic union is not treated in detail until chapter eighteen, near the end of the book. For its statement and defense, it seems Owen felt the doctrine had been satisfactorily handled by others, but some exposition was still necessary.

The first of two purposes for the treatment of the doctrine in the *Christologia* is "to help those that believe, in the regulation of their thoughts about this divine person" (1:223). The knowledge of the person of Christ, or his two natures and the hypostatic union, is foundational for understanding "the whole work of his mediation, with the design of God's love and grace therein, with our own duty thereon" (1:223). This should have been apparent from the fact that the whole treatise up to this point, in both its doctrinal and practical dimensions, was built upon this foundation, but it would seem that now it was necessary to spell it out for the reader. The second aim was "to manifest in particular how ineffably distinct the relation between the Son of God and the man Christ Jesus is, from that relation and union which may be between God and believers, or between God and any other creature" (1:223).

"The Glory of His People Israel"

Owen's greatest exegetical accomplishment was the publication of his *Exposition of the Epistle to the Hebrews* (1668 - 1684) in four folio volumes. It is said that upon finishing this work Owen exclaimed, "Now my work is done; it is time for me to die" (1:lxxxvi). It is evident throughout the work that Owen's great objectives were the defense and proclamation of the person and work of Jesus the Divine Messiah and the application of these truths to the lives of his contemporaries. As Goold accurately describes it,

> The nature of the Exposition is threefold;—partly critical, in the brief comment sometimes made on the text and language of the Epistle; partly doctrinal, in the ample and thorough discussion of the great truths of which the language is the vehicle; and partly practical, in the observations immediately bearing on the life and duty with which these discussions are generally followed up. That so much of the Exercitations, and of the earlier portion of the Exposition, should be occupied with a refutation of Socinian and Jewish errors, is a circumstance admitting of explanation, from the progress which Socinianism was making in the times of Owen, and from the lingering deference that was paid to the notions of the Jews on all matters of Hebrew literature and learning. The space occupied with these controversial discussions may sometimes lead the reader away from the direct consideration of the Epistle, but it was professedly to meet these errors that the work was undertaken; and the Epistle itself gives prominence to the very doctrines on which a Christian author comes most directly into collision with those who impugn the divinity of Christ, or deny that he was the promised Messiah. (18:ix-x)

The Hebrews commentary is the product of over twenty years of research and reflection (1:lxxxiv-lxxxv),

"Who Do You Say That I Am?"

giving us the most mature form of his thought on nearly every topic to be considered in the present work.

Owen's final written work was his *Meditations and Discourses on the Glory of Christ*. "It is a striking circumstance," says Andrew Thomson,

> that each of the three great Puritan divines wrote a treatise on the subject of heaven, and that each had his own distinct aspect in which he delighted to view it. To the mind of Baxter, the most prominent idea of heaven was that of rest; and who can wonder, when it is remembered that his earthly life was little else than one prolonged disease?—to the mind of Howe, ever aspiring after a purer state of being, the favourite conception of heaven was that of holy happiness;—while to the mind of Owen, heaven's glory was regarded as consisting in the unveiled manifestation of Christ. (1:c)

Actually, the *Glory of Christ* is not strictly a treatise on heaven, but a treatise on the vision, by faith here and by sight hereafter, of the Mediator's glory. While the *Christologia* describes the glorious mystery of the person of Christ in order to move the reader to be found built on him as the sure foundation (1:5), these meditations focus attention upon the glory of Christ to help the reader in the duty and privilege of beholding Christ by faith, and so be carried "cheerfully, comfortably, and victoriously through life and death, and all that we have to conflict withal in either of them," afterwards attaining the beatific vision of Christ in heaven (1:277, 284).

The treatise builds upon the principle that the representation of God's nature and will through Christ is the means of conformity to him. This is scripturally expressed in two of Owen's most universally employed biblical texts: 2 Corinthians 4:6 ("For God, who commanded the light to shine out of darkness, hath shined in our hearts to give the light of the knowledge of the glory of God in the face of Jesus Christ") and 2 Corinthians 3:18 ("But we all, with open face beholding as in a glass the glory of the Lord, are changed into the same image from glory to glory, even as by the Spirit of the Lord"). These texts, or near paraphrases, appear in a great number of Owen's writings, whether the subject is Christ, the Holy Spirit, the Christian life, or the church.[6] The message in these phrases is no less significant for Owen's thought than "the candle of the Lord" is for Whichcote. (Nor was Owen inclined to forget the difference between this candle and the "effulgence" of glory in the face of the "sun of righteousness.")[7] Jesus Christ is the theanthropic medium for the knowledge of the glory of God. To provide a view of this glory is the aim of the church, the work of the Spirit, and the purpose of the Father. Christ is the archetype, conformity to him is the motive, and steadfastly beholding him by faith is the means, for the restoration of the image of God. As Owen says, "To know God, so as thereby to be made like unto him, is the chief end of man. This is done perfectly only in the person of Christ, all other means of it being subordinate thereunto, and none of them of the same nature therewithal" (1:65).

Conclusion

In addition to these works, Owen's Christology may be observed in his sermons and sacramental discourses, and his treatises upon justification, the Holy Spirit, sanctification, and worship. Across four decades, Owen labored to promote the knowledge of Christ. The "one thing needful" for the saints was their progress in this knowledge; the principal obstacles to their good were the forces at work in the nation, and within their own hearts, which tended to deny, pervert, or overshadow the biblical doctrines necessary for the right understanding and due esteem of Christ's person and work. However, Owen realized it was not sufficient to expound the scriptural

"Who Do You Say That I Am?" 75

doctrine of Christ when the one infallible authority for that doctrine was in question. In the following chapter, we will look at Owen's doctrine of the authority and interpretation of Scripture.

---

[1] See as examples, *The Unsearchable Riches of Christ*, by Thomas Brooks (1866, 3:3-232); *The Saint's Knowledge of Christ's Love; or, The Unsearchable Riches of Christ*, by John Bunyan (1853, 2:1-40); *The Fountain of Life* by John Flavel (1820, 1: xvii-561); *The Mediator* by Thomas Goodwin (1863, 5:10-436); *A Discourse of the Knowledge of God in Christ*, by Stephen Charnock (1865, 4:110-63), or his *The Knowledge of Christ Crucified* (1865, 4:494-506); "Christ's All in All" (Burroughs 1654, 31-62); *Christ, A Christian's Only Gain* (Vines 1660, 1-235); and *The Excellent Knowledge of Christ*, by David Clarkson (1696, 201-21). For a typical ordination exhortation to preach Christ, see Edward Reynolds, *Preaching of Christ* (1679, 1031-40)

[2] None of the recent apologies for Arminianism provides an equally comprehensive treatment or succeeds in answering Owen's argument. Terry Miethe, for example (Pinnock, 1989, 71-96), merely contradicts several arguments commonly offered by Calvinists, without really facing Owen's general argument or answering the rejoinders Owen made to the same Arminian points when they were raised in the seventeenth century.

[3] As far as I have been able to determine, no significant study has been made of this controversy which involved at least six Puritan and two Latitudinarian writers for four years in a vigorous theological war over the very issues which most distinguished them.

[4] *Theologuoumena* and *Pro Sacris Scripturis* have been translated by Stephen P. Westcott, and published in English under the title, *Biblical Theology* by Soli Deo Gloria Publications (Pittsburgh: 1994), 856 pages.

[5] Richard A. Muller's treatment of the issue of "fundamental articles of religion" (2003, 406-30) shows that the use of Christ as the doctrinal foundation of the church was fairly standard during the Reformation and post-Reformation periods.

[6] Quotations or allusions to 2 Corinthians 4:6 occur at least 85 times across 20 volumes of Owen's works.

[7] This significance of this difference is not missed by Charnock who remarks, "Reason, though it be 'the candle of the Lord,'...yet it is but a candle, and can no more discover the nature of God as he is to be known in Christ, than a candle can help us to see the sun when it is masked by a thick cloud" (1865, 4:154).

CHAPTER
4

"Flesh and Blood Has Not Revealed it unto You"

The principal authority for John Owen's Christology was the Bible.[1] This might appear to be a simplistic assertion in that ancient Arians and Socinians and even many modern opponents of incarnational Christology claim that their doctrine is agreeable with what the Bible teaches about Jesus. The issue, therefore, is one of theological method. The subject of the present chapter is Owen's theological method, with particular attention to the way it fits into and influenced his Christology.

Can the Scriptures teach or compel men to believe that which is not comprehensible to human reason? The Arminians, Socinians, Quakers and Latitudinarians generally denied that it could (7:5-6), encouraging the rise of a religion which lay "within the limits of reason alone," and which ultimately dispensed with anything in the Scripture not discoverable by the light of nature alone. The great issue between Owen and his opponents was ultimately over the authority of Scripture. The principal objections raised by his opponents were essentially denials of some explicit or necessarily inferred teaching of Scripture on the grounds that such a teaching was contrary to "right reason" (e.g., 12:208-209). To Owen, this

"Flesh and Blood Has Not Revealed it unto You"

rationalism was clearly opposed to "right reason" because it failed to appreciate the infinite difference between God's knowledge and our own. This was significant enough when it came to "natural things," but when it comes to "supernatural things," even though there is natural revelation of these, nothing short of a "supernatural knowledge" of them is sufficient for saving faith or for true understanding.

Supernatural knowledge, the *sine qua non* of true theology, is the "illumination of the minds of men" by the Holy Ghost. This illumination is "that supernatural knowledge that any man hath or may have of the mind and will of God, as revealed unto him by supernatural means, for the law of his faith, life, and obedience" (4:7). As this definition makes clear, supernatural *knowledge* depends upon a supernatural *means*, namely, supernatural *revelation*. As Owen explains it,

> unto this supernatural illumination it is required both that its object be things only supernaturally revealed, or as supernaturally revealed, 1 Cor. ii. 9, 10, and that it be wrought in us by a supernatural efficiency, or the immediate efficacy of the Spirit of God, Eph. i. 17-19; 2 Cor. iv. 6. This David prays for, Ps. cxix. 18,... "'Reveal,' or uncover mine eyes, bring light and spiritual understanding into my mind, 'that I may behold' ... 'wondrous things out of thy law.'" The light he prayed for within did merely respect the doctrine of the law without.... The various supernatural revelations that God hath made of himself, his mind and will,... are the sole and adequate object of supernatural illumination. (4:7-8)

These two requirements of supernatural *content* and supernatural *efficiency* should be kept in mind, as they will reappear under the consideration of the revelatory role of Christ, and so demonstrate the Christocentric nature of Owen's doctrine of Scripture. In this particular context, however, Owen is making two points: against the rationalists of his day he is arguing the necessity and certainty of supernatural revelation from the Holy Spirit, and against the Quakers he is arguing that this illumination comes as the Spirit opens the mind to the light of Holy Scripture.

The Divine Origin and Authority of Scripture

Owen's basic argument for the authority of Scripture is its divine origin. Though the mystics of the seventeenth century liked to call attention to the fact that God had spoken long before there was any written revelation, reasoning that we might as easily expect a similar revelation afterward, the Reformed tradition had always affirmed this, without drawing the same inference.[2] According to Owen, "divine external revelation" was given out "immediately" to the patriarchs (Adam, Enoch, Noah, Abraham, etc.) to be communicated to the church until it was set down in writing by Moses. Owen follows Calvin in his emphasis that this word of revelation was self-evidencing (4:8; *Institutes*, I.vi.2). However, he emphasizes that this revelation was self-evidencing "to faith and not to sense." That is, as the creation bears witness to the being and power of God when men "exercise the best of their rational abilities in the consideration and contemplation of them," so men must receive these divine revelations with the exercise of "the faith, conscience, obedience, and reason of them," because "therein they gave full assurance of their proceeding from him" (4:9).

Though this method of revelation was "sufficient, to guide in all required duty to God," nevertheless, "as it was in itself imperfect and liable to many disadvantages, so through the weakness, negligence, and wickedness of men, it proved insufficient to retain the knowledge of God in the world." There was need of a "certain standard of divine truth," which was supplied by the inscripturation of "all divine revelations given out by himself from the beginning of the world, and all that ever shall be so to the end thereof, which are of general use unto the church, that it may be thoroughly instructed in the whole mind and will of God, and be directed in all that worship of him and obedience unto him which is necessary to give us acceptance with him here, and to bring us unto the eternal enjoyment of him hereafter" (4:11).

Of this revelation Owen says God obliged the church to the use of it alone, that all other revelation for the Old Testament church was comprised in the Old Testament books, and that the full revelation was committed to and perfected by Jesus Christ. Scripture, therefore, is the "only external means of divine supernatural illumination, because it is the only repository of all divine supernatural revelation" (4:12).

Owen gives two general prerequisites if the Scriptures are to be "a sufficient external cause of illumination unto us": we must believe with a faith which is "divine and supernatural," knowing "assuredly the Scripture to be the word of God" (4:14; cf. 4:15-20, 47-82), and we must have an understanding of its teaching (4:14). The concept of a "divine and supernatural faith" is important to Owen and will require some attention here.

First, faith is described in terms of its material object (the thing believed in), and its formal object (the reason we believe it). In *The Reason of Faith*, Owen names as the material object of faith the "things revealed in the Scripture, declared unto us in propositions of truth," and mentions as examples the Trinity and the death, burial, and resurrection of Christ. Owen says "sometimes, indeed, this expression of 'believing the Scriptures' by a metonomy, denotes both the formal and material objects of our faith, the Scriptures themselves as such, and the things contained in them," as when the disciples "did... believe what was declared in the Scriptures because it was so declared in them" (4:16). In his *Christologia*, however, he will emphasize the person of Christ as the formal object of our faith.

Owen's position differs greatly from the view often advanced against the Orthodox doctrine of Scripture—that Scripture, or a doctrine concerning it, became the formal object of faith as opposed to Christ. If Owen refers to the propositions of truth as the formal objects of faith, he does so in a general way, not in contrast to Christ himself. When he distinguishes between Christ and the propositions made known in the gospel, he relates the person of Christ, the propositions made known in the gospel of Christ, and the illumination of the Holy Spirit in the following manner. The person of Christ is the "'*Objectum reale et formale fidei*'—the real, formal object of our faith in this matter." The gospel, however, is the "'*Medium revelans*,' or '*lumen deferens*' [bearing or carrying light]—the means of its revelation, or the objective light whereby the perception and knowledge of it is conveyed unto our minds," and without which we "can behold nothing of this image of God." To these two, Owen adds the "*Lumen preparans, elevans, disponens subjectum* ['Light preparing, elevating, and disposing the subject']—the internal light of the mind in the saving illumination of the Holy Spirit, enabling us—by that means, and in the use of it," that is, by means of the Bible and the preaching of the gospel, "spiritually to behold and discern the glory of God in the face of Christ: 2 Cor. iv. 6" (1:74-75).

This "divine and supernatural faith" is the only faith that will suffice. "The authority of God,... the first and only absolute Truth, whose word is truth—speaking in and by the penmen of the Scriptures—evinced singly in and by the Scripture itself—is the sole bottom and foundation, or formal reason, of our assenting to those Scriptures as his word, and of our submitting our hearts and consciences unto them with that faith and obedience which morally respect him, and are due to him alone" (16:307). The same self-evidencing power that accompanied the word when it was given to the prophet is present in the written word. The Scriptures

> abundantly and uncontrollably manifest themselves to be the word of the living God; so that, merely on the account of their own proposal of themselves unto us in the name and majesty of God, as such—without the contribution of help or assistance from tradition, church, or any thing else without themselves—we are obliged, upon the penalty of eternal damnation,... to receive them, with that subjection of soul which is due to the word of God. The authority of God shining in them, they afford unto us all the divine evidence of themselves which God is willing to grant unto us, or can be granted us, or is any way needful for us. (16:307)

Owen assumes this presuppositional stance for the very reason that since there can be no higher authority than this, none can be required or expected. If Scripture is the word of God, there can simply be no higher court of appeal. But how may we be sure that God has in fact revealed himself by his word, and that the claims of Scripture are not "deceivable pretences"? Owen answers that every revelation that God makes of himself carries within itself sufficient evidence that it comes from him. "Wherever they are seen and considered, they undeniably evince that they are so, and that what they teach concerning him, they do it in his name and authority" (16:310). In a manner similar to Calvin, Owen argues that all God's self-revelation is self-evidencing.

> Let us consider the issue of this general induction: As God, in the creation of the world, and all things therein contained, hath so made and framed them, hath left such characters of his eternal power and wisdom in them and upon them, filled them with

such evidences of their Author, suited to the apprehensions of rational creatures, that without any other testimony from himself, or any else—under the naked consideration and contemplation of what they are—they so far declare their Creator, that they are left wholly inexcusable who will not learn and know him from thence; so in the giving out of his Word to be the foundation of that world which he hath set up on this world,... his church—he hath, by his Spirit implanted in it and impressed on it such characters of his goodness, power, wisdom, holiness, love to mankind, truth, faithfulness, with all the rest of his glorious excellencies and perfections, that...it declares itself to be his, and makes good its authority from him; so that the refusal of it upon its own evidence brings unavoidable condemnation on the souls of men. (16:312)

Owen's Theological Method

The second necessity for supernatural illumination is the understanding of the Scripture. As he was the author of Scripture, so also is the Holy Spirit the "principal efficient cause" in the understanding of it. *"There is an especial work of the Spirit of God on the minds of men, communicating spiritual wisdom, light, and understanding unto them, necessary unto their discerning and apprehending aright the mind of God in his word, and the understanding of the mysteries of heavenly truth contained therein"* (4:124-25). The true understanding of Scripture, i.e., the true theology, is limited to the regenerate (Owen 1994, 603-604).

This understanding comes not through direct revelations or "enthusiasms," but by the Spirit's *"enlightening our minds* and enabling our understandings to perceive and apprehend his mind and will" (4:125). Owen's directions for understanding the mind of God in Scripture grow out of and answer to this conviction.

The "general and absolutely necessary" means for

understanding the mind of God in the Scripture" is the *"diligent reading of the Scripture, with a sedate, rational consideration of what we read"* (4:199). Owen complains that many diligently study other writings, but "their reading of the Scripture is for the most part superficial, without that intension of mind and spirit, that use and application of means, which are necessary unto the understanding of it, as the event doth manifest" (4:201). For the better understanding of what is read, Owen adds the use of a number of means that he calls spiritual, disciplinary, and ecclesiastical. The same means, in general, are urged by Owen upon theological students as providing the best preparation for dealing with Socinianism (12:48-53).

Spiritual Means
Agreeably to his fundamental conviction of the need of the Holy Spirit for the understanding of the mind of God, Owen emphasizes the importance of *"fervent supplications, in and by Jesus Christ, for supplies of the Spirit of grace...to give him an understanding of the Scriptures and the will of God therein"* (4:204). Applying this to the theological conflict of the time, he adds that "the practical neglect of this duty is the true reason why so many that are skilful enough in the *disciplinary means of knowledge* are yet such strangers to the true knowledge of the mind of God" (4:202; cf. 21:311).

To prayer Owen adds that there must be a *"Readiness to receive impressions from divine truths as revealed unto us,* conforming our minds and hearts unto the doctrine made known" (4:205). This is because the "end of all divine revelations" is to "beget the image and likeness of themselves in the minds of men" (4:205). The relationship of this practice to the person of Christ will appear below, when we consider Owen's doctrine of sanctification as consisting of conformity to Christ. One of the most forceful applications of this principle, however, may be found in Owen's preface to the *Vindiciae Evangelicae*. Owen says,

> When the heart is cast indeed into the mould of the doctrine that the mind embraceth; when the evidence and necessity of the truth abides in us; when not the sense of the words only is in our heads, but the sense of the things abides in our hearts; when we have communion with God in the doctrine we contend for,—then shall we be garrisoned, by the grace of God, against all the assaults of men. And without this all our contending is, as to ourselves, of no value. What am I the better if I can dispute that Christ is God, but have no sense or sweetness in my heart from hence that he is a God in covenant with my soul? What will it avail me to evince, by testimonies and arguments, that he hath made satisfaction for sin, if, through my unbelief, the wrath of God abides upon me, and I have no experience of my own being made the righteousness of God in him,—if I find not, in my standing before God, the excellency of having my sins imputed to him and his righteousness imputed to me. (12:52)

His conclusion illustrates an important emphasis in Puritan piety: the difference between the knowledge that "puffs up," and the knowledge that belongs to eternal life and sanctification:

> It is the power of truth in the heart alone that will make us cleave unto it indeed in an hour of temptation. Let us, then, not think that we are any thing the better for our conviction of the truths of the great doctrines of the gospel, for which we contend with these men, unless we find the power of the truths abiding in our own hearts, and have a continual experience of their necessity and excellency in our standing before God and our communion with him. (12:52)

In addition, there must follow the "*Practical obedience*

in the course of our walking before God" (4:206). Also, "*A constant design for growth and a progress in knowledge, out of love to the truth and experience of its excellency*, is useful, yea, needful, unto the right understanding of the mind of God in the Scriptures" (4:206). Owen expects "no great or useful discoveries of the mind of God" from those who rest satisfied in the knowledge of a system of theology (4:206-207). This might be surprising when we consider Owen's own systematic prowess, but that is just the point: Owen believes that divine truths are inter-related, but he is equally convinced that the "stores of truth laid up" in the Scriptures are "inexhaustible," that those who have gone before "are yet far from having discovered the depths of this vein of wisdom" (4:205). This reflects another important aspect of Puritan piety; the Christian is a *viator*, a pilgrim, who feeds upon Zion's "thousand sacred sweets" as he makes his journey. Finally, Owen stresses participation in "ordinances of spiritual worship" (4:207). These are God-ordained means for growth in the knowledge of himself.

Disciplinary Means
By disciplinary means Owen refers to "the due use and improvement of *common arts and sciences*" (4:209). Owen cannot be accused of obscurantism, as his knowledge in this area was vast; but his use of the arts and sciences was regulated by his Christianity. They "have no moral good in themselves, but being indifferent in their own nature, their end, with the manner of their management thereunto, is the only measure and standard of their worth and value" (4:209).

The most important of these for the interpreter of Scripture was skill in the original languages. Of course, this was needed for the interpretation of the Scripture in general, but in the preface to the *Vindiciae Evangelicae*

Owen stresses its special importance in dealing with Socinianism:

> He that is not in some measure acquainted with these will scarcely make thorough work in dealing with them. There is not a word, nor scarce a letter in a word (If I may so speak), which they do not search and toss up and down; not an expression which they pursue not through the whole Scripture, to see if any place will give countenance to the interpretation of it which they embrace. (12:50)

One example of fallacious Socinian exegesis mentioned by Owen is their use of Hebrew words related to the doctrine of satisfaction. Knowledge of the original language is essential:

> Unless a man can debate the use of words with them in the Scripture, and by instances from other approved authors, it will be hard so to enclose or shut them up but that they will make way to evade and escape. Press them with any testimony of Scripture, if of any one word of the testimony, whereon the sense of the whole in any measure depends, they can except that in another place that the word in the original hath another signification, and therefore it is not necessary that it should here signify as you urge it, unless you are able to debate the true meaning and import of the word with them, they suppose they have done enough to evade your testimony. (12:50)

However, knowledge of the languages alone would not suffice. This skill must be exercised "with that humility, sobriety, reverence of the Author of the Scripture, and respect unto the *analogy of faith*, which ought to bear sway in the minds of all men who undertake to expound the oracles of God" (4:216). Owen emphasizes that this lack of humility, a tendency of "effecting *eminency by singularity*," was "a snare of Satan" which had done much harm to the cause of evangelical theology (4:217-19, 224-26; 12:49-50).

After knowledge of the languages, Owen stresses the importance of "the *history and geography of the world*," and "*chronology*" (4:219). Owen gives two general reasons for this: the first pertains to the observation of God's witness to himself in the creation and providential rule in the world (i.e., in natural revelation); the second pertains to the observation of redemptive history. Knowledge of history is necessary for the due exposition of prophecies, while biblical chronology, when applied to the prophecy of Daniel 9:24-27, affords a strong testimony to Jesus' identity as the Messiah, despite the difficulties involved in being precise (4:219-23; 18:262-348).[3]

The student also needs "skill in the ways and methods of reasoning" (4:223). Owen says, "An *ability to judge of the sense of propositions*, how one thing depends on another, how it is deduced from it, follows upon it, or is proved by it; what is the design of him that writes or speaks in any discourse or reasoning; how it is proposed, confirmed, illustrated,—is necessary unto any rational consideration to be exercised about whatever is so proposed unto us" (4:223). At the same time, Owen insists that

> this must be admitted with its limitations; for whatever perfection there seems to be in our art of reasoning, it is to be subject to the wisdom of the Holy Ghost in the Scripture.... In the consideration of all the effects of infinite wisdom, there must be an allowance for the deficiency of our comprehension; when humble subjection of conscience, and the captivation of our understandings to the obedience of faith, is the best means of learning what is proposed unto us. (4:224)

This is very important to Owen, as we see from the many criticisms made of the so-called "right reason" employed by his Socinian and Arminian opponents.

Especially important is the observance of the "analogy of faith": "And this is that pride which is the source and original of *heresy*,—namely, when men will prefer their seemingly wise and rational conceptions of the sense of *particular places* before the *analogy of faith* (4:224). Owen points to the Quaker's abuse of John 1:9 as a particular example (21:316). It is obvious from all of Owen's works that this is a basic principle of his methodology.

The abuse of these means (i.e., dependence upon them as sufficient of themselves), Owen insists, arises from the "secret persuasion that the Scripture indeed is not, what it pretends to be, *the word of the living God*, or that it doth not indeed express the *highest effect of his wisdom* and deepest counsel of his will" (4:225). It is also from a failure to appreciate God's purpose in giving the Scripture as "a sanctified means of our *illumination*" (4:225).

Ecclesiastical Means
The only understanding of ecclesiastical means which Owen allows in the interpretation of Scripture is "the due consideration and improvement of that *light, knowledge, and understanding* in, and those *gifts* for the declaration of, the mind of God in the Scripture, which he hath granted unto and furnished them withal who have gone before us in the ministry of the gospel" (4:228). It is with this in mind that we consider the possible sources of Owen's Christology.

Sources for Owen's Christology
The principal source for Owen's Christology was obviously the Holy Scriptures, as understood by the means just recited. Within the general category of "ecclesiastical means," however, a great many individuals might be mentioned who have contributed to Owen's Christological thought.

Apostolic Fathers and Apologists

Owen's works demonstrate an interest in and acquaintance with the works of the Apostolic Fathers and Apologists. Clement of Rome, Ignatius, Justin Martyr, Origen (despite his "fooleries and mistakes" [4:228]), Clement of Alexandria, Irenaeus, and Tertullian are all appealed to in the support of some Christological point. Irenaeus, in particular, seems to hold the Puritan's interest, as noted in chapter 9 below.

Ante-Nicene & Post-Nicene Fathers

Consistent with his professed interest in the tradition of the church Owen possessed a broad and intimate acquaintance with the writings of the Ante-Nicene and Post-Nicene Fathers, including Cyprian, Basil, Ambrose, Cyril of Alexandria, Cyril of Jerusalem, Eusebius, Athanasius, Lactantius, Dionysius of Rome, Theodoret, Gregory Nazianzen, Augustine, Chrysostom, Jerome, John of Damascus, Leo I, Leontius of Byzantium, and Prosper. Of these, Owen possessed such an over-arching interest in the works of the great bishop of Hippo that one is tempted to regard him as the single most significant influence upon Owen. Owen is not uncritical of the Fathers, however, even Augustine.

Owen's Assessment of Medieval Christology

With the exception of the individuals named above, Owen had a low regard for medieval Christology, particularly the abuse of power in enforcing the decisions of the counsels, and the "curious" investigations of the Scholastics. Anselm and Bernard are quoted with approval. Abelard, Rupert, Albertus Magnus, and Duns Scotus receive Owen's censure. Thomas is often quoted, but also criticized.

Sixteenth & Seventeenth Centuries

With regard to Owen's general theological method, particular attention might be given to Thomas Barlow, Owen's tutor at Oxford, who advocated a philological approach to Scripture and the use of commentaries by Reformed divines (Wallace 1965, 15). The breadth and depth of Owen's acquaintance with the writings of sixteenth and seventeenth century Reformed, Lutheran, Arminian, Roman, and Socinian authors makes it extremely difficult clearly to identify points of direct dependence. It is possible to show Owen's acquaintance with the works of Luther and Calvin, Bucer, and Martyr. Beza figures prominently in Owen's Christology, not only as the editor of the Greek New Testament, but also as the author of several important works. His interest in Zanchius is principally directed towards his work on the Holy Trinity. As noted earlier, Owen approvingly cites Richard Hooker's *Laws of Ecclesiastical Polity* for its description of the believer's participation of and union with Christ. Other Anglicans are appealed to as teaching essentially the same doctrine: Jewell, Whitgift, Abbot, Morton, Ussher, Hall, Davenant, Reynolds, Whitaker, and Sutcliffe (2:304).

Some other authors whose Christological opinions are cited (not necessarily with approval) or works are recommended are Altingius, Maccovius, Zarnovitius, Casmannus, Salinarius, Paraeus, Piscator, Twisse, Rutherford, Spanheim, Ames, Lubbertus, Lucius, Cameron, Baxter, Voetius, Amyraldus, Placaeus, Rivetus, Walaeus, Thysius, Maresius, Essenius, Arnold, Hoornbeek, Turretin and the Lutherans Tarnovius, Meisnerus, Calovius, Stegmannus, Martinius, and Franzius. In his defense of the doctrine of the perseverance of the saints, he extols Reynolds, Whitaker, Perkins, Greenham, Dodd, Preston, Bolton, Sibbes, Rogers, Culverwell, and Cotton as men who had not only written on that doctrine but adorned it by their godliness (11:487). On the question of the free offer of the gospel, he commends works by Piscator,

Perkins, Twisse, the Synod of Dort, Du Moulin, Baronius, Rutherford, Spanheim, and Ames.

While it is difficult to prove a direct influence, special attention might justifiably be given to Richard Sibbes (1777-1635), who provided a model for the Puritan ministers of Owen's generation. The following description by Samuel Clarke should demonstrate the fact more conveniently than a great number of examples:

> And though he were a wise master-builder, and that in one of the eminentest auditories for learning and piety that was in the land,... yet according to the grace which was given to him, *he was still taking all occasion to preach of the FUNDAMENTALS to them*: and amongst the rest, of the incarnation of the Son of God, one of the chief fundamentals of our faith, one of the chief of those wonders in the mercy-seat which the cherubim gaze at, which the angels desire to pry into, 1 Pet. i.12. And preaching at several times, and by occasion of so many several texts of Scripture concerning this subject, there is scarce any one of those incomparable benefits which accrue to us thereby, nor any of those holy impressions which the meditation hereof ought to make on our hearts, which was not by him sweetly unfolded, as may appear by those sermons now in print. 'And therefore,' saith a reverend divine, "the *noted humility of the author* I less wonder at, finding how often his thoughts dwelt upon the humiliation of Christ. (Quoted in Sibbes 1862, I:cxxiv-v)

The "reverend divine" referred to by Clarke was Thomas Fuller who likewise confirms: "Of all points of divinity, he most frequently pressed that of Christ's incarnation."

There can be no doubt that Sibbes was a major influence in spreading the doctrinal system and experiential piety of English Puritanism among the men of his generation and that which followed. The "sweet dropper" made a deep impression upon John Cotton, John Preston, Thomas Goodwin, Thomas Manton, and many others. However, there is one motif so important to John Owen, so often and so broadly cited by him, that this writer would go so far as to call it the focal point of Owen's theology. It was also a theme developed in a major treatise by Sibbes, published in 1639, under the supervision of Thomas Goodwin and Philip Nye, namely, the doctrine that in the gospel we behold, by the Christ-given Holy Spirit, the glory of God "in the face of Christ" and are thereby changed into his image (Sibbes 1862, 4:200-305; see also, 312-49).

Though not in any major way, Thomas Goodwin, Owen's senior by sixteen years, friend, academic colleague, and fellow worker, might have had an influence upon Owen's Christological thought. True dependence is difficult to establish, but Goodwin's works on Christ antedate Owen's by several years, and a comparison shows many common ideas. In a number of areas (which will appear below), Owen seems to pick up a thought of Goodwin's and develops it. Nevertheless, on the doctrine of Christ Owen does not quote Goodwin or refer to him, as he does to those previously mentioned.

Hebrew Literature
One of the most fascinating aspects of Owen's Christology is the wealth of Hebrew literature employed in his exposition of Scripture. He quotes from a colossal array of rabbinical writings, Targums, and Talmuds, ancient and more recent commentaries and grammars.

Conclusion
Owen's Christology was formed within the context of Puritan England. It reflects the major Christological categories and themes developed by Luther and Calvin, their associates and immediate successors to the Reformed tradition. While Owen valued these as God's gifts to the

church for its edification, his authority, and the authority to which he insisted that all others must yield, was the voice of God speaking in the Scriptures.

In understanding the content of that revelation, Owen employed the hermeneutic that he understood to be required by the Scriptures themselves. That is, as the Scriptures were the voice of God given for the purpose of man's restoration in the divine image through the revelation of Jesus Christ, they must be humbly received as such, and can only be rightly understood when employed by regenerate people in the pursuit of growth in grace, continuing in prayer and holding fast the analogy of faith. At the same time they are the words of God speaking rationally to men in a particular historical context, so the Christian use of logic and the knowledge of history and biblical languages are also necessary.

In the following two chapters, we will be able to observe how these principles were applied in Owen's investigation of the Bible's testimony to the doctrines of the Trinity and the Deity of Christ.

---

[1] On Owen's doctrine of Scripture, see Gundry (1884, 189-222), and Ferguson (1987, 184-201).

[2] See, for example, Calvin, *Institutes*, I.vi.2-4; and Bullinger, *Decades*, I.i.

[3] After examining several theories for the computation of Daniel's seventy weeks, Owen decides that the decree referred to is that of Artaxerxes Longimanus (18:344-48).

CHAPTER 5

The Doctrine of the Trinity

In his preface to the *Christologia*, Goold correctly observes that the work "is not occupied with a formal induction from Scripture in proof of the supreme Godhead of the Saviour." Instead, Owen "assumes the truth of this doctrine, and applies all his powers and resources to expound its relations in the Christian system, and its bearings on Christian duty and experience" (1:2). This is certainly not due to any thought on Owen's part that the doctrine needed no proof: ten years earlier he had published his *Brief Declaration and Vindication of the Doctrine of the Trinity*. The doctrine of the Trinity is an appropriate place to begin the study of Owen's Christology, with this treatise supplying several important principles to be observed in the management of these two complex and controversial doctrines.

Owen wrote the *Brief Declaration* for the establishment of the *"meanest sort of professors,"* that is, "to assist and direct those who are less exercised in the ways of managing controversies in religion, that they may have a brief comprehension of the truths opposed, with the firm foundations whereon they are built, and be in a readiness to shield their faith…and secure their minds" (2:272, 276).[1] Since the doctrine was under attack at the time, this

The Doctrine of the Trinity

task would require vindication as well as declaration, as Owen explains:

> I have no mind to contend and dispute about these things, which I humbly adore and believe as they are revealed. It is the importunity of adversaries, in their attempts to draw and seduce the souls of men from the truth and simplicity of the gospel in these great fundamentals of it, that alone can justify any to debate upon, or eristically [in the form of controversy] to handle these awful mysteries. (2:367)

This conviction that the doctrine of the Trinity is an "awful mystery" pervades Owen's thought. The problem with the adversaries, however, is that they are too proud to bow before the heavenly mystery. The result of this confidence in man's rational powers in the face of overwhelming biblical testimony to that which is above reason is the adoption of a hermeneutic which was, in the judgment of the orthodox, marked by outrageous distortions of the biblical data.

> I know our adversaries could, upon the matter, decry any thing peculiarly mysterious in these things, although they are frequently and emphatically in the Scriptures affirmed so to be. But, whilst they deny the mysteries of the things themselves,—which are such as every way become the glorious being and wisdom of God,—they are forced to assign such an enigmatical sense unto the words, expressions, and propositions wherein they are revealed and declared in the Scripture, as to turn almost the whole gospel into an allegory, wherein nothing is properly expressed but in some kind of allusion unto what is so elsewhere: which irrational way of proceeding, leaving nothing certain in what is or may be expressed by word or writing, is covered over with a pretence of *right reason*; which utterly refuseth to be so employed. (2:367-68)

Method

So solemn is the subject of the treatise that Owen feels constrained to request that the reader "not look on the subject...as the matter of an ordinary controversy in religion"; that he would "bring with him a due reverence of the majesty, and infinite, incomprehensible nature of God, as that which is not to be prostituted to the captious and sophistical scanning of the men of corrupt minds, but to be humbly adored, according to the revelation that he hath made of himself"; and that he would willingly "submit his soul and conscience to the plain and obvious sense of Scripture propositions and testimonies, without seeking out evasions and pretences for unbelief" (2:368).

The study of the doctrine of the Trinity utilizes two avenues of approach. First, consideration is to be given to its revelation in Scripture, along with its practical religious application. This revelation consists of *propositions* that we are required to "*understand the terms of*," and to believe. It is required that we "assent unto the assertions and testimonies of God concerning himself according to their natural and genuine sense," because God will be "known, believed in, feared, and worshipped by us," and because "he himself hath, by his revelation, not only warranted us so to do, but also made it our *duty*, necessary and indispensable" (2:377).

Given the catholic character of his theology, Owen's statement of the doctrine of the Trinity is not at all unique:

> Now, the sum of this revelation in this matter is, that *God is one*;—that this one God is *Father, Son, and Holy Ghost*;—that the *Father is Father of the Son*; and *the Son, the Son of the Father*; and *the Holy Ghost, the Spirit of the Father and the Son*; and that, in respect of this their mutual relation, they are distinct from each other. (2:377; cf. Heppe 1950, 110)

Such a definition suits his purpose in this treatise. Its

parts are each capable of a scriptural defense which when made will constitute Owen's proof of the doctrine. To expound his doctrine more fully, however, will require consideration of more detailed definitions below.

Secondly, the doctrine of the Trinity is to be considered as it is expounded in scripturally based expressions "meet to direct and keep the mind from undue apprehensions of the things it believes and to declare them, unto farther edification" (2:377). Edification is the important word here: the teaching is to inform and enlighten the mind, so that, as far as possible, and "by *divine assistance,*" faith may be increased. At the same time, the exposition should not "beget or occasion any *undue apprehensions concerning God, or our obedience unto him*" (2:378). It is not altogether clear what Owen means by Trinitarian expressions that beget undue apprehensions of our *obedience* to God. Perhaps they do so indirectly, i.e., because of undue apprehensions of God himself. Of these misapprehensions of God, however, there were many. The difficulty of avoiding them becomes apparent when one observes some of the attempts that were made to remove the "mystery" of the Trinity. During the debate that raged over the doctrine of the Trinity during the last decade of the seventeenth century, the Unitarian Stephen Nye was very happy to expose the weaknesses of some of these in his criticisms of so-called "orthodox" expositions of the Trinity. Of course, Nye also rejected the concept of mystery, attributing its use to "laziness or...ignorance" (Nye, 1697, 12). However, Nye never answered Owen's scriptural case for the Trinity, nor successfully dealt with the question of the divine incomprehensibility.

This exposition of the doctrine thus asserted will employ these two methods to address three crucial questions: 1) how God is one, 2) how the being of God subsists in three distinct persons, and 3) "what are their mutual respects to each other, by which, as their peculiar properties, giving them the manner of their subsistence, they are distinguished one from another" (2:378-79). That is, it will present scriptural propositions and explain them with "such words and expressions as, it may be, are not literally and formally contained in the Scripture; but only are, unto our conceptions and apprehensions, expository of what is so contained" (2:378-79).

Owen realizes it is at just this critical point that the opponents of the doctrine of the Trinity brought in their most subtle and yet destructive objection. Though expressed in various ways, the objection amounted to this: "In the Bible, God has revealed to us everything we need for a godly life. Since He has not employed such terms as essence, subsistence, nature, person, etc., He can not have made salvation dependent upon belief in a doctrine dependent upon such extra-biblical words." Out of this assumption, there arose a number of treatises purporting to expound the "Scripture doctrine" of the Trinity, atonement, etc.

Against this tendency Owen maintains that objection to the use of extra-scriptural words in theological discourse is not only groundless but also contrary to God's intent in giving us the Scripture. It is,

> to deny all interpretation of the Scripture,—all endeavors to express the sense of the words of it unto the understandings of one another; which is, in a word, to render the Scripture itself altogether useless. For if it be *unlawful* for me to *speak or write* what I conceive to be the sense of the words of the Scripture, and the nature of the thing signified and expressed by them, it is unlawful for me, also to think or conceive in my mind what is the sense of the words or nature of the things; which to say, is to make brutes of ourselves, and to frustrate the whole design of God in giving unto us the great privilege of his word. (2:379)

The Doctrine of the Trinity

For this reason, Owen argues,

> in the declaration of the doctrine of the Trinity, we may *lawfully*, nay, we must *necessarily*, make use of other words, phrases, and expressions, than what are literally and syllabically contained in the Scripture, but teach no other things. (2:379)

The divines at Westminster had asserted the "whole counsel of God" to be "either expressly set down in Scripture," or deduced "by good and necessary consequence" from it (*Westminster Confession of Faith*, I:vi). Like them, Owen regarded the "necessary consequence" of scriptural propositions to be "no less true and divine" than the propositions themselves (2:379). Necessary consequences "rightly drawn" from a divine revelation are equally of divine authority. "Hence it follows that when the Scripture revealeth the Father, Son, and Holy Ghost to be one God, seeing it necessarily and unavoidably follows thereon that they are one in essence (wherein alone it is possible they can be one), and three in their distinct subsistences (wherein alone it is possible they can be three),—this is no less of divine revelation than the first principle from whence these things follow" (2:379).

Nevertheless, Owen is very emphatic that the proper course in the presentation of the doctrine of the Trinity is first to assert and vindicate the scriptural evidence for the constituent parts of the doctrine (i.e., prove the unity of God, and the deity and distinction of the three persons); and only afterwards to explain the doctrine. This sequence is required because the enemies of the doctrine will

> always begin their opposition not unto the *revelation* of it, but unto the *explanation* of it; which is used only for farther edification. Their disputes and cavils shall be against the *Trinity, essence, substance, persons, personality, respects, properties* of the divine persons, with the modes of expressing these things; whilst the plain *scriptural revelation* of the things

> themselves from whence they are but explanatory deductions, is not spoken to, nor admitted into confirmation...these explanations, so excepted against, are indeed not of any *original consideration* in this matter. Let the direct express revelations of the doctrine be confirmed, they will follow of themselves, nor will be excepted against by those who believe and receive it. Let that be rejected, and they will *fall of themselves*, and never be contended for by those who did make use of them. (2:380)

An examination of the works of South, Wallis, and Stephen Nye will reveal how little these remarks of Owen's were heeded in the next two decades (South, 1693; Wallis, 1690, 1691; Nye, 1697).[2]

Owen begins his proof of the doctrine of the Trinity with the uncontested assertion that *God is one*, with the usual references to Deuteronomy 6:4 and Isaiah 44:6, 8 (cf. Goodwin, 1863, 4:349-50). At the same time, he points out that in both of these passages a *plurality of persons* is "included and expressed." Indeed, as he explains, "although there be no more absolute and sacred truth than this, that God is one, yet it may be evinced that it is nowhere mentioned in the Scripture, but that, either in the words themselves or the context of the place, a *plurality of persons* in that one sense is intimated" (2:381). Owen does not stop to prove this assertion, claiming to have previously done so.[3]

Next, he proceeds to the doctrine of the deity of the Father. This, one might think, is uncontested by the opponents of the doctrine of the Trinity. "But," says Owen,

> there is a mistake in this matter. Their...presumptuous error, casts all the conceptions that are given us concerning God in the Scripture into disorder and confusion. For the Father, as he whom we worship, is often called so only with reference unto his Son; as the Son is so with reference to the Father.... But

now, if this Son had no pre-existence in his divine nature before he was born of the Virgin, there was no God the Father seventeen hundred years ago, because there was no Son. (2:381)

On the presupposition that the Son had no pre-existence, Owen explains, Marcion was led to reject the Father. The church Fathers retained this logic as an argument for the pre-existence of the Son. Owen merely reintroduces the argument here against those who want the Father without the pre-incarnate Son, concluding "he who is not the Father, who was not so from eternity, whose paternity is not equally co-existent unto his deity, is not God unto us" (2:382).

The remainder of the treatise is a defense of the deity of the Son and of the personality of the Holy Spirit. As the vindication of the deity of the Son occupies so much of Owen's Christological labors, this will be addressed in a separate chapter. Nor will we examine Owen's proof of the personality of the Spirit, which is delivered at length in his major work on the third Person, *Pneumatologia* (3:64-92). We turn from proof of the doctrine of the Trinity to the further examination of the relations of the persons of the Godhead and to the significance of the doctrine of the Trinity for Owen.

Relations between the Persons of the Godhead and their Work

Owen's doctrine of the Trinity is noteworthy for the following reasons. First, an obvious feature of Owen's theology is his emphasis upon the fact that every work of God is a perfect work of the entire Trinity. This conviction is so strong that it might fairly be considered a regulative principle in his theological thinking, often appearing in his exposition. Yet equally obvious is the great emphasis he places upon the order of subsistence among the persons of the ontological Trinity as providing the pattern for their operations. This is, of course, not new in theory, but Owen's *emphasis* upon, and *development* of, the idea is rare.[4] Conversely, since God is known only by his works, the works of the triune God are deliberately designed for the revelation of his triune nature, particularly the work of redemption. Finally, not only the fact that God is triune, but *even the order of the subsistence* of the divine persons of the Godhead is deliberately to be considered in our worship (cf. Heppe 1950, 117-18).

Concerning the works of God, Owen adopts the familiar classification into internal works (*opera ad intra*), i.e., "internal acts in one person whereof another person is the object," and external works (*opera ad extra*), or external acts, either toward the creature, or to one of the other persons "with respect unto some peculiar dispensation and condescension" (3:66, 67). The former are,

> natural and necessary, inseparable from the being and existence of God. So, the Father knows the Son and loveth him, and the Son seeth, knoweth, and loveth the Father.... And they are absolute, infinite, natural, and necessary unto the being and blessedness of God. (3:66-67)

While many of Owen's opponents rejected all discussion of the internal works of the Trinity as vain speculation, Owen's approach, when considering those things beyond his understanding, was, like Calvin's, to bow his understanding to the Holy Scripture.

> The manner hereof unto us, in this life, is incomprehensible; therefore it is rejected by some, who will believe no more than they can put their hands into the sides of. And yet they are forced, in things under their eyes, to admit of many things which they cannot perfectly comprehend! (3:117)

External works, on the other hand are distinct actings of the persons "which are voluntary, or effects of will and choice, and not natural or necessary." In addition to works upon the creation, the external works include "external acts of one person towards another" when the latter is not considered "absolutely as a divine person, but with respect unto some peculiar dispensation and condescension." Among these are included the divine counsels concerning our redemption, including the incarnation of the Son and the sending of the Holy Spirit (3:67; cf. Heppe 1950, 118-20).

Owen agrees with classical orthodoxy: "*all divine operations* are usually ascribed unto *God absolutely*." Since the divine nature is undivided by the three persons, and acts in each, "the several persons are undivided in their operations, acting all by the same will, the same wisdom, the same power." However, "as to the manner of subsistence therein, there is distinction, relation, and order between and among them; and hence there is no divine work but is distinctly assigned unto each person, and eminently unto one" (3:93). If the works of God are of God absolutely,

> How come they, then, eminently to be assigned one to one person, another to another? as unto the Father are assigned *opera naturae*, the works of nature, or the old creation; to the Son, *opera gratiae procuratae*, all divine operations that belong unto the recovery of mankind by grace; and unto the Spirit, *opera gratiae applicatae*, the works of God whereby grace is made effectual unto us. (3:93)

Owen supplies the answer: "this is done," he says,

> (1.) When any especial impression is made of the especial property of any person on any work; then is that work assigned peculiarly to that person. So there is of the power and authority of the Father on the old creation, and of the grace and wisdom of the Son on the new. (2.) Where there is a peculiar condescension of any person unto a work, wherein the others have no concurrence but by approbation and consent. Such was the susception of the human nature by the

Son, and all that he did therein; and such was the condescension of the Holy Ghost also unto his office, which entitles him peculiarly and by way of eminence unto his own immediate works. (3:93-94)

"The person of the Father is the *'fons et origo Trinitatis'* [spring and origin of the Trinity], the Son is from him by eternal generation, and is therefore his Son, the Son of God; whose denomination as the Father is originally from hence, even the eternal generation of the Son" (3:60). As noted already, the Father is the *eternal Father*, because of the eternal generation of the Son. Describing the order of the three persons of the Trinity, Owen emphasizes,

> The Father is of none, is αὔταυτος [of himself]. The Son is begotten of the Father, having the glory of the only-begotten Son of God, and so is αὐτόθεος [God in and of himself] in respect of his nature, essence, and being, not in respect of his personality, which he hath of the Father. (12:392)

In this paragraph, we find an explicit reference to Christ as "*autotheos.*" This word is rare in Owen; the truth of it, however, is necessary as the foundation his doctrine of the true and full deity of the Son. Owen saw no contradiction between eternal generation of the person and the *autotheotes*, or self-deity of the nature, the divine essence, of the Son.[5] With this firmly established, Owen's emphasis is on the person of the Son, and on his *economic* subordination to the Father.

The Holy Spirit, by an eternal procession from the Son, as well as the Father, "is also called the *Spirit of the Son*...and the Spirit of Christ" (3:60). The biblical evidence for the procession from the Son seems more directly to indicate a procession in the *application* of redemption. Owen is aware of this, but on the assumption that the order of application follows the order of subsistence he argues backwards to the eternal procession of the Spirit from the Son. Hence,

The Doctrine of the Trinity

> The Spirit is of the Father and the Son. He is often so called the Spirit of God and the Spirit of the Son. For the term of "proceeding," or "going forth," I profess myself ignorant whether it concern chiefly his eternal personality or his dispensation in the work of the gospel. The latter I rather like; of which this is no time to give my reasons. But be those expressions of what import soever, he is equally the Spirit of the Father and the Son, and is of them both and from them both. (12:392)

Owen wrote this in 1655. By 1674, under the stimulus of Socinian objections, it appears he had come to the opinion that the sending of the redemptive gift of the Spirit followed the pattern set by the eternal procession from the Father and the Son, and that this rested upon the fact that the Spirit was "antecedently" the Spirit of the Son.

> Nor is he otherwise the Spirit of Christ, originally and formally, but as he is the Spirit of God,—that is, as Christ is God also. On this supposition I grant, as before, that he may consequently be called the "Spirit of Christ," because promised and sent by him, because doing his work, and communicating his grace, image and likeness to the elect. (3:60-63)

Speaking of the procession of the Spirit, Owen emphasizes the "economic," or "dispensatory," or "external" operations (*ad extra*) of God over the "ontologic," "natural," "personal," or "internal" operations (*ad intra*). Nevertheless, he retains the ontologic as the ground of the economic. That is, the Spirit's eternal procession from the Father and the Son is the basis for his being called the "third person" of the Trinity. "This constitutes the *natural order* between the persons which is unalterable" (3:92). Consequent to this natural order of subsistence is the "order of operation" in the plan of salvation, wherein the

Spirit proceeds from the Father and the Son in the application of redemption (3:92, 116-18; 2:226-27). Thus,

> in the whole economy of the Trinity, as to the works that outwardly are of God, especially the works of grace, the order of subsistence of the persons in the same nature is represented unto us, and they have the same dependence on each other in their operations as they have in their subsistence. The Father is the fountain of all, as in being and existence, so in operation. The Son is of the Father, begotten of him, and, therefore, as unto his work, is sent by him; but his own will is in and unto what he is sent about. The Holy Spirit proceedeth from the Father and the Son, and therefore, is sent and given by them as to all the works which he immediately effecteth; but yet his own will is the direct principle of all that he doth,—he divideth unto every one according to his own will. (3:92)

This order of subsistence is also reflected in the works of creation and redemption. For instance, Owen applied the order of subsistence to God's work upon creation in the following manner:

> The beginning of divine operations is assigned unto the Father,..."the fountain of the Deity itself:" "Of him, and through him, and to him, are all things," Rom. xi. 36. The subsisting, establishing, and upholding of all things," is ascribed unto the Son: "He is before all things, and by him all things consist," Col. i. 17. As he made all things with the Father, so he gives them a consistency, a permanency, in a peculiar manner, as he is the power and wisdom of the Father. He "upholdeth all things by the word of his power," Heb. i. 3. And the finishing and perfecting of all these works is ascribed to the Holy Spirit, as we shall see.

Owen is endeavoring to demonstrate three things: 1) that the entire Godhead, "God," is the great worker in all di-

The Doctrine of the Trinity

vine operations; 2) that, nevertheless, there are distinct operations for each person; and 3) these outward operations reflect, as it were, the inward relationship because they arise out of it. He continues:

> I say not this as though one person succeeded unto another in their operation, or as though where one ceased and gave over a work, the other took it up and carried it on; for every divine work, and every part of every divine work, is the work of God, that is, of the whole Trinity, inseparably and undividedly: but on those divine works which outwardly are of God there is an especial impression of the order of the operation of each person, with respect unto their natural and necessary subsistence, as also with regard unto their internal characteristical properties, whereby we are distinctly taught to know them and adore them. And the due consideration of this order of things will direct us in the right understanding of the proposals that are made unto our faith concerning God in his works and word. (3:94-95)

The same principle operates with regard to the redemptive acts of the triune God:

> Unto this great work there are peculiarly required, authority, love, and power—all directed by infinite wisdom. These originally reside in the person of the Father, and the acting of them in this matter is constantly ascribed unto him. He sent the Son, as he gives the Spirit, by an act of sovereign authority. And he sent the Son from his eternal love;—he loved the world, and sent his Son to die. This is constantly assigned to be the effect of the love and grace of the Father. And he wrought in Christ, and he works in us, with respect unto the end of this mystery, with the "exceeding greatness of his power," Eph. i. 19. The Son, who is the second person in the order of *subsistence, in the order of operation* puts the

whole authority, love, and power of the Father in execution. (1:220)

These remarks from Owen's *Christologia* were written, remember, with the pastoral design of getting "ordinary Christians" to admire the love of God in the great mystery of godliness, the glorious person of the Son of God. This question of the order of subsistence and operation is undoubtedly raised to explain the data of Scripture, for the purpose of spiritual illumination and the deepening of Christian piety. He continues,

> This order of subsistence and operation thereon is expressly declared by the apostle, 1 Cor. viii. 6, "To us there is but one God, the Father, of whom are all things, and we in him; and one Lord Jesus Christ, by whom are all things, and we by him." The Father is the original fountain and spring,...*from whom*—[from] whose original authority, love, goodness, and power—are all these things. That expression, "from him," peculiarly denotes the eternal original of all things. But how are this authority, goodness, love, and power in the Father, whence all these things spring and arise, made effectual—how are their effects wrought out and accomplished? "There is one Lord," even Jesus Christ a distinct person from the Father,..."by whom are all things." He works in the order of his subsistence, to execute, work and accomplish all that originally proceedeth from the Father. By the Holy Spirit, who is the third person in order of subsistence, there is made a *perfecting application* of the whole unto all its proper ends. (1:219)

It is this order of subsistence in the Trinity that provides part of the rationale for the *choice of the Son* as the divine person who becomes incarnate for man's redemption (1:220).

Owen provides a further example of this reflection of the natural in the economic by the incident of the Lord's breathing upon his disciples. He says,

> As the vital breath of a man hath a continued emanation from him, and yet is never separated utterly from his person or forsaketh him, so doth the Spirit of the Father and the Son proceed from them by a continual divine emanation, still abiding one with them: for all those allusions are weak and imperfect wherein substantial things are compared with accidental, infinite things with finite, and those that are eternal with those that are temporary.... And from hence, or the subsistence of the Holy Spirit in an eternal emanation from the Father and Son, as the breath of God, did our Saviour signify his communication of his gifts unto his disciples by breathing on them: John xx: 22,... and because in our first creation it is said of Adam that God... "breathed into his nostrils the breath of life," Gen. ii. 7. (3:55, 100)

It is by the external works of God alone that we may come to any knowledge of his nature. In the "new creation," or the gospel, Owen says,

> God hath revealed himself in an especial manner as *three in one*. There was no more glorious mystery brought to light in and by Jesus Christ than that of the holy Trinity, or the subsistence of the three persons in the unity of the same divine nature. And this was done not so much in express propositions, or verbal testimonies unto that purpose,—which yet is done also, as by the declaration of the mutual, divine, internal acts of the persons towards one another, and the distinct, immediate, divine, external actings of each person in the work which they did and do perform,—for God revealeth not himself unto us merely doctrinally and dogmatically, but by the declarations of what he doth for us, in us, and towards us, in the accomplishment of "the counsel of his own will;" see Eph. i. 4-12. And this revelation is made unto us, not that our minds might be possessed with the notions of it, but that we may know

aright how to obtain and exercise communion with him, until we come to the enjoyment of him. (3:158)

As a particular example of this, we see Owen pointing to the priesthood of Christ as providing a needed revelation of the Triune nature of God:

> All the natural and essential properties of that being are absolutely and essentially the same; and all the operations of this divine essence or being, according to its properties, are undivided, as being the effects of one principle, one power, one wisdom. Hence it could not by any such acts be manifested that there was more than one person in that one nature or being. But now, in these actings of the persons of the Trinity in such ways as firstly respect themselves, or their operations *"ad intra,"* where one person is as it were the object of the other person's acting, the sacred truth of the plurality of persons in the same single, undivided essence is gloriously manifested. The Son undertaking to the Father to become a high priest for sinners, openly declares the distinction of the Son, or eternal Word from the person of the Father. And in these distinct and mutual actings of the persons of it is the doctrine and truth of the holy Trinity most safely contemplated. (21:413-14; see 3:158)

Finally, Owen applies this relation of the internal and external works of God to Christian piety by demonstrating the ultimate ground of our obligation to love Christ: *"The person of Christ is the principal object of the love of God"* (1:144). As Owen explains,

> No small part of the eternal blessedness of the holy God consisteth in the mutual love of the Father and the Son, by the Spirit. As he is the only-begotten of the Father, he is the first, necessary, adequate, complete object of the whole love of the Father.... In him was the ineffable, eternal, unchangeable delight and complacency of the Father, as the full object of his love....His being the only-begotten Son declares his

> eternal relation unto the person of the Father, of whom he was begotten in the entire communication of the whole divine nature. Hereon he is in the bosom of the Father—in the eternal embraces of his love, as his only-begotten Son. The Father loves, and cannot but love, his own nature and essential image in him. (1:144)

The creation of man in his own image, Owen says, was "to express his holiness and righteousness; and he implanted love in our natures to express this eternal mutual love of the holy persons of the Trinity" (1:145).

With regard to God incarnate, however, Owen says "the person of Christ in his divine nature is the adequate object of that love of the Father which is '*ad intra*'...; and the person of Christ as incarnate, as clothed with human nature, is the first and full object of the love of the Father in those acts of it which are '*ad extra*,' or are towards anything without himself" (1:145). Christ as the "first object" of the love of God is the one in whom the church partakes of that love (1:146). Owen's genius for applying "speculative theology" to Christian piety is observable in his conclusion to this part of his argument:

> our love unto Christ being the only outward expression and representation of this love of the Father unto him, therein consists the principal part of our renovation into his image. Nothing renders us so like unto God as our love unto Jesus Christ, for he is the principal object of his love;—in him doth his soul rest—in him is he always well pleased. Wherever this is wanting, whatever there may be besides, there is nothing of the image of God. He that loves not Jesus Christ, let him be Anathema Maranatha; for he is unlike unto God,—his carnal mind is enmity against God. (1:146-47)

The Trinity and History

The importance of the doctrine of the Trinity for Owen is

also reflected in his belief that its revelation is the purpose of history. By the progressive revelation of His triune nature, God has made increasing demands upon its recipients; he has more precisely defined the nature of covenantal fidelity.

> From the foundation of the world, the principal revelation that God made of himself was in the oneness of his nature and his monarchy over all. And herein the person of the Father was immediately represented with his power and authority; for he is the fountain and original of the Deity, the other persons as to their subsistence being of him: only, he did withal give out promises concerning the peculiar exhibition of the Son in the flesh in an appointed season, as also of the Holy Spirit, to be given by him in an especial manner. Hereby were their persons to be signally glorified in this world, it being the will of God that all "men should honour the Son as they honoured the Father," and the Holy Spirit in like manner. In this state of things the only apostasy of the church could be polytheism and idolatry. (3:43)

With the coming of Christ came the obligation to receive and obey the Son, followed by an ultimate obligation to receive the person and work of the Holy Spirit (3:43-4). Owen is implying that the seventeenth-century Unitarian rejecting the deity of Christ or denying the necessity of regeneration is, despite his confession of the divine monarchy, guilty of apostasy as the Israelite worshipping at the altar of Baal; for he has rejected that revelation of God which defines the content of covenant fidelity. This principle underlies the argument employed by the author of Hebrews (21:127).

The Trinity and Worship

The purpose of this revelation is religious—that we might "fear him, believe, worship, obey him, and live unto him, as God," that we might duly worship the *one*

The Doctrine of the Trinity

true God who is Father, Son, and Holy Spirit. Clear confirmation of this by "positive divine testimonies" provides faith with its *"formal object,"* and enables it to be *"directive* of divine worship and obedience" (2:378). As he says in his treatise on the Holy Spirit, *"The nature and being of God is the foundation of all true religion and holy religious worship in the world,"* the revelation of that God is "the rule and measure of all religious worship and obedience," and "God hath revealed or manifested as three in one, and, therefore, as such is to be worshipped and glorified by us;—that is, as three distinct persons, subsisting in the same infinitely holy, one, undivided essence" (3:64-66). This is the reason for the baptismal formula, namely, that this constitutes the initiation of our worship of the triune God: "Unto this service we are solemnly dedicated, namely, of God, as Father, Son, and Holy Spirit; as they are each of them equally participant of the same divine nature" (3:64-66, 72-74).

But beyond the fact that God is Triune, "God…by us is to be worshipped as he hath revealed the subsistence of the three persons in this order, and so are we to deal with him in our approaches to him: not that we are to frame any conception in our minds of distinct substances, which are not; but by faith closing with this revelation of them, we give up our souls in contemplation and admiration of that we cannot comprehend" (12:392). With this in mind, Owen shows us in an unprecedented manner that each person of the Trinity *distinctly* and *equally* is the due object of this worship. Owen's detailed but glowing exposition of the communion which the Christian holds with the Father, Son, and Holy Spirit is contained in his treatise *On Communion with God*.

The Trinity and the Understanding of Scripture
Another definition of the Trinity is found in Owen's treatise, *The Divine Original of the Scripture*:

The sum of it is: That God is one—his nature or his being is one: that all the properties or infinite essential excellencies of God, as God, do belong to that one nature and being: that this God is infinitely good, holy, just, powerful; he is eternal, omnipotent, omnipresent; and these things belong to none but him—that is, that one God: that this God is the Father, Son, and Holy Ghost; which are not diverse names of the same person, nor distinct attributes or properties of the same nature or being, but one, another, and a third, all equally that one God, yet really distinguished between themselves by such incommunicable properties as constitute the one to be that one, and the other to be that other and the third to be that third. Thus, the Trinity is not the union nor unity of three, but is a trinity in unity, or the ternary number of persons in the same essence; nor doth the Trinity, in its formal conception, denote the essence, as if the essence were comprehended in the Trinity, which is in each person; but it denotes only the distinction of the persons comprised in that number. (16:340)

The placing of this definition in a treatise devoted to the written word is very significant. In *The Divine Original*, Owen is arguing for the necessity of Scripture for answering man's inquiries concerning his relationship with God. Apart from Scripture, man has no knowledge of the doctrine of the Trinity, the incarnation, etc. The Trinity is used as an example of one of several biblical revelations at which "nature startles, shrinks, and is taken with horror,... but yet, gathering itself up to them, it... finds that unless they are accepted and submitted unto ...not only all that hath been received must be rejected, but also the whole dependence of the creature on God be dissolved, or rendered only dreadful, terrible, and destructive to nature itself" (16:340). The communion between God and man, with God's communication of

His love, and man's return of obedience, is so "wrapped up in the doctrine of the Trinity, that without the belief, receiving, and acceptance of it, it is utterly impossible that any interest in them should be obtained or preserved" (16:340, 341). The fact that the Scripture teaches this doctrine, so beyond the light of nature to discover, yet providing a necessary principle of religious and epistemological integration, is an evidence of Scripture's necessity and its divine origin.

This is Owen's argument; it illustrates the pervasive Trinitarianism of his thought. Apart from the Triune God of Scripture, man can have no right understanding of himself, of the Scripture, or of God's creation.

---

[1] Bunyan's brief unpublished treatise *Of the Trinity and a Christian* is subtitled "How a young, or shaken Christian should demean himself under the weighty thoughts of the Trinity, or plurality of persons in the eternal godhead" (Bunyan 1853, 2:387). For more detailed expositions of the doctrine see, e.g., Thomas Goodwin, *The Knowledge of God the Father and His Son Jesus Christ,* Book 1 (1863, 4:347-404), and Francis Cheynell (1650).

[2] Of the controversy which took place between Dr. Wallis (accused of Sabellianism) and Sherlock (accused of Tri-theism), William Cunningham remarked that "it would have been much better had they confined themselves to an exposition of the scriptural evidence in support of the specific positions which make up, or involved in [the first of the Thirty-nine Articles], and restricted their more abstract speculations to the one precise and definite object of merely bringing out what was indispensable to show that none of the positions taught in Scripture, and embodied in this general statement, could be proved necessarily to involve a contradiction or a denial of the divine unity.... This discussion afforded a handle to the enemies of the doctrine of the Trinity at the time, who made it the subject of a plausible pamphlet, entitled 'Considerations on the different explications of the doctrine of the Trinity'" (1862, 2:202-203).

[3] He most likely intends his discussion of the plurality of persons, which is included in his treatment of the origin of the priesthood of Christ, published the previous year (19:42-76; cf. Goodwin 1863, 4:353-61).

[4] See Muller, on the discussion of this by several Reformed theologians of the period, including Vermigli, Musculus, Calvin, Polanus, Wollebius, Perkins, and Witsius (2003, 4: 255-60).

[5] Isaac Ambrose: "Now, as he is a Son, he is the thing begotten, but not as he is a God. As he is God, he is of himself, neither begotten, nor proceeding: the Godhead of the Father, and the Godhead of the Son is but one and the same thing, and therefore *essentia filii est a seipso, et hac ratione dici potest* [*auto Theos*] [the essence of the son is from himself, and for this reason may be said to be God of himself]. The Son, as he is God, he is God of himself, without beginning, even as the Father;... But as he is Son, he is not of himself, but the Son of the Father, begotten of him; and hereupon it follows, that the Son is begotten of the Father as he is a Son, but not as he is a God" (1855, 45f.). For the crucial importance of the *autotheotes* of Christ in the thought of Calvin, see Warfield, 1991, 233-84. See also MacLeod 1998, 149-51, and Muller 2003, 4:324-32.

CHAPTER

6

Owen's Formal Proof of the Deity of Christ

Having declared that God is one, the next thing to be established is *"that Jesus Christ is God, the eternal Son of God;*—that is, he is proposed, declared, and revealed unto us in the Scripture to be God, that is to be served, worshipped, believed in, obeyed as God, upon the account of his *own divine excellencies"* (2:382; see Goodwin 1863, 4:404-54; Brooks 1866, 5:149-56; Manton 1870, 1:427-53). Again, Owen takes a two-fold approach, variously applied, in his proof of the deity of Christ. First, he presents positive scriptural evidence of the doctrine. Owen's scriptural proof of the deity of the Son as delivered in *A Brief Declaration* uses the standard texts, but does not exhaust his arsenal. Second, for the edification of the church it was necessary to answer the objections of those who were undermining the doctrinal foundation of the faith by rendering these testimonies invalid, a necessity brought about by men's not being "acquainted with the Scriptures as they ought to be" (2:386-87). Vindication of the scriptural evidence required the exposure of the opponents' faulty exegesis and the exposure of the logical fallacies involved in their arguments. The vindication of the evidence for the deity of Christ constituted a large part of Owen's labor in this controversy.

Some Rules of Thumb

Before observing Owen's argument in detail it may be helpful to look at several general guidelines that he would have us remember in order to avoid the logical fallacies and other errors commonly encountered in Socinian theology. Antitrinitarians make three basic errors: they limit the divine nature, they fail to distinguish between the Son as God and the Son as mediator, and, rationalistically presupposing the impossibility of the incarnation and the two-natures doctrine, they unwarrantably reject the testimony of Scripture to the deity of Christ. Owen's first rule addresses the first of these:

> Distinction of persons..., it being in an infinite substance, doth no way prove a difference of essence between the Father and the Son. Where therefore, Christ, as the Son [or "as mediator" (12:170)], is said to be *another* from the Father, or God, spoken personally of the Father, it argues not in the least that he is not partaker of the same nature with him. That in one essence there can be but one person, may be true where the substance is finite and limited, but hath no place in that which is infinite. (2:388)

To help us avoid all the errors that arise from failing to distinguish the Son as God and the Son as Mediator, he insists,

> Secondly. Distinction and inequality in respect of *office* in Christ, doth not in the least take away his equality and sameness with the Father in respect of nature and essence, Phil. ii. 7, 8. A son, of the same nature with his father, and therein equal to him, may in office be his inferior,—his subject.

> Thirdly. The *advancement* and exaltation of Christ as mediator to any dignity whatever, upon or in refer-

ence to the work of our redemption and salvation, is not at all inconsistent with the essential honour, dignity, and worth, which he hath in himself as God blessed for ever. Though he humbled himself, and was exalted in office, yet in nature he was one and the same; he changed not. (2:388-89)

His fourth rule is the simple assertion that according to Scripture, deity and humanity are not contradictory, and that testimony for one must not be rejected because of the other. He says, "The Scriptures, asserting the *humanity* of Christ, with the concernments thereof, as his birth, life, and death, do no more thereby deny his *Deity* than by asserting his Deity, with the essential properties thereof, they deny his humanity." Finally, "God working in and by Christ as he was a mediator, denotes the Father's sovereign appointment of the things mentioned to be done,—not his immediate efficiency in the doing of the things themselves." That is, when God is said to do something in the person of Christ, it is not to be attributed to the person of the Father acting, to the denial of the deity of the Son. These rules, he says, "contain a sufficient ground for the resolution and answering of all the sophisms and objections" of the adversaries (2:389).

Evidence from Scripture

In the *Brief Declaration*, Owen chooses to answer the objections raised against only a few key passages and to set down several general rules for the "improvement" of the rest. Much more thorough vindication of the scriptural evidence was carried out in the *Vindiciae Evangelicae*, in which Owen provides valuable criticism of the Socinian methodology in its treatment of particular texts. Additionally, his Hebrews commentary contains many significant texts from the Old Testament to which he appeals in order to establish the nature of the expected Messiah. While these Scriptures are commonly (and pejoratively) referred to as "proof texts," it should be kept in mind that in most cases a text used by Owen as a proof receives an exegetical analysis somewhere in his writings that supports the use he makes of it. Whether his exegesis is correct is a question the reader must decide; the point is that Owen does not *indiscriminately* appeal to proof texts out of context. The Socinians often appear satisfied to diminish the force of a Scriptural testimony by proposing an alternative interpretation. Owen is not arguing unfairly when he writes, "These Scriptures perhaps *may be answered thus or thus*,...but the question is, How *ought* they to be interpreted, and what is their sense and intendment?" (12:330). In the *Vindiciae*, therefore, Owen assumes the responsibility of supplying this proper interpretation.

We may summarize his strategy by observing that Owen presents four main types of evidence for the deity of Christ, which we will follow. Naturally, we can only consider a small portion of Owen's very extensive effort in this regard.

Old Testament References to Christ Quoted in the New Testament

Numerous Old Testament passages, which reference "God," "Lord," etc., are cited in the New Testament to identify Jesus or describe some of his activity. Psalm 45:6, for example, says "Thy throne, O God, is for ever and ever." This is applied to Christ in Hebrews 1:8 where it stands as a clear testimony to the deity of the Son. The purpose of the quotation is not directly to prove the deity of the Son, but the Son's superiority over the angels. The argument, however, rests upon the truth of the assertion that God addresses Christ as God and ascribes eternity to his throne, which he could not have done were Christ less than God by nature. Owen points out that the *Targum* applied the Psalm to the Messiah; and he argues, contrary to those who apply it to Solomon, that as "the Messiah is *principally*, so there is no cogent reason to prove that he is not *solely*, intended in this psalm" (20:180; 179-95). He also critiques alternative translations pleaded by Socinians.

A second, very important, text is Psalm 68:17, 18; which is applied by Paul to Christ in Ephesians 4:8-10. Christ's relationship to the church is described in terms of the psalm's depiction of Yahweh at Sinai. It is difficult to escape the conclusion that Paul thinks of the exaltation of Christ as parallel to, and even greater in significance than, the Sinai theophany. Owen does not put it in these terms, but under his exegesis the relationship between the two passages receives a great deal of light, and the significance of the parallel becomes quite clear (1:247-48, 350; 4:488-89; 9:438-39; 12:329-30; 21:409).

Psalm 102:25-27 is applied to Christ in Hebrews 1:10-12.[1] Owen realizes that, despite the apostolic application to Christ, in view of the deference paid to the Jews on these matters he must demonstrate that the words of the psalmist refer to the Messiah. He argues that the ancient Jews obviously understood it in this way, or the author of Hebrews could not have so used it in his argument. Moreover, the psalm contains a prophecy applicable to the Messiah: it prophesies "redemption of the people, with the re-edification of the temple, as a type of that spiritual temple and worship which were afterwards to be erected," (vv. 13, 16); and the *"calling of the Gentiles* to the church and worship of God" (vv. 15, 21, and 22). With great insight Owen points out that verse 18 points to "the *creation of a new people*, a new world": a new creation of Jews and Gentiles that "shall praise the LORD" (20:197). As he explains,

> These are the heads of the prophetical part of the psalm, and they all respect things everywhere peculiarly assigned unto the Son, who was to be

incarnate, or the days of the Messiah, which is all one; for,—

[1.] The redemption and deliverance of the church out of trouble is his proper work. Wherever it is mentioned, it is he who is intended, Ps. xcviii. So signally, Zech. ii. 8-13, and other places innumerable.

[2.] The bringing in of the Gentiles is acknowledged by all the Jews to respect the time of the Messiah; it being he who was to be a light unto the Gentiles, and the salvation of God unto the ends of the earth. (20:197-98)

[3.] Also, "the generation to come," and "people to be created," the Jews themselves interpret of the... "world to come," or the new state of the church under the Messiah. These two last put together, the gathering of the people, and the world to come, created for the praise of God, make it evident that it is the Son whom the psalmist hath respect unto. (20:198)

One may observe here that Owen has not simply quoted the psalm as a proof text; a study of the remainder of Owen's exposition of the passage would demonstrate this even further.

First Corinthians 10:9 is a warning against tempting Christ,[2] "as some of them also tempted, and were destroyed of serpents." Owen concludes, "He whom the people tempted in the wilderness, and for which they were destroyed by serpents, was the Lord Jehovah; now, this doth the apostle apply to Christ: he therefore is the Lord Jehovah" (12:280).

Another example of this kind of New Testament witness to the Old Testament revelation of Christ is found in John 12:40-41, which is a quotation of Isaiah 6:10 followed by the words "these things spake Esaias, when he saw his glory, and spake of him." From this Owen argues, "He whose glory Isaiah saw, chap. vi., was 'the Holy, holy, holy, LORD of hosts,' verse 3, 'the King, the LORD of hosts,' verse 5; but this was Jesus Christ whose glory Isaiah then saw, as the Holy Ghost witnesses in these words of John xii. 41" (12:281). Against the Socinian assertion that "his glory" does not refer to God the Son, Owen shows that the context of the passage supports the identification of the one speaking and appearing to Isaiah as the one who was then doing miracles in Jerusalem, in whom no one was believing (12:282; cf. Goodwin, 1863, 4:358-59).

There are many such Old Testament texts applied to Christ in the New Testament, more than can be mentioned here. Some of them will appear in the course of the present chapter, in chapter ten, and various other places where their significance to particular points of Owen's Christology will appear.

Divine Names and Titles of Christ
Jehovah
The second main type of evidence is the ascription of various divine names and titles to Christ. Commenting on the name "Jehovah," Owen makes the syllogism, "He who is Jehovah, God, the only true God, he is God properly by nature; but Jesus Christ is Jehovah, the true God, etc.: therefore he is God properly by nature" (12:248). Owen does not give us a listing of the "innumerable testimonies" of Christ's being called Jehovah, but we may observe his opinion of these texts in his vindication of several more familiar ones from the objections of John Biddle (namely, Jer. 23:6; Zech. 2:8; 1 John 5:20; Jude 4; Titus 2:13; Rev. 1:8; 4:8; Acts 20:28; and 1 John 3:16), to which Owen adds several others (Isa. 40:3; Mal. 3:1; 1:23; Isa. 45:22-25; Rom. 14:10-12; Hos. 13:14; 1 Cor. 15:54, 55).

One which Owen regards as a particularly forceful testimony is Jeremiah 23:6: "In his days Judah shall be saved, and Israel shall dwell safely: and this is his name whereby he shall be called, JEHOVAH OUR RIGHTEOUSNESS." The "subject matter" of this text, Owen argues, is Christ. He is the Branch raised up to David; he is "our Righteousness," as the New Testament asserts in many places. After showing that this name refers to the Branch, and not to Israel, Jerusalem, nor Zerubabel (12:252-53), Owen concludes:

> Where God simply says his name is Jehovah, we believe him; and where he says the name of the Branch of the house of David is Jehovah, we believe him also. And we say hence that Christ is Jehovah, or the words have not a tolerable sense. (12:251)

Again, Owen does not merely cite Zechariah 2:8 as a proof text, with a simple assertion that "the LORD of hosts is sent from the LORD of hosts," as Biddle alleges against the orthodox. Owen argues that the speaker

> is the man who was upon the red horse, chap. i. 8, who is called *"Angelus Jehovae"* ["Angel of the LORD"], verse 11, and makes intercession for the church, verse 12; which is the proper office of Jesus Christ. And that he is no created angel, but Jehovah himself, the second person of the Trinity, we prove, because he calls himself "The LORD of hosts;" says he will destroy his enemies with the shaking of his hand; that he will convert a people, and make them his people; and that he will dwell in his church. And yet unto all this he adds three times that he is sent of the Lord of hosts. We confess, then, all these to be spoken of him who was sent; but upon all these testimonies conclude that he who was sent was the Lord of hosts. (12:254)

To Grotius' assertion that the messenger is Michael, a created angel, Owen responds, "If he who speaks be Michael, how comes the temple of Jehovah to be his?" (For Owen's comments on the "Angel of Jehovah," see chapter ten below.)

The Lord

Christ is "Lord." According to the Socinians Jesus Christ was the Lord of Christians (Eph. 4:5), having been made Lord upon his resurrection as a reward for his obedience. The inference is that because Christ is "made Lord" he is not Lord by nature. Owen replies that "unless he were one God with his Father, it is utterly impossible he should be the one Lord of Christians," since by his Lordship he necessarily obtains the right of divine worship, which cannot be given to any but God without the guilt of idolatry (12:171, 172). Furthermore,

> His being Lord, then, distinctly in respect of his mediation hinders not his being God in respect of his participation in the same nature with his Father. And though here he be not spoken of in respect of his absolute, sovereign *lordship*, but of his lordship over the church, to whom the whole church is spiritually subject…, yet were he not Lord in that sense also, he could not be so in this.… And the mention of "one God" is here, as in other places, partly to deprive all false gods of their pretended deity, partly to witness against the impossibility of polytheism, and partly to manifest the oneness of them who are worshipped as God the Father, Word, and Spirit: all which things are also severally testified unto. (12:172)

Against Biddle's claim that the humiliation and exaltation of Christ related in the second chapter of Philippians is inconsistent with his having a divine nature, Owen answers that this inconsistency has "yet to be proved." Against the Socinian appeal to Romans 14:9, Owen directs our attention to the following verse, explaining,

> As another argument to that of the dominion and lordship of Christ, to persuade believers to a mutual forbearance as to judging of one another, he adds, verse 10, "We shall all stand before the judgment-seat of Christ." And this, verse 11, the apostle proves

> from that testimony of the prophet Isaiah, chap. xlv. 23, as he renders the sense of the Holy Ghost, "As I live, saith the Lord, every knee shall bow to me, and every tongue shall confess to God." So that Jesus Christ our Lord is that Jehovah, that God, to whom all subjection is due, and in particular that of standing before his judgment-seat. (12:173-74)

The great problem is not with the biblical evidence, which is abundant. The problem is that the Socinians are devoid of the Holy Spirit, for it is by him alone that confession is duly made that "Jesus is Lord." In this early confession of the church, Owen says, they

> professed that he was the Lord; and thereby avowed their faith in him and obedience unto him. Principally, they owned him to be Jehovah, the Lord over all, God blessed for ever; for the name יְהֹוָה [Yahweh] is everywhere in the New Testament expressed by κύριος, [Lord] here used. He who thus professeth Jesus to be Lord, in the first place acknowledgeth him to be the true God. And then they professed him therewithal to be their Lord, the Lord of their souls and consciences, unto whom they owed all subjection and performed all obedience; as Thomas did in his great confession, "My Lord and my God," John xx. 28.... Hereby then, the apostle informs them wherein the foundation of all church relation, order and worship did consist; for whereas they all had respect unto the Lordship of Christ and their acknowledgement thereof, this was not from themselves, but was a pure effect of the operation of the Holy Ghost in them and towards them. (3:17, 18)

God

Christ is "God." In 1 John 5:20, Christ is called "the true God, and eternal life." This is asserted against Biddle who claims that the reflexive pronoun ὀυτος, "this" in the phrase "This is the true God" is a reference to God the

Father. Owen argues that, while theoretically the pronoun might modify the remote rather than the nearest antecedent when the context requires it, in this particular context the antecedent is Christ (12:256). The wider context of the epistle is also relevant:

> ....That Jesus Christ is by John peculiarly called "life," and "eternal life," is evident both from his Gospel and this Epistle; and without doubt, by the same term in his usual manner, he expresses here the same person. Chap. i. 2, v. 12, 20, "The Son of God is life, eternal life: he that hath the Son hath life: we are in him, in his Son Jesus Christ: this is the true God, and eternal life." So he began, and so he ends his Epistle. (12:256)

Christ is also called God in Titus 2:13: "Looking for that blessed hope, and the glorious appearance of the great God and our Saviour Jesus Christ." Owen maintains the argument, against Biddle's attempted refutation, that the text employs one definite article for both expressions ("great God" and "our Saviour Jesus Christ"), and that the "glorious appearing" is of the Son, and not the Father (12:258).

In Revelation 1:8 and 4:8, Christ is identified as the one who was, is, and is to come, as the Holy One, and as the Lord God Almighty. Owen soundly answers Biddle's objections against these strong testimonies to Christ's deity (12:259-61). Other Scriptures of this nature receiving vindicated by Owen include Acts 20:28 (12:261-63); 1 John 3:16 (12:263-65); John 20:28; and Romans 9:5 (12:305-307).

The Word
Christ is "the Word of God." Owen explains that by the "word" of God it is possible to understand either the word spoken by him, or his "essential Word or Wisdom." Owen reasons that since Christ, being a person, is not the

word spoken by God; he must be the essential eternal Wisdom of God, and therefore must be God (12:321). To the objection that Christ is the Word of God and therefore cannot be God himself, Owen points to John 1:1 with "the Holy Ghost affirming the flat contrary" (12:321).

One particularly interesting observation on the "Word of God" is found in Owen's comments on Hebrews 4:12. He has no difficulty observing the distinction between the "essential" word, and the "enunciative word, or the Scripture, as inspired and written" (21:350). Owen certainly realizes that his equation, in this particular context, of the "word of God" with the Son places him in the minority, and is well acquainted with the reasons why the majority of interpreters reject it. Nevertheless, he answers the objections and offers several reasons in support of his interpretation. The habit of the Hebrews to call the "*second subsistence in the Deity* by the name of 'The Word of God'" forms the basis for his argument from the more general context of the passage (21:354). As proof of this Owen refers to several instances of the Jewish use of the "Word of God." Of course, if these are all understood to be personifications of the "enunciative word" Owen's argument would not hold, but he does not believe they can be so understood: "And whosoever will take the pains to consider what occurs in the Targums concerning their …'Word of God,' and compare it with what the apostle here speaks, and the manner of its introduction, will, if I greatly mistake not, be of the same mind with myself" (21:355). The immediate context also refers to Christ.

As a further argument, Owen points to the description and attributes of the word. While the word of the gospel is the *instrument* of quickening, it does not have life in itself. Christ is the "living" word, having life in himself and being the "Prince of life" (21:357; cf. Goodwin, 1863, 4:365-66). "Wherefore," Owen concludes, "to stir us up to carefulness,…that we give not place to any decays or declensions in our profession, we are especially minded that he is the *living one*, and one that continually exerciseth acts of life toward us" (21:366).

This word is also "powerful." The author of Hebrews adds this "to manifest that the Lord Christ, the Word of God, would effectually put forth his power in dealing with professors" (21:357). It exercises its power in "cutting," which refers to the "spiritual, almighty, penetrating efficacy of the Lord Christ, in his dealing with the souls and consciences of men by his word and Spirit" (21:359). Here we find the basis for Owen's association of the *"essential Word,"* and the *"word preached"* which will be dealt with below under the subject of Christ's prophetic office.

Finally, it is "a discerner of the thoughts and intents of the heart." This feature provides Owen with the occasion to give an interesting and practical exposition of Christ's omniscience (21:359-85).

Son of God
Christ is the "Son of God." Biddle, Episcopius, and Grotius had allowed that the title might be given to Jesus for other reasons than His eternal generation. Owen considers each of the alternative explanations for this title and explains that they are all dependent upon this original filiation, which alone is sufficient for this title. The alternative reasons include the following: Christ's conception by the Holy Ghost; his virgin birth; his likeness to God by his growth in grace; "His mission, or sending into the world by the Father; adoptive sonship; His resurrection ("as it were born again from the womb of the earth without the help of any mother"); and His exaltation, making Him "heir of all things."

Owen's general answer to these is "If Jesus Christ be called the 'Son of God' antecedently to his *incarnation, mission, resurrection, and exaltation,* then there is a reason and cause of that appellation before and above all these considerations, and it cannot be on any of these accounts that he is called the 'Son of God'" (12:177; cf. 12:190-205). Consequently, it becomes Owen's task to "show that the filiation of Christ consists in his generation of the substance of his Father from eternity, or that he is the Son of God upon the account of his divine nature and subsistence therein, antecedent to his incarnation" (12:184). His argument rests upon the premise that this will be the case if, and only if, Christ is a "true," "proper" son of God, as opposed to a son in a metaphorical sense: "He is properly a father who begets another of his substance; and he is properly a son who is so begotten" (12:185). Christ is such a son. He is God's own, proper, natural, "only-begotten Son," in contrast to others who are his sons by adoption (12:185, 186).

Replying to the Socinian interpretation of Psalm 2:7 ("Thou art my Son; this day have I begotten thee"), Owen explains,

> God hath other sons, and believers are said to be begotten of God;" but how? By regeneration, and turning from sin, as in the places quoted is evident. That Christ is so begotten of God is blasphemous once to imagine. Besides, he is the only-begotten Son of the Father, so that no other is begotten with a generation of the same kind with him. It is evident, then, by this testimony, and from these words, that Christ is so the Son of God as no angels are his sons in the same kind; for that the apostle produceth these words to prove, Heb. i. 5, "For unto which of the angels said he at any time, Thou art my Son, this day have I begotten thee? And again, I will be to him a Father, and he shall be to me a Son?" Now, the angels are the sons of God by creation, Job i. 6, xxxvii. 7. He is also such a Son and so begotten as believers are not; for they are begotten by *regeneration* from sin and adoption into the family of God. Therefore Christ, who is the Son of God in another kind than

angels and men, who are so by creation, regeneration, and adoption, is the natural Son of God by eternal generation; which is also proved from this place. (12:241-42)

However, Owen has failed to state the best meaning of the text: the words spoken to the Son refer to something associated with his resurrection as the mediator, when he was "born again" into the world to come, "the first begotten from the dead," and "declared to be the Son of God with power" (see below, chapters 12 and 15). As Owen will demonstrate, Christ's *mediatorial* enthronement depends upon his *natural* sonship, but he seems not to be thinking along this line in the present argument.[3]

According to Owen, Christ is "such a son as is equal to his father in essence and properties," and so is *"begotten of the essence* of his Father" (12:186-89). Owen argues from Psalm 2:7; John 3:18; Proverbs 8:25, 31; Micah 5:2; John 1:1 and 17:5; and Hebrews 1:6 that Christ was begotten "by an eternal communication of his divine essence" (12:189). To correct the error that the divine essence is divided among the persons of the Godhead, Owen corrects Biddle's statement that the Son is begotten out of the divine being by insisting that He is begotten "*in it*, not by an eternal act of the Divine Being, but of the person of the Father" (12:177).[4]

The First-born of Every Creature
Christ is said to be the "first-born of every creature," a favorite phrase among Arians. However, as Owen accurately expounds it, it gives them no more support than it does Socinians. Owen points out that the text does not call Christ the first created, but the "first-born," a term which calls attention to Christ's dominion over creation as one above it, rather than his being a part of it.

> The word which the apostle intends to express is בְּכוֹר, which oftimes is used in the sense now pleaded for, namely, to denote not the birth in the

first place, but the privilege that belonged thereunto. So Ps. lxxxix. 27, God is said to make David his בְּכוֹר, his "first-born;" which is expounded in the next words, "Higher than the kings of the earth." So that the Lord Christ being the first-born is but the same which we have insisted on, of his being heir of all, which was the privilege of the first-born; and this privilege was sometimes transmitted unto others that were not the first-born, although the natural course of their nativity could not be changed, Gen. xxi. 10, xlix. 3, 4, 8. The Lord Christ, then, by the appointment of the Father, being intrusted with the whole inheritance of heaven and earth, and authority to dispose of it, that he might give out portions to all the rest of God's family, is and is called "the first-born" thereof. (20:159; cf. 24:341 and 12:311-12)

"The Brightness of His Glory and Express Image of His Person"
One of Owen's most impressive treatments of the deity of Christ is found in his comments upon Hebrews 1:3, where Christ is called the "brightness of glory, and the express image of his person" (20:87-97). After identifying the errors of several other views of the text, Owen shows that the text does not speak "absolutely of either nature of Christ, his divine or human, but only of his *person*" (20:90). It is the person of Christ, God incarnate, which is the "brightness of glory." Interpreting the phrase as it would most likely be understood by its first readers, Owen directs our attention to the "glory" which dwelt with the people of God, the Ark of the Covenant. As he expresses it,

> Now, on the filling of the tabernacle with the signs of God's presence in cloud and fire, the Jews affirm that there was a constant..."majestic shining glory," resting on the ark; which was "the splendour of the glory of God," in that typical representation of his presence. And this was to instruct them in the way

Owen's Formal Proof of the Deity of Christ 133

and manner whereby God would dwell amongst them. The apostle, therefore, calling them from the types, by which in much darkness they had been instructed in these mysteries, unto the things themselves represented by them, acquaints them with what that typical glory and splendour of it signified, namely, the eternal glory of God, with the essential beaming and brightness of it in the Son, in and by whom the glory of the Father shineth forth unto us. (20:93)

Owen reinforces this with a number of rabbinical examples where the "glory" is understood to be "the essential presence or majesty of the glorious God" (20:94). The glory is also called the *Shechinah*, indicating that God is dwelling there. The association with John 1:14 ("the Word became flesh and tabernacled among us,") and Colossians 2:9 ("in whom the fullness of the Godhead dwelleth bodily") is obvious.

Christ is also affirmed to be the "express image" or "character" of God's (i.e., the Father's) "person" (χαρακτὴρ ὑποστάσεώς αὐτοῦ). "Character," according to Owen, indicates that "the Son in himself is ἐν μορφῇ Θεοῦ, 'in the likeness of God,' Philippians 2:6," and that "unto us he is εἰκὼν Θεοῦ, "the image of God," representing him unto us, Colossians 1:15" (20:95). Owen supports this with a quotation from Philo, that the "most ancient Word is the image of God." In explaining it, Owen says the word alludes, perhaps, to the engraving of God's name, "Holiness to Jehovah" upon the golden plate worn on the head of the high priest (20:96):

> Aaron was to wear this engraven name of God on his forehead, that he might bear the iniquity of the holy things and gifts of the children of Israel; which could really be done only by him who was Jehovah himself. And thus, also, when God promiseth to bring forth the Son as the corner stone of the

> church, he promiseth to engrave upon him the seven eyes of the Lord, Zech. iii. 9, or the perfection of his wisdom and power, to be expressed unto the church in him. There having been, then, this representation of the presence of God, by the character or engraving of his glorious name upon the plate of gold. which the high priest was to wear that he might bear iniquities; the apostle lets the Hebrews know, that in Christ the Son is the real accomplishment of what was typified thereby, the Father having actually communicated unto him his nature, denoted by that name, whereby he was able really to bear our iniquities, and most gloriously represent the person of his Father unto us. (20:96)

Again, we see the emphasis placed not upon the Son's ontological relation to the Father, nor solely upon a view of Christ "from below," but upon the appearing of God to man.

Divine Attributes and Activities Ascribed to Christ

Pre-Eternity

"It is enough," Owen reminds us, "to prove Christ eternal if we prove him begotten of his Father, for no such thing can be new in God" (12:236-37). Nevertheless, there are several particular texts of Scripture which support the pre-eternity, or the eternal generation, of the Son that Owen finds necessary to vindicate from the objections of the Socinians (Micah 5:2; Psalm 2:7, 110:3; and Proverbs 8:23). Biddle's answer to these and similar texts as demonstrating the eternal generation of the Son was a typical, simple, philosophic denial: Christ could not take a part of the Father's essence because it is "impartable; nor the whole, for it being one in number is incommunicable" (translated by Owen, 12:237). Owen's answer is likewise typical, very much like Calvin's, and illustrative of the importance of presuppositions:

And this is the fruit of measuring spiritual things by carnal, infinite things by finite, God by ourselves, the object of faith by corrupted rules of corrupted reason. But,—1. That which God hath revealed to be so is not impossible to be so. Let God be true, and all men liars. That this is revealed hath been undeniably evinced. 2. What is impossible in finite, limited essences, may be possible and convenient to that which is infinite and unlimited, as is that whereof we speak. 3. It is not impossible, in the sense wherein that word must here be used, if any thing be signified by it. "It is not, it cannot be so in limited things, therefore not in things infinite;"—"We cannot comprehend it, therefore it cannot be so;"—"But the nature of the thing about which it is inconsistent with it." This is denied, for God hath revealed the contrary. 4. For the *parting* of the divine essence, or receiving a part of the divine essence, our catechists might have left it out, as having none to push at with it, none standing in the way of that horn of their dilemma. 5. We say, then, that in the eternal generation of the Son, the *whole essence* of the Father is communicated to the Son as to a *personal existence* in the same essence, without multiplication or division of it, the same essence continuing still one in number; and this without the least show of impossibility in an infinite essence, all the arguments that lie against it being taken from the properties and attendancies of that which is finite. (12:237; cf. Calvin, *Institutes*, I. 13. i-iii, xxv-xxvi)

In this way, Owen dismisses the philosophical argument against the eternal generation of the Son. There remains the necessity to vindicate the passages used in its defense from the objections of the Socinians. A text commonly introduced to prove the eternal generation was Micah 5:2. The following will provide an example of Owen's strategy when dealing with a problem of translation such as the one in this text that brings into question the meaning of the words, "from eternity." Owen says,

> the word *gnolam* [עוֹלָם], translated "*seculi*," it hath in the Scripture various significations. It comes from a word signifying "to hide," and denotes an unknown, hidden duration. Principally "*perpetuum, aeternum, sempiternum*,"—that which is pre-eternal and eternal. Sometimes a very long time, Gen. ix. 12, and verse 16, that is perpetual: so Gen. xvii. 13, and in other places, with a reference to the sovereignty of God. Gen. xxi. 33, it is ascribed to God as a property of his and signifies "eternal," *Jehova gnolam* [יהוָה עוֹלָם]:so Ps. lxxxix. 2, as also Isa. xlv. 17. Let all places where the word in Scripture in this sense be reckoned up (which are above three hundred), and it will appear that in far the greatest number of them it signifies absolutely "eternity." In the places of Isa. lxiii. 9, 11, and Mal. iii. 4, only a long time, indeed, is signified, but yet that which reaches to the utmost of the thing or matter treated of. And upon the same rule, where it is put absolutely it signifies "eternity." So doth αἰών in the New Testament, by which the LXX. often render *gnolam* [עוֹלָם], whence πρὸ χρόνων αἰωνίων may may be "from eternity," 2 Tim. i. 9, Tit. i. 2; wherein, also, with a like expression to that under consideration, the "times of eternity" are mentioned. Though perhaps with a peculiar respect to something at the beginning of the world. This, then, is here expressed: He that was in the fulness of time born at Bethlehem, had his goings forth from the Father from eternity. (12:238-39)

Omniscience

Owen's attention has two foci with regard to the Son's omniscience. The first is the Son's full comprehension of the Father, a knowledge of which no creature is capable. The second is his exhaustive knowledge of the hearts of man, by which the "hearts and ways of professors, were 'evident, open, and naked before him,' as the body of the sacrificed beast was to the priest when flayed, opened, and cut to pieces" (21:361-73).

Omnipotence
Owen comments upon Christ's omnipotence in his description of the "O most Mighty" King of Psalm 45:3. Of course, the Son acted omnipotently in the creation of the worlds and in the exercise of providence. In this context Owen focuses upon five ways in which he exercises his mighty power: the building and preservation of the church, "the subduing of his enemies," "the raising of the dead," and "the judging of all flesh, and distributing of eternal rewards and punishments" (9:487-90).

Unity of Essence with the Father
Christ's unity of essence with the Father is evident in John 10:29-31:

> 1. From the apprehension the Jews had of his meaning in those words, who immediately upon them took up stones to stone him for blasphemy, rendering an account of their so doing, verse 33, "Because he, being a man, did make himself God." 2. From the exposition he makes himself of his words, verse 36, "I am the Son of God;"—"That is it I intended; I am so one with him as a son is with his father,"—that is, one in nature and essence. 3. He is so one with him as that the Father is in him, and he in him, by a *divine immanency of persons*. (12:307-308)

Against Grotius' opinion that the context points to a unity of authority (*potestatis*) delegated by the Father to the Son, Owen rightly argues that the context actually points to a unity of potency (*potentiae*), and not authority. Furthermore, "*potestas* is ...'authority,' and may belong to office; but *potentia* is ... 'force,' 'virtue,' or 'power,' and belongs to essence." Owen continues:

> It is not *potestas* or authority that Christ speaks of, but strength, might, and power, which is so great in God that none can take his sheep out of his hand. Now, though *unitas potestatis* doth not prove unity of essence in men, yet *unitas potentiae*, which is here spoken of, in God evidently doth; yea, none can have *unitatem potestatis* with God but he who hath *unitatem essential*. (12:308-309)

Against the allegation that John 17:11 works against this understanding of the unity with the Father, by comparing the unity of believers to it, Owen answers that the words "do not argue a *parity*" between these two unities, "but a *similitude*" (12:308).

Creator of Heaven and Earth
That Christ is the creator of heaven and earth, and therefore is God, is argued from Colossians 1:15-17. When Paul says all things were created by Christ, he is not (as alleged by the Socinians) referring to the gospel state, over which Christ is also the head. Owen argues very persuasively, "the creation of all things simply and absolutely is most emphatically expressed" in the text (12:266). Having emphasized the extent of the "all things" described in the passage, Owen adds,

> They were created for him εἰς αὐτόν, as it is said of the Father, Rom. xi. 36; which, Rev. iv. 11, is said to be for his will and "pleasure." ... For a farther description of him, verse 17, his pre-existence before all things, and his providence in supporting them and continuing that being to them which he gave them by creation, are asserted: "And he is before all things, and by him all things consist." (12:266)

The foundation for the Messiah's pre-eminence, according to Hebrews 1:2 ("By whom also he made the worlds,") is his relation to the world. That is, since the worlds were made by him, "it was meet that, in the new condition which he underwent, he should be Lord of them all" (20:69). Enjedinus and Hugo Grotius had denied this very strong testimony to Christ's deity arguing that δι οὑ, "by whom" should be read as δι ὃν "for whom," making Christ the purpose rather than the agent in creation; but Owen shows that there is no justification for the change, and that the translation making Christ the efficient cause in the creation is correct. Some Socinians argued that the universe is never said to be made through an intermediate cause. "This," says Owen, is "begging the question (*petitio principii*) that this expression doth denote any such intermediate cause as should interpose between the Father and the creation of the world, by an operation of its own, diverse from that of the Father." Such an objection does not have any weight here. "By whom," does not denote "an *instrument*, or an inferior, intermediate, created cause: for then also must he be created by himself, seeing all things that were made were made by him, John i. 3." Rather, it is

> as God's own eternal Word, Wisdom, and Power,... the same individual creating act being the work of Father and Son, whose power and wisdom being one and the same undivided, so also are the works which outwardly proceed from them. And as the joint working of Father and Son doth not infer any other subordination but that of subsistence and order, so the preposition dia doth not of itself intimate the subjection of an instrumental cause, being used sometimes to express the work of the Father himself, Gal. i. 1. (20:74, 71; cf. 12:267-70)

Other Socinians had taken exception not with the prepositional phrase but with the meaning of "worlds." They understood this term, as well as other references to the object of Christ's creative work, to mean not the *first* creation, the physical universe, but only the new creation, i.e., the gospel. The Socinian author Schlichtingius, demonstrating the Socinian emphasis upon Christ's prophetic office, argues to the effect that Christ is, by his word, the source of the new creation. Owen, after pointing out the numerous fallacies in Schlictingius' reasoning emphasizes that the word αἰών, taken absolutely, does not signify "the new creation or state of the church under the gospel; but the whole world, and all things therein contained," and that the immediate context of Hebrews 1 requires this use of the term (20:73, 74; cf. 12:271-73).

John 1:3 also clearly ascribes to the Logos the divine activity of creation. Again, with respect to the δι᾿ αὐτοῦ ["through him," or "by him"] of verse three, Biddle objected that this affirms that Christ was the instrumental, not the immediate, cause of all things. Though this "might help the Arians," it offers no help to the Socinians who deny that Christ had any pre-existence. What about the Arians? Owen does not as often directly address Arian positions, but in this case, his remarks are pertinent to them. The expression, δι᾿ αὐτοῦ, "is sundry times used concerning God the *Father himself*,...the principal efficient cause of the things ascribed to him" (12:221). While the Socinians were used to identifying the "all things" of verse 2 with the gospel itself, Arians extend it to all things excepting the Logos. Owen shows that neither of these positions is adequate (12:221-25). After a comparison of Acts 4:24, Hebrews 1:10, and Colossians 1:16, Owen asks,

> In what words possible could a divine revelation of the eternal power and Godhead of the Son of God be made more plain and clear unto the sons of men? or how could the truth of any thing more evidently be represented unto their minds? If we understand not the mind of God and intention of the Holy Ghost in this matter, we may utterly despair ever to come to an acquaintance with any thing that God

reveals unto us; or, indeed, with any thing else that is expressed or is to be expressed by words. (2:394)

An All-Ruling and Disposing Providence
"That as the great and wise Creator of all things, he doth also govern, rule, and dispose of the things by him created, is another evidence of his eternal power and Godhead" (12:278). Owen's teaching on this will be observed in detail in chapter eight.

"The Incarnation of Christ and His Pre-Existence Thereunto"

The significance of the pre-existence of Jesus Christ to the modern Christological debate is no less crucial than it was to the Socinian controversy. Of both controversies it may reasonably be said,

> it is sufficient for the disproving of their hypothesis concerning Christ if we prove him to have been existent before his incarnation, whether the testimonies whereby we prove it reach expressly to the proof of his eternity or no. That which they have undertaken to maintain is, that Christ had no existence before his conception and birth of the Virgin;—which if it be disproved, they do not, they cannot, deny but that it must be on the account of a divine nature; for as to the incarnation of any pre-existing creature (which was the Arians' madness), they disavow and oppose it. (12:215-16)

Following the order of argument in Biddle's catechism, Owen begins with an exposition and vindication of the witness of the first chapter of the gospel of John. First, he addresses the introductory question of the historical context of the epistle, arguing that John's intent was to "disprove and condemn sundry that were risen up in those days" denying the deity of Christ. The precise translation of *logos*, into word (*verbum*) or speech (*sermo*) is immaterial to the issue at hand: "Jesus Christ is intended" (12:216). Owen says, "Here, then, if any where, we may learn what we are to believe concerning the person of Christ; which also we may certainly do, if our minds are not perverted through prejudice, 'whereby the god of this world doth blind the minds of them which believe not, lest the light of the glorious gospel of Christ, who is the image of God, should shine unto them,' 2 Cor. iv. 4" (2:389-90).

From the overall teaching of the prologue, Owen concludes the following:

> He that was in the beginning before the creation of the world, before any thing of all things that are made was made, who was then with God and was God, who made all things, and without whom nothing was made, in whom was life,—he is God by nature, blessed for ever; nor is there, in the whole Scripture, a more glorious and eminent description of God, by his attributes, names, and works, than here is given of him concerning whom all these things are spoken. But now all this is expressly affirmed of the "Word that was made flesh;" that is, confessedly, of Jesus Christ: therefore he is God by nature, blessed for ever." (12:217)

Several aspects of the prologue of John tending to confirm the pre-existence of Christ were challenged by the antitrinitarians. They objected, for example, that the phrase "in the beginning" did not necessarily indicate "eternity." To this, Owen replied, "To affirm that Christ did exist before the whole creation, and made all things, doth no less prove him to be no more a creature, but the eternal God, than the most express testimony of his eternity doth or can do." Secondly, "in the beginning" is descriptive of eternity, as is evident from the parallel use of the same phrase in Gen. 1:1, and the use of "from everlasting," and "In the beginning, before the earth was," in

Proverbs 8:23. Owen exposes the absurdities present in the Socinian interpretation of this passage (12:217-19; cf. 2:390-91).

Biddle is no more successful in his attempt to impugn the testimony of John 1:14. After vindicating the text from Biddle's various attempts to prove that it merely means that God's servant was a man, Owen concludes: "The place evidently affirms the Word to be made something that he was not before, when he was the Word only, and cannot be affirmed of him as he was man" (12:228).

Biddle's catechism denied the testimony of John 6:62 to the pre-existence of Christ by asserting, "the Scripture witnesseth that the Son of man, that is a man, was in heaven, who without all controversy was not eternally pre-existent" (quoted by Owen, 12:228). To this Owen responds:

> It is expressly affirmed that Christ *was in heaven* before his coming into the world. And if we evince his pre-existence to his incarnation against the Socinians, the task will not be difficult to prove that pre-existence to be in an *eternal divine nature* against the Arians. It is sufficient, as to our intendment in producing this testimony, that it is affirmed that Christ was ἦν πρότερον [previously] in heaven before his coming forth into the world; in what nature we elsewhere prove. (12:229)

He continues,

> ...It is said, indeed, that the *Son of man* was in heaven; which makes it evident that he who is the Son of man hath another nature besides that wherein he is the Son of man, wherein he is the Son of God. And by affirming that the Son of man was in heaven before, it doth no more assert that he was eternal and in heaven in that nature wherein he is the Son of man, than the affirmation that God redeemed his church with his own blood doth prove that the blood shed was the blood of the divine na-

ture. Both the affirmations are concerning the person of Christ. As he who was God shed his blood as he was man, so he who was man was eternal and in heaven as he was God. So that the answer doth merely beg the thing in question, namely, that Christ is not God and man in one person. (12:229)

With regard to other Johannine texts which refer to Christ coming into the world, the Socinians took the same approach of denying to Christ as a man what orthodox Christians had always affirmed concerning the person of the Son of God, or Christ according to his divine nature. Alternatively, they interpreted Christ's coming into the world as his coming into public ministry. Along with showing the weakness of several of Biddle's arguments for this alternative, Owen points out that the Socinians "utterly omit and take no notice of that place where Christ says he *so came from heaven* as that he was *still in heaven*; nor do they mention any thing of that which we lay greatest weight on,—his affirming that he was in heaven before,—but merely insist on the word 'descending' or 'coming down'; and yet they can no other way deal with that neither but by begging the thing in question" (12:230). They had also apparently failed to notice that the texts in question depict Christ as being "so sent into the world *as that he was in heaven before*, and so came forth from the Father, and was with him in heaven before his coming forth" (12:230).

Biddle's exegesis of John 8:58 ("Before Abraham was, I am") is simply ridiculous, being an example of the absurd "shifts" for which the Socinians were (in the esteem of the Orthodox) famous. It seems that only the importance of the text in question elicits Owen's terse refutation (12:234-35). Positively, Owen explains the text thus: "He who in respect of his human nature was many hundred years after Abraham, yet was in another respect existing *before him*; he had an existence before his birth, as

Owen's Formal Proof of the Deity of Christ   145

to his divine nature" (12:234). Any other sense is a "gross equivocation" on the part of Christ (2:390).

Conclusion

Owen's case for the deity of Christ is both more extensive and more powerful than the previous survey of major arguments and interesting features could begin to convey. Many additional texts of Scripture could have been considered and none were examined as carefully as Owen actually does in his exegesis. His general outlook on the Scriptural evidence for Christ's deity may perhaps best be summarized in his conclusion to the evidence from John's prologue: "The sum is,—all the ways whereby we may know God are, his name, his properties, and his works; but they are all here ascribed by the Holy Ghost to the Son, to the Word: and he therefore is God, or we know neither who nor what God is" (2:394).

Particularly important is Owen's emphasis upon the Scripture for the source of the doctrines of the Trinity and the deity of Christ. Owen's method of beginning with the Scriptural testimony to Christ's deity (or the personality of the Holy Spirit), before proceeding to the reconciliation of this testimony with that of the Divine Unity, demonstrates that the orthodox doctrine is neither unscriptural nor dependent upon Greek philosophy. On the contrary, Owen saw, as did the Patristic theologians of the Trinity, that the doctrine of the Trinity was required by the Scriptural evidence, and that its rejection in the face of such overwhelming evidence was due to a non-Christian rationalism, asserting itself against divine revelation.

---

[1] Owen sees Hebrews 1:10-12 as a testimony to Christ's eternity, omnipotence, immutability, sovereignty, and his being called "Jehovah" (see vol. 12, p. 273).

[2] Owen is aware of Grotius' notation of ms. with the variant reading of "θεόν" [God] for "Χριστόν" [Christ], and (from the standpoint of

subsequent textual criticism) rightly dismisses it. A variant with about equal support with "Χριστόν" reads "κύριον" [Lord] Owen seems unaware of this alternate reading. If he had been faced with the choice of these two words it is likely he would have argued that the point holds regardless, since verse four indisputably speaks of Christ and determines the context of verse nine. "From the example of God's dealing with the children of Israel in the wilderness upon their sins and provocations, there being a parity of state and condition between them and Christians as to their spiritual participation of Jesus Christ, verses 1-4, he dehorts believers from the ways and sins whereby God was provoked against them" (12:280).

[3] Cf. Ambrose, commenting on Psalm 2:7, "But we distinguish betwixt generation itself, and the manifestation or declaration of it. Jesus the Son of God from all eternity was begotten, but when he was incarnate, and especially when he was raised again from the dead, then was he mightily declared to be God's Son by nature. And of this declaration or manifestation of this eternal generation is that of the apostle understood" (Ambrose 1855, 46; on the eternal generation see 45-49).

[4] For additional examples of Puritan exposition of the deity of Christ see Brooks (1866, 5:149-56) and Manton (1870, 1:427-53).

CHAPTER 7

God's Eternal Counsels

"The Person of Christ is the foundation of all the counsels of God, as unto his own eternal glory in the vocation, sanctification, and salvation of the church" (1:54). Thus Owen introduces his treatment of the doctrine of the divine eternal counsels. His analysis is sober, centered upon Christ, and scriptural. It is marked by hesitancy toward speculation combined with willingness to follow the implications of his scriptural exegesis to their logical conclusions.

Owen emphasizes the importance of the knowledge of the eternal counsels for the strength and consolation of the church, reasoning that "all the transactions between the Father and the Son, concerning his offices, undertakings, and work of our redemption have respect unto the faith of the church, and are declared for our consolation" (22:491). Because the tidings of the gospel are "great and marvelous" and therefore liable to be doubted by the weak in faith (as too good to be true),

> God discovers the fountains of these things, that we may apprehend the truth and reality of them. His eternal covenant with his Son about them, his oath that he hath made unto him, whereby he was established in his office, and the glorious transactions of his wisdom and grace, are revealed unto this very

end, that we might not be faithless in these things, but believe. (22:492)

The Origin and Design of the Divine Counsels

The "original" or spring of the divine counsels was "in the divine will and wisdom alone, without respect unto any external moving cause" (1:62). We can have no knowledge of the *"absolute* original" of these counsels, which belong to the unsearchable depths of his wisdom and knowledge, but we know they are for the manifestation of God's "nature, in its being, existence, and essential properties," particularly in glorifying himself "as existing in three distinct persons, and himself in each of those persons distinctly." The divine counsels were "from all eternity personal transactions in the Holy Trinity concerning mankind in their temporal and eternal conditions" (19:43).

Counsels of wisdom and delight

Though the absolute original of the counsels is inscrutable, the *"design* of their accomplishment was laid in the person of the Son alone" and they were *"effected* in Christ" (1:62, 54, emphasis mine). To prove this Owen appeals first to Proverbs 8:22, 23.[1] This text has had a long history as a testimony to the pre-incarnate Logos, the eternal essential wisdom of God. Owen sees this as assumed in the text, but explains that it principally regards Wisdom's future incarnation for the accomplishment of the counsels of God. It is with respect to these counsels that

> God "possessed him in the beginning of his way, and set him up from everlasting." God possessed him eternally as his essential wisdom—as he was always, and is always, in the bosom of the Father, in the mutual ineffable love of the Father and Son, in the eternal bond of the Spirit. But he signally possessed him "in the beginning of his way"—as his wisdom

God's Eternal Counsels

acting in the production of all the ways and works that are outwardly of him. The beginning of God's ways," before his works, are his counsels concerning them—even as our counsels are the beginning of our ways, with respect unto future works. And he "set him up from everlasting," as the foundation of all the counsels of his will, in and by whom they were to be executed and accomplished. (1:54)

What was "set up"? It was not the person of the Son absolutely—not the divine nature. The text refers rather to the peculiar glory of the Son that belongs to him as the foundation of the counsels of God. This is the glory referred to in John 17:5, the glory which Christ had with the Father before the world was. Owen explains that in John 17 Jesus neither prays for the communication of divine attributes to his human nature, nor for the manifestation of the glory of his divine nature, but for the manifestation of "the glory of his goodness, grace, and love—in his peculiar undertaking of the execution of the counsels of God" (1:55-56).

Continuing his exposition of Proverbs 8:22, Owen says that there was an "ineffable delight between the Father and the Son in his setting up or exaltation" (1:56). "The Father delights in the Son," but the text is not referring to the eternal delight of the Father in the Son, *per se*—that is, in the Son as bearer of the divine excellencies—but in his delight in the Son *as the mediator* undertaking the salvation of the church. It is his eternal wisdom in the "contrivance" of the counsels, and the "means of their accomplishment in his future incarnation" (1:57). This "counsel of Peace" between Jehovah and the Branch, i.e., between the Father and the to-be-incarnate Son (*incarnandus*), is the basis for the Scriptures which testify of the Father's delight in the Son and the elect servant (1:57). This also explains how, according to Titus 1:2, God promised eternal life before the world began: "There was eternal life with the Father—that is, in his counsel treasured up in Christ, and in him afterwards manifested unto us: 1 John i. 2" (1:56).

Owen emphasizes that God delights not only in his Son, but also in his eternal counsels. First, he delights in them as the acts of infinite wisdom and as the way in which the Divine wisdom is principally revealed (1 Cor. 1:24; Eph. 3:10; Rom. 11:33-36). As Owen explains elsewhere, the wisdom of God's counsel is an "abyss which we cannot dive into," and which men and angels "may adore, but cannot comprehend." The "end of all the free acts and purposes of the will of God" is the glorification of himself in the manifestation of this wisdom (22:261). Furthermore,

> On this account are *all the treasures of wisdom* and knowledge said to be hid in Jesus Christ, Col. ii. 3. There is not only in him, and the work of his mediation, "the wisdom of God,"—that is, both exerted and manifested,—but "all the treasures of it"; that is, God will not produce any effect out of the stores of his infinite wisdom but what is suitable and subservient unto what he hath designed in and by Jesus Christ. (22:262)

The purpose of God is referred to as a "counsel" precisely because it is an act of infinite wisdom. The same infinite wisdom renders the purpose of God immutable and certain of accomplishment, since "in his wisdom he fixeth on such means for its accomplishment as shall not depend on anything whereby their efficacy might be frustrated" (22:264).

Secondly, God delights in his counsels because, of all the acts of God, they are the "greatest exercise and emanation of divine goodness," even, "acts of infinite goodness," because these counsels concern nothing short of the communication of the greatest of all good to man—God Himself. Reading Owen, one is struck by the absurdity of the idea that in the Reformed doctrine of redemption God begrudgingly forgives sinners upon the payment of their ransom. If a good man takes pleasure in doing good, Owen argues,

> what shall we conceive concerning eternal absolute infinite, perfect, immixed goodness, acting itself in the highest instance (in an effect cognate and like unto it) that it can extend unto! So was it in the counsels of God, concerning the incarnation of his Son and the salvation of the church thereby. No heart can conceive, no tongue can express, the least portion of that ineffable delight of the holy, blessed God, in these counsels, wherein he acted and expressed unto the utmost his own essential goodness. (1:59)

Thirdly, God delights in his counsels because in them he communicates his love and grace unto his elect. Owen is obviously moved at the idea of God's "delight and complacency in the actings of his love towards the church," over which he "rejoiceth with joy and joyeth with singing" (1:60, quoting Zephaniah 3:17).

Laid in the person of Christ
The divine counsels have for their origin, "the divine will and wisdom alone." However,

> the design of their accomplishment was laid in the person of the Son alone. As he was the essential wisdom of God, all things were at first created by him. But upon a prospect of the ruin of all by sin, God would in and by him—as he was fore-ordained to be incarnate—restore all things. The whole counsel of God unto this end centered in him alone. (1:62)

How are the divine counsels laid in the person of Christ? Owen answers with a review of the creation and fall, emphasizing that the purpose of man's creation in the image of God was that the creator might "receive the glory that he aimed at in and by the whole inanimate creation" (1:61). Upon the entrance of sin, however, it became impossible that God would receive this glory. Nevertheless, "God had from all eternity laid in provision of counsels for the recovery of all things into a better and more permanent state than what was lost by sin." This new state Owen calls the "revivification, the restitution of all things," and the "ἀνακεφαλαίωσις" i.e., "the gathering all things in heaven and earth into a new head in Christ Jesus," according to Acts 3:21 and Ephesians 2:10 (1:61-62). In this restoration of all things, Christ is the "provisional wisdom of God." There is nothing here to support Reid's conclusion that the divine counsel is "that of a God into whose counsels Christ has not been admitted, and the inmost recesses of whose wisdom Christ has not illuminated" or that Christ lacks "a secure and effective part in the design and preparation of the decree of election" (Reid 1948, 10).[2]

The assertion that the counsels have their origin in the will and wisdom of God in no way diminishes the fact that they arise from the love of God:

> The *eternal disposing cause* of the whole work wherein the Lord Christ was engaged by the susception of this office, for the redemption and salvation of the church is the *love of the Father*.... And this love of the Father acted itself in his eternal decrees, . . . Originally, it is his eternal election of a portion of mankind to be brought unto the enjoyment of himself, through the mystery of the blood of Christ, and the sanctification of the Spirit. (1:333-34)

Owen describes the counsels of God in terms equivalent to the love of God, which is "the eternal spring which is derived unto the church through the mediation of Christ" (1:334).

On the part of Christ, Owen adds,

> The sole spring of all the mediatory actings of Christ, both in the susception of our nature and in

all that he did and suffered therein, was his own mere love and grace, working by pity and compassion. It is true, he undertook this work principally with respect unto the glory of God, and out of love unto him. But with respect unto us, his only motive unto it was his abundant, overflowing love. (1:166)

The love of the Son is "that which put all the design of this eternal love of the Father into execution, and wrought out the accomplishment of it (1:334). Considering our state as having fallen, "the *first act* of love in Christ towards us was in *pity* and compassion,... but as he looketh on us as recoverable out of that state, his love worketh in and by *delight*. It was an inconceivable delight unto him, to take a prospect of the deliverance of mankind unto the glory of God; which is also an act of love" (1:334; cf. 20:369).

The Covenant of Redemption

Owen describes the eternal transactions between the Father and the Son as being carried on "'*per modum foederis,*' 'by way of Covenant,' compact, and mutual agreement" (19:77). It has been a matter of some debate as to whether the use of the language of a pact or covenant (*pactum*) is appropriate to describe this "inter-Trinitarian economy of salvation" (cf. Murray, 1977, 130). The principal objections to the terminology are these: It leads to tri-theism, it separates the purpose of God in salvation from election, and it is based upon Roman law rather than the Bible.

Owen anticipates the first of these objections, which was still being discussed by Barth and Kuyper in the twentieth century; namely, whether the idea of a covenant between the Father and the Son poses a threat to the doctrine of the Trinity. It is alleged to presuppose a division in the divine will, and a subordination that is incompatible with the idea of the Trinity. Owen answers,

Although it should seem that because they are single

acts of the same divine understanding and will, they cannot be properly federal, yet because those properties of the divine nature are acted distinctly in the distinct persons, they have in them the nature of a covenant. Besides, there is in them a supposition of the *susception of our human nature* into personal union with the Son. On the consideration hereof he comes to have an absolute distinct interest, and to undertake for that which is his own work peculiarly. (19:77)

By his reference to the properties of the divine nature distinctly acting in the distinct persons, Owen seems to be anticipating Geerhardus Vos, who says that in the *pactum salutis* the divine will "appears as having its own manner of existence in the Persons." Vos also maintains that the unity of the being of God is not threatened hereby, for "to emphasize that unity so strongly that the Persons can no longer enter into judicial terms with each other would lead to Sabellianism and would undermine the reality of the work of salvation with its relations between Person and Person" (*De Verbondsleer in de Gereformeerde Theologia*, pp. 25, 27, as quoted in Berkouwer 1960, 161). Berkouwer asks whether "in the doctrine of the *pactum salutis* [covenant of redemption] a deeply religious motif lies embedded," a question to which Vos had already spoken by affirming that the doctrine of the covenant of redemption originates from an inclination to concentrate the decree in the Mediator. This is precisely Owen's point, as will appear shortly.

Owen's strategy for the exposition of the covenant of redemption is first to prove that such a covenant existed and secondly to "insist on that in it in particular which is the original of his priesthood."

The Name and Nature of a Covenant
Owen realizes that he must first prove that the transactions between the Father and the Son are federal in

God's Eternal Counsels

character. His most extensive treatment of this subject may be found in the second introductory volume to his *Exposition of the Epistle to the Hebrews*. There are three general senses in which the Hebrew word בְּרִית may be taken. "Sometimes," he says, "it intends no more but peace and agreement, although there were no compact or convention unto that purpose: for this is the end of all covenants," referring to Job 5:23 and Hosea 2:18 as examples of this use (19:80). Secondly, "synecdochically, the law written on the two tables of stone was called the covenant." Explaining how this may be considered a covenant, Owen says,

> Now, this law was purely preceptive, and an effect of sovereign authority, yet is it called a covenant. But this it is not absolutely in its own nature, seeing no mere precept, nor system of precepts as such, nor any mere promise, can be a covenant properly so called; but it was a principal part of God's covenant with the people, when accepted by them as the rule of their obedience, with respect unto the promises wherewith it was accompanied. (19:80)

"Thirdly," he continues, "an absolute promise is also called בְּרִית, "a covenant," the covenant of God," for example, Isaiah 59:21, or the "decree constitutive of the law of nature and its continuance" as alluded to in Jeremiah 33:20 (19:81). The conclusion Owen comes to is that the precise meaning must be learned from the context (19:81).

What is a covenant? "An absolutely complete covenant is a voluntary convention, pact, or agreement, between distinct persons, about the ordering and disposal of things in their power, unto their mutual concern and advantage" (19:82). Explaining this definition Owen emphasizes that covenants have the following characteristics. First, covenants "properly so called" are *mutual compacts* requiring two or more parties (19:82). Second, the agreement must be "*voluntary* and of choice upon the election of the terms covenanted about." A proper covenant is

> founded on a free election of the terms of it.... Hence, when one people is broken in war or subdued by another, who prescribe terms unto them, which they are forced as it were to accept for the present necessity, it is but an imperfect covenant, and...not like to be firm or stable. (19:82-83)

Third, "The matter of every righteous and complete covenant must be of *things in the power* of them who convent and agree about them." Owen explains that this is the reason God in the covenant of grace undertakes for man to ensure man's faith and obedience. Fourth, "The end of a covenant is the disposal of the things about which the covenant is made to the *mutual content and satisfaction* of all persons concerned" (19:83).

To these four aspects of every equal compact, Owen adds that there is "an especial kind of covenant, depending solely on the personal undertakings and services of one party in order unto the common ends of the covenant, or the mutual satisfaction of the covenanters." These covenants have three parts also: a proposal of service, a promise of reward, and an acceptance of the proposal. Owen is well aware of the objections that may arise from ascribing such characteristics to the divine counsel, but demonstrates that the Scriptures describe just such a covenant between the Father and the Son. Accordingly, this arrangement

> indispensably introduceth an inequality and subordination in the covenanters as to the common ends of the covenant, however on other accounts they may be equal; for he who, prescribes the duties which are required in the covenant, and giveth the promises of either assistance in them or a reward upon them, is therein and so far superior unto him,

God's Eternal Counsels 157

or greater than he who *observeth* his prescriptions and *trusteth* unto his promises. (19:83)

The Covenant Between the Father and the Son
Assuming that the Father and the Son are two distinct persons and that there were eternal transactions between them concerning the redemption of mankind, Owen proceeds in his demonstration of the covenant of the redeemer by proving that these transactions were indeed federal in nature. His method is to appeal to Scripture texts that testify to the subordination of the Son to the Father, particularly those in which the Father is called the "God" or "Lord" of the Son. "This expression of being a God unto any one is declarative of a covenant, and is the word whereby God constantly declares his relation unto any in a way of covenant, Jer. xxx. 33, xxxii. 38; Hos. ii. 23" (19:84; 20:185; 1:249). He explains that "God, declaring that he will be a God unto any, engageth himself unto the exercise of his holy properties, which belong unto him as God, in their behalf and for their good; and this is not without an engagement of obedience from them" (19:84). Scriptures referring to the Father as "God" or "Lord" to the Son express their relationship in the economy of redemption. They "argue both a covenant and a subordination therein," i.e., in the covenant, rather than a subordination of the human nature only, or an *ontological* subordination of the Son. For example, when, in John 14:28, Jesus says, "the Father is greater than I," he

> speaks with respect unto the covenant engagement that was between the Father and himself as to the work which he had to do: for therein, ... the Father was the *prescriber*, the promiser, and lawgiver; and the Son was the *undertaker* upon his prescription, law, and promises." (19:84-85)

Here Owen, like Calvin before him, points out that the text was misused by both the Arians and the orthodox fathers.[3] While Calvin emphasized the redemptive-historical significance of the mediator's words at his last supper, Owen saw them as expressing the relation of Father and Son in the pre-mundane covenant.

At this point in the exposition, Owen makes it clear that the Son is not subordinate to the Father by his eternal generation, but is so only in and by the covenant of redemption. He says Christ is indeed, in respect of his divine personality, said to be "God of God."

> No more is intended hereby but that the person of the Son, as to his personality, was of the person of the Father, who communicated his nature and life unto him by eternal generation. But the Father on that account is not said to be his God, or to be a God unto him, which includes the acting of divine properties on his behalf, and a dependence on the other side on him who is so a God unto him. And this hath its sole foundation on that covenant and the execution of it which we are in the consideration of. (19:85)

This emphasis upon the "personality" is a way of setting apart the person from the essence, and provides another testimony to Owen's belief that the Son is God-in-himself (*autotheos*).

The second criterion of a proper covenant was that the two parties take counsel together concerning the covenant. The counsel referred to was between the Lord and "the Branch." He explains,

> And this was not spoken of him absolutely as he was a man, or was to be a man, for so there was not properly..."counsel," between God and him...Rom. xi. 34. And, besides, the Son in his human nature was merely the servant of the Father to do his will, Isa. xlii. 1. But God takes this counsel with him as he was his *eternal Wisdom*, only with respect unto his future incarnation; for therein he was to be both the "Branch of the Lord," and "the fruit of the earth,"

Isa. iv. 2. Hereunto regard also is had in his name: Isa. ix. 6, "He shall be called Wonderful Counselor;" for these titles, with those that follow, do not absolutely denote properties of the divine nature, though they are such divine titles and attributes as cannot be ascribed unto any but to him who is God; but there is in them a respect unto the work which he had to do as he was to be a "child born" and "a son given" unto us. And on the same account is he called "The everlasting Father," a name not proper unto the person of the Son with mere respect unto his personality. There is, therefore, a regard in it unto the work he had to do, which was to be a father unto all the elect of God. (19:85)

The Father is taking counsel with one who is his eternal wisdom. Such an understanding of the unity of the divine will can hardly justify a charge of tritheism. But in taking this counsel with the Son, he does so with him "with respect unto his future incarnation." Hence, the counsel is not with someone who is ontologically subordinate, but with someone considered as having identified himself with mankind and assuming the role of mediator.

Owen continues, "Particularly, the *will* of the Father and Son concurred in this matter: which was necessary, that the covenant might be of voluntary and of choice" (19:86). Though they concurred, "the original of the whole is referred to the will of the Father constantly." His is the part of the "enjoiner, prescriber, and promiser, whose will in all things is to be attended unto." Owen's emphasis here is on the Father's liberty, and thus the gracious character of salvation. "Whatever, therefore, we may afterwards assert concerning the necessity of satisfaction to be given unto his justice, upon the supposition of this covenant, yet the entering into this covenant, and consequently all that ensued thereon, is absolutely resolved into the mere will and grace of God" (19:86).

Owen goes on, however, to show that the will of the Son was "distinct" in this counsel, and the significance of that distinction with respect to the will of the Father.

> In his divine nature and will he undertook voluntarily for the work of his person when the human nature should be united thereunto, which he determined to assume; for what is spoken of the second person is spoken with respect unto his purpose to assume our nature, for the obedience whereof in all that was to be done upon it or by it, he undertook. This the Scripture fully declares, and that for a double end:—First, To demonstrate that the things which he underwent in his human nature were just and equal, inasmuch as himself whose it was voluntarily consented thereunto. Secondly, To manifest that those very acts which he had in command from his Father were no less the acts of his own will.... And this his voluntary susception of the discharge of what he was to perform, according to the nature and terms of this covenant, was the ground of the *authoritative mission*, sealing, and commanding of the Father towards him. (19:86-87)

Owen wishes to show that Christ voluntarily entered into the covenant, and that on this basis he "owns himself the servant of the Father," and "acknowledgeth him to be his Lord."

It is noteworthy that Owen extends this voluntary susception of the discharge of the covenanted duties to the human nature of Christ as "but a representation of the will of the Son of God when he engaged into this work from eternity" (19:87). Here, however, Owen, makes the application of the principle that the Son voluntarily accepted the discharge of the terms of the covenant with a view to his incarnation, by arguing that "whereas, therefore, he had a sovereign and absolute power over his own human nature when assumed, whatever he sub-

God's Eternal Counsels

mitted unto, it was no injury unto him, nor injustice in God to lay it on him" (19:87).

It is important to note Owen's consistent use of such phrases as "as unto the nature which he was to assume." There is no hint that he entertains any idea of a pre-existent human nature, as conceived by Isaac Watts (Watts 1753, 820).

At this point in his exposition Owen addresses the objection that the divine will, as a natural property of the one God, cannot act distinctly in the three persons of the Trinity. Previously he had shown that the acts of the Father and the Son were federal because the "properties of the divine nature acted distinctly in the distinct persons"; now he must prove that such a distinct acting is possible. He says,

> This difficulty may be solved from what hath been already declared; for such is the distinction of the persons in the unity of the divine essence, as that they act in natural and essential acts *reciprocally* one towards another,—namely, in understanding, love, and the like; they know and mutually love each other. And as they subsist distinctly, so they also act distinctly in those works which are of external operation. And whereas all these acts and operations whether reciprocal or external, are either with a will or from a freedom of will and choice, the will of God in each person, as to the peculiar acts ascribed unto him, is his will therein peculiarly and eminently, though not exclusively to the persons, by reason of their mutual *in-being*. The will of God as to the peculiar actings of the Father in this matter is the will of the Father, and the will of God with regard unto the peculiar actings of the Son is the will of the Son; not by a distinction of sundry wills, but by the distinct application of the same will unto its *distinct acts* in the persons of the Father and the Son. (19:87-88)

Next, Owen expounds the principle that "a covenant

must be about the disposal of things *in the power of them that enter into it*, otherwise it is *null* or fraudulent." He considers this in two ways. The first and more obvious understanding of this principle is that persons may rightly enter a covenant when they have the right and power to fulfill their parts in it. That is, when "the things to be disposed of according to the limitations of the covenant are lawful and good antecedently unto any agreement made about them, and because they are in the power of the covenanters" (19:88). The second way looks at those aspects, or "limitations," of the covenant which are not good antecedently, but are only so because of the covenant. These include

> most of the things that are disposed in the covenant between the Father and the Son under consideration. They become good and desirable, and suited unto their glory and honor, not as considered absolutely and in themselves, but with respect unto that order, dependence, and mutual relation, that they are cast into by and in the covenant. (19:89)

In his discussion of this, Owen, without identifying it as such, addresses an issue which had been a point of dispute with Socinians from the beginning: What righteousness can there be in the penal sufferings of an innocent being? Apart from the covenant of redemption, Owen argues, none. Owen adds,

> It was utterly impossible that an innocent person, considered absolutely as such, should suffer penally under the sentence and curse of the law; for the law denounceth punishment unto no such person. Guilt and punishment are related; and where the one is not, real, or supposed, or imputed, the other cannot be. But now, in the terms of this covenant, leading unto the limitations and use of these sufferings, they are made good, and tend unto the glory of God, as we shall see. (19:89)

Besides, the argument works in both directions. What glory can there be in the pardoning of sinners? "But, as we shall see, through the terms and conditions of this covenant, this is rendered righteous, holy, and good, and eminently conducing to the glory of God" (19:89).

The Matter and Ends of the Covenant
The covenanters enter into a covenant for the purpose of attaining certain ends; the "matter" of the covenant is the "thing agreed about" for the attaining of those ends. In the case of the covenant of redemption the matter is "the saving of sinners, in and by ways and means suited unto the manifestation of the glory of God." It is God's purpose "in and by Jesus Christ to save his elect from sin and death, to bring his many sons unto glory, or the full enjoyment of himself unto eternity" (19:89, 90). Owen distinguishes between the covenant and the "disposition of all things made thereby." The former refers to the pact between the Father and the Son; the latter refers to the contents of the pact. The end of both the making of the covenant and of the disposition of all things made thereby" is the manifestation of the glory that is in God.

Owen shares the Reformed conviction that as God is "absolutely, infinitely, eternally perfect in himself and all his glorious properties," nothing can add glory to him. Rather, God's external works are for the *manifestation* of the glory that belongs to his being.

> When the holy properties of his nature are exercised in external works, and are thereby expressed,... then is God glorified. The end therefore in general of this covenant, which regulated the disposal of the whole matter of it, was the exercise, exaltation, and manifestation, of the glorious properties of the divine nature; other supreme end and *ultimate it could have none*, as hath been declared. (19:90)

As God is one, and all of his works are the works of

that one divine nature, there is a sense in which any one of his works will glorify all of his divine properties (19:90). However, "in several particular works of God, his design is firstly, immediately, and directly, to exercise in a peculiarly eminent manner, and therein to advance and glorify, one or more of his glorious properties, and the rest consequentially in and by them." In the case of the covenant of redemption, God designs peculiarly to exalt his "wisdom, attended with sovereignty," his "justice, springing from holiness," and his "grace, mercy, goodness, love, which are various denominations of the same divine excellency" (19:91). The point to be emphasized here is that the covenant of redemption "sprang from these properties of the divine nature, that the execution of it is the work and effect of them all, and that it is designed to manifest and glorify them, or God in and by them unto eternity" (19:91). Reflecting his Trinitarianism, Owen points out that these are the properties which "God, even the Father, aims at in this covenant, and which supplies the place of that security or advantage which amongst men is intended in such compacts" (19:91).

There was also a twofold honor intended for the Son. The Son enjoys the honor which belongs to him "*conjunctly* with the Father, as he is of the same nature with him, 'over all, God blessed for ever.'" In addition, due to his "peculiar" undertaking in the covenant, there is a "peculiar honour and glory thereby, not as God, but as the Mediator of the covenant of grace, which sprang from hence" (19:92).

The Condition and Limitation of the Covenant
The conditions of the covenant are comprised in promises made unto, and requirements laid upon, the Son. Owen divides the promises into those concerning the Person of the Mediator, and those concerning the prosperity of his work. First, Owen emphasizes that the

promises concern not the Son "absolutely considered," but "with respect unto his future incarnation." In this state of humiliation and dependence, the Son is promised divine assistance:

> Whatever opposition hell and the world,—which were to prevail unto the bruising of his heel,—could make against the Son of God acting in the frail nature of man, he was to encounter withal; whatever the law and the curse of it could bring on offenders, he was to undergo it. Hence in that nature he stood in need of the presence of God with him; in respect whereunto he placed his trust and confidence in God, even the Father, and called upon him in all his distresses. See Isa. xlii. 4,6; Ps. xvi. 10, 11, xxii., lxxxix. 28; Isa. l. 5-9. This God promised him, and gave him that assurance of, which at all times he might safely trust unto,—namely, that he would not leave him under his troubles, but stand by and assist him to the utmost of what had a consistency with the design itself whose execution he had undertaken. (19:93)

The phrase concerning the help given, that it would be consistent with the design of the covenant, is very significant, since it precludes the objection that Jesus Christ had an "unfair advantage" in living the life required of him.

To these Owen adds certain promises that were made "concerning his *exaltation*, his kingdom and power, with all that glory which was to ensue upon the accomplishment of his work" (19:93). These promises motivated Christ in the accomplishment of the conditions of the covenant, upon which he "made his request, and expected that they should be made good and fulfilled" (19:94; cf. Goodwin 1863, 5:27-30).

In addition to these promises concerning the person of the mediator, there were promises concerning his work. First, the Son is "assured that the children whom he undertook for should be delivered and saved, should be made partakers of grace and glory" (19:94). It is this promise made in the covenant that renders the obedience and suffering of Christ meritorious toward the salvation of the elect. The intrinsic value of his obedience and suffering is an "indispensable condition" of his meriting this salvation (no other being could have undertaken this task), but, as Owen puts it, "there must not only be a *proportion*, but a *relation* also, between the things whereof the one is the merit of the other" (19:94). In other words, Christ not only renders an obedience of infinite value, but he obeys *for the sake of* their salvation; therefore, their salvation is merited by his obedience.

Of the three requirements placed upon the Son, the first was the assumption of human nature.

> In this his readiness, willingness, and delight, springing from love and compassion, the *counsel* of God concerning the way of our recovery is, as it were, proposed unto him. Now, this was a way of great difficulties and perplexities unto himself,—that is, unto his person as it was to be constituted. To the divine nature nothing is grievous,—nothing is difficult; but he was to have another nature, wherein he was to undergo the difficulties of this way and work. It was required of him that he should pity us until he had none left to pity himself when he stood in need of it,—that he should pursue his delight to save us until his own soul was heavy and sorrowful unto death,—that he should relieve us in our sufferings by suffering the same things that we should have done. But he was not in the least hereby deterred from undertaking this work of love and mercy for us; yea, his love rose on this proposal like the waters of a mighty stream against opposition. For hereon he says, "Lo, I come to do thy will, O God;"—it is my delight to do it, Heb. x. 5-7; Isa. l. 5-7. (1:335)

Owen says, "This condescension, which was the foundation of all his obedience, gave the nature of merit and purchase unto what he did" (19:94-95). There is no contradiction between this and the statement just made concerning the relation of the promise and the merit of Christ's obedience. There must be a promise if obedience is to have a ground for a plea; there must be an incarnation, that there might be a person suited to render the obedience which the ends of the covenant require.

This leads us to the second requirement of the covenant, that "in this nature so assumed he should be the *servant of the Father*, and yield universal obedience unto him, both according to *the general law* of God obliging all mankind, and according unto the *especial law* of the church under which he was born and made, and according unto the *singular law* of that compact or agreement" between himself and the Father (19:95). The first of these laws is self-evident, the second means that the mediator would be required to fulfill any further laws revealed to his people. In the actual event, this refers to the laws of the Mosaic administration, which Jesus fully satisfied. The third refers to the covenant of redemption itself, which is to say his unique and specific duties as the Mediator. These three laws make up the "whole will of God" required of Christ. The third condition of the covenant is that he should make atonement for sin.

Christ as Surety of his People
One of the most important motifs of Owenian Christology, shared with Puritan theologians generally, was the biblical concept of the union of Christ with his people. It is important to grasp the significance of this union if one is to appreciate such important doctrines as the covenant of redemption, the substitutionary atonement, justification by the imputation of Christ's righteousness, communion with Christ in the Holy Spirit, and the church. It may not be too much of an exaggeration to say that this is the most

important doctrine in Puritan theology. This is not to assert that it was so *explicitly*. Jonathan Won, in comparing certain Puritans to Calvin has observed that, relative to the Reformer, these Puritans spoke more of communion than union (1989, 351).[4] Two things should be kept in mind, however. First, in so doing, they were commenting upon a consequence of that union. Second, more of their theology was dependent upon that union than what may be generally understood by the term "communion with Christ." For instance, Owen makes all communion with Christ to flow not merely from our union with him by faith, but from this antecedent union with us in the eternal compact. As he says,

> There is almost nothing that Christ hath done, which is the spring of that grace whereof we speak, but we are said to do it with him.... In the actings of Christ there is, by virtue of the compact between him as mediator, and the Father, such an assured foundation laid of the communication of the fruits of those actings unto them in whose stead he performed them that they are said, in the participation of those fruits, to have done the same things with him. (2:155; cf. Brooks 1866, 5:513-15)

Again, this union is not to be confused with that vital union which is constituted between Christ and the saints by the mutual indwelling of the Holy Spirit, which is its consequence (21:146-52).

The importance of this appears, for example, in his description of the imputation of Christ's righteousness to sinners. Owen asserts that,

> The principal foundation hereof is,—that *Christ* and the *church*, in this design, were one *mystical person*; which state they do actually coalesce into, through the *uniting efficacy* of the Holy Spirit. He is the head, and believers are the members of that one person, as the apostle declares, 1 Cor. xii. 12, 13. Hence, as what

he did is imputed unto them, as if done by them; so what they deserved on the account of sin was charged upon him. (5:176; cf. Goodwin, 1863, 5:30-31)

Owen emphasizes that, although the word "person" may be taken in a number of senses,

> Christ and believers are neither one *natural* person, nor a *legal* or *political* person, nor any such person as the *laws, customs*, or usages of men do know or allow of. They are *one mystical* person; whereof although there may be some imperfect resemblances founded in *natural* or *political* unions, yet the union from whence that denomination is taken between him and us is of that nature, and ariseth from such reasons and causes, as no *personal union* among men... hath any concernment in. And therefore, as to the *representation* of it unto our weak understandings, unable to comprehend the depth of heavenly mysteries, it is compared unto *unions* of divers kinds and natures. (5:178-79)

After several examples, Owen proceeds to explain the *causes* of this union: "The first spring of this *union*, and of all the other causes of it, lieth in that *eternal compact* that was between the Father and the Son concerning the recovery and salvation of fallen mankind" (5:178). One of the effects of this compact was the assumption of our nature. This assumption of human nature unto the person of the Son of God results in a union that becomes the principal among other causes of the mystical union of Christ and believers.

Secondly,

> The Lord Christ, as unto the nature which he was to assume, was hereon *predestinated* unto grace and glory. He was..."fore-ordained," predestinated, "before the foundation of the world," 1 Pet. i. 20; that is, he was so, as unto his office, so unto all the grace and glory required thereunto, and consequent thereon. All the grace and glory of the human nature of Christ

was an effect of free *divine pre-ordination*. God chose it from all eternity unto a participation of all which it received in time. Neither can any other cause of the glorious exaltation of that portion of our nature be assigned. (5:180)

Owen adds, "This grace and glory whereunto he was pre-ordained was twofold: . . . That which was *peculiar unto himself;*" and "That which was to be *communicated*, by and through him, unto the church" (5:180). The first of these is the,

> χάρις ἑνώσεως,—the grace of personal union; that single effect of divine wisdom (whereof there is no shadow nor resemblance in any other works of God, either of creation, providence, or grace), which his nature was filled withal: "Full of grace and truth." And all his personal glory, power, authority, and majesty as mediator, in his exaltation at the right hand of God, which is expressive of them all, do belong hereunto. These things were peculiar unto him, and all of them effects of his eternal *predestination*. (5:180)

Owen lists six ways in which Christ was predestinated with respect to the church. He was, first, "the *pattern and exemplary cause* of our predestination." This is the meaning of our being "predestined to conformed unto the image of the Son of God" (Rom. 8:9). Second, he was predestinated as "the *means and cause of communicating all grace and glory unto us*" (Eph. 1:3-5): "He was designed as the only procuring cause of all spiritual blessings in heavenly things unto those who are chosen in him." Third, "He was thus *fore-ordained* as the head of the church; it being the design of God to gather all things into a head in him, Eph. i. 10." Fourth, "All the *elect of God* were, in his eternal purpose . . . and in the everlasting covenant between the Father and the Son, committed unto him.... Hence was that love of his unto them wherewith he loved them, and gave himself for them, antecedently unto any good or love in them, Eph. v. 25, 26; Gal. ii. 20; Rev. i. 5, 6." Fifth, "In the prosecution of this design of God,...in the fullness of time he took upon him our nature, or took it into personal subsistence with himself. The especial relation that ensued hereon between him and the elect children the apostle declares at large, Heb. ii. 10 - 17." Sixth, "On these foundations" concludes Owen, "he undertook to be the *surety of the new covenant*, Heb. vii 22" (5:180-81). Seventh, all of the "precedent causes of the *union* between Christ and believers ... centre" upon the "*communication of his Spirit*, the same Spirit that dwelleth in him, unto them, to abide in, to animate and guide, the whole mystical body and all its members" (5:196).

Christ's suretyship is extremely important for the covenant of redemption and the doctrine of justification. As Owen puts it, "on these foundations" which constitute his union with his people, he becomes their surety in the covenant of redemption, and thereby provides the foundation for their justification. Occupying such a critical place in Puritan theology, it receives an extended exposition by Owen both in his treatise on justification and in his Hebrews commentary.

After a brief lexical survey of ἔγγυος [surety, sponsor], Owen concludes that "A *surety* is an undertaker for another, or others, who thereon is justly and *legally* to answer what is due to them, or from them; ... one that voluntarily takes on himself the cause or condition of another, to answer, or undergo, or pay what he is liable unto, or to see it done; whereon he becomes justly and legally obnoxious unto performance" (5:182). First, the surety is a volunteer: "His own *voluntary susception* of the office and work is all that is required, however he may be designed or induced to undertake it." This was in opposition to the Socinians, who argued that since Christ is ordained *by the Father* to be surety of the covenant, it follows that He is surety for God to us rather than for us to God. In this way, Christ's suretyship was employed by the Socinians as an expression of his prophetic office.

Along with "the generality of expositors, ancient and modern, of the Roman and Protestant churches," Owen argued that Christ was "a surety or undertaker unto God for us." In the exercise of his great love, in order that "the covenant might be established and made effectual unto us," he "willingly and voluntarily" assumed our nature, so as to make atonement for us (Heb. 10:5, 7). By assuming our nature,

> although we neither did nor could appoint him so to be, yet he took *from us* that wherein and whereby he was so; which is as much as if we had designed him unto his work, as to the true reason of his being our surety. Wherefore, notwithstanding those antecedent transactions that were between the Father and him in this matter, it was the *voluntary engagement* for himself to be our *surety*, and his taking our nature upon him for that end, which was the *formal reason* of his being instated in that office. (5:183, 184)

Secondly, and to the same purpose against the argument of the Socinians, Owen argues that a surety undertakes for another "wherein he is *defective, really* or in *reputation*." For this reason God can have no surety. It is man who stands in need of a surety, for "without the interposition of such a surety, could any covenant between God and us be firm and stable, or an *everlasting covenant*, ordered in all things and sure" (5:186). Man's breach of the Adamic covenant, demonstrated that

> it was necessary, that upon the making of the *new covenant*,...with a design and purpose that it should *never be disannuled*, as the former was, we should have a *surety* and undertaker for us; for if that *first covenant* was not firm and stable, because there was no *surety* to undertake for us, notwithstanding all

that ability which we had to answer the terms of it, how much less can any other be so, now [that] our natures are become depraved and sinful! (5:186)

In order that we might "enjoy the benefits of the covenant," the Lord Christ, as our surety, must perform all that was required of us in it. This required his "answering for our transgressions against the first covenant," and "his purchase and procurement of the grace of the new."

(1.) He undertook, as the *surety of the covenant*, to answer for all the sins of those who are to be, and are, made partakers of the benefits of it;—that is, to undergo the *punishment due unto their sins*; to make atonement for them by offering himself a propitiatory sacrifice for the expiation of their sins, *redeeming* them, by the price of his blood, from their state of misery and bondage under the law, and the curse of it....(5:187-88)

(2.) That those who were to be taken into this covenant should *receive grace* enabling them to comply with the terms of it, fulfil its conditions, and yield the obedience which God required therein; for, by the ordination of God, he was to procure, and did merit and procure for them, the Holy Spirit, and all needful supplies of grace, to make them new creatures, and enable them to yield obedience unto God from a new principle of spiritual life, and that faithfully unto the end: so was he the *surety* of this better testament. (5:188)

Mediator of the New Testament

Christ is called the "surety," or "mediator" of a "better testament." Owen distinguishes between the "covenant that God made *with men concerning Christ,* and the covenant that he made *with his Son concerning men*" (19:78). The main tenets of contemporary Reformed thought on the covenant are assumed: "That God created man in and under the terms and law of a covenant, with a prescription of duties and promise of reward, is by all acknowledged." This refers to the "covenant of works," though it was a gracious covenant in fact (cf. Ferguson, 1987, 22-24). "After the fall he entered into another covenant with mankind, which, from the principle, nature, and end of it, is commonly called the *covenant of grace*" (19:78).

With respect to this covenant of grace Owen explains,

> That the Lord Jesus Christ was the principal *subject-matter* of this covenant, the undertaker in it and surety of it, the Scriptures expressly declare: for the great promise of it was concerning him and his mediation, with the benefits that should redound unto mankind thereby in grace and glory; and the preceptive part of it required obedience in and unto him new and distinct from that which was exacted by the law of creation, although enwrapping all the commands thereof also. And he was the *surety* of it, in that he undertook unto God whatever by the terms of the covenant was to be done, for man, to accomplish it in his own person, and whatever was to be done *in* and *by* man, to effect it by his own Spirit and grace; that so the covenant on every side might be firm and stable, and the ends of it fulfilled. (19:78)

Owen's treatment of the covenants is quite lengthy, and has been conveniently summarized by Ferguson (1987, 20-31). In addition to what has already been said on the covenant of redemption, and what must be added later with regard to the new covenant, it is necessary at this point to consider Owen's understanding of "testament."

A διαθήκη, according to Owen, is "such a covenant, as wherein the covenanter, he that makes it, bequeatheth his goods unto others in the way of a legacy" (23:111). Owen says that "as unto their *"especial regulation,"* testaments "owe their original unto the Roman civil law, yet as unto the substance of them, they were in use amongst all mankind from the foundation of the world" (23:335). Owen observes that the sealing of a covenant does not require the blood of the covenanter, and that the death of a testator does not need to be a bloody one for a testament to be in force. But,

> the apostle, declaring the necessity of the death of Christ, both the manner of it, that it was by the effusion of his blood: and that from the consideration of the two covenants, the old and the new testament, and what was required unto them; he evinceth it by that which was essential unto them both, in a covenant as such, and in a testament precisely so called....
>
> ...Hereon the apostle, in the use of the word διαθήκη, doth diversely argue both unto the nature, necessity, and use of the death of the mediator of the new testament. He was to die in the confirmation of it as it was a testament, he being the testator of it; and he was to offer himself as a sacrifice in his blood, for the establishment of it, as it had the nature of a covenant. (23:336-37)

How, in particular, is Christ a testator? Owen answers by showing the similarities between Christ and other testaments and testators. All require the death of the testator. All involve the bequeathing of some goods. These goods are given without condition, "and what there is in the gospel, which is the instrument of this testament, that prescribes conditions unto them, that exacts terms of obedience from them, it belongs unto it as it is a covenant, and not as a testament" (23:341). This is very significant. When one sees the covenant of grace in this way it is clear that there is no reason to see it as a movement towards Arminianism, or as a retrogression from the high doctrine of predestination taught by Luther and Calvin.[5] Furthermore, the testator may "assign and determine both the *time, season, and way*, whereby those to whom he hath bequeathed his goods shall be admitted unto the actual possession of them" (23:341).

Of what are the saints to be heirs? Owen answers, "all the goods of grace and glory were the property, the inheritance of Christ, firmly instated in him alone" (23:340). By "goods of grace," Owen would have meant Christ himself, with his merits for their justification; the regenerating, sanctifying, and preserving work of the Holy Spirit; the gifts of the Spirit; adoption; the ordinances of gospel worship; and access to God (to mention the most obvious). "Goods of glory" would include the glory of the resurrected state. All of these things are the "inheritance of the saints" coming from the testament of Christ.

---

[1] See Goodwin, 1863, 5:31-33. In this interpretation of Proverbs 8 Owen may be influenced by Goodwin's earlier work. If so, he has refined and developed Goodwin's thought.

[2] Owen's position fully answers Reid's desire to find for Christ a central role in the formulation of the decree of predestination. The following comments by Thomas Goodwin should remove all doubt about the Puritan ability to give Christ this role. Arguing for the divinity of Christ from his participation in the covenant of redemption, Goodwin says, "God may say to all the creatures as he said to Job, Where were you when the plot of redemption was laid, and the platform thereof drawn, and the book of life penned, and the names of my redeemed ones put in? None but he whose name is Wonderful, Counselor, the mighty God, and everlasting Father;... was capable of all this; which names of his are put into that promise of him as mediator, because it was requisite that our mediator should be all this. And now he being the mighty God, he might be of counsel with God from eternity, he was present at the first pricking down our names, and foreknew all God's choice. He stood at God's elbow and consulted with him whose names to put in..., and so became their everlasting Father, begetting them in the womb of eternal election." (Goodwin 1863, 5:37-38). See also, Goodwin's more general detailed description of the eternal counsels in *Of Christ the Mediator* (1863, 5:1-33).

[3] Of John 14:28, Calvin comments, "Christ does not now speak either of his human nature, or of his eternal Divinity, but, accommodating himself to our weakness, places himself between God and us; and, indeed, as it has not been granted to us to reach the height of

God, Christ descended to us, that he might raise us to it." For Owen, the redemptive-historical does not appear here, though it is not absent from his thought elsewhere (e.g., 1:249).

⁴ This union and the communion which depends upon it was addressed by Jonathan Won in "Communion With Christ: An Exposition and Comparison of the Doctrine of Union and Communion with Christ in Calvin and the English Puritans," Westminster Theological Seminary, Ph.D. Dissertation, 1989.

⁵ In this regard we should consider Luther's very interesting observation of Chrysostom's comments on Hebrews 9:16, 17: "First: he did not bequeath to all because 'he disinherited certain ones.' As John 17:9 says, 'I pray for them, not for the world.' Or the same, 'Neither pray I for these alone, but for them also which shall believe in me through their word' (1 John 17:20). The same thing, too, in that he did not say that his blood was shed for all but for many (Mark 14:24; Matt. 26:28). Also in this passage under discussion 'that...they which are called might receive the promise of eternal inheritance' (Heb. 9:15). But this touches upon the subject of predestination, a subject at once too difficult and too unyielding for our feeble intellect to grasp" (Luther 1962, 197-98). Luther's observation of the connection between predestination, testament, the death of the testator, and the reception of the inheritance, illustrates the Christological foundation for the Reformed doctrine of particular and efficacious redemption. The fact that it is made by Luther, the "unsystematic" exegete, demonstrates that the position taken by Owen might as likely grow out of his own interpretation of Scripture's teaching on the mediator of the new testament, as out of any commitment to a predestinarian "central dogma."

CHAPTER

8

Creation and Providence

In chapter five, it was noted that creation, as an act of the Godhead, was a triune activity with distinguishable roles associated with each person of the Trinity. With regard to specific creative acts, Owen gives considerably more attention to the work of the Holy Spirit than to the Father and the Son. The work of the Holy Spirit denotes, for Owen, the "forming and perfecting" of the creation, which is to be understood "not exclusively to the other persons" (3:96, 97). With this in mind, there is no reason to accuse Owen of inconsistency when he expounds the creation as the work of Christ, for in creation as in redemption Christ works by the Spirit according to the purpose of the Father.

The Purpose of Creation

With regard to the Father's purpose for the creation, however, Owen places a peculiar emphasis upon the Son:

> The holy and blessed Trinity could have so ordered the work of creation as that it should not immediately, eminently, and signally have been the work of the Son, of the eternal Word; but there was a further design upon the world to be accomplished by him, and therefore the work was signally to be his,—that is, as to immediate operation, though as to authority

Creation and Providence

and order it peculiarly belonged to the Father, and to the Spirit as to disposition and ornament, Gen. i. 1, 2; Job xxvi.13. (20:78-79)

Why did he not do this? "God in infinite wisdom ordered all things in the first creation, so as that the whole of that work might be subservient to the glory of his grace in the new creation of all by Jesus Christ" (20:77). In creating the universe "by the Son," he makes it fitting that the Son should become, upon that account, the "heir and lord of all" (20:77). This, as might be guessed from what has already been said concerning the counsels of God for man's redemption, is indicated in Proverbs 8:22-31, where Christ, according to Owen,

> declares his presence and co-operation with him in the whole work of making the world and the several parts of it, verses 27-30; which in other places is expressed, as here [in Hebrews 1:2] by the apostle, that God by him made the worlds. After which he declares the end of all this dispensation, namely, that he might rejoice in the habitable parts of the earth, and his delight be with the sons of men. (20:78)

The connection between the Son's role in creation and in redemption is also evident in the prologue of the Gospel of John where the apostle compares the creation by the "Word absolutely" with the new creation by the word "as incarnate." Owen explains:

> "The Word was with God," saith he, "in the beginning," and "all things were made by him; and without him was not any thing made that was made," verses 1-3. But what was this unto the gospel that he undertook to declare? Yes, very much; for it appears from hence that when this Word was made flesh, and came and dwelt among us, verse 14, he came into the world that was made by him, though it knew him not, verse 10; he came but to his own, whatever were the entertainment that he received,

verse 11. For this end, then, God made all things by him, that when he came to change and renew all things, he might have good right and title so to do, seeing he undertook to deal with or about no more but what he had originally made. (20:78)

The creation of all things by the Son was "peculiarly subservient to the glory of the grace of God in the reparation and renovation of all things by him as incarnate." The worlds were created by him "that when they were lost, ruined, scattered, they might again, in the appointed season, be gathered together into one head in him." "It was the eternal design of God that the whole creation should be put in subjection unto the Word incarnate" (20:79).[1]

It should be emphasized that this in no way diminishes the significance of the original creation or the glory that redounds to God by it. In his description of Psalm 8, Owen observes that the works of God "are indeed in themselves exceedingly glorious.... And the more we contemplate on them, the more skilful we are in the consideration of their nature, order, and use, the more excellent do they appear unto us" (20:342-43). They show the "infinite glory," greatness, self-sufficiency, infinite and eternal power, wisdom, and goodness of their creator (20:344-50). Nevertheless, the glory of the creation serves the more to magnify the condescension of him who was mindful of man and "visited him" in the incarnation (20:366-69). They are "ever to be admired and adored" because they are the "whole theatre which he hath erected for the manifestation of his glory unto eternity" through his "condescension and grace" (20:369). It is difficult to conceive of a more Christocentric view of the purpose of God in creation than this, which subjects the creation and history of the universe to the manifestation of the glory of God in its renovation by the Son. Owen's explanation of this is worth quoting in full.

God designed from eternity that his great and everlasting glory should arise from the new creation and the work thereof....God had not resolved ultimately to commit the manifestation of his glory unto those works [of the old creation], though very glorious; and therefore did he suffer sin to enter into the world, which stained the beauty of it, and brought it wholly under the curse. But he never suffered spot or stain to come upon the work of the new creation,... Yet God hath so ultimately laid up his glory in the new creation, as that he will not lose any thing of that which also is due unto him from the old; but yet he will not receive it immediately from thence neither, but as it is put over into a subserviency unto the work of the new. Now God ordered all things so as that this might be effected without force, coaction, or wrestling of the creation, or putting it beside its own order. And is there any thing more genuine, natural, and proper, than that the world should come into subjection unto Him by whom it was made, although there be some alteration in its state and condition, as to outward dispensation, in his being made man? (20:80-81)

The Creation and the Coming of Christ
In the beginning God looked upon the creation and saw that it was good, taking satisfaction and delight in his work. However, with the fall of man,
> the creation "fell under the power of the devil," and became debased or, in the language of Scripture, "subject to vanity." This debasement was its new inability to "answer the end for which it was made and erected, namely, to declare the glory of God, that he might be worshipped and honoured as God; but was as it were left, especially in the earth, and the inhabitants of it, to be a stage for men to act their enmity against God upon, and the means for the fulfilling and satisfaction of their filthy lusts." (20:81)

For this reason Owen explains Romans 8:19-22 as describing a state "unsuitable unto its primitive constitution, preternatural, occasional, and forced," so that the creation is said "to dislike it, to groan under it, to hope for deliverance, doing that in what it is by its nature, which it would do voluntarily were it endowed with a rational understanding" (20:81). The creation thus yearns for the "glorious liberty of the sons of God," that is, "the bringing forth of the kingdom of Christ in glory and power" (20:81).

All of this is changed through the incarnation, life, death, and exaltation of Christ. The creation, he says,

> receiveth a real advancement and honour in the Son's being made 'the first-born of every creature,' that is, the especial heir and lord of them all.... God setting up the kingdom of Christ, and making him the first-born, the whole creation hath a right unto a new, glorious lord and master. And however any part of it be violently for a season detained under its old bondage, yet it hath grounds of an "earnest expectation" of a full and total deliverance into liberty, by virtue of this primogeniture of Christ Jesus. (20:167)

The Use of the Creation

The "advancement" of the creation to its new status under Christ, determines what "improvement ... we are to make of the work of the creation unto his glory." Concerning the significance of the creation, Reformed theology had already made a great advance over the middle ages, but this was primarily with respect to the exposition of the first article of the creed. Owen's exposition is more redemptive-historical, emphasizing the significance of the work of Christ. With respect to the use of the creature, Owen says,

> It is his will that we should not use any thing as merely made and created by him, though originally for that purpose, seeing as they are so left they are under the curse, and so impure and unclean unto

them that use them, Tit. i. 15; but he would have us to look upon them and receive them as they are given over unto Christ. For the apostle, in his application of the 8th Psalm unto the Lord Christ, Heb. ii. 6-8, manifests that even the beasts of the field, on which we live, are passed over in a peculiar manner unto his dominion. And he lays our interest in their use, as to a clear, profitable, and sanctified way of it, in the new state of things brought in by Christ.... This God instructs us in, namely, to look for a profitable, sanctified use of the creatures in Christ, in that himself ordered them in the very first creation to fall at length naturally under his rule and dominion, making them all by him. (20:81-82)

A sanctified use, therefore, is one that is mindful of Christ's dominion and is made with thanksgiving.

This will naturally mean that, just as man was originally to "learn the glory of God from them" in their primitive state, he will now learn this glory in a new way. This is demonstrated by the use of the eighth Psalm in Hebrews 2, which illustrates why a Christ-centered use of the creation is necessary, and in what it consists. Apart from Christ, there can be no proper use of the world:

Whereas there is but a twofold holy use of the works of the creation,—the one suited unto the state of innocency, and the moral-natural worship of God therein, which they had lost; the other to the state of grace, and the worship of God in that, which they had not attained,—the world and the inhabitants thereof, being otherwise involved in the curse and darkness wherewith it was attended, exercised themselves in fruitless speculations about them ("foolish imaginations" as the apostle calls them), and glorified not God in any due manner, Rom. i. 21. Neither do nor can men unto this day make any better improvement of their contemplation on the works of creation, who are unacquainted with the recapitulation of all things in Christ, and the beauty of it, in that all things at first were made by him.

When and how can men make a proper use of the world? Owen answers,

> But when men shall by faith perceive and consider that the production of all things owes itself in its first original unto the Son of God, in that by him the world was made, and that unto this end and purpose, that he being afterwards incarnate for our redemption, they might all be put into subjection unto him, they cannot but be ravished with the admiration of the power, wisdom, goodness, and love of God, in this holy, wise, beautiful disposition of all his works and ways. (20:82, 83)

As God's chief end in the creation of the world was to glorify himself in his Son, man's chief end in the use of the world must be the same, so that in all things Christ would have the preeminence.

A Christocentric Doctrine of Providence[2]

Reformed theology understood God's providence as operating in three ways: 1) in the "preservation" of all things; 2) in "concurrence" (God's working with second causes, "by an influence of causality into the agents themselves," or by "determining and restraining second causes to such and such effects" [10:34]); and 3) in "government," (Heppe, 1950, 256). In *A Display of Arminianism*, Owen discusses these aspects of God's providence in a manner representative of the more scholastic form of Reformed Orthodox polemic.

Owen understands providence as "an ineffable act or work of Almighty God, whereby he cherisheth, sustaineth, and governeth the world, or all things by him created, moving them, agreeably to those natures which he endowed them withal in the beginning, unto those ends which he hath proposed" (10:31). This providence is

Creation and Providence   185

made known to us by "God's works and his word." It is exercised in a general sense over all his works, including the reprobate and the "least thing in the world," but with a special regard to his church (10:32-34).

In keeping with other exponents of the Reformed doctrine of providence, Owen points to scriptural evidence of preservation, concurrence, and government, in terms of God's "sustentation or upholding of all things in his powerful continuing of their being, natural strength, and faculties bestowed on them at their creation," "God's working in and together with all second causes for producing their effects," "His supreme dominion" which "exerciseth itself in disposing of all things for his own glory," and his "predetermination of second causes . . . according to his eternal purpose" (10:34-36). While Owen's scriptural evidence for this doctrine of providence includes several explicit references to Christ, the mere use of these "proof texts" does not demonstrate a Christocentric view of providence. However, the Christocentrism of his view of providence is unmistakably clear when one compares the above description with his description of the dominion of Christ (cf. chap. 15, below).

The extent of God's providential control is absolute, as Owen asserts in his sermon, "A Vision of Unchangeable Free Mercy": "All things below in their events are but the wax, whereon the eternal *seal* of God's purpose hath left its own impression; and they every way answer unto it" (8:10). Owen says that "the creature can by no means deviate from that eternal rule of providence whereby it is guided" than can (among other examples) "the wheels in Ezekiel's vision move irregularly to the spirit of life that was in them" (8:10). The importance of this unusual illustration will appear shortly. Along with this assertion of the absolute character of Divine providence, Owen insists that this does not prejudice the liberty of second causes nor involve God in the fault of his creature's sin.

These basic features of the Reformed doctrine of providence are briefly asserted, but the sermon is principally designed to produce in his hearers humility and gratitude to God that He sent the gospel to England, and to encourage a grateful Parliament to settle ministers in neglected parts of the kingdom. The entire sermon is based upon God's special providence concerning the kingdom of Christ, as most of Owen's expositions of God's providence are. We find Owen's most elaborate exposition of Christ's providential role in his Hebrews commentary, where we will see the aforementioned features of providence given a particularly Christocentric cast.

The Word of His Power
According to the author of Hebrews, Christ "upholds all things by the word of his power" (Heb. 1:3), which Owen understands as a "further evidence of his glorious power, and of his exercise of it." This is supported by the meaning of φέρων, which may be understood as "upholding, supporting, bearing, carrying," or by "ruling, governing and disposing of all things by him made" (20:100, 101). Both ruling and bearing apply to the providence of Christ; "for as absolutely it is the same divine power and providence which is exercised in the upholding and ruling or disposing of all things, so all rule and government is a matter of weight and burden" (20:101). The word which most eminently expresses the meaning of φέρων as used in this Scripture, however, is the Hebrew רֹכֵב, derived from רָכַב ("to ride"). The most eminent illustration of God upholding all things by the word of his power is Ezekiel's vision of the chariot of cherubim, "over which sat the God of Israel, in his disposing and ruling of all things." Owen understands the vision to be of God

> governing, ruling, influencing all second causes, as to the orderly production of their effects, by the communication of life, motion, and guidance unto

Creation and Providence

them…by a mere intimation of the mind and will of Him who guides the whole; and that because there was a living, powerful spirit passing through all, both living creatures and wheels, that moved them speedily, regularly, and effectually, as he pleased; that is, the energetical power of divine Providence, animating, guiding, and disposing the whole as seemed good unto him. (20:103)

Owen's application of Ezekiel's vision to this text arises from the fact that the vision appears to be describing just such a divine activity. One interesting support for the interpretation is found in a comment of Rabbi Kimchi upon the vision in Isaiah 6, which the apostle John identifies as Christ. According to Owen, Kimchi says that Isaiah had a vision of "the glory of God, that glory which Ezekiel saw in the likeness of a man" (20:103). Furthermore, Owen notes that the voice of the living creatures "was as the voice…of 'the Almighty,' 'the powerful,' 'the all-' or 'self-sufficient'" which he says "is fully expressed in this of the apostle, 'bearing, upholding, disposing of all things'" (20:103). Christ, the essential word, upholds all things by his "powerful word, that is, by his *effectual and operative* word which works omnipotently, as Owen explains.

This in the vision of Ezekiel is the communication of a spirit of life to the cherubs and wheels, to act and move them as seems good to Him by whom they are guided; for as it is very probable that the apostle in these words, setting forth the divine power of the Son in ruling and governing the whole creation, did intend to mind the Hebrews that the Lord Christ, the Son, is he who was represented in the form of a man unto Ezekiel, ruling and disposing of all things, and the שַׁדָּי "the Almighty," whose voice was heard amongst the wheels, so it is most certain that the same thing is intended in both places.... The Son being over all things made by himself, as on a throne over the cherubim and wheels, influenceth the whole creation with his power, communicating unto it respectively subsistence, life, and motion, acting, ruling, and disposing of all according to the counsel of his own will. (20:104-105)

From all of the above considerations Owen draws two conclusions concerning Christ and the creation. First, Christ "hath the weight of the whole creation upon his hand, and disposeth of it by his power and wisdom." Second, "Such is the nature and condition of the universe, that it could not subsist a moment, nor could any thing in it act regularly unto its appointed end, without the continual supportment, guidance, influence, and disposal of the Son of God" (20:105). Preservation, concurrence, and government, in a general as well a special providence, are each clearly evident in Owen's description of the way Christ "upholds all things":

> The things of this creation can no more support, act, and dispose themselves, than they could at first make themselves out of nothing.... Were there not a mighty hand under them all and every one, they would all sink into confusion and nothing; did not an effectual power influence them, they would become a slothful heap. It is true, God hath in the creation of all things implanted in every particle of the creation a special natural inclination and disposition, according unto which it is ready to act, move, or work regularly; but he hath not placed this nature and power *absolutely* in them, and *independently* of his own power and operation. The sun is endued with a nature to produce all the glorious effects of light and heat that we behold or conceive, the fire to burn, the wind to blow, and all creatures also in the like manner; but yet neither could sun, or fire, or wind preserve themselves in their being, nor retain the principles of their operations, did not the Son of God, by a constant, continual emanation of his eternal power, uphold and preserve them; nor could

they produce any one effect by all their actings, did not he work in them and by them. (20:105-106)

This divine providence reaches the rational creation also:

> And so is it with the sons of men, with all agents whatever, whether natural and necessary, or free and proceeding in their operations by election and choice. Hence Paul tells us that "in God we live, and move, and have our being," Acts xvii. 28. He had before asserted that he had "made of one blood all nations," verse 26; that is, all men of one, whom he first created. To which he adds, that we may know that he hath not so left us to stand by ourselves on that first foundation as that we have any power or ability, being made, to do or act any thing without him, that in him,—that is, in his power, care, providence, and by virtue of his effectual influence,—our lives are supported and continued, that we are acted, moved, and enabled thereby to do all we do, be it never so small, whereon there is any effect of life or motion.... (20:106)

The point Owen is making is that the upholder and controller of all things is Christ:

> Now, what is thus spoken of God in general is by Paul particularly applied unto the Son: Col. i. 16, 17, ... He did not only make all things, ... but also he continues at the head of them; so that by him and by his power they consist,—are preserved in their present state and condition, kept from dissolution, in their singular existence, and in a consistency among themselves. (20:106)

As Owen explains, this preservation is necessary from the nature of created things which have a "derived and dependent being" (20:106). Though he does not identify it as such, this also explains the necessity of concomitance: "that which cannot subsist in and by itself cannot act so neither" (20:106). Owen is clearly opposed to the encroaching Deism as he writes that God "did not create the world to leave it to an uncertain event,—to stand by and to see what would become of it, to see whether it would return to its primitive nothing…; but the same power and wisdom that produced it doth still accompany it, powerfully piercing through every parcel and particle of it (20:107). Why is this the work of the Son? This he explains in terms of the covenant of the mediator.

> This work is *peculiarly* assigned unto the *Son*, not only as he is the eternal power and wisdom of God, but also because by his *interposition*, as undertaking the work of mediation, he reprieved the world from an immediate dissolution upon the first entrance of sin and disorder, that it might continue, as it were, the great stage for the mighty works of God's grace, wisdom, and love to be wrought on. Hence the care of the continuance of the creation and the disposal of it is delegated unto him, as he that hath undertaken to bring forth and consummate the glory of God in it, notwithstanding the great breach made upon it by the sin of angels and men. This is the substance of the apostle's discourse, Col. i. 15-20. Having asserted him to be the image of God, in the sense before opened and declared, and to have made all things, he affirms that all things have also their present consistency in him and by his power, and must have so, until the work of reconciliation of all things unto God being accomplished, the glory of God may be fully retrieved and established for ever. (20:107)

Hence, it is a covenanted mediatorial exercise of "divine properties…for the good and advantage of them for whom he hath undertaken, and whom he designed to bring again into favour and communion with God" (20:212-13).

Consequently, it would seem that this mediatorial exercise of providence has an end coincident with the mediatorial kingdom of Christ. In his exposition of Hebrews 1:10-12, Owen notes that two things are attributed to Christ regarding the heavens and the earth: their cre-

Creation and Providence

ation, and their *"abolition or change"* (20:208). The creation is as a garment disposed of by its wearer. It is now as a garment which displays, yet hides the full manifestation of, the glory of God, but at the last day the heavens and the earth "shall be laid aside...from their use as a garment to clothe and teach the power and wisdom of God to men," because at that time "God shall unclothe or unveil all his glory to his saints, and they shall know him perfectly" (20:210-11, 209). The garment itself, however, "waxeth old," undergoing decay.

In view of these facts (Christ's absolute authority over and control of the creation, and the dependent and perishing nature of the world), Owen draws several conclusions which further emphasize and clarify his Christocentric view of providence. For instance, Owen emphasizes "the vanity of expecting any thing from the creatures, but only what the Lord Christ is pleased to communicate unto us by them." Therefore, "They who rest upon them or rest in them, without the consideration of their constant dependence on Christ, will find at length all their hopes disappointed, and all their enjoyments vanish into nothing" (20:107, 108). We are "dying persons using dying creatures," and therefore we must "use them for our present service and necessity, but not as those that look after rest or satisfaction in them, which they will not afford us." The only way to obtain lasting rest or satisfaction in this changing world is in the unchanging Christ: "Use the world, but live on Christ" (20:217).

Owen emphasizes the "full, absolute, plenary *self-sufficiency and sovereignty* of the Son, our Saviour." In contrast to an earthly king's limited power of his subjects, Christ,

> not only rules over all the whole creation, disposing of it according to the rule and law of his own counsel and pleasure, but also they all have their beings, natures, inclinations, and lives from him; by his power are they continued unto them, and all their

actions are influenced thereby.... And this should teach us our constant dependence on him and our universal subjection unto him."(20:108)

Moreover, this sovereignty is exercised toward the good of believers, therefore, "there is not just cause of fear unto believers from any thing in heaven or earth, seeing they are all of the making and at the disposal of Jesus Christ" (20:214).

This also provides a powerful answer to those who are in opposition to Christ and his cause:

> His own power is the very ground that they stand upon in their opposition unto him, and all things which they use against him consist in him. They hold their lives absolutely at the pleasure of him whom they oppose; and they act against him without whose continual supportment and influence they could neither live nor act one moment: which is the greatest madness and most contemptible folly imaginable. (20:108)

It is not clear if Owen has a particular form of opposition in mind here. This comment was written under the rigors of the Clarendon code, and may reflect his confidence in the same providence which he had often observed exercised for the relief of Christ's own in England's recent past. Equally well, it addresses fallen man's perpetual abuse of his rational powers, particularly when one considers that man's "wisdom, learning, skill and cunning in arts and sciences," are all the gifts of Christ (20:63), despite their employment against him by England's rational theologians.

---

[1] In a sermon entitled "Christ the Creator of All Things" (Manton, 1870, 1:434-44), Thomas Manton uses identical words to describe the design of God in the creation (p. 438). This was one of a series of sermons, *Christ's Eternal Existence*, published against Socinianism

Creation and Providence

(pp. 417- 504). See also Part 3 of Goodwin's *The Knowledge of God the Father and of His Son Jesus Christ* (1863, 4:454-570).

[2] Flavel's practical treatise on the doctrine of providence does not center so much upon Christ as Owen does here. However, his treatment of Christ's providential rule in *The Fountain of Life* (1820, 1:211-22) is similar. According to Charnock, "All the providences of God are for the glorifying of his grace in Christ" (1684, 62; see 62-67).

CHAPTER 9

Cur Deus Homo: The Manifestation of the Glory of God

> That which God designeth herein, in the first place, is not the justification and salvation of sinners. His utmost complete end, in all his counsels, is his own glory. He doth all things for himself; nor can he who is infinite do otherwise. But in an especial manner he expresseth this concerning this way of salvation by Jesus Christ. (5:97)

In the Middle Ages, someone asked whether Christ would have become incarnate even if sin had not entered the world; the question became the subject of ongoing debate. Those who answered in the affirmative were separated by Owen into two groups: those who actually believe in a pre-existent Christ who would become incarnate, such as Duns Scotus and Osiander, and those who deny this pre-existence but assert the existence of Christ as the head of the new creation, such as the Socinians (19:21f.).

The principal motive for the doctrine was to provide a work for Christ to do which would have no respect to sin. Ostensibly, to argue that the Son would have become incarnate regardless of the fall is to add to the significance of the incarnation by freeing it from dependence upon anything so contingent and evil, and by emphasizing the dependence of man upon the Son of God. Owen is not unsympathetic to the latter of these reasons. Even in the state of innocence, he says,

> all immediate transactions with the creatures should have been by the Son; for by him, as the power and wisdom of God, were they made,...He therefore, should have immediately guided and conducted man unto his happiness, and that both by confirming him in his obedience and by giving him his reward; an express document whereof we have in the angels that sinned not. (19:22)

On the other hand, it results in a diminution of the atonement and of the love of God it manifests. This was especially evident in the case of Socinians, who, according to Owen, "hope to evince by this means that the Lord Christ may discharge his whole office without making any atonement for sin by sacrifice" (19:21).

The principal objections to the doctrine are that it is not revealed in Scripture, is contradictory to its plain assertions, and even contrary to "spiritual reason" (19:22-25).

> The first promise, and consequently first revelation, of the *incarnation* of the Son of God, was after the entrance of sin, and with respect unto the recovery of the sinner, unto the glory of God. Hereby are all other promises, declarations, and revelations concerning it, as to their end, to be regulated; for that which is the first in any kind, as to the end aimed at, is the rule of all that follows in the same kind. And therefore that which men ground themselves upon in this opinion is indeed neither argument nor testimony, but conjecture and curiosity. (19:22)

Owen's comment on the theological method of those who seek to ground the incarnation in God's desire to communicate himself to human nature reflects his commitment to a scriptural theology as opposed to the Christology of idealism:

> They frame to themselves a notional state of things, which they suppose beautiful and comely, (as who are not enamoured of the fruits of their own imaginations?) and then assert that it was meet and according unto divine wisdom that God should so order things unto his own glory as they have fancied! Thus they suppose, that without respect unto sin or grace, God would take unto himself the glory of uniting our nature unto him. Why so? Because they find how greatly and gloriously he is exalted in his so doing. (19:22)

It does not follow that the incarnation in and of itself brings glory to God. Apart from the entrance of sin and the need of redemption,

> the assumption of human nature into union with the divine, in the person of the Son of God, is no way suited unto the exaltation of divine glory, but rather to beget false notions and apprehensions in men of the nature of the Godhead, and to disturb them in their worship thereof; for the assumption of human nature absolutely is expressed as a great condescension,...and that which served for a season to *obscure* the glory of the Deity in him that assumed it,...but the glory of it lies in that which caused it, and that which ensued thereon; for in them lay the highest effects and manifestations of divine love, goodness, wisdom, power, and holiness, Rom. iii. 24-26. (19:23)[1]

The design of the incarnation is best understood in the light of the consideration of the relation of God's external works to his attributes. As Owen reminds us, "There are three divine attributes to be considered in all the external works of God": His *goodness*, which is the "spring of all divine communication"; his *wisdom*, "which is the directive ...excellency of the divine nature"; and his *power*, "which is the effective excellency of the divine nature" (1:179, 180). To the "due apprehensions" of the roles of these attributes in the plan of redemption, Owen says we must add the "consideration of that state and condition of our own wherein they are so concerned" (1:180). This will provide necessary background not only for the motive of the incarnation, but also for the doctrine of the work of Christ (i.e., what God intended and what Christ actually accomplished.)

Man's Creation and Fall
In order to understand Owen's Christology, particularly as it concerns the motive of the incarnation, it is necessary to consider the "ends" for which the incarnation of Christ is the "means." As Owen observes, it is the universal teaching of the Scripture that "Christ came into the world to save sinners." Therefore, to understand Owen's doctrine of the person and work of Christ it will be necessary to observe in some detail the state of man resulting from the Fall and the *"nature of our sin and apostasy from God"* (1: 181). The Fall had a number of objective and subjective consequences that must be effectively addressed if man is to be restored. Without a due appreciation of these consequences, Owen insists, "we cannot have the least view of the glorious actings of divine wisdom in our deliverance by Christ" (1:187-88).

First, Owen points to the *"reflection* on the honour of the holiness and wisdom of God in *the rejection of his image"* (1:181). The divine image which man bore was God's "representation of his holiness and righteousness among his creatures" (1:182). Secondly, it was the "means of rendering actual glory unto him from all other parts of the creation" (1: 183). Thirdly, the divine image was God's means of bringing man "unto that *eternal enjoyment of Himself*, which he was fitted for and designed unto" (1:183). In the words of the Westminster Shorter Catechism, "man's chief end is to glorify God and to enjoy him forever." Man was created in the image of God in order that he might attain this end. The way unto this end was the way of obedience, and the rule of obedience was the law of God.

The Fall was man's rejection and defacement of the divine image, that is, of God's holiness, his wisdom, and power. Sin was "destructive of all that order of things, which ensued on the creation and giving of the law." This was true for several reasons. The "representation" of "God's holiness, and righteousness," and other moral perfections had become despoiled, with the most horrible of consequences:

> The nature of man under the loss of this image—fallen, depraved, polluted, and corrupted—gives rather a representation and image of Satan than of God. Hence—instead of goodness, love, righteousness, holiness, peace, all virtues usefully communicative and effective of the good of the whole race of mankind, which would have been effects of this image of God, and representatives of his nature—the whole world, from and by the nature of man, is filled with envy, malice, revenge,... and all engines of promoting self, whereunto man is wholly turned, as fallen off from God. (1:184)

With the "loss" of the image of God in man, "there was no way left whereby glory might redound unto God from the remainder of the creation here below" (1:184). Furthermore, "Man lost all power and ability of attaining that end for which he was made" (1:184).

If man is to be saved, this image of God must be restored: God must receive *from man* the glory due to him, and man must be enabled once again to glorify God. As Owen says, "It was not...consistent with the glory of God, that mankind should be restored..., unless his holiness be more exalted, be more conspicuously represented *in the same nature*, than ever it was depressed or despised

The Manifestation of the Glory of God

thereby" (1:186, emphasis mine). However, two further consequences of man's defection must be remedied if this is to happen: 1) "Sin brought *disorder* and *disturbance* into the whole rule and government of God," requiring the vindication of the justice of God; and 2) man *"put himself into the power of the devil,"* making the breaking of that power a further need if man is to be saved (1:185-87).

The Vindication of the Justice of God

As the author of Hebrews asserts, it "was fitting" for God to make the Captain of salvation perfect through suffering (Heb. 2:10). The reason for this is explained by Owen in terms of the vindication of God's justice (20:399-400). The gospel is designed to manifest the glory of the righteousness of God (1:97). Owen asserts, "it belonged unto the nature of God to be the rector and disposer" of his creation, which is to say that the government of God is necessary, not free. To suffer the disorder to continue unrectified was not consistent with the wisdom and righteousness of God (1:185-87). The necessity of the punishment of sin is one of the most crucial issues in the Christological debate, and one that Owen was particularly determined to demonstrate (see Burgesse 1654, 1-48).

Sin-Punishing Justice is Natural to God
In his *Dissertation on Divine Justice,* Owen argues that "sin-punishing justice," is "natural, and in its exercise necessary to God" (10:496; see 2:84; 19:98-138). "Our first idea ... of the Divine Being, and the natural conception of all men, demand and enforce the necessity of justice being ascribed to God." Just as nature bears witness to the existence of God, it also testifies to the justice of God. Men will even question the existence of God before they will allow that he can be unjust (an opinion for which the "God is dead" movement of the post-war twentieth century provides a recent illustration).

In this *Dissertation*, as well as his comments on "The Necessity of The Priesthood of Christ on the Supposition of Sin and Grace" (19:98-138), Owen begins his discussion of "sin-punishing justice" with an Aristotelian classification of the various kinds of righteousness. Even so, he prefers to simplify the discussion by considering justice "in a twofold manner": "absolutely," and "in respect of its egress and exercise (10:498; 19:99, 100). Considered "absolutely," the righteousness or justice of God is "nothing but the *universal rectitude of the divine nature.*" In respect of its "egress," it is "considered as consequent, or at least concomitant to some acts of the divine will, assigning or appointing to it a proper object" (10:498-99). In this manner, Owen lays the foundation for describing God's righteousness in terms of the various ways in which it is expressed. For instance, in God's words of "legislation" God's righteousness is exercised in their equity, in words of "declaration," it is exercised in "truth." With regard to God's deeds, this rectitude of the divine nature expresses itself "either in the government of all things according to what is due to them by the counsel and will of God, or in judgments rewarding or punishing, according to the rule of his right and wisdom" (10:499). In all of these respects the "egresses of the divine justice" are "*necessary*, and such that they could not possibly be otherwise" (10:499; cf. 19:99, 100).

It is clear that Owen does not believe, nor will his description allow, that by this position God is made subject to something outside of himself, such as the law or justice. The justice which the atonement is designed to satisfy has *all* of its existence from the divine nature itself. Since this justice is "the power and readiness of God to do all things rightly and becomingly, according to the rule of his wisdom, goodness, truth, mercy, and clemency" (10:502-503), it follows that this attribute of

The Manifestation of the Glory of God 201

God is not to be conceived as in conflict with God's mercy. Rather, it

> presides, as it were, in all the divine decrees, actions, works, and words, of whatsoever kind they be. There is no egress of the divine will, no work or exercise of providence, though immediately and distinctly breathing clemency, mercy, anger, truth, or wisdom, but in respect thereof God is eminently said to be just, and to execute justice. Hence Isa. li. 6, he is said to be just in bringing salvation; Rom. iii. 25, 26, just in pardoning sin; Rev. xvi. 5, 6, just in avenging and punishing sin; Rom. iii. 5, 6, just in all the exercises of his supreme right and dominion, Job xxxiv. 12-14; Rom. ix. 14, 15, 18, he is just in sparing according to his mercy; just in punishing according to his anger and wrath. In a word, whatsoever, by reason of his right, he doeth or worketh "according to the counsel of his will," whatever proceeds from his faithfulness, mercy, grace, love, clemency, anger, and even from his fury, is said to be done by, through, and because of his justice, as the perfection inducing to, or the cause effecting and procuring, such operations. It is evident, then, that justice, universally taken, denotes the highest rectitude of the divine nature, and a power promptitude of doing all things in a manner becoming and agreeable to his wisdom, goodness, and right. (10:503)

As all created things are "placed in an universal, indispensable, and absolutely unchangeable dependence" on him, God has a natural and necessary rule of government (*jus domini*) over them. God's essential rectitude has its egress in "governing and administering created things according to the rule of his rectitude and wisdom." This Owen calls the "justice of government," of which "frequent mention is made in the sacred writings" (10:504; Zeph. 3:5; 2 Chron. 12:6; Ps. 7:9; Jer. 12:1; 2 Tim. 4:8). In the outgoing of this justice of government, God makes righteous laws according to the "rule of his right." When these laws are broken by "rational beings, to whom a law hath been given," God punishes the crime. This punishment is the exercise of "vindicatory justice" (10:505; cf. 20: 407-408).

To help the reader "avoid mistakes" over the doctrine of vindicatory justice, Owen supplies five important principles to be borne in mind. First, some of God's attributes require no "determined object antecedent to their egress" but must "be entirely free, and dependent upon the mere good pleasure of God only." God is free to exercise these in action or to not act; if he chooses to act, however, he must act in accordance with his attributes. On the other hand, other attributes require some object antecedent to manifesting themselves. An example of these is punitive justice, "for the exercise of which there would be no ground but upon the supposition of the existence of a rational being and its having sinned; but these being supposed, this justice must necessarily act according to its own rule" (10:503). Secondly, "that rule is... *a supreme, intrinsic, natural right of Deity*, conjoined with wisdom, to which the entire exercise of this justice ought to be reduced." Owen says this to offset objections by those who annex "certain absurd conclusions of their own...to a supposition of the necessity of punitive justice, as to its exercise" (10:503). Owen has in mind the objection that God must punish every sin to the utmost of his power to eternity. In answer to this, Owen says God punishes "so far as it just; and all modes and degrees of punishment are determined by the standard of the divine right and wisdom" (10:509). Thirdly, "the existence of a rational creature...being supposed, the first egress of this justice is in the constitution of a penal law; not as a law which, as was before observed, originates from the justice of government, but as a penal law." Why does the existence of a rational creature necessitate a penal law? Owen answers that otherwise God might lose his natural right and dominion over his creatures, and thus he would not be God; or, that right being established, that the creature might not be subject to him, which implies a contradiction:... for in case of a failure in point of obedience,... that dependence could be continued in no way but through means of a vicarious punishment, and there must have been a penal law constituted necessarily requiring that punishment. Hence arises a secondary right of punishing, which extends to every amplification of that penal law, in whatever manner made. But it has a second egress, in the infliction of punishment. (10:509)

Fourthly, and very importantly, "this justice necessarily respects *punishment in general*, as including in it the nature of punishment, and ordaining such a vindication of the divine honour as God can acquiesce in: not the time or degrees, or such like circumstances of punishment, yea, not this or that species of punishment; for it respects only the preservation of God's natural right and vindication of his glory, both which may be done by punishment in general, however circumstanced" (10:509). This leads to his fifth observation, that God exercises this justice freely. The necessity of exercising it

doth not exclude a concomitant liberty, but only an antecedent indifference." This only we deny,— namely, that supposing a sinful creature, the will of God can be indifferent (by virtue of the punitive justice inherent in it) to inflict or not inflict punishment upon that creature, or to the volition of punishment or its opposite. (10:509-10)

This is important to Christology, as it provides the possibility of a substitutionary atonement.

Anticipating the objection that since it is God's nature to be merciful, he must as necessarily be merciful to, as to punish sinners, Owen points out that between the act of mercy and its object no natural obligation intervenes, for God is not bound to any one to exercise any act of mercy, neither is he bound to reward obedience, for this is a debt due from his natural right, and from the moral dependence of the rational creature.... But between the act of justice and its object a natural obligation intervenes, arising from the indispensable subordination of the creature to God: which supposing disobedience or sin, could not otherwise be secured than by punishment. (10:511)

The question is whether or not the punishment of sin is "an *essential attribute of the divine nature*," making sin's punishment necessary if God is to be true to Himself, or whether it is "a free act of the divine will, which he may exercise at pleasure" (10:505).[2] To prove the former position, Owen appeals to four ways by which God has revealed Himself: the written word, rational conscience, works of providence, and "by the person of Jesus Christ, his only-begotten Son, and by the mystery of godliness manifested in him" (10:512-49).

Proof
There are three types of scriptural testimony to the vindicatory justice of God. First, Owen mentions those passages which "certify that the purity and holiness of God hostilely oppose and detest sin." Owen is arguing that God's exercise of moral purity in punishing his creature is necessary. One clear proof of this is found in Habakkuk 1:13; God does not hate sin because he wills to, but because of "the purity of God's eyes." As Owen explains, "The incomprehensible, infinite, and most perfect holiness or purity of God is the cause why he hates and detests all sin" (10:513; cf. 20:405-406). Among other texts appealed to, a particularly strong argument is made from the declaration of God's name to Moses, (Ex. 34:5-7), where God "manifestly leads us to the contemplation of

The Manifestation of the Glory of God 205

that excellence essentially inherent in his nature, which induces him" to punish the guilty. A second class of Scriptures "ascribe to God the office of a judge," and "affirm that he judges and will judge, all things with justice" (10:514). A third class asserts the just infliction of punishment upon sin, e.g., Romans 1:34; 2 Thessalonians 2:6; Hebrews 2:2; and Jude 7. Owen sums up his argument with the following syllogism:

> to that Being whose property it is to "render unto every man according to his deeds," not to clear the guilty, to condemn sinners as worthy of death and to inflict the same upon them, to hate sin, and who will in no wise let sin pass unpunished, and all this because he is just, and because his justice so requires, sin punishing justice naturally belongs, and that he cannot act contrary to that justice; but the passages of Scripture just now mentioned, with many others, assert that all these properties above recounted belong to and are proper to God, because he is just: therefore, this justice belongs to God, and is natural to him. (10:516-17)

Owen's second argument is drawn from the "universal consent of mankind." Scripture, the testimony of conscience, and public consent of all nations bear witness to God's justice. Owen believes that "what common opinion and the innate conceptions of all assign to God, that is natural to God; but this corrective justice is so assigned to God: therefore, this justice is natural to God" (10:517).

Thirdly, Owen argues that sin-punishing justice is demonstrated in the works of providence (i.e., as scripturally described). Here Owen argues with considerable strength. First he points out the undeniably vivid manner in which the Scripture pictures the *anger* of God:

> Certain it is that God assumes no affection of our nature so often to himself in Scripture as this; and that, too, in words which for the most part, in the Old

> Testament, denote the greatest commotion of mind. Wrath, fury,... indignation, hot anger,... wrathful anger, anger appearing in the countenance, inflaming the nostrils, rousing the heart, flaming and consuming, are often assigned to him, and in words, too, which among the Hebrews express the parts of the body affected by such commotions. (10:542)

However, the fact of "God's holy and unchangeable nature" requires us to view these passionate expressions as accommodations (cf. 20:404-405). The anger of God is therefore concluded to mean, first, "the effects of anger" or the threatened punishment of sin. "But secondly," Owen says,

> It denotes a *constant and immutable will in God of avenging and punishing, by a just punishment, every injury, transgression, and sin.* And hence that expression, Rom. ix. 22, "What if God, willing to show his wrath,"—that is, his justice, or constant will of punishing sinners; for when any external operations of the Deity are described by a word denoting a human affection that is wont to produce such effects, the holy Scripture means to point out to us some perfection perpetually resident in God, whence these operations flow, and which is their proper and next principle ["That is, the principle from which they immediately flow.—Tr."]. (10:543)

This "perfection" is his "vindicatory justice." When Paul says, "the wrath of God is revealed from heaven," Owen argues convincingly that this is equivalent to saying that the vindictive righteousness of God is manifested in the works of providence (10:543-46). Perhaps one of the most forceful of his arguments in this regard is found in his conclusion: since providence testifies as clearly of God's wrath as of his goodness, "he, then, who shall deny this justice to be essential to God, may, for the same reason, reject his goodness and long-suffering patience" (10:548).

Owen's fourth argument is the most difficult to answer as it appeals to God's most forceful demonstration of his righteousness—namely, the righteousness "exhibited to us in and through Christ." Christ is God's definitive word to the human race, "but in the whole matter of salvation by the Mediator, God-man, there is no excellence of God, no essential property, no attribute of his nature,... that he hath more clearly and eminently displayed than this punitory justice," so it must be as natural to him as are the love, wisdom, etc., which it demonstrates (10:547-48).

The Necessity of the Punishment of Sin
Having shown that "sin-punishing justice" is natural to God, it remains for Owen to prove that "the existence and sin of a rational creature being supposed, the exercise of this justice is necessary" (10:549). Owen argues first, "He who cannot but hate all sin cannot but punish sin; for to hate sin is, as to the affection, to will to punish it, and as to the effect, the punishment itself...he cannot possess an indifference of will to punish" (10:550). Secondly, Scripture describes the "divine nature in respect of its habitude to sin" as a "consuming fire," and God as one who "will by no means clear the guilty." That is, it is as natural for God to do so as it is for fire to "consume stubble," though he does so in a different manner (10:553-54; 20:407). Thirdly, "the non-punishment of sin is contrary to the glory of God's justice." Since the Scriptures emphasize that "God punishes because he is just" (as it is easy for Owen to demonstrate), it follows that for God to "clear the guilty" would be unjust and contrary to the glory of his justice (10:555; 20:407). Furthermore, "a proper regard is not shown to divine holiness, nor is its glory manifested, unless the punishment due to sin be inflicted." Nor could God's "natural dominion" be preserved other than "by means of a *vicarious punishment*"

(10:554-56). Fourthly, and to Owen most importantly, "were we to suppose that God might will the salvation of any sinner"—that is merely, without the punishment of sin—"it will be difficult, if not impossible, to assign any sufficient and necessary cause to the death of Christ" (10:556). As he expressed it elsewhere, to look upon God's justice in not sparing his only Son "as that which God may exercise or forbear, makes his justice not a property of his nature, but a free act of *his will*; and *a will to punish where* one may do otherwise without injustice, is rather ill-will than justice" (2:84). In the course of his argument in the *Dissertation*, Owen undertakes an extensive, fair, and satisfactory examination of objections to his position. The positive exposition of this doctrine may also be found in his *Exposition of the Epistle to the Hebrews*, in exercitation twenty-nine, and in his commentary on Hebrews 2:19 (19:97-131; 20:401-10).

Deliverance of Man from the Power of the Devil

"Man by sin *put himself into the power of the devil*, God's greatest adversary." Owen explains man's subjugation to Satan in the following way. Satan, being under the eternal displeasure of God, was

> designing his dishonor and the impeachment of his glory with the utmost of his remaining abilities. In this state of things, man voluntarily leaves the rule and conduct of God, with all his dependence upon him, and puts himself into the power of the devil; for he believed Satan above God—that is, placed his faith and confidence in him, as unto the way of attaining blessedness and true happiness. And in whom we place our trust and confidence, them do we obey, whatever we profess. Herein did God's adversary seem for a season to triumph against him, as if he had defeated the great design of his goodness, wisdom, and power. So he would have continued to

do, if no way had been provided for his disappointment. (1:178)

This subjugation takes place in two principle ways. First, man is taken captive to Satan and enslaved. This, of course refers to that mental, spiritual enslavement which results from the depravity of our hearts and minds. Second, Satan has power "in and over death." Owen explains four ways in which Satan may be said to have this power. First, he "was the means of bringing it into the world." That is, by introducing sin, he had the power to bring in death also, and thereby Satan became its "efficiently-procuring cause" (20:448). Second, "sin and death being thus entered into the world... Satan came thereby to be their *prince*, as being the prince or author of that state and condition." Third, "God having passed the sentence of death against sin, it was in the power of Satan to terrify and affright the consciences of men with the expectation and dread of it, so bringing them into *bondage*." Fourth, "God hath ordained him to be the executioner of the sentence of death upon stubborn sinners unto all eternity; partly for the aggravation of their punishment, when they shall always see, and without relief bewail, their folly in hearkening unto his assurements; and partly to punish himself in his woeful employment" (1:449).

Demonstrating the Attributes of God
Mankind's Purpose
Given all that has been expressed so far in this chapter concerning the effects of the Fall—the reflection upon the wisdom and holiness of God, the rejection of his image and defacing of the representation of his glory below, the disorder and disturbance of his government, and the subjection of man to his enemy—the question arises as to whether it was "meet, with respect unto the holy properties of the divine nature, that all mankind should be left

eternally in this condition, without remedy or relief? or whether there were not a condecency and suitableness unto them, that at least our nature in some portion of it should be restored" (1:188).

Arguing for the latter position, Owen says that it was not

> consistent with the wisdom and goodness of God that an entire species capable of glory in the eternal enjoyment of Him should be excluded from it. That such a thing should fall out as it were accidentally, without divine provision and disposal, would argue a defect in wisdom, and a possibility of a surprisal into the loss of the whole glory he designed in the creation of all things." (1:189)

In the case of the angels which fell this did not happen, seeing that a part of that "species" kept their integrity. In the sin of Adam, however, the whole race sinned and died. To permit a race so to perish which had been created to enjoy and glorify God, "if any way of relief for any portion of it were possible unto infinite wisdom," would have argued against the glory of God (1:189-90; cf. 18:158-59).

Owen makes the pivotally significant point that man's recovery required the exertion of divine attributes beyond those which were demonstrated in the creation: "Were there not other properties of the divine nature than what were discovered and revealed in the creation of all—were not some of them so declared capable of an exercise in another way or in higher than what had as yet been instanced—it must be acknowledged that the reparation of mankind could not be conceived compliant with the divine excellencies, nor to be effected by them" (1:191).

Conversely, Owen argues that the "salvation of sinners conduceth, yea, is necessary, unto the manifestation of some of those divine excellencies wherein no small part of the glory of God doth consist" (18:159). This does not diminish the gracious character of salvation. Far from it, so serious was the first sin that God might "righteously, and suitably unto all the holy properties of his nature leave mankind to perish eternally in that condition whereinto they had cast themselves." For this reason it is no reflection upon the goodness of God if the majority are left to perish (1:191). When Owen refers to this manifestation of attributes as "necessary" (18:159, 160) he is not asserting that a necessity lies upon God to manifest his "goodness, grace, mercy, and readiness to forgive." Rather, he is arguing against the false conclusion that God's judgment upon the apostate angels requires a similar judgment upon mankind, and on behalf of the "*expectation* . . . just, and firmly grounded" of the "discovery" of his attributes in the salvation of sinners (18:160).

Some attributes of God are "undiscoverable" apart from the redemption of sinners by Christ: love, grace, and mercy, for example (1:191; 2:81-83; 21:132-33). "With these it was that the reparation of our nature was compliant—unto them it had a condecency; and the glory of them infinite wisdom designed therein" (1:191). Other attributes displayed in creation are more evident, more brilliantly displayed, in the redemption of sinners by Christ, such as his goodness (1:191), his vindicatory justice, patience, forbearance and longsuffering, wisdom and his all-sufficiency (2:83-90). So, the divine goodness awaits incarnation for the recovery of sinners before it finds its most glorious expression.[3]

Man's Insufficiency
Given that it was meet that some portion of man should be restored, Owen next observes that this restoration cannot be done by man himself through a return in obedience to God, nor by rendering satisfaction for himself (through works, suffering, his own death, etc.). Owen's arguments against the first point show a measure of insight often lacking in the modern opponents to the

doctrine of the incarnation and atonement, who argue that the biblical way of restoration is simple repentance. First, man cannot do it: in the Fall he lost the ability to "yield any acceptable obedience unto God." As Owen explains, man's power consisted in the image of God. Having by the Fall defaced this image he had deprived himself of his original power of living unto God, and would require even more power to make a return to that condition from which he had fallen (1:192-93; 2:97-99). Second, "As man *could not* effect his own recovery, so he *would not* attempt it" (1:193). Owen is not saying that man would not attempt many things, but that man will not attempt the return which is necessary.

> He likes it not, as that which is incompliant with his dispositions, inclinations, and desires,—as inconsistent with everything wherein he placeth his interest. And hence, as he *cannot* do what he should through impotency, he will not do even what he can through *obstinacy*. (1:193)

Man lacks the "love unto the divine goodness, without which he cannot choose to return to God" (1:193). Third, assuming the impossible (i.e., the sinner's return), "yet no reparation of the glory of God, suffering in the loss of the former state of all things would thereon ensue" (1:193). Owen is not surprised that apostate men would want salvation without regard to the glory of God, but in his own view, such thoughts are "highly contradictory unto all equity, justice, and the whole reason of things, wherein the glory of God is the principal and centre of all" (1:194). As Owen will make very clear, it is not enough simply to point to scriptural examples of return and forgiveness, since these examples are not inconsistent with an effectual grace which brings about that repentance, nor with forgiveness given within the context of a covenantal relation founded upon the mediation of Christ.

If man is to be saved in a manner which repairs the

loss suffered to the glory of God, returning must be accompanied with the rendering of satisfaction. However, as Owen points out, this would effect restitution only; there would still be no addition to the glory of God.

> But this became not the nature and efficacy of divine wisdom. It became it not merely to retrieve what was past, without a new manifestation and exaltation of the divine excellencies. And therefore, *in our restitution by Christ*, there is such a manifestation and exaltation of the divine properties as incomparably exceeds whatever could have ensued on, or been effected by, the law of creation, had man continued in his original condition. (1:194)

Rendering the necessary satisfaction, however, is an even greater impossibility than making the necessary return. Since "whatever he can do towards God is antecedently and absolutely due from him in that instant wherein he doth it, and that in the manner wherein it is done," it follows that "it is impossible…by anything a man can do well, he should make satisfaction for anything he hath done ill" (1:194; cf. 2:104).

If man can render neither acceptable obedience nor sufficient satisfaction, what is required for his recovery? First, an obedience must be yielded to God "bringing more glory than the dishonor accrued from the disobedience of man" (1:195; cf. 2:104-105). God had given a law, suitable to his holiness, to the creature. If that law is broken, the glory of God which belongs to him as the giver of that law must be diminished. Owen expresses the issue in terms of the purpose of the giving of the law, saying,

> how should the holiness of God be represented by it?—how should it be evident that the transgression of it was not rather from some defect in the law itself, than any evil in them that should have yielded obedience unto it?… But if the law given unto man should never be complied withal in perfect obedi-

ence by any one whatever, it might be thought that the law itself was unsuited unto our nature, and impossible to be complied withal. Nor did it become *infinite wisdom* to give a law whose equity, righteousness, and holiness, should never be exemplified in obedience—should never be made to appear but in the punishment inflicted on its transgressors. Wherefore the original law of personal righteousness was not given solely nor primarily that *man might suffer justly* for its transgression, but that God *might be glorified* in its accomplishment.... If the law be not fulfilled by obedience, man must suffer evermore for his disobedience, or God must lose the manifestation of his holiness therein. (1:196)

Holiness must be restored to our nature, "and that with advantages above what it had in its first communication," if man is to be "recovered unto the glory of God (1:196). Second, "it was necessary that the *disorder brought into the rule* and government of God by sin and rebellion should be rectified." This could not be done without the punishment of sin. God having threatened death for man's disobedience, his failure to inflict death would argue for the truthfulness of the devil and against God's righteousness. Third, Satan must be "*justly* despoiled of his advantage and power over mankind, unto the glory of God" (1:196).

"That Man of God's Own Choosing"

So great was the work of man's restoration Owen concludes that "from the eternal springs [of infinite wisdom] must this work arise, or cease for ever" (1:197; cf. Goodwin, 1863, 5:19). This wisdom will be more evident after we consider the necessary qualifications of the restorer of mankind.

First, it is evident that he must partake of human nature. The required obedience must be wrought in our own nature, the nature which sinned, as the Scripture declares. Moreover, this nature must be "derived from the common root or stock of the same nature, in our first parents," since in a man otherwise created "there would be no cognation or alliance between him and us, so that we should be any way concerned in what he did or suffered." Despite this requirement, however, he must also be free from the "*same taint of sin*, and the same *liableness unto guilt*," since defilement would render him unable to render the obedience required and personal guilt would disqualify him from rendering satisfaction for others.

Consequently, he can be no *mere* man (Goodwin, 1863, 5:35-50). "There was no one act which he was to perform, in order unto our deliverance, but did require a divine power to render it efficacious" (1:200). Owen supplies five reasons why the restorer of mankind must be divine. He argues first, that no mere creature may yield obedience to God bringing more glory than the dishonor which accrued from man's disobedience, "for to suppose that God should be pleased and glorified with the obedience of any one man, more than he was displeased and dishonoured by the disobedience of Adam and all his posterity, is to fancy things that have no ground in reason or justice, or are any way suitable unto divine wisdom and holiness" (1:201). Furthermore, such obedience of a mere man must be for himself. The Savior of man cannot have been originally obliged to this obedience, but "every mere creature is so obliged" (1:201). Thirdly, the sins of the "great multitude" to be redeemed were "next to absolutely infinite." In each of those sins "there was something reductively infinite as committed against an infinite Majesty," and the miseries to which these sinners were "obnoxious unto were *infinite*, because eternal; or all that evil which our nature is capable to suffer was by them all eternally to be undergone." Every sin of every person makes "an inroad" against the glory of God.

Hence Owen reasons, "to suppose that a mere man, by his temporary suffering of external pains, should make satisfaction unto the justice of God for all the sins of all these persons, so as it should be right and just with him not only to save and deliver them from all the evils they were liable unto, but also to bring them unto life and glory, is to constitute a mediation between God and man that should consist in appearance and ostentation, and not be an effect of divine wisdom, righteousness, and holiness, nor have its foundation in the nature and equity of things themselves" (1:202). Owen emphasizes that

> God doth not do these things for show or appearance, but according unto the real exigence of the holy properties of his nature. And on that supposition, there must be a *proportion* between the…sufferings of the *one* and the deliverance of *all*. (1:202)

Owen's fourth principle is that the restorer of mankind must take on himself to perform his acts in the way of an office committed unto him. The acts of his office required a divine power to make them efficacious, as we will observe in the study of Christ's official acts.[4] Fifth, he must restore man to the same state, at least, from which he fell. Consequently, man would have him as the author of that new status. This raises a considerable problem, however: if the restorer were a mere creature, man would be reduced from immediate dependence upon God, to dependence upon a creature. "But, on this supposition, we are so far from an advancement in state and dignity by our restoration, that we do not recover what we were first instated in" (1:203-204).

Christ: the Revelation of the Wisdom of God

One principal effect of the gospel is the revelation of the wisdom of God "in the contrivance of the work of redemption by Jesus Christ" (1:206). Owen's exposition of the way the gospel demonstrates the wisdom of God is simple,

The Manifestation of the Glory of God   217

clear, and remarkably stimulating. Owen suggests nine ways in which the gospel manifests the wisdom of God.

First, it must be remembered that the Fall was a move on the part of man to exalt himself out of the status of a creature, a condition of "universal subjection and service unto the Creator," and into "a condition of *self-sufficiency*— of dominion and rule" (1:206). The attempt brought man into "absolute and eternal ruin." In the work of restoring man in a manner which would bring glory to God, infinite wisdom determined that the Son of God, to whom belonged self-sufficiency, absolute dominion, and no law of obedience, would become a second Adam and "take on him a state of absolute service" (1:206). Or, as Owen explains the significance of Philippians 2:6-8,

> Adam being in the form—that is, the state and condition—of a servant, did by robbery attempt to take upon him the "form of God," or to make himself equal unto him. The Lord Christ, being in the "form of God"—that is, his essential form, of the same nature with him—accounted it no robbery to be in the state and condition of God, to be "equal to him;" but being made in the "fashion of a man," taking on him our nature, he also submitted unto the form or the state and condition of a servant therein. He had dominion over all, owed service and obedience unto none, being in the "form of God," and equal unto him—the condition which Adam aspired unto; but he condescended unto a state of absolute subjection and service for our recovery. (1:207)

In this manner "more glory did arise unto the holiness and righteousness of God from his condescension unto universal service and obedience who was over all, God blessed for ever, than dishonour was cast upon them by the self exaltation of him who, being in all things a servant designed to be like unto God" (1:207).

Second, Adam was *"poor in himself,"* and in the attempt to enrich himself "by the rapine of an equality with God," he "brought on him and us all...all things we were entrusted with": the image of God, our "right to the creatures here below," and our souls. On the other hand, when Christ was "rich in himself, he became poor, that we through his poverty might be made rich, 2 Cor. viii. 9" (1:208). God was more glorified in this condescension than he was dishonored by man's self-love.

In addition to being glorified by Christ's condescension and self-denial, God was glorified in his *obedience*. "For man—by all that he was, by all that he had received, by all that he was expected or was farther capable of, by the constitution of his own nature, by the nature and authority of God, with his relation thereunto—was indispensably obliged unto universal obedience." This being the case, man's disobedience could only be compensated by one who owed no obedience, namely, one who is God. Yet "it could be performed only by him who was man." The crucial significance of the hypostatic union now appears:

> Wherefore, for the accomplishment of this obedience, he who, in his own person as God, was above the law, was in his human nature, in his own person as man, made under the law. Had he not been made under the law, what he did could not have been obedience; and had he not been in himself above the law, his obedience could not have been beneficial unto us....
>
> Unto the glory of God in all these ends, the person of Christ, as an effect of infinite wisdom, was meet and able to be a mediator and undertaker between God and man. In the union of both our natures in the same person, he was so meet by his relation unto both;—unto God by *filiation*, or sonship; unto us by *brotherhood*, or nearness of kindred, Heb. ii. 14. And he was able from the dignity of his person; for

the temporary sufferings of him who was eternal were a full compensation for the eternal sufferings of them who were temporary. (1:208-209)

In the Fall, man forfeited his right and title to the earth. God designed a new heir "who was meet and able" to enter upon the inheritance and possess it "as that no detriment or damage might arise unto the riches, the revenue, the glory of God, from the waste made by the former possessor" (1:210).

The fifth way Owen identifies the manifestation of the wisdom of God was the way he restores mankind from a state of enmity and unbelief to faith in God, and "unto the love of him above all." By this argument, Owen expresses the truth contained in "subjective" theories of the work of Christ. What, he asks, "could confirm our faith and hope in God... like this ineffable testimony of his good will unto us" in our own nature (1:210)? In addition to encouraging our faith, the gospel "consists in a *divine declaration*, that all the causes of *fear* and dread upon the account of sin are removed and taken away." Further, we are to return unto God in *love*; and what greater motive can there be unto it than that infinite love displayed here (1:211)? This point is made very forcefully in *Communion with God* (2:22-40), where Owen describes communion with God the Father in love. Since the Fall, however, "there was no *example* left unto them to manifest how excellent, how glorious and comely a thing it is, to live unto God,—to believe and trust in him—to cleave unto him unchangeably by love." However, "this is given us most conspicuously in the *human nature of Christ*" (1:211).

At Satan's instigation, man had sought to become wise through disobedience.

> To cast an everlasting reproach of folly on this contrivance of the devil and man, and uncontrollably to evince wherein alone true wisdom doth consist, God would glorify a state of obedience. He would

> render it incomparably more amiable, desirable, and excellent, than ever it could have appeared to have been in the obedience of all the angels in heaven and men on earth, had they continued therein. This he did in this way of our recovery—in that his own eternal Son entered into a state of obedience, and took upon him the "form" or condition "of a servant" unto God. (1:212)

Owen's argument is simple and striking: "What greater evidence could be given, that the nature of man is not capable of a better condition than that of service and universal obedience unto God?" The eternal Son of God "delighted" in it (1:212-13).

As a seventh example Owen points to God's wisdom in securing "the whole inheritance of this life and that which is to come from a second forfeiture." Owen explains that "whatever God will bestow on the children of men, he grants it unto them in the way of an inheritance"; but through the Fall, Adam had forfeited this inheritance. Owen does not say that it was forfeited into the hand of Satan, but "into the hand of the great Lord, the great possessor of heaven and earth" who graciously was "pleased again to restore it... unto the former tenants; and that with an addition of grace and a more exceeding weight of glory" (1:213). This "addition of grace," demonstrating the wisdom of God, consisted in the entrusting of the inheritance no more to any fallible creature, but to his only Son (1:213-16).

Eighth, "*the wisdom of God was gloriously exalted in the righteous destruction of Satan and his interest*, by the incarnation and mediation of the Son of God" (1:216). Owen gives several reasons for this. By bringing about the fall of man, Satan brought man under his power and deprived God of his glory.

> It belonged unto the honour of the wisdom of God that he should be defeated in this triumph. Neither

was it meet that this should be done by a mere act of sovereign omnipotent power; for he would yet glory in his craft and the success of it,—that there was no way to disappoint him, but by crushing him with power, without respect unto righteousness or demonstration of wisdom." (1:216)

In explaining the manner in which this was done Owen says, "The web which he had woven to clothe himself withal, as the god of this world, was unravelled to the last thread. And although all this seems to represent a work of power, yet was it indeed an effect of wisdom and righteousness principally." Since Satan obtained and possessed his rule over man unjustly (on Satan's part), God might justly have taken it from him by force. But since man was justly "given up unto him in a way of punishment, he was a lawful captive, and was not to be delivered but in a way of justice" (1:217). This was accomplished by the satisfaction which Christ made to the justice of God, in consequence of which,

> Immediately hereon all the charms of Satan were dissolved, all his chains loosed, his darkness that he had brought on the creation dispelled, his whole plot and design defeated;— whereon he saw himself, and was exposed unto all the holy angels of heaven, in all the counsels, craft, and power he had boasted of, to be nothing but a congeries—a mass of darkness, malice, folly, impotency, and rage....

> To find that which he contrived for the destruction of the glory of God—the disappointment of his ends in the creation of all things—and the eternal ruin of mankind, to issue in a more glorious exaltation of the holy properties of the divine nature, and an unspeakable augmentation of blessedness unto mankind itself, is the highest aggravation of his eternal torments. (1:217-18)

The idea that "it belonged unto the wisdom and righteousness of God, that Satan should be conquered and subdued in and by the same nature which he had prevailed against, by his suggestion and temptation," and that God did this "not with force," but "redeeming us with his own blood, giving his soul for our soul, and his flesh for ours," Owen finds "divinely" asserted by Irenaeus (1:24, quoting Irenaeus, *Against Heresies*, bk. 3, chap. 20).

Ninth, Owen says, "It became the wisdom of God that the second person, the Son, should be incarnate" (1:218; cf. Goodwin, 1863, 5:41-44). While the reason of this is the divine will alone, and it is "not curiously to be inquired into" God has revealed certain things pertaining to this glorious mystery on which we may "meditate… unto the improvement of faith and love towards God" (1:218). For instance, by sin we had lost the image of God. In the work of our recovery, in the restoration of that image, there was a "condecency unto divine wisdom, that this work should be done by him who was the essential image of God" the Father, because "it consists in the communication of the effects and likeness of the same image unto us which was essentially in himself" (1:218-19). Secondly, by sin we had lost our status as sons of God, with all the privilege which was attached to it:

> Without a recovery into this estate we cannot be restored, nor brought into the enjoyment of God. And this cannot be done but by adoption. Now, it seems convenient unto divine wisdom that he should recover our sonship by adoption, who was himself the essential and eternal Son of God. (1:219)

Third, the order of the operations of the persons of the Trinity follows the order of their subsistence (1:219). Owen explains that the work of our redemption requires "authority, love, and power—all directed by infinite wisdom." "These originally reside in the person of the Father," and are operative in his sending of the Son. "The Son, who is the second person in the order of *subsistence*, in the order of *operation* puts the whole authority, love, and power of the Father in execution," while the Holy Spirit "makes a *perfecting application* of the whole unto all its proper ends" (1:219). Christ was thus the executor of this divine purpose, and as such was the one to become incarnate.

In all of these ways the wisdom of God is manifested unto the eternal praise of his saints and angels. Again, the importance of Christology to Owen is seen in his conclusion to his description of this:

> Is it not much to be lamented that many Christians content themselves with a very superficiary knowledge of these things? How are the studies, the abilities, the time, and diligence of many excellent persons engaged in, and laid out about, the works of nature, and the effects of divine wisdom and power in them, by whom any endeavour to inquire into this glorious mystery is neglected, if not despised! Alas! the light of divine wisdom in the greatest works of nature holds not the proportion of the meanest star unto the sun in its full strength, unto that glory of it which shines in this mystery of God manifest in the flesh, and the work accomplished thereby! A little time shall put an end unto the whole subject of their inquiries, with all the concernment of God and man in them for evermore. This alone is that which fills up eternity, and which, although it be now with some a nothing, yet will shortly be all. (1:220-21)

"Bringing Many Sons To Glory"

In the incarnation of Christ, God designed to bring "many sons to glory." In his exposition of this Owen brings together all of the main points referred to earlier in this chapter, and perhaps better than any place in his works, provides us with the integration of his theology of redemption in its briefest compass (20:378-410; see also,

20:410-87). Man had come short of God's glory by sin (20:378). To bring them to glory he first takes them into a state of sonship and reconciliation. Thus they are the objects of a two-fold predestination: sinners to grace and adoption, sons to glory. Both are wrought by Christ. This designation of them to glory is "peculiarly assigned" to the Father, who is the *"spring and fountain"* of the covenant of redemption (20:379-80). Owen says, "Rather than his love should not be satisfied and his counsel accomplished, he spared not his own Son, but gave him unto death for us" (20:380). The Father also establishes the covenant of grace, with the Son as its mediator. He sends the Son, draws the elect unto him, reconciles them unto himself, sanctifies them, adopts them, confirms and comforts them by the Holy Spirit in such a way that, as Owen says, "all the sovereign acts of power, wisdom, love, and grace exerted [in bringing many sons to glory], are peculiarly assigned unto the Father as all ministerial acts are unto the Son as mediator" (19:380-81; see Goodwin 1863, 5:34-66). The design of the incarnation is to provide such a "Captain of Salvation" as will be able to accomplish this redemption, which will involve not only the making of atonement, but also the priestly work of intercession, the exercise of his prophetic office in leading the people, and the exercise of *"power, authority, and majesty"* as their king going before them (20:384-96).

Recapitulation

In chapter seven, mention was made of the "ἀνακεφαλαίωσις" or recapitulation of all things, as the provision which God had laid in his counsels "for the recovery of all things into a better and more permanent estate than what was lost by sin" (1:61). According to Owen the apostle Paul calls this "the most signal effect of divine wisdom, and sovereign pleasure of God" (1:367). For this reason, and because this motif is sometimes presented as if it were a theory of the motive for the incarnation which is contrary to the Reformed position rather than a part of it, Owen's use of the idea will be examined here. Actually, Owen sheds much light on the dispute by not recognizing it. He simply does not view recapitulation, as taught by Irenaeus, as an alternative to the doctrine of substitution, but apparently as a description of the work which God accomplishes by all the subordinate means such as the incarnation, atonement, and the sending of the Spirit. Irenaeus' "recapitulation" says Owen, is "nothing but the ἀνακεφαλαίωσις mentioned by the apostle, Eph. i. 10—and he here affirms, that, unto this end, the Lord was made flesh" (1:25).[5] Owen appeals to Irenaeus as a witness from the early church with respect to several of the ideas mentioned in the present chapter: such as the idea that redemption must be "in and by the nature that sinned,... free from all that contagion which invaded our nature by the Fall"; that man should be restored unto the image of God by him who was the essential image of the Father; "that he was made like unto us, that we might be made like unto him, and unto God through him"; and that we are redeemed from the devil's power through Christ's substitutionary death (1:20-26; cf. Irenaeus, *Against Heresies*, 5:1, 14; 3:20, 21).

While recapitulation is used in a sense that is comprehensive of the whole change wrought by Christ, it nevertheless communicates a particular emphasis concerning that change: Christ's glory. To show the glory of Christ in the recapitulation of all things, Owen begins by reminding his reader of the situation of "all things beforehand. Before the Fall, he emphasizes, all creation depended *immediately* on God himself, without the interposition of any other head of influence or rule" (1:369). This included "two distinct, rational families, that should depend on him according to a law of moral obedience, and thereby give glory to him; with two distinct habitations for them," i.e., heaven for the angels and earth for man. The beautiful order of this creation, wherein these two families together in their respective ways brought glory to God, was destroyed, Owen explains,

> by the entrance of sin; for hereby part of the family above, and the whole family below, fell off from their dependence on God; and ceasing to centre in him as their head, they fell into variance and enmity among themselves. For the centre of this union and order being removed and lost, nothing but enmity and confusion remained among them. Hereon, to show that its goodness was lost, God cursed the earth and all that was in it; for it was put in subjection unto man, who was now fallen from him. (1:370)

"Howbeit," says Owen, "God would not restore them to their former state, so as to have two distinct families, but would gather them into one, under a new head, in whom the angelic part would be preserved, and the human would be delivered, from sin" (1:370). God's solution was to make Jesus Christ the new head of all things in heaven and on earth, "on whom they should have their immediate dependence, and be reconciled again among themselves" (1:371). Whereas "all power in heaven and earth, all fullness of grace and glory," is committed to Christ, Owen says,

> There is no communication from God, no act of rule towards this family, no supply of virtue, power, grace, or goodness unto angels or man, but what is immediately from this new head whereinto they are gathered. In him they all consist, on him do they depend, unto him are they subject; in their relation unto him doth their peace, union, and agreement among themselves consist. This is the *recapitulation of all things* intended by the apostle. (1:371)

As their needs differ, so Christ "acts distinctly and variously towards the two parts of the re-collected family of angels and men": preserving the one and repairing, exalting, and preserving the other.

In this work Christ is "transcendently glorious" with a glory for which he alone is "a meet and capable subject." Again, Christ's divine mediatorial glory appears in the consideration that no mere creature no matter how exalted "was meet to be thus in the place of God, to have all things depend upon him, and be put in subjection unto him; so as that there should be no communication between God and the creation but by and through him alone" (1:371-72; cf. 1:375).

Further, this glory was *designed* for him. Here, again, we see Owen's perspective on the purpose of the work of Christ:

> What is his design in this incomprehensible work of his wisdom, love, and power? Indeed, in the first place, it was for the redemption of the church, by the sacrifice of himself, and other acts of his mediation. But there is that which is *more general and comprehensive, and wherein all the concerns of the glory of God do centre*. And this was that he might "gather all things into one" in him. (1:372, emphasis mine)

Along similar lines Owen speaks of the restoration of a loveless world: All things were at first made in a state of love.

> That rectitude, order, peace, and harmony, which were in the whole creation, was an expression of the love of God. And our love towards him was the bond of that perfection, and the stability of that state and condition. The whole beauty of the creation below consisted in...*man's loving God above all*, and *all other things in him and for him*, according as they did participate of and express his glory and properties. (22:168)

The Fall, Owen says, broke "the first link of this chain of love," introduced confusion and hatred into the created order so that "nothing of original love" remained in the world. The promise of Christ was the "stop made unto that confusion...because it was a new discovery that there was yet love in God towards fallen mankind (22:168-69).

In an ardent exhortation to the reader to "live more in the contemplation of this glory of Christ," Owen provides several additional points to meditate upon. First, "the whole breach made on the glory of God in the creation, by the entrance of sin, is hereby repaired and made up"; in fact, "the whole curious frame of the divine creation is rendered more beautiful than it was before" (1:373). Furthermore, Christ is "appointed as the only means of exerting and expressing all the treasures of the infinite wisdom of God towards his creatures." Finally, *"hereby, firmness and security is communicated unto the whole new creation"* (1:374). In other words, there can never be another Fall.

With respect to the establishment of the angels and to the restoration of order and harmony to the creation, Owen's views on the meaning of Ephesians 1:10 are similar to those expressed by Calvin. A much more detailed exposition of this passage may be found in three sermons by Thomas Goodwin (Goodwin 1863, 1:148-83).

Conclusion

Owen strongly disagrees with those who argue that the Son would have become incarnate even if man had not sinned, but this should not be construed as in any way diminishing the importance of the incarnation. God's ultimate design was the manifestation of his glorious attributes in the Son, by the salvation of sinners (cf. 21:191-92). In this way the glory of God is seen "in the face of Jesus Christ" (5:97).

Thus far in our study we have observed Owen's strongly Christocentric exposition of three themes of major significance in Reformed theology: predestination, creation, and providence. In the present chapter, by an interesting but not surprising twist, we have seen a very theocentric doctrine of the work of Christ in the restoration of a sin-ruined world. Again, Christ is the focus, as he is the mediator between God and man, manifesting the glory of God through his human nature, giving all God's goodness to man by uniting that nature with the divine. As the following chapter will demonstrate, Owen understood the Bible as teaching that the hope of this restoration by Christ was the principal part of true religion since the beginning of the world, until its manifestation in the flesh.

---

[1] For details of the various arguments which were raised against Owen's position and his specific replies, the reader may refer to his twenty-sixth "exercitation" in the exposition of Hebrews (19:14-42).

[2] In addition to Twisse and Rutherford, Goodwin asserts, "God might have pardoned sin without satisfaction, yet he would not" (Goodwin, 1863, 5:14-16). See the discussion of this by John Murray (1955, 1-18).

[3] Goodwin says, "Is not the plot of reconciliation his masterpiece, wherein he means to bring all his attributes upon the stage" (Goodwin, 1863, 5:16).

[4] *Infra*, Chapters 13-15.

[5] "That in the dispensation of the fullness of times he might gather together in one all things in Christ, both which are in heaven, and which are on earth; *even* in him."

CHAPTER
10

"Beginning with Moses..."

> The great design, whose lines are drawn in the face, and whose substance lies in the bowels of the Old Testament, and which is the spirit that enlivens the whole doctrine and story of it, the bond of union wherein all the parts do centre, without which they would be loose, scattered, and deformed heaps, is the bringing forth of the Messiah, the Saviour of the world. Without an apprehension of this design, and faith therein, neither can a letter of it be understood, nor can a rational man discover any important excellency in it. *Him* it promiseth, *him* it typifieth, *him* it teacheth and prophesieth about, *him* it calls all men to desire and expect. (18:370)

In the middle of the seventeenth century, Socinian and Jewish writers vigorously attacked the Christocentricity of the Old Testament. Latitudinarian thinkers were inclined to defer to the Jews, and Deists looked upon the solemn rites of the Mosaic administration as superstitious priest-craft of which modern men of reason have no need. Owen rose to the challenge posed by these contemporary opponents of salvation history (*heilsgeschichte*) by demonstrating that the Hebrew Scriptures present a genuine and progressive revelation of God's redeeming work, directing its readers to, and preparing them for, the manifestation of the long expected divine Messiah (see Warfield 1991, 3-49).

Owen recognized this as a problem addressed in the New Testament—a difficulty faced by early Hebrew Christians and answered by the epistle addressed to them. Given the divine origin of the Old Testament, there must be a compelling reason for departing from its prescribed religion. According to Owen, the author of the epistle to the Hebrews shares this conviction with his readers. The argument of that epistle depends upon the premise that the religion of the fathers was of divine revelation and that no change in doctrine and worship may be introduced but by divine authority. The author then proceeds with the demonstration that God had, in fact, in the sacred Scriptures, promised such a change: a *new covenant* to be introduced by the Messiah. The old covenant being no longer in effect, and all of its institutions soon to be finally and irretrievably set aside, it was imperative that the Hebrews persevere in the faith of the new covenant. The message of this entire epistle rests upon Christ's divine messiahship as the compelling reason why the ancient Hebrews (and contemporary Christians as well) should persevere in the Christian faith. Apart from a genuine Old Testament prediction of and hope for a new covenant and new priesthood, the Epistle to the Hebrews loses its most important premise. With this in mind we can better understand Owen's motivation for his *magnum opus*, and his rationale for including protracted examinations of the Old Testament witness to the promise, the priesthood, and the divinity of Christ.

The Old Testament's witness to Christ is multifaceted, so Owen approaches it from a number of perspectives. Owen's most exhaustive exposition of the history of redemption constitutes a major portion of his introductory "exercitations" to his commentary on the Epistle to the Hebrews, the first one addressing the Old Testament expectation of a "Divine Messiah." When the author began to exhort the Hebrews to persevere in the Christian faith he "took for granted" their consent to certain foundational "first maxims," namely:

> First, That there was a Messiah, or Saviour of mankind from sin and punishment, *promised* upon, and from, the first entrance of sin into the world, in whom all acceptable worship of God was to be founded, and in whom all the religion of the sons of men was to centre.
>
> Secondly, That this Messiah, long before promised, was *now actually exhibited* in the world, and had finished the work committed unto him, when the apostle wrote this Epistle.
>
> Thirdly, That *Jesus of Nazareth* was this Messiah, and that what he had done and suffered was the work and duty promised of old concerning him. (18:142)

These maxims were the "great verities ... of the *Christian profession*," which were in need of "explanation and vindication."

The second historical treatment provided in the Hebrews commentary centers upon the priesthood. Owen includes this to provide background information for his exposition of the relevant portions of the epistle, and to vindicate the orthodox interpretation of the priesthood from the alternative theories of the Socinians.

The Hebrews commentary, however, is not the only place where Owen describes the importance of the witness of the Old Testament, nor is vindication from Socinianism his only rationale. In *The Glory of Christ*, Owen makes the following comment on Luke 24:27:

> It is...manifest that Moses, and the Prophets, and all Scriptures, do give testimony unto him and his glory. This is the line of life and light which runs through the whole Old Testament; without the conduct whereof we can understand nothing aright

therein: and the neglect hereof is that which makes many as blind in reading the books of it as are the Jews,—the veil being upon their minds. It is faith alone, discovering the glory of Christ, that can remove that veil of darkness which covers the minds of men in reading the Old Testament, as the apostle declares, 2 Cor. iii. 14-16. (1:348)

In this treatise, Owen's objective is the elucidation of the several ways in which Christ's glory was "represented unto believers under the Old Testament" (1:348). He mentions the "institution of the *beautiful worship of the law*, with all the means of it," the *"mystical account...*of his communion with his church in love and grace," personal appearances of God the Son and, of a different character, *"prophetical visions," "promises, prophecies, predictions, concerning his person, his coming, his office*, his kingdom, and his glory in them all, with the wisdom, grace, and love of God to the church in him," the specific declaration of the incarnation, and a multitude of *"metaphorical expressions"* which declare "the power of things spiritual in what we naturally discern" (1:348-52). Owen only touches upon these themes in *The Glory of Christ* in order to "stir up" the reader's souls "unto a contemplation" of that glory as it is declared in the Old Testament. However, in his earlier works he had written extensively on each, leaving us in no doubt as to how we should understand him. The present chapter will look at most of these various ways in which Christ's glory was manifest to the church in the Old Testament.

The Promise of Deliverance

The first testimony to the coming of a divine Messiah is found in the *protoevangelion*, the first message of glad tidings delivered to Adam and Eve after the Fall. To better appreciate Owen's position it will help to review the background to this promise. With regard to man's creation, Owen says,

> ...as he was not *liable* unto any evil which is the effect of God's displeasure, nor *defective* in any good necessary to preserve him in the condition wherein he was made, so he was *destitute* of nothing that was any way requisite to carry him on unto that further enjoyment of God whereunto he was designed. (18:143)

In the creation of man God had demonstrated his immense power, wisdom, and goodness. He also demonstrated his righteousness "whereby, as the supreme rector and governor of all, he allotted unto his rational creatures the law of their obedience, annexing a reward thereunto in a mixture of *justice and bounty*" (18:144). To reward obedience is a matter of justice, "but that such a reward should be proposed unto the temporary obedience of a creature as is the eternal *enjoyment of God*, was of mere grace and bounty" (18:144). This is the covenant of works.

The Fall and its Consequences
It is evident to all, however, that the world did not continue in such a state. Owen observed "that there is a corrupt spring of sin and disorder in the nature of man; that the whole world lieth in ignorance, darkness, evil and confusion; that there is an alienation and displeasure between God and mankind, God revealing his wrath and judgements from heaven,...*reason* itself, with prudent observation, will discover" (18:144). The explanation why so great a world of evils should exist, however, was beyond the power of reason and observation, beyond the ability of this "light of nature." It was clearly discernable in the light of revelation: "by one man sin entered into the world," says Paul in Romans 5:2, "and death by sin." "*Sin* and *death*," Owen explains,

> are comprehensive of all that is *evil* in any kind in the world. All that is *morally* so is sin; all that is *pe-*

nally so is death. The entrance of both into the world was by the sin of one man, that is, Adam, the common father of us all. (18:145)

Whatever may be considered evil in the world finds its origin in the Fall of Adam.

Since the work of the Messiah is the deliverance of mankind from this state and condition, knowledge of the consequences of the Fall is a prerequisite for an adequate understanding and admiration of the work of God in Christ for man's redemption. For this reason, Owen describes the consequences of the Fall at considerable length in his four principal Christological treatises. He does this not simply to expound a theological *locus*, but to make his reader's hearts "burn within them" with "admiration" for the wisdom of God in the marvelous contrivance of this way of salvation.

The first effect of the Fall for Adam was punishment for himself and his posterity. Concerning the divine sanction, "Dying thou shalt die," Owen asserts, "Whatever is or might be *evil* unto himself and his whole posterity, with the residue of the creation, so far as he or they might be any way concerned therein, hath grown out of this commination." From this, and from the fact that it would be unjust with God to "increase the penalty after the offence was committed," Owen argues,

> The *threatening*, therefore, was the rule and measure of the curse. But this is here extended by God himself, not only to all the miseries of man (Adam and his whole posterity) in this life, in labour, disappointment, sweat, and sorrow, with *death under* and by virtue of the curse, but to the *whole earth* also, and consequently unto those *superior regions* and orbs of heaven by whose influence the earth is as it were governed and disposed unto the use of man, Hos. ii. 21, 22. (18:146)

Furthermore, this curse must be of everlasting duration.

God having given no indication of an expiration, man is left to spend a miserable life, "and then to *die under the curse of God*, without hope of emerging into a better condition" (18:147).

The punishment must also be visited upon Adam's posterity: "What was threatened unto, what was inflicted upon, those who *first* sinned, they are all liable and obnoxious unto" (18:148). Owen appeals to Manasseh Ben Israel, Aben Ezra, and Menahem Rakanatensis to demonstrate rabbinical belief that Adam was the common head to all mankind, and that "his sin was imputed unto all his posterity." The covenantal nature of this relationship is gathered from his translation of Rabbi Rakanatensis:

> It is no wonder why the sin of Adam and Eve was engraven, and sealed with the signet of the King, to be propagated unto all following generations; for in the day that Adam was created, all things were finished, so that he was the perfection and complement of the whole workmanship of this world. Therefore when he sinned, the whole world sinned; whose sin we bear and suffer, which is not so in the sin of his posterity. (18:149)

Owen adds, "to be 'sealed with the signet of the King,' is their expression of God's constitution" (18:149). By this and several other testimonies he shows rabbinical support for the imputation of Adam's sin to his posterity—support which disappeared in the Christian era when, Owen concludes, it became expedient to deny this doctrine because of the advantage it rendered to the Christians (18:151).

"The SECOND consequent of the first sin of man is the *moral corruption of nature*, the spring of all that evil of actual sin that is in the world" (18:151). Owen notes with approval the rabbinical use of "יצר הרע, — the *'figmentum malum;'* the evil figment of the heart." This term, found in Genesis 6:5, is "a more proper name" for man's moral corruption than "original sin." In their descriptions of "inbred and indwelling sin," Owen observes that the Talmudists have employed a number of terms "not unsuited unto those descriptions of it which are given us by the Holy Ghost in the New Testament" (18:152). The result of these two consequents of the Fall is that mankind "can justly expect nothing but a *confluence of evil* in this world, and at the close of their pilgrimage to perish with a ruin commensurate unto their existence" (18:155).

In this manner Owen begins to expound an Old Testament "biblical theology" as the history of the revelation of the promised coming Messiah who would destroy the devil by nullifying his work. Appealing to earlier rabbinical commentaries to answer the objection that Satan is not expressly identified here, Owen argues that the objection arose out of resistance to the Christian use of the passage. After identifying several New Testament passages which confirm the identification of the serpent with Satan, Owen (who seldom hesitates to appeal to the self-authenticating Scriptures) chooses to "forbear to press them on the Jews." Owen was living at the dawning of the age of criticism which would soon render obsolete his dispute with those "sottish" persons who attribute the Fall to a brute beast. At the time, however, it was vital that he do so: at stake was the definition of the work of the Messiah in the destruction of Satan, with the redemption of the cosmos from the evil introduced by him.

The Promise Made

> The first intimation that God gave of this work of his grace in redeeming mankind from sin and misery, is contained in the *promise* subjoined unto the curse denounced against our first parents, and their posterity in them: Gen. iii. 15, ... The things are contained in these words;—a *promise of relief* from the misery brought on mankind by the temptation of Satan;

and an *intimation of the means or way* whereby it should be brought about. (18:170)

This, Owen insists, is a "promise of deliverance," as is evident from three things. First, without this promise of an "*intervention* satisfactory to the righteousness and truth of God" there is no just basis for God's suspension of the death sentence: the serpent speaks the truth and God's threat of death is rendered empty. This liability to immediate death was acknowledged by the Jews, as Owen demonstrates (18:170-71). Secondly, by this promise, God has assured that He would break the "league" which the woman had made with the serpent. "A change of condition, therefore, on the part of the woman and her seed is plainly promised; that is, by a deliverance from the state of sin and misery wherein they were" (18:171). Thirdly,

> In pursuit of this enmity, the Seed of the woman was to *bruise the head of the serpent*. The head is the seat of his power and craft. Without the destruction of the evil and pernicious effects which by his counsel he had brought about, his head cannot be bruised. By his head he had contrived the ruin of mankind; and without the destruction of his works and a recovery from that ruin, he is not conquered nor his head bruised....
>
> In the bruising of his head, the defeat of his counsel, the destruction of his work, and the deliverance of mankind, are contained.... Death must be removed, and righteousness brought in, and acceptance with God procured, or the head of Satan is not bruised. (18:171, 176)

Here we find three of the basic parts of the redemption accomplished by Christ: objective righteousness established by God, spiritual conversion of the sinner, and Satan overcome.

In addition to a promise of deliverance there is an indication of the manner in which the deliverance would come. "*I* will put..." is an indication that "it is an issue of his sovereign wisdom and grace." "*The Seed of the Woman*," however, is an indication that deliverance would come "in and by the nature of man." Furthermore, it is by the conquering of Satan, in a way of suffering "from, and by means of, Satan." "This," says Owen, "is the MESSIAH, or God joining with mankind to deliver mankind from sin and eternal misery" (18:171).

The important question at this point is, to whom does "seed" refer. Owen explains:

> This seed is twice repeated in the words: once expressly, "and her seed;" and, secondly, it is included in the pronoun... "it." And as by "seed," in the first place, the posterity of the woman, some to be born of her race, partakers of human nature, may be intended, as the subject of the enmity mentioned; so in the latter some *single person* some *one* of her posterity or seed, that should obtain the victory, is expressly denoted: for as all her seed in common do never go about this work, the greatest part of them continuing in a willing subjection unto Satan, so if all of them should combine to attempt it, they would never be able to accomplish it, as we have before proved at large. Some one, therefore, to come of her, with whom God would be present in an especial and extraordinary manner, is here expressly promised; and this is the Messiah. (18:176)

It is important to realize that this is the only way of deliverance, and the first discovery in God of grace, mercy, compassion, and pardon. It is a message concerning Christ. Hence, faith in Christ has been "the foundation of all acceptable religion in the world since the entrance of sin" (1:120). This promise of deliverance through the mediator holds quite a different significance for Owen than for the modern opponents of salvation history:

> This is the very foundation of the faith of the church; and if it be denied, nothing of the economy or dispensation of God towards it from the beginning can be understood. The whole doctrine and story of the Old Testament must be rejected as useless, and no foundation be left in the truth of God for the introduction of the New. (1:120)

For Owen, the Puritan pastor, alongside its hermeneutical interest, the consideration of the circumstances of the giving of this promise provides a powerful encouragement for guilt-laden sinners to believe in God's forgiveness. Adam, guilty of the "greatest sin that ever was in the world," and fully expecting the "vengeance due for a broken covenant," hears the "blessed word" of the *protoevangelion*. This is the first revelation that there is forgiveness with God. As such, it gives the highest of reasons to believe in forgiveness with God, seeing its revelation was an act of pure sovereign grace. Furthermore, since from the created order alone there is no revelation of forgiveness for sinners, it provides the *only ground* for the hope of forgiveness from God. Owen concludes that "this revelation of forgiveness with God in this one promise was the bottom of all that worship that was yielded unto him by sinners for many ages; for we have shown before, that without this no sinner can have the least encouragement to approach unto him" (6:433; 434).

The Promise Confirmed

By the institution of expiatory sacrifices God revealed the forgiveness of sin. Owen stresses and takes great pains to prove that atonement for sin was to be made by substitution and satisfaction (1:121), and that all bloody sacrifices "respect atonement, expiation and consequently forgiveness" (6:435). The precise occasion of the institution of sacrifice is not revealed in the Scripture, "But as the sacrifices of beasts could not have been before the entrance of sin, so it may be evidenced that they were instituted from the foundation of the world,—that is presently after the entrance of sin" (6:435-36; cf. 1:122). Owen supports this by declaring his understanding of the description of Christ as the Lamb of God, which was "slain from the foundation of the world." This, he says,

> could not be unless some sacrifice, prefiguring his being slain, had been then offered; for it denotes not only the efficiency of his mediation, but the way. Besides, the apostle tells us that "without the shedding of blood there was no remission," Heb. ix. 22,—that is, God to demonstrate that all pardon and forgiveness related to the blood of Christ from the foundation of the world gave out no word of pardon but by and with blood. Now, I have showed before that he revealed pardon in the first promise; and therefore there ensued thereon the shedding of blood and sacrifices; and thereby that testament or covenant "was dedicated with blood" also, verse 18. Some think that the beasts, of whose skins God made garments for Adam, were offered in sacrifices. Nor is the conjecture vain; yea, it seems not to want a shadow of a gospel mystery, that their nakedness, which became their shame upon their sin (whence the pollution and shame of sin is frequently so termed), should be covered with the skins of their sacrifices: for in the true sacrifice there is somewhat answerable thereunto; and the righteousness of Him whose sacrifice takes away the guilt of our sin is called our clothing, that hides our pollution and shame. (6:436; cf. Owen, 1994, 180)

Owen may call this idea of the origin of Adam's garments a "conjecture," but of the origin of sacrifices there is nothing conjectural. Any other origin for them would mean "the foundation of all acceptable religion in the world was laid in, and resolved into, the wisdom and wills of men, and not into the wisdom, authority, and will of God" (1:122). Since "after the giving of the law, the greatest most noble, and solemn part of the worship of God consisted in *sacrifices*" (6:436), the entire sacrificial system, assuming its institution by God, must be reduced to the divine approval of such a human institution; and this is an intolerable solution.

> All expiatory sacrifices were, from the beginning, types and representations of the sacrifice of Christ; whereon all their use, efficacy, and benefit among men—all their acceptance with God—did depend. Remove this consideration from them, and they were as irrational a service, as unbecoming the divine nature, as any thing that reasonable creatures could fix upon." (1:122; cf. Owen, 1994, 177-83)

The promise of deliverance and its declaration were committed unto the faithful from the beginning of the world, who believed the promise and were saved thereby (18:176). In fact, Owen emphasizes, all the promises and covenants afterward given to the church were founded upon this one and confirm it.

The Promise to Abraham[1]

The call of Abraham was God's means for the "provision of a peculiar stock, from whence the Seed of the woman should spring," which he prepared by raising them "into a civil, regal, and church state, that he might in them typify and prefigure the offices and benefits of the promised Messiah, who was to gather to himself the nations that were to be blessed in the seed of Abraham" (20:12).

The promise made to Abraham was a promise of Christ (22:221; 21:232-33). Made to "Abraham and his seed," it may be considered in two ways, as Owen explains,

> For the promise which is made *concerning* Christ in one sense, is made *unto* him in another. As to the benefit and effects of the coming of Christ, it was made concerning him unto Abraham and all his

seed; but as unto the first grant, intention and stability of the promise, it was made unto Christ himself, with respect unto that everlasting covenant which was between the Father and him, in his undertaking the work of meditation. Or, the Lord Christ may be considered either as the *undertaker of the covenant* with God, and so the promise was made unto him; or as the accomplishment of the terms of it for us, so the promise was made concerning him. (22:229-30)

The promise contained elements which were "carnal and typical," and others "spiritual and eternal." Abraham's material blessing was "a type and pledge of that full administration of grace and spiritual things which was principally intended"; that is, the number and success of his posterity, which though it had literal fulfillment in the conquests of Israel, was typical of the "more numerous subjects of the kingdom of Christ, and of his spiritual conquests for them and in them of all their spiritual adversaries. See Luke i. 70-75" (22:226-27). More than a type, the land was a "sacrament"; the "visible pledge of the love, power, and faithfulness of God in performing and accomplishing the spiritual and invisible part of the promise, or the gospel, in sending the blessing and blessed Seed to save and deliver from sin and death, and to give rest to the souls of them that do believe" (21:233). Thus, the promise was also "spiritual and eternal." Abraham received the promise that he would be a blessing by being a channel for the promised blessing— that is, "That *the Lord Christ should come of his seed according to the flesh*" (22:227), and hence, that all the families on earth would be blessed in him. As Owen explains,

> Being the *first* that received or embraced this promise, he became the *spiritual father of all that do believe*, and in them the 'heir of the world' in a spiritual interest, as he was in his carnal seed the heir of Canaan in a political interest. No men come to be ac-

cepted with God but upon the account of their faith in that promise which was made unto Abraham; that is, in him who was promised unto him. (22:228)

Furthermore, they are not blessed in general, but in a manner which insured a true restoration from the Fall unto the glory of God:

> They were all cursed in Adam, ... and God here promiseth that they shall be blessed in the seed of Abraham, and by him the Seed of the woman. And this blessing must inwrap in it all the good things whereof by the curse they were deprived, or it will be of no use or benefit unto them; a blessing, indeed, it will not be. For a while he intended to leave mankind to walk in their own ways; partly that he might show his severity against sin; partly that he might evidence the *sovereignty* and undeserved freedom of that grace wherein he had provided a Deliverer; and partly that they might try and experiment their own wisdom and strength in searching after a way of deliverance. But in this promise was the ore laid up, which, after many generations, was brought forth and stamped with the image of God. (18:179)

Owen emphasizes that the promise of the blessing made to Abraham "was the life of the church of the old testament, the spring of its continuance unto its appointed season; which could never be dried up" (22:230). As he expresses it elsewhere, "After the giving of this promise, the whole Old Testament beareth witness that a person was to be born, of the posterity of Abraham, in and by whom the nations of the earth should be saved; that is, delivered from sin and curse, and made eternally happy" (18:179). This ultimately determined the history of Israel. Against all opposition, by this promise, this particular church-state continued until, and only until, the coming of Christ (22:230). Hence,

> They lost not their civil state until he came unto

whom was "the gathering of the nations." After that, though many of the individuals obtained mercy, yet their being a nation or people was of no peculiar use, as to any special end of God. Therefore was it immediately destroyed and irrecoverably exterminated.... The end of the days was come; and it was to no purpose for men to endeavour to keep up that which God, having accomplished the utmost of his design by and upon, would lay aside. And this season was fully evidenced to all the world by the gathering of the people to the Shiloh, or the coming in of the nations to partake in the blessing of faithful Abraham, Mic. iv. 1,2.

...The nation, state, temple, sacrifices, being set apart, set up, and designed for no other end but to bring him forth, he was to come whilst they were standing and in use; after which they were none of them to be allowed a being upon their old foundations. This is that which the apostle pointed at in mentioning the last days, that they might consider in what condition the church and people of the Jews then were. (20:13)

Promises From the Remainder of the Old Testament
"After the giving of this promise, the whole Old Testament beareth witness that a person was to be born, of the posterity of Abraham, in and by whom the nations of the earth should be saved; that is, delivered from sin and curse, and made eternally happy" (18:179). Owen mentions several very significant texts to prove the Old Testament expectation of this deliverer. The first, Genesis 49:10, receives considerable attention. The text refers to a coming "Shiloh," which the Targums identify as the Messiah, unto whom the people of the world shall gather "for safety and deliverance, or to be made partakers of the promised blessing" (18:180). This text was very important for Owen's argument that the Messiah had "long since

come," because it provides a final point in time for the Messiah's appearance: the cessation of the ruling line of Judah. Owen argues at length that rule had not passed from "Judah" (loosely considered) until the destruction of the Jewish state by Vespasian and Titus. This destruction took place after the gathering had already begun; the Gentiles were coming to faith in Christ through the spreading of the gospel.

Several other texts are appealed to in confirmation of this expectation in the Old Testament, including Numbers 24:17, 19 and Job 19:25, which bear witness to this expectation among the Gentiles. Commenting on Job 19:25, Owen says,

> Though he was among the Gentiles, yet he believed the promise, and expected his own *personal redemption* by the blessed Seed. And thus, although God confined the posterity of Abraham after the flesh unto the land of Canaan, yet, because in the promised Seed he was to be "heir of the world," he gives unto the Messiah "the heathen to be his inheritance, and the uttermost parts of the earth of his possession," Ps. ii. 8. And upon the accomplishment of the work assigned unto him, he promiseth that "all the ends of the world shall remember and turn unto the LORD, and all the kindreds of the nations shall worship before him," Ps. xxii. 27,—a plain declaration of the Gentiles coming in for their share and interest in the redemption wrought by him. (18:181)

Several other texts direct the attention of the Old Testament believer to the expectation of the Messianic kingdom of God when the Gentiles shall be blessed in the seed of Abraham.[2]

Because of the great number of Messianic prophecies available for comment, Owen decides against an intensive treatment of them all, but summarizes them under the three general ways in which the prophets testified of him. The first of these was, "*By preferring the promised relief and remedy above all the present glory and worship of the church, directing it to look above all its enjoyments* unto that which in all things was to have the pre-eminence" (18:183). Owen lists over forty Scripture passages as examples, asserting that "they all teach, with one consent, that there was in the promise which they assert and confirm an excellency of blessings far exceeding in glory and worth, and in advantage unto believers, all that which they outwardly enjoyed, in their peace, prosperity, kingdom and temple worship," namely, "the spiritual and eternal deliverance of their persons from sin, curse, and misery, with the enjoyment of the favour of God in this life, and blessedness hereafter in his presence for evermore" (18:183).

The second way was in the description they give the person and work of the promised one. Concerning his person they declare that he was to be "God and man in one person, Ps. ii. 7, cx. 1; Isa. ix. 6, 7; Jer. xxiii. 5, 6; Zech. ii. 8-10;... whereby the church was further instructed how God would join with the nature of man in the *seed of the woman*, for the conquest of the old serpent and the destruction of his works." Concerning the redeemer's *work*, the prophets foretell his suffering,

> bearing the effect of and punishment due to sin,... teaching, ruling, and governing of his people, in their obedience unto God by him, until they are saved unto the uttermost, as the great prophet and king of his church,... Yea, herein all the prophets greatly abound, it being the principal work that God raised them up for, and inspired them by his Holy Spirit in their several generations, as Peter declares, 1 Epist. i. 10-12. (18:184)

Owen naturally points to Isaiah 53 and Psalm 22 as examples of revelations of Messiah's sufferings (1 Peter 1:11), adding,

> Nevertheless their conceptions concerning them were dark and obscure. It was his person that their faith principally regarded. Thence were they filled with desires and expectations of his coming, or his exhibition and appearance in the flesh. With the renewed promises hereof did God continually refresh the church in its straits and difficulties. And hereby did God call off the body of people from trust in themselves, or boasting in their present privileges, which they were exceedingly prone unto. (1:102)

The third activity of the prophets according to Owen was the "taking off the *expectations* of men from looking after relief and deliverance by any other way or means whatsoever, Ps. xl. 6, 7" (18:184). Such single-minded expectation is also to characterize our faith in Christ (24:237).

The Personal Revelation of the Son

In addition to the promises, God used other means to establish the Old Testament saints and to reveal the glory of Christ. It is no surprise that these means reveal a message in common with that of the prophets. Nor is it surprising, considering the unity of the Old and New Testament church, to find Owen emphasizing the common elements of their common foundation.

> There are two things concerning the Messiah which are the pillars and foundation of the church. The one is his *divine nature*; and the other, his work of mediation in the *atonement* for sin, which he was to make by his suffering, or the sacrifice of himself. For the declaration of these unto them who, according unto the promise looked for his coming, there were two especial ways or means graciously designed of God. (18:216)

The first of these, his divine nature, was revealed by means of "*visions and appearances* of the Son of God, as the head of the church, which were granted unto the fathers under the old testament" and which very significantly, amounted to the revelation "of a *distinct person* in the Deity, who in a peculiar manner did manage all the concernments of the church after the entrance of sin" (18:216). This allusion to Christ as the manager of the concerns of the church should not be passed over lightly. In it Owen directs our attention to an important motif in Biblical Theology: the peculiar presence of Yahweh with his covenant community. The fact that this presence points to a distinct person in the deity may be questioned by modalists, but Owen's perspective preserves something the modal model does not: the concept of the mediatorial. "A mediator is not of one," is a principle which, while properly applied to God incarnate, seems applicable to the one who appeared to the fathers. The fact that this presence of God with his people is mediatorial argues against the idea of it being a modal presence, since, it would seem, "a mode is of one." Owen does not put it this way. As we will see, his reasons for understanding this presence of Yahweh as that of a distinct person of the Godhead are somewhat different. Nevertheless, such a conclusion seems a plausible inference from his exposition of the divine presence.

The Word of the Lord
Taking his cue from the Targumist's use of מימרא דיי, (the word of the Lord), as well as the evidence from Scripture, Owen points out that those works of creation or providence assigned to "the voice of the Lord" or "the word of his power" are, in the New Testament, "immediately wrought...by the essential Word of God, John i. 3, Col. i. 16; which was with God 'in the beginning,' or at the creation of all things, John i. 1, 2, as his eternal wisdom, Prov. viii. 22-26, and power" (18:216-17). This was the Word, or voice—קוֹל יְהוָה, which Adam and Eve

heard walking in the garden (Gen. 3:8). Owen supports this with quotations of the Targums which he believed "denote a distinct person in the deity" (18:217). Philo, likewise, is appealed to, not as if he believed the "first begotten Word" was the eternal and consubstantial Son of God, but because he identified the Word with the Angel which appeared unto the fathers and with the eternal image of God.

> How these things answer the discourses of our apostle about Jesus Christ, Col. i. 15-18, Heb. i. 3, is easily discerned. And this conception of theirs was so far approved by the Holy Ghost, as suitable unto the mind of God, that John in the beginning of his Gospel, declaring the eternal deity of Christ, doth it under this name of...'the Word.' (18:218)

Owen's explanation of the voice in the garden is noteworthy as a particularly strong indication of the mediatorial character of the divine presence. He says,

> It is...*most probable*, that, in the great alteration which was now coming upon the whole creation of God,—mankind being to be cast out of covenant, the serpent and the earth being to be cursed, and a way of recovery for the elect of God to be revealed,—He by whom all things were made, and by whom all were to be renewed that were to be brought again unto God, did in an especial and glorious manner appear unto our first parents, as he in whom this whole dispensation centred, and unto whom it was committed. And as, after the promise given, he appeared...'in a human shape,' to instruct the church in the mystery of his future incarnation, and under the name of Angel, to shadow out his office as sent unto it and employed in it by the Father; so here before the promise, he discovered his distinct glorious person, as the eternal Voice or Word of the Father. (18:219-20)

The Lord who Appeared to Abraham
In his interpretation of the account of God's visit to Abraham in Genesis 18, Owen observes that the Lord had a twofold agenda: the renewal of the promise to Abraham concerning his Seed, and, as a work of "vindictive justice," the destruction of Sodom and Gomorrah.

> And both these were the proper works of him on whom the care of the church was in an especial manner incumbent,—all whose blessedness depended on that promise,—and to whom the rule of the world, the present and future judgment thereof, is committed; that is, the person of the Son. And hence, in the overthrow of those cities, he who is to be their judge is said to set forth an ensample of his future dealing with ungodly men, 2 Pet. ii. 6. (18:220-21)

Owen denies the preposterous suggestion that the three visitors signify the persons of the Trinity, but argues that a distinction of persons in the Deity (not their precise number) is "demonstrable" from the observation that "he of the three that spake unto Abraham, and to whom he made his supplication for the sparing of Sodom, was Jehovah,...and yet all the three were sent upon the work, that one being the Prince and Head of the embassy; as he who is Jehovah is said to be sent by Jehovah, Zech. ii. 8, 9" (18:221). Owen's conclusion, after considering and refuting several other objections, is that

> one distinct person in the Godhead, who now represented himself unto Abraham in the form and shape wherein he would dwell amongst men, when of his seed he would be "made flesh,"...was one signal means whereby Abraham saw his day and rejoiced; which himself lays upon his *pre-existence* unto his incarnation, and not upon the promise of his coming, John viii. 56, 58. A solemn preludium it was unto his taking of flesh, a revelation of his divine nature and person, and a pledge of his coming in human nature to converse with men. (18:222)

Again, it should be born in mind that Owen does not simply present these passages as "proof texts," but endeavors to draw out the significance of the appearance, in its context, for salvation history.

The Angel of the Covenant
An even better example of this is his exposition of the appearance to Jacob in Genesis 32, when Jacob wrestles with the angel before confronting Esau.

> In the promise about which their contest was, the blessed Seed, with the whole church-state and worship of the old testament, was included; so that it was the greatest controversy, and had the greatest weight depending on it, of any that ever was amongst the sons of men. Wherefore, to settle Jacob's right, to preserve him with his title and interest, he who was *principally concerned in the whole matter* doth here appear unto him. (18:223, emphasis mine)

Certain very important facts are available concerning this person. He appeared as a man. He is called an "angel": "The Angel that redeemed me." Owen says, "'The Angel the Redeemer';... is the name of the promised Messiah, as the Jews grant, Isa. lix. 20." Furthermore, "This man in appearance, this angel in office, was in name and nature God over all, blessed for ever." He is "expressly said to be 'God, the LORD God of hosts,' Hos. xii. 3, 5," and the one with whom he entered into covenant at Bethel (18:223, 224). From this Owen concludes "it is evident that he who appeared unto Jacob,... was God; and because he was sent as the angel of God, it must be some distinct person in the Deity condescending unto that office; and appearing in the form of a man, he represented his future assumption of our human nature" (18:224-25). The appearance of God to Moses in the burning bush and at the giving of the Law was also an appearance of an "Angel":

namely, the Angel of the covenant, the great Angel of the presence of God, in whom was the name and nature of God. And he thus appeared that the church might know and consider who it was that was to work out their spiritual and eternal salvation, whereof that deliverance which then he would effect was a type and pledge. (18:225)

In the appearance at the giving of the law, the presence of God is called his "glory"—a designation which will appear often.

A particularly strong support for the distinction of persons in the deity is found in Exodus 23:20-22, where God promises to send his Angel with the Israelites. Owen distinguishes between two angels referred to in Exodus 33:2, 3 and verses 13-16, the Angel of God's presence, which had been with them during their journey so far, and a "ministering angel, to execute the judgments and vengeance of God" (18:226). The people are distressed when God says that he (i.e., his presence) shall not go with them. Owen understands that God is giving the angel of his presence characteristics which can only properly be attributed to God. The first of these is his *sovereign authority*, so strongly expressed in Exodus 23:21-24. The second is his divine name: "my name is in him." Third, this angel is called by God, "my presence," or "my face," "which presence Moses calls his 'glory,' verse 18, his essential glory: which was manifested unto him, chap. xxiv. 6, though but obscurely in comparison of what it was unto them who, in his human nature...'beheld his glory'" (18:228). Owen approvingly quotes Rabbi Moses Nachmanides Gerundensis's comment that the Angel is the "face of God," and that the "'face of God' signifieth God himself, as all interpreters acknowledge" (18:231).

One further example is that of the appearance of the "Prince of the LORD's host" to Joshua, in Joshua 5. The strength and significance of Owen's argument becomes clearer if his words are quoted in full:

> And this was another illustrious manifestation of the Son of God unto the church of old, accompanied with many instructive circumstances: as,—(1.) From the *shape* wherein he appeared, namely, that of a man, as a pledge of his future incarnation. (2.) From the *title* that he assumes to himself, "The Captain of the LORD'S host," he unto whom the guidance and conduct of them unto rest, not only temporal but eternal, was committed; whence the apostle, in allusion unto this place and title, calls him "The Captain of our salvation," Heb. ii. 10. And, (3.) The *person* unto whom he spake when he gave himself this title was the captain of the people at that time; teaching both him and them that there was another, supreme Captain of their eternal deliverance. (4.) From *the time and place* of his appearance, which was upon the first entrance of the people into Canaan, and the first opposition which therein they met withal; so engaging his presence with his church in all things which oppose them in their way unto eternal rest. (5.) From the *adoration and worship* which Joshua gave unto him; which he accepted of, contrary to the duty and practice of created angels, Rev. xix. 10, xxii. 8, 9. (6.) From the *prescription of the ceremonies* expressing religious reverence, "Put off thy shoe;" with the reason annexed, "For the place whereon thou standest…, "it is holiness,"—made so by the presence of God: the like precept whereunto was given to Moses by the God of Abraham, Isaac, and Jacob, Exod. iii. 5. (18:228-29)

Owen's summary conclusion of this appearance to Joshua is a concise expression of his general assessment of them all: "By all these things was the church instructed in the person, nature, and office, of the Son of God, even in the mystery of his eternal distinct subsistence in the Deity, his future incarnation and condescension unto the office of being the Head and Saviour of his church" (18:228-29; cf. 20:378-93).

Types of the Messiah

Another of the principal means for the revelation of Messiah's person and work to the Old Testament church was the use of types (τύποι, 1 Cor. 10:6). Owen is aware of two general errors with regard to the interpretation of these types: "expositors either pass by these things without any notice, or indulge unto various conjectures without any certain rule of what they assert" (23:213). His description of types and their interpretation is worth noting, especially given his estimate of their value for the church in the revelation of Christ.

Owen distinguishes between three varieties of types. The first includes "such as were *directly instituted* and appointed for this end, that they should signify and represent something in particular in the Lord Christ and his kingdom" (21:33). These "were materially either *persons*, as vested with some certain office in the church, or *things*" (21:33). Persons were types of Christ "in the *discharge of their offices and present duties*" representing, as he puts it,

> in a way of prefiguration the Lord Christ and his offices, who was to come. They were a transcript out of the divine idea in the mind and will of God, concerning the all-fulness of power and grace that was to be in Christ, expressed by parcels and obscurely in them, so as by reason of their imperfection they were capable. (21:33)

The typical "things" consisted primarily of all the parts of the solemn and glorious worship of the Old Testament church. These were apparently "transcripts" as well. God "first...made a glorious representation" of his glory "immediately by his own power" on Sinai, but also "showed a pattern of it in the mount; which was not only an exemplar of what he would have framed here below, but expressive of the idea in his own mind of good things to come" (23:213; cf. Vos, 1956, 55-59).

The general features of this "representation" contribute to Owen's approach to the interpretation of the details. For instance, they were "earthly" in nature, befitting the "imperfect" state of the church. They were also "outwardly glorious and venerable; for the people being comparatively carnal were affected by such things." Moreover, the "resemblance of heavenly things in them was but dark and obscure." However, what provides Owen with a rule for their interpretation, he says, is

> that God chose this way and these means to represent his glorious presence in and with the Lord Christ, unto all the ends of his mediation. For with respect unto them it is said that "in him dwelleth all the fulness of the Godhead bodily," Col. ii. 9; namely, as it dwelt *typically* in the tabernacle by the outward pledges of his especial presence. Whence he concludes that they were all "a shadow," whereof "the body was Christ," verse 17. (23:213-14)

In addition to persons and things Owen mentions a second general sort of type: "Such things and actions as had only a *providential ordination* to that purpose,—things that occasionally fell out, and so were not capable of a solemn institution, but were as to their events so guided by the providence of God as that they might prefigure and represent somewhat that was afterwards to come to pass" (21:33-34). Of these, Owen says, some "receive a *particular application* unto the things of the new testament, or unto spiritual things belonging to the grace and kingdom of Christ, by the Holy Ghost himself in the writings of the Gospel" but as the apostolic example illustrates, many others "were ordained in the providence of God" for our instruction. As members of the covenant people of God, Owen reminds us, we "may expect answerable dispensations of God towards ourselves; and they were all written for our sakes" (21:34).

A third sort of type arises because "there are things that fell out of old which are meet to illustrate present things, from a proportion or similitude between them." These are "allegories," but not because the events had no literal significance, nor because they have any other "*mystical* or allegorical" sense. As Owen puts it, "the words which have not one determinate sense have no sense at all: but the things mentioned in any place holding a proportion unto other things, there being a likeness between them, the words whereby the one are expressed are applied unto the other" (21:35). In the interpretation of these he emphasizes the application of three rules. First, there must be a "*due proportion*" between them. Second, there must be "a *designed signification* in them." For example, Hosea 11:1 ("Out of Egypt I have called my son") "did firstly and properly express God's dealing with the people of Israel; but there was also an intention included in them of shadowing out his future dealing with his only Son, Christ Jesus" (21:35-36). Owen might be accused of understatement when he adds, "The discovery hereof is a matter of great skill and wisdom; and great sobriety is to be used in such applications and allusions" (21:36). Third, "the first, *original sense* of the words" must be "sacredly observed."

Mystical Communion with the Messiah

Another way in which the "glory of Christ was represented unto believers under the Old Testament" was in what Owen calls the "*mystical account* which is given us of his communion with his church in love and grace" (1:348-49). Owen says, "As this is intimated in many places of Scripture, so there is one entire book designed unto its declaration," the Song of Solomon. Jonathan Won has explored the use of the Song of Solomon by several leading Puritans, rightly concluding, "The most significant difference from Calvin," in the matter of union and communion with Christ, "lies in the Puritan use of the allegorical interpretation of the Song of Songs to develop an experimental theology of communion with Christ" (1989, 356). In the light of what was said above concerning the interpretation of types, "develop" would most accurately be understood in the sense of to *illustrate* rather than to *invent*. No point of Owenian experimental theology rests solely on the allegorization of the Song of Solomon that cannot be gathered from other Scriptures depicting the marriage between God and his people.[3]

The point here is that faithful worshippers under the Old Testament actually experienced "inward communion" with Christ as they beheld his glory in the *"beautiful worship of the law."* Moreover, the Song describes the "holy strains of delight and admiration," "raptures of joy," "solemn and divine complacency," "ardency of affection, and diligence in attendance unto the means of enjoying" this communion (1:349; cf. Sibbes 1862-64, 2:6-195). The strength of Owen's position rests upon the accuracy of his assumptions that Christ, as revealed to the Old Testament believer, was the object of his faith and love, that this faith and love was not in name only, but a true "spiritual affection," and that there was a real communication of grace to the saint. Owen adds, "if we, whose revelations of the same glory do far exceed theirs, should be found to come short of them in ardency of affection unto Christ, and continual holy admiration of his excellencies, we shall one day be judged unworthy to have received them" (1:349).

Christ: The Object of Old Testament Faith

Owen undertakes the description of the faith of the Old Testament church concerning the Messiah in the eleventh exercitation of his exposition of Hebrews. He begins with the assumption, allowable in the case of the truly faithful, that "what God revealed, that they *believed*" (18:234). As he explains,

> They of old saw not, indeed, clearly and fully into the sense of the promises,—as to the way and manner whereby God would work out and accomplish the mercy and grace which they lived and died in the faith and hope of; but this they knew, that God would, in his *appointed* time, in and by the *nature of man*, in one to be born of the seed of Abraham and house of David, cause *atonement to be made for sin, bring in everlasting righteousness*, and work out the salvation of his elect. This was abundantly revealed, and this they steadfastly believed, and in the faith hereof "obtained a good report," or testimony from God himself that they "pleased him," inherited the promises, and were made partakers of life eternal. (18:234)

As the time of Christ's advent was approaching, the expectations of the Jews for the accomplishment of the promise were very high. Nevertheless, by then, the people in general

> had utterly lost the light and faith of their fore-fathers about the nature, work, and office, of the promised Messiah; for, being grown carnal, and minding only things earthly and present, they utterly overlooked the spiritual genealogy of the Seed of the woman from the first promise and . . . fancied him unto themselves as one that was to deliver them from all *outward trouble*, and to satisfy them with the glory and desirable things of this world, without respect to sin and the curse, or delivery from them. (18:235)

As Owen explains, "All things which concern the Messiah, his person, office, and work, are exceedingly mysterious, as containing the principal effect of the eternal wisdom and goodness of God, and the sacred counsel of his will" (18:240). Consequently, to "carnal reason" the Old Testament is filled with numerous inconsistencies concerning the Messiah. After a lengthy catalogue of these, Owen points to the wonderful way all are resolved in person and work of Christ (18:240).

"The Promised Messiah Has Long Since Come"
In order to confirm that the Old Testament witness to the Messiah has been fulfilled in Jesus, Owen points to a number of texts that define the time and circumstances of the event, together with the activities of the Messiah, and the Old Testament's description of the rise of what he calls the "gospel-state." These are shown not only to be fulfilled in Christ, but also to be incapable of any chance of fulfillment since the Roman destruction of Jerusalem (18:269-305). The objection that many promises of the Messiah were not fulfilled by Christ receives Owen's lengthy and cogent response (18:424-46). Owen's discussion on this point is exceedingly rich in rabbinical commentary, and provides many additional and valuable examples of his exegesis of Messianic texts.

One illustration of Owen's historical perspective on the incarnation of Christ is his exegesis of the "the last days" as found, for example, in Hebrews 1:1. Owen understands this eschatological term to be a reference to the *"last days of the Judaical church"*: a period which coincides with the days of the coming of the Messiah, who will "put an end to their station and condition" (20:11, 12; see also Owen 1994, 597-99). Owen refers here to the transformation which will accompany the inauguration of the New Covenant.

Conclusion
When we look at Owen's interpretation of the Old Testament, two facts stand out. First, he understands Christ to

be the central figure, either as the promised Seed who is revealed in the promises and institutions of worship, or as the present Mediator who undertakes for the people of God, and in whom they find participation with the Divine. The unity of the people of God through time is thereby firmly established. Second, there nevertheless is a difference between the Old Covenant and the New which is all-important: Christ has come. Henceforth, a new creation exists which has Jesus of Nazareth as its head. All things have become new in him. In the next chapter we consider with Owen how Jesus of Nazareth is constituted the "head of the new creation."

---

[1] See also Owen, 1996, 359-69.

[2] For example, Psalms 45:16 and 68:18; Isaiah 2:2-4; 11:10-12; 19:25; 40:5; 42:4; 49:6; 51:5; 53:12; and 55:1-4.

[3] John Owen wrote the commendatory letter to James Durham's *An Exposition of the Song of Solomon*, in which he supports Durham's allegorical approach to the book (Durham 1840, 19-22; see pp. 30-61, and Burrowes 1853, 10-140).

CHAPTER
11

"God Was Manifest in the Flesh"

In the theological system of John Owen, the "first" foundation of religion is the Divine Being. This foundation, however, is hidden, and cannot be known but by its "outward acts and effects." Therefore, it cannot be the cause of religion, for religion, Owen says, is "nothing but the due respect of rational creatures unto the divine nature, and its infinite excellencies" (1:44-45). In such a manner Owen introduces his doctrine of the person of Christ: "The person of Christ is the most glorious and ineffable effect of divine wisdom, grace and power; and therefore is the next [i.e., second] foundation of all acceptable religion and worship" (1:44). Here we find an important summary of Owen's fundamental approach to Christology. To be born uppermost in the mind is the "glorious and ineffable" person of the Mediator. The creation of man and all other things was so great as to be the "immediate ground of all natural religion," as these declare the glory of God. Nevertheless, "of all the effects of the divine excellencies, the constitution of the person of Christ as the foundation of the new creation, and as 'the mystery of Godliness,' was the most ineffable and glorious" (1:45).

The Humiliation of Christ
"Infinite love prevailed with the Son of God to lay aside

the privilege of his infinite dignity, that he might suffer for us and our redemption" (21:525). In his exposition of Philippians 2:5-8, Owen describes the humiliation of Jesus Christ as having two parts: His self-emptying (ἐκκένωσις), and his humbling of himself (ταπείνωσις). Christ was in the form of God, and equal with God. Owen says, "As long as he would make use of this privilege, it was impossible he should be exposed to the least suffering" (21:526). Turning our attention now to the state of humiliation, Owen says, "He emptied himself to take the form of a servant; and he humbled himself in that form, to engage in obedience, to undergo death." These are not equivalent:

> There is an infinite distance between the ἐκκένωσις, the self-emptying of Christ, when, "being in the form of God, he took upon himself the form of a servant," and the ταπείνωσις, the taking on him the form of a servant to obey and die. The one infinitely excels the other. (16:494)

The point of this passage for Owen is that it is an "infinite, mysterious self-humiliation and condescension in Jesus Christ, the Son of God to take our nature upon him, with reference unto the office of a mediator" (16:494). In this condescension and love, we behold the glory of Christ (1:323). Owen begins his exposition of this infinite condescension by illustrating the infinite distance between the natures, beings, and essences of God and the creature.

That the divine nature was his is evident from Philippians 2:6 (cf. 12:285-92). Though the words of this controversial passage are "not without their difficulty," Owen follows the translation found in the King James Version: Christ "thought it not robbery to be equal with God," i.e., he "did not esteem it to be any wrong, on that account of his being in the form of God, to be equal to his Father" (12:291-92).[1] This is to say,

Because he was 'in the form of God,' partaking of the divine essence, therefore he was 'equal with God,' in dignity, power, and authority: which nothing could give him but only his being in the form of God; for though there is an order in the persons of the Trinity, there is no distinction or inequality in the nature of God. (16:497)

From Isaiah 40:15-17, Owen concludes that "there can be no reason why an infinite Being should have regard unto that which is as nothing, but its own infinite condescension" (16:495). Given the divine aseity, and the divine blessedness which it secures, "there can be no addition made unto God. It must be an infinite condescension in him and a humbling of himself, to behold the things done in heaven and on earth" (16:495-96; 1:324-25). And if it is a humbling of God "so much as to behold the most glorious things in heaven or the greatest things on earth," Owen exclaims, "what great humiliation is it in the Son of God, who did not only look upon and behold us, and act kindly towards us, but took our nature upon him to be his own" (16:496; 1:325). This point becomes even more effective when one considers Owen's description of the nature that God regarded in this condescension (20:351-52).

How did Owen understand the *kenosis*? Negatively, it did not consist in a relinquishing of the divine nature. "He that is God can no more cease to be God, by any act of his own, or act upon him, than he that is not God can become God by any act of his own, or any act upon him" (16:497; cf. 1:325; 21:526). Nor did it "consist in the substantial conversion of the divine nature into the human" (1:326). The Arian belief in the conversion of the pre-existent nature of the Son into human nature results in "a human nature...that is of no affinity and cognation unto us; not derived of Adam as we, but made of the substance of the divine Word" (16:497). The divine and human natures were not "mixed and compounded into one nature"

(1:327). Owen emphasizes that the divine nature "acts suitably unto itself; it acts nothing but what becomes it and is proper unto the divine nature." Finally, as he says elsewhere, "the Son of God could not absolutely and really part with his eternal glory.... Neither by any thing he underwent, did he really forego, nor was it possible he should so do, any thing of his divine glory" (21:526). Making a point that is often overlooked by kenotic theologians, Owen observes,

> The apostle doth not say that Christ made that form of no reputation, or Christ ἐκένωσε that form; but Christ, being in that form, ἑαυτὸν ἐκένωσε "made himself of no reputation," not by any real change of his divine nature, but by taking to himself the human, wherein he was of no reputation, it being he that was so, in the nature and by the dispensation wherein he was so. And it being not possible that the divine nature of itself, in itself, should be humbled, yet he was humbled who was in the form of God, though the form of God was not. (12:287)

Positively, "What did Christ do with reference to his divine nature, when he took our nature upon him?" Owen answers,

> He veiled himself, he shadowed himself, he hid his divine nature, he eclipsed the glory of it. Not absolutely; all things under heaven cannot veil, eclipse, or hide, the glory of the divine nature. But he eclipsed, shadowed, hid, and laid it aside, as to himself and his interest in it: for upon his taking our nature upon him, men were so far from looking on him as God, that they did not look on him as a good man. (16:498; cf. 21:527; 1:327)

Christ veiled his glory in taking the nature of man upon himself. Owen never tired of expounding the glory of this mystery. Two years before his death, in the sermon to which we have been referring, he summarized the condescension of Christ thus:

> What, then did Christ do in his condescension? Pray remember it, for it is the principal object of your faith, and the life of your souls. This was that which he did: The person of the Son of God, or the divine nature in the second person, continuing God in his essence and God in his state and dignity, did take "upon" him (I use that word rather than take "unto" him) the nature of man, into an individual subsistence in his own person, whereby he became that man; and what was done and acted in it by that man was done and acted by the person of the Son of God. (16:499)

Here, in a sermon for the "ordinary sort of Christian," Owen explains the wonderful significance and practical importance of the subsistence of Christ's human nature in the person of the Son of God.

> This is that condescension of Christ that is here spoken of. Every man hath his own individual subsistence, whereby the human nature is divided in particular. We have all of us the same nature in general;—that is, the same specific human nature belongs unto us equally and unto all men in the world; yet every man and woman hath this nature entire and absolutely unto himself, as if there were no other man or woman in the world. And Adam was not more a single person when there was none in the world but himself, than everyone of us is a single person now the world is full of men, as if there were but one man. And every one comes into the world in his own individual subsistence unto himself, whereby he becomes a man as much as any of us. Here is the great act of self-denial in Christ. (16:499)

The point of the exposition is to emphasize that God the Son, without ceasing to be God, really became the man Jesus, for Christ's humanity was really his own, as any man's humanity is his own (1:329). Modern opponents of the incarnation object to the non-personal (*anhypostatic*) subsistence as a denial of the humanity of Christ. Here, in a way of in-personal (*enhypostatic*) union, as argued by Leontius in the sixth century, we see that the manhood's person truly exists: it is the person of the Son. Furthermore, the Son truly possesses the manhood, precisely because, as with all other men, the manhood subsists in his person as his own nature. Owen does not apologize, but regards it as redounding to the glory of God, that "flesh and blood can reveal that unto no man." This is the very thing that renders Christ a "stumblingstone and rock of offence" (1:328).

The ταπείνωσις consists of what he did in that nature having assumed it: "He did not immediately take the nature he had assumed into glory; but he first became a 'servant' in it,—a servant to God, to do his will, and that in the most difficult service that ever God had to do in this world" (21:526). Owen emphasizes that Christ "made himself of no reputation," in this service, undertaking this honorable work in a manner which "exposed him unto scorn, reproach, and contempt in the world." It consisted in obedience unto death, even the death of the cross (21:527).

Though an "infinite distance" exists between the ἐκκένωσις and the ταπείνωσις, this fact does not negate the significance of the latter. All that Christ ever "did or doth, all that ever he underwent or suffered as mediator," was for the saints, not only the condescension of kenosis, but all that he suffered in his life: fulfilling all righteousness, enduring all manner of persecutions and hardships, doing all manner of good to men (2:135).

An Act of the Triune God

The Role of the Father

In his exposition of Hebrews 10:5, Owen assigns the preparation of the body of Christ in a peculiar way to the

Father. It is to the Father that the Son addresses the words "A body thou hast prepared for me." This is because in the covenant of redemption "the Father proposed to him what was his will," and undertook to provide whatever things were necessary for its accomplishment. "Among those the principal was, that the Son should have a body prepared for him, that so he might have somewhat of his own to offer," that is, as a high priest offering for the sins of his people (23:460, 461). Owen explains that this preparation may be considered in two ways. The first is "In the *designation and contrivance of it*," in the eternal counsels of God. This is not to be understood as a pre-incarnate human existence, but as a "resolution for the effecting" of the incarnation (23:461-62; 1 Pet. 1:20). The second way was in "the *actual effecting*, ordering, and creating of it, that it might be fitted and suited unto the work that it was ordained to." This is the sense it is used in Hebrews 10:5 (23:462).

It is this idea that the body of Christ is "suited unto the work that it was ordained to" that is particularly important for Owen, since it is this which demonstrates the wisdom of God, and renders the person of Christ an object of the everlasting admiration of saints and angels. Owen assigns ten ways in which this is so. This human nature was so prepared as that it "*might be of the same nature as ours.*" It was in "*no way subject unto that depravation and pollution* that came upon our whole nature by sin" (23:462). It consisted "*of flesh and blood, which might be offered as real substantial sacrifice…wherein he might suffer for sin.*" It was "*animated with a living, rational soul,*" which was "*obnoxious unto all the sorrows and sufferings which our nature is liable unto,*" was "*exposed unto all sorts of temptations* from outward causes," was "*liable unto death,*" and "*meet to be raised again from death.*" "This body and soul," Owen adds, "being capable of a real separation, and being actually separated by death, though not for any long continuance, yet no less truly and really than they who have been dead a thousand years, a *demonstration was given therein of an active subsistence of the soul in a state of separation from the body.*" Lastly, Owen mentions, this body was "*visibly taken up into heaven, and there resides.*" This entire "contrivance" was of the Father, who prepared the body of Christ "in the authoritative disposition of all things" (23:463, 464).

The Role of the Holy Spirit
The work of the Holy Spirit in the incarnation of the Son of God receives only slight treatment in the *Christologia* compared to that in the third chapter of *Pneumatologia*, which must receive our attention now. The Socinians had raised an objection which, if granted, would render the discussion pointless, so Owen begins his treatment of the doctrine by addressing the question, "Could not the Son of God himself, in his own person, perform all things requisite both for the forming, supporting, sanctifying, and preserving of his own nature, without the especial assistance of the Holy Ghost?" There seemed no "*need*, nor indeed, room" for a work of the Spirit (3:160). Owen replies that the "only singular immediate act of the person of the Son on the human nature was the *assumption* of it into subsistence with himself," and "the only *necessary consequent* of this assumption of the human nature, or the incarnation of the Son of God, is the *personal union of Christ*, or the inseparable subsistence of the *assumed nature* in the person of the Son" (3:160-61). Furthermore,

> The Holy Spirit is the *Spirit of the Son*, no less than the Spirit of the Father.... Whatever the Son of God wrought in, by, or upon the human nature, he did it by the Holy Ghost, who is his Spirit, as he is the Spirit of the Father. (3:162)

Owen had already demonstrated that the Holy Ghost is the "*immediate, peculiar, efficient cause* of all external divine operations," by whom God "immediately applies the power and efficacy of the divine excellencies unto their operation." The external works of the Trinity are undivided since the principle of all divine operations is the nature of God, undivided in the three persons. However,

> in every divine act, the authority of the Father, the love and wisdom of the Son, with the immediate efficacy and power of the Holy Ghost, are to be considered. Yea, and there is such a distinction in their operations, that one divine act may produce a peculiar respect and relation unto one person, and not unto another; as the assumption of the human nature did to the Son, for he only was incarnate. (3:162)

With this introduction to his subject, Owen meets the Socinian objection to the work of the Spirit in the incarnation. He has shown that it is possible and reasonable to expect such a work of the Spirit in distinction from the Son. He next proceeds to describe and prove that operation of the Spirit: "The *framing, forming, and miraculous conception of the body of Christ in the womb of the blessed Virgin* was the peculiar and especial work of the Holy Ghost" (3:162). Hebrews 10:5 ascribes this work to the Father with respect to its "designation, and the authoritative disposal of things," but as Matthew and Luke make evident, "the immediate divine *efficiency* in this matter was a peculiar work of the Holy Ghost" (3:163). This is illustrated in the angel's reply to Mary's inquiry concerning how she, a virgin, should conceive: "'The Holy Ghost,' saith the angel, 'acting the power of the Most High,' or in the infinite power of God, 'shall accomplish it'" (3:163). Secondly, the Spirit will "come upon" Mary. This is an expression

> often used to declare his actings with reference unto the production of miraculous works.... "He will so come upon you as to put forth the power of the Most High in you and by you, in gifts and opera-

tions miraculous;" for he is said to come, with respect unto his beginning of any marvellous operation, where before he did not work to the like purpose.

Thirdly, he says,
> The act of the Holy Ghost in this matter was a creating act; *not, indeed, like the first creating act, which produced* the matter and substance of all things out of nothing, causing that to be which was not before, neither in matter nor form, nor passive disposition; but like those subsequent acts of creation, whereby, out of matter before made and prepared, things were made that which before they were not, and which of themselves they had no active disposition unto nor concurrence in. (3:163-64)

The point to be stressed in this last consideration is that the Holy Ghost prepared this body with pre-existent matter, namely, the "substance of the blessed Virgin," in order that the promises should be fulfilled and that Christ might be a partaker of our nature.

There are several important consequences of this work of the Spirit. First, Owen argues, "the Lord Christ could not on this account, no, not [even] with respect unto his human nature only, be said to be the *Son of the Holy Ghost*, although he supplied the place and virtue of a *natural father* in generation; for the relation of filiation dependeth only on and ariseth from a perfect generation, and not on every effect of an efficient cause." The only relation of the Holy Ghost to the human nature of Christ was that of creator to creature. Filiation is uniquely from the Father, "and belongs unto Christ as he was a divine person, and not with respect unto his human nature. But that nature being assumed, *whole Christ* was the Son of God" (3:164-65). Second, there is a clear distinction between the creating act of the Holy Spirit and the assumption of that newly created nature by the Son. The Holy Spirit "made the human nature of Christ, body and soul, with, in, and unto a subsistence in the second person of the Trinity, not [in] his own" (3:165). Third, "the conception of Christ in the *womb*, being the effect of a *creating act*, was not accomplished *successively* and in process of time, but was perfected in an *instant*" (3:165). Owen draws this conclusion from his understanding of the original creative acts which, though spread over six days, were "instantaneously produced." "So was the forming of the body of Christ, with the infusion of a rational soul to quicken it, though it increased afterwards in the womb unto the birth" (3:165). The significance of this lies in the doctrine of the *enhypostasia*: Christ's human nature is preserved from impersonal existence because its existence is simultaneous with its subsistence in the person of the Son. That is,

> it was necessary that nothing of the human nature of Christ should exist of itself antecedently unto its union with the Son of God: for in the very instant of its formation, and therein, was the Word made flesh," John i. 14; and the Son of God was "made of a woman," Gal. iv. 4; so that the whole essence of his nature was created in the same instant. (3:165)

Fourth, "From this miraculous creation of the *body of Christ*, by the immediate power of the Holy Ghost, did it become a *meet habitation for his* holy soul, every way ready and complying with all actings of grace and virtue" (3:167). The importance of this will be observed under the life of Christ, considered below.

Interestingly, Owen says, "it is probable that this conception was immediate upon the angelical salutation" (3:166), but offers no reason for this.[2] He rejects scholastic speculations into the manner of the Spirit's work in the formation of Christ's human nature. It is something hidden, that we "may learn to adore that holy work here, which we hope to rejoice in and bless God for unto eternity" (3:166). He suggests, however, that in the angel's answer to Mary there is "an allusion unto the expression of the original acting of the Holy Spirit towards the newly-produced mass of the old creation" (3:166).

"The Word Became Flesh"

For Owen, the incarnation was the most glorious of the acts of God:

> His conception in the womb of the Virgin, as unto the integrity of human nature, was a miraculous operation of the divine power. But the prevention of that nature from any subsistence of its own—by its assumption into personal union with the Son of God, in the first instance of its conception—is that which is above all miracles, nor can be designed by that name. (1:45)

Owen is particularly impressed with the incarnation *per se*, as it manifests the divine wisdom. As he explains it,

> The wisdom of God in this great work may be reduced unto these four heads:—I. The assumption of our nature into personal subsistence with the Son of God. II. The union of the two natures in that single person which is consequential thereon. III. The mutual communication of those distinct natures, the divine and human, by virtue of that union. IV. The enunciations or predications concerning the person of Christ, which follow on that union and communion. (1:224)

The Assumption of Human Nature

The assumption of human nature was "the greatest and most admirable effect of divine love wisdom and grace"; by it, "the scattered light" of divine glory apparent in creation "is gathered into one sun, giving out most glorious beams, unto the manifestation of his infinite excellencies far above all other things" (20:445, 446). Owen defines assumption as "that ineffable divine act whereby the person of the Son of God assumed our nature, or took it into a personal subsistence with himself." The Scripture describes this assumption actively on the part of the divine nature acting in the person of the Son, and passively on the part of the human nature assumed. This active assumption of human nature is clearly expressed in such texts of Scripture as Hebrews 2:14, 16, and Philippians 2:6-7, where it is emphasized that he "took," i.e., assumed, human nature.

> The eternal Word, the Son of God, was not made flesh, not made of a woman, nor of the seed of David, by the conversion of his substance or nature into flesh; which implies a contradiction,—and besides, is absolutely destructive of the divine nature. He could no otherwise, therefore, be made flesh, or made of a woman, but in that our nature was made his, by his assuming of it to be his own. The same person—who before was not flesh, was not man—was made flesh as man, in that he took our human nature to be his own. (1:225)

To "take it to be his own, his own nature, can be no otherwise but by giving it a subsistence in this own person; otherwise his own nature it is not, nor can be" (1:225). The importance of this is apparent from the emphasis given to its clarification and implications for Christian piety.

In his exposition of Hebrews 2:16 ("For verily not anywhere doth he take angels, but he taketh the seed of Abraham"), Owen demonstrates that the words indicate the assumption of the nature of man, and then makes the following important observations. First, the text presupposes Christ's pre-existence. He took on another nature, not ceasing to be what he was before. Moreover, he took it to be his own nature, and this "by taking that nature into *personal subsistence* with himself, in the hypostasis of the Son of God." This assumption is done "without a *mul-*

tiplication of persons in him; for the human nature can have no personality of its own, because it was taken to be the nature of another person who was pre-existent unto it, and by assuming of it prevented its proper personality." This assumption occurs without the mixture, confusion, or separation of the natures (20:461-62).

Again we see Owen's appreciation of the significance of the doctrine of *enhypostasia*: by means of the assumption of human nature, that nature becomes the nature of the Son, making Christ truly a man.

> The nature he assumed could no otherwise become his. For if he had by any ways or means taken the person of a man to be united unto him, in the strictest union that two persons are capable of, a divine and a human, the nature had still been the nature of that other person, and not his own.... But he took it to be his own nature; which it could no ways be but by personal union causing it to subsist in his own person. And he is therefore a true and perfect man: for no more is required to make a complete and perfect man but the entire nature of man subsisting; and this is in Christ as a man, the human nature having a subsistence communicated unto it by the Son of God. (20:461; cf. Goodwin 1863, 5:50-55)

Owen emphasizes that Christ "took to himself the *nature of all men*, and not the *person* of any man." One consequence of this, along with making the human nature truly his, is that it is not subject to the "infirmities and weaknesses following that nature, as existing in our sinful persons" (20:445).

Hebrews 2:16 asserts further that the nature of *angels* was not taken. The reason given for this assumption of human nature, as opposed to angelic, is the "sovereign grace, pleasure, and love of God" (20:462). Owen says, "For a *sinning nature* to be saved, it was indispensably necessary that it should be assumed." In a manner reminiscent of Irenaeus, he adds, "we were carrying away all human nature into endless destruction; for so it is intimated: whence Christ's assumption of it is expressed by his putting forth his hand and taking hold of it, to stop it in its course of apostasy and ruin" (20:462). When we compare "our own vileness and low condition" to the greater dignity of angelic nature, "we may have matter of eternal admiration suggested to us" (20:462).

The Resulting Union of the Two Natures
While it often appears that Owen is using "hypostatic union" as a synonym for the incarnation, this is not the case, as the following explanation of the distinction between assumption and hypostatic union shows.

> This *assumption* and the *hypostatical union* are distinct and different in the formal reason of them. (1.) *Assumption* is the *immediate* act of the divine nature in the person of the Son on the human; *union* is *mediate*, by virtue of that assumption. (2.) *Assumption* is unto personality; it is that act whereby the Son of God and our nature become one person. *Union* is an act or relation of the natures subsisting in that one person. (3.) *Assumption* respects the *acting* of the divine and the *passion* of the human nature; the one *assumeth*, the other is *assumed*. *Union* respects the *mutual relation* of the natures unto each other. Hence the divine nature may be said to be united unto the human, as well as the human unto the divine; but the divine nature cannot be said to be assumed as the human is. Wherefore *assumption* denotes the acting of the one nature and the passion of the other *union*, the mutual relation that is between them both. (1:225-26)

The hypostatic union is an effect of the *gratia unionis*. This term does not refer to the grace which dwells in the person of Christ by virtue of union with the Godhead, but to the grace shown toward and bestowed upon the man Christ Jesus in the "predestinating, designing, and taking him into actual union with the person of the Son, without respect unto, or foresight of, any precedent dignity or merit in him, 1 Pet. i. 20" (1:227). As per Augustine (*On the Predestination of the Saints*, chap. 30), even the man Christ Jesus was elect according to free grace, and not because of the merit of that obedience which would flow from the union with the divine nature. The term also expresses "the peculiar dignity of the human nature of Christ," unique among all created being. "This is the fundamental privilege of the human nature of Christ, which all others, even unto his eternal glory, proceed from, and are resolved into." It also expresses,

> the *glorious meetness* and ability of the person of Christ, for and unto all the acts and duties of his mediatory office. For they are all resolved into the union of his natures in the same person, without which not one of them could be performed unto the benefit of the church. And this is that "grace of our Lord Jesus Christ," which renders him so glorious and amiable unto believers. Unto them "that believe he is precious." (1:228)

A Unique Union

The hypostatic union is unique. "There is no other union in things divine or human, in things spiritual or natural, whether substantial or accidental, that is of the same kind with it;—it differs specifically from them all" (1:228).

It is not the same as the union of the divine persons of the Trinity because, as Owen explains,

> that is of *many distinct persons* in the same nature;— this is of *distinct natures* in the same person. That union is *natural*, substantial, essential, in the same nature; this, as it is not accidental,... so it is not properly substantial, because it is not of the same nature, but of diverse in the same person, remaining dis-

tinct in their essence and substance, and is therefore peculiarly hypostatical or personal. (1:228)

In this respect he approves of Augustine's dictum, "The man is more in the Son of God, than the Son is in the Father" (*De Trinitate*, Book I, chap. 10), i.e., that the man is one person with the Son, while the Son is not one person with the Father. "In all other respects it must be granted that the in-being of the Son in the Father—the union between them, which is natural, essential, and eternal—doth exceed this in glory, which was a temporary, external act of divine wisdom and grace" (1:228).

It also differs from the union of soul and body. Though there are some "similitude between this union and that of the different natures in the person of Christ," they are not of the same nature, and "the dissimilitudes . . . are more, and of greater importance." Human nature is the union of soul and body, and neither by itself constitutes human nature. "But the union of the natures in the person of Christ doth not constitute a new nature, that either was not or was not complete before. Each nature remains the same complete nature after this union" (1:229).

Next, Owen explains the in-personal subsistence of the humanity:

> The union of the soul and body doth constitute that nature which is made essentially complete thereby,—*a new individual person*, with a subsistence of its own, which neither of them was not had before that union. But although the person of Christ, as God and man, be constituted by this union, yet his person absolutely, and his individual subsistence, was perfect absolutely antecedent unto that union. He did not become a new person, another person than he was before, by virtue of that union; only that person assumed human nature to itself to be its own, into personal subsistence. *3dly.* Soul and body are united *by an external efficient cause*, or the

power of God, and not by the act of one of them upon another. But this union is effected by that act of the divine nature towards the human which we have before described. *4thly*, Neither soul nor body have any personal subsistence before their union; but the sole foundation of this union was in this, that the Son of God was a self-subsisting person from eternity. (1:229)

Owen contrasts this union with other "natural" unions produced by mixtures, and with unions consisting of the conversion of one substance with another, such as the Eutychian and Arian heresies. He also dismisses the old illustration of the fire and iron in the one sword as a "weak and imperfect representation of this mystery, on many accounts" (1:230).

However, while the illustration of fire and iron in the one sword fails to win Owen's approval, he uses the type of the burning bush to illustrate the indwelling of the divine with the human nature of Christ. This is an illustration of "mutual in-dwelling" however, and not an explanation of how the two natures are united in the one person. He says,

> This fire was a type or declaration of the presence of God in the person of the Son. For with respect unto the Father he is called an Angel, the Angel of the covenant; but absolutely in himself, he was Jehovah, the "God of Abraham," &c. And of his presence the fire was a proper representation. For in his nature he is a "consuming fire" and his present work was the delivery of the church out of a fiery trial. This fire placed itself in a bush, where it burned; but the bush was not consumed. And although the continuance of the fire in the bush was but for a short season, a present appearance, yet thence was God said to dwell in the bush: 'The good-will of him that dwelt in the bush,' Deut. xxxiii. 16. And this is so spoken, because the being of the fire in the bush for

> a season was a type of him in whom "the fullness of the Godhead dwelt bodily," and that for ever, Col. ii. 9,—of him who was "made flesh, and dwelt among us," John i. 14. The eternal fire of the divine nature dwells in the bush of our frail nature, yet is it not consumed thereby. God thus dwells in this bush, with all his good-will towards sinners. (1:311)

(In other contexts Owen will apply the theophany of the burning bush to Christ's dwelling in and preserving his mystical body, the church [8:89-90; 24:310]. It is perfectly consistent for him to make this application, given his doctrine of the headship of Christ.) He continues:

> Moses looked on this sight as a marvelous and wondrous thing. And if it were true in the type, what is it in the truth, substance, and reality of it?
>
> And by direction given unto him to 'put off his shoes,' we are taught to cast away all fleshly imaginations and carnal affections, that by pure acts of faith we may behold this glory,—the glory of the only begotten of the Father. (1:311-12)

Of particular concern is the comparison with the spiritual union of Christ and believers, since this suggests the error of Nestorius.[3] According to its seventeenth-century proponents,

> The eternal Word was so united unto the man Christ Jesus, as that thereby he was exalted inconceivably above all other men, though ever so holy, and had greater communications from God than any of them. Wherefore he was on many accounts the Son of God in a peculiar manner; and by a communication of names is called God also. (1:230)

Owen identifies five ways in which Nestorius thought of the divine presence in Christ. First, "*by inhabitation*, as a man dwells in a house or a ship to rule it." Although this is true with respect to the presence of the

"God Was Manifest in the Flesh"

Holy Spirit, who dwells in Christ and in believers, in different degrees,

> this answers not that divine testimony, that in him dwelt "all the fullness of the Godhead bodily," Co. ii. 9. The fullness of the Godhead is the entire divine nature. This nature is considered in the person of the Son, or eternal Word; for it was the Word that was made flesh. And this could no otherwise dwell in him bodily, really, *substantially*, but in the assumption of that nature to be his own. (1:231)

At first sight Owen's conclusion may not seem necessary; upon further reflection it is difficult to escape the force of his logic. Of no believer, no matter how sanctified, nor of any heavenly creature for that matter, could it be said that the entire divine nature dwells in him bodily. However, the infinite person who takes to himself human nature to be his own proper nature, may indeed be said to "dwell in" that nature; nor is it necessary that his infinity should be thereby diminished. Second, Owen says Nestorius allowed a presence of the deity "by such a *union of affections* as is between intimate friends." Again, this is true as far as it goes, but the scriptural allusions to the love between God and Christ have in mind the mutual delight between the Father and the Son, "with reference unto the work that he was sent of the Father to accomplish, and his own delight therein" (1:231). Third, Nestorius supposed that divine honor and dignity should be given to the manhood of Christ, as well as the deity, "without a supposition of the subsistence of his human nature in the person of the Son of God"; Owen says he was introducing idolatry into the church (1:231). Fourth, Nestorius identified this union as one of *"consent and agreement*...between the will of God and the will of the man Christ Jesus,"* to which Owen responds that there is a perfect unity of will between God and the angels in heaven, but it is not said that God took on the nature of angels (1:232). Finally, Nestorius affirmed a union "by an *equivocal denomination*, the name of the one person, namely, of the Son of God, being accommodated unto the other, namely, the Son of man," to which Owen replies: "But this no way answers any one divine testimony wherein the name of God is assigned unto the Lord Christ... wherein no homonymy or equivocation can take place" (1:232). Owen's principal objection to all of these is that they, contrary to Scripture, "constituted a separable accidental union, wherein nothing in kind, but in degree only, was peculiar unto the man Christ Jesus" (1:232). This is the Christology of Owen's opponents, a "spirit-Christology" of the seventeenth century.[4] To the extent that these expressions of union are true, they are so only by virtue of the communication of the two natures in one person.

Two scriptural descriptions of this union are to be found in the Epistle to the Hebrews. In Hebrews 2:11-13, we find the Son of God as having been made "ἐξ ἑνός," ("of one") with man. Commenting upon the phrase as it appears in Acts 14:26 ("ἐξ ἑνός αἵματοσ," or "of one blood"), Owen explains that the word denotes one common nature, or the same human nature, the same mass of human nature. "Being made 'of one blood' gives humankind a common brotherhood among themselves." In Hebrews 2, the author speaks of Christ becoming of one nature with them in order he and they might become one. This was in order that Christ might be "meet to suffer for them," bringing them into "a capacity of enjoying the benefit of his sufferings" (20:418). Owen illustrates this from the second chapter of Leviticus: "For as in an offering made unto the Lord of the firstfruits, of meat or of meal, a parcel of the same nature with the whole was taken and offered, whereby the whole was sanctified,... so the Lord Jesus Christ being taken as the first-fruits of the nature of the children, and offered unto God, the

"God Was Manifest in the Flesh" 283

whole lump, or the whole nature of man in the children,—that is, all the elect,—is separated unto God, and effectually sanctified in their season" (20:419). To this Owen adds, that Christ's

> participation of their nature was that which brought him into such a condition as wherein it was needful for him to put his trust in God, and to look for deliverance from him in a time of danger; so being the principal head and firstfruits of our nature, and therein the author and finisher of our salvation, he is a father unto us, and we are his children: which the apostle proveth by his last testimony from Isa. viii., "Behold I and the children which the Lord hath given unto me." And further upon the close of these testimonies, the apostle assumes again his proposition, and asserts it unto the same purpose, verse 14, showing in what sense he and the children were of one, namely, in their mutual participation of "flesh and blood." (20:419)

Thus the apostle shows that it was necessary "on the part of God, intending to bring many sons unto glory, to constitute such a union between them and the captain of their salvation as that it might be just for him to suffer in their stead" (20:437).

Next, Owen says, the apostle shows what that nature is in which they partake of union. He describes the state and condition of the children thus: Naturally, they are all common partakers of "flesh and blood." Morally, they are under the penalty of death, and therefore in fear of it, they are subject to bondage." The captain of their salvation is said to do two things for the children directed at meeting the needs arising from their state and condition: he partakes of the same nature, and he delivers them from their condition by means of his incarnation and death (20:438-41). Owen's exposition of the "Captain of Salvation" encapsulates much of his Christology: the motive of the incarnation, the covenant, the attributes the Messiah, his manner of leading his people, his various works of salvation for them and, of course, the use we are to make of this doctrine (20:378-95; also 3:384).

The Two Natures and the One Divine Person
With respect to the "communication of attributes" (*communicatio idiomatum*) Owen says there is "a threefold *communication* of the divine nature unto the human." The first is the immediate communication of the divine nature in the person of the Son which he identifies as "subsistence." In itself the human nature has no

> subsistence of its own, which should give it individuation and distinction from the same nature in any other person. But it hath its subsistence in the person of the Son, which thereby is its own. The divine nature, as in that person, is its *suppositum*. (1:233)[5]

Second, "By the Holy Spirit he filled that [human] nature with an all-fullness of habitual grace." Third, "In all the acts of his office, by the divine nature, he communicated worth and dignity unto what was acted in and by the human nature." From these ideas arise certain principles which "the Scripture, reason, and the ancient church do all concur in," and which, as we find repeatedly in Owen's works, are very important for a true understanding and esteem of the work of God in our redemption.

First, Owen stresses, "*Each nature* doth preserve its own natural, essential properties, entirely unto and in itself; without mixture, without composition or confusion, without such a real communication of the one unto the other, as that the one should become the subject of the properties of the other." Second, "*Each nature operates in him according unto its essential properties.…* the one nature being his no less than the other." Third, as a consequence of this,

> *The perfect, complete work of Christ, in every act of his*

mediatory office,—in all that he did as King, Priest, and Prophet of the church,—in all that he did and suffered,—in all that he continueth to do for us, in or by virtue of whether nature soever it be done or wrought,—is not to be considered as the act of this or that nature in him alone, but it is the act and work of the whole person,—of him that is both God and man in one person. (1:234)

Consequent "Predications Concerning the Person of Christ"
The hypostatic union of the two natures in Christ gives rise to four crucial principles for understanding Scripture statements concerning him. First, "Some things are spoken of the person of Christ, wherein the enunciation is verified with respect *unto one nature only*" (1:234). Second, "Sometimes that is spoken of the person which belongs not distinctly and originally unto either nature, but doth belong unto him on account of their *union* in him,—which are the most direct enunciations concerning the person of Christ" (1:234-35). It is significant that Owen affirms that these are the "most direct enunciations" of the person of Christ, for it demonstrates and justifies his emphasis upon the relation of the incarnation to the mediatorial work of Christ: "So is he said to be the Head, the King, Priest, and Prophet of the church; all which offices he bears, and performs the acts of them, not on the singular account of this or that nature, but of the *hypostatical union* of them both" (1:235). Third, "Sometimes his person being denominated from *one nature*, the properties and acts of the other are assigned unto it. So they 'crucified the Lord of glory'" (1:235). Finally, "Sometimes the person being denominated from one nature, that is ascribed unto it which is common unto both; or else being denominated from both, that which is proper unto only one is ascribed unto him" (1:235). This obscure statement is clarified by his example of Romans 9:5, where

Christ is said to be descended from human ancestors but identified as "God over all, blessed forever."

These are very simply mentioned in *Christologia* because, as Owen indicates, they are ancient principles which have been handled at length by others. However, as one reads Owen's Christology it is clear that these are his own cardinal principles, devoutly employed in the exposition and vindication of the doctrine of Christ, as illustrated in what follows.

Characteristics of The Human Nature of Christ

The human nature of Christ, or more accurately, Christ according to his human nature, receives considerable attention from Owen.

Freedom from Sin

"The purity of the snow is not to be compared with this lily, of this rose of Sharon, even from the womb" (2:64). To Owen this is more remarkable than the purity of Adam and the angels because, unlike them, "Jesus Christ is a plant and root out of dry ground, a blossom from the stem of Jesse, a bud from the loins of sinful man." (This was true of his humanity regardless of his virgin birth.) "That the human nature of Christ should be derived" from the corrupt flesh of fallen humanity, "free from guilt, free from pollution, this is to be adored" (2:64).

This comment naturally raises the question of how Christ could have avoided the guilt and pollution of original sin. Of this guilt and pollution, Owen says, Christ was "most free," because of the relationship he bore to Adam, and because of the work of the Holy Spirit. Christ, he says, "was *never federally in Adam*, and so not liable to the imputation of sin on that account." The sin which was imputed to him was not imputed to him on account of the covenant of *Adam*, resulting in that "*legal imputation*" of his transgression to those who are in Adam, having

Adam as their federal head; rather, sin was imputed to him "in the covenant of the Mediator, through his voluntary susception." Owen explains this in terms of the order of the decrees (cf. 19:30-37):

> Had Adam stood in his innocency, Christ had not been incarnate, to have been a mediator for sinners; and therefore the counsel of his incarnation, morally, took not place until after the fall. Though he was in Adam in a natural sense from his first creation, in respect of the purpose of God, Luke iii. 23, 38, yet he was not in him in a law sense until after the fall: so that, as to his own person, he had no more to do with the first sin of Adam, than with any personal sin of [any] one whose punishment he voluntarily took upon him; as we are not liable to the guilt of those progenitors who followed Adam, though naturally we were no less in them than in him. Therefore did he, all the days of his flesh, serve God in a covenant of works; and was therein accepted with him, having done nothing that should disannul the virtue of that covenant as to him. This doth not, then, in the least take off from his perfection. (2:65; 3:168)

Freedom from the Pollution of Sin
Along with freedom from the guilt of sin, Christ was free from its pollution:

> For the *pollution of our nature*, it was prevented in him from the instant of conception, Luke i. 35,...He was 'made of a woman,' Gal. iv. 4; but that portion whereof he was made was sanctified by the Holy Ghost, that what was born thereof should be a holy thing. Not only the conjunction and union of the soul and body, whereby a man becomes a partaker of his whole nature, and therein of the pollution of sin, being a son of Adam, was prevented [preceded] by the sanctification of the Holy Ghost, but it also

accompanied the *very separation of his bodily substance* in the womb unto that sacred purpose whereunto it was set apart: so that upon all accounts he is 'holy, harmless, undefiled.' (2:65)

Fullness of Grace
By the Holy Spirit, Christ was "endowed with all grace"; he had every kind of grace, and "all degrees of grace for its perfection" (3:168). This variety and degree of grace,

> make up that fullness that was in him. It is created grace that I intend; and therefore I speak of the kinds of it: it is grace inherent in a created nature, not infinite; and therefore I speak of the degrees of it. (2:66)

In his sermons on Psalm 45 describing "The Excellency of Christ," Owen describes how Christ is "fairer than the children of men." The dignity of Christ's person consists in the glory of the divine nature and the "immeasurable, unspeakable *fullness of grace* that was given to his human nature." The latter is represented in Psalm 45:2. Owen distinguishes "inherent grace and holiness, or the graces of the Spirit," from external grace which is favor and love. It is the first which poured into the lips of the king:

> It is what I have as much thought of as any one thing, concerning the immeasurable fullness of grace which is in the human nature of Christ. So saith the apostle, John iii. 34, "God gave not the Spirit by measure unto him." How by measure? "To every one of us is given grace according to the measure of the gift of Christ," Eph. iv. 7. *We* have every one of us a *measure*; but it is given to him without a measure. There is an immeasurable fullness of grace in the human nature of Christ, which we are partakers of; "for of his fullness we all receive, and grace for grace." It is an infinity in the divine nature, transferred into the human nature of Christ, and through

him communicated unto our souls. From the eternal fountain of the divine nature, through the human nature of Christ, which hath an immeasurable fullness, as the head of the church, it is, I say, transfused to all his members. In this he is "fairer than the children of men." (9:480)

It is also this grace which Owen calls "the endowment that renders the human nature of Christ so exceedingly desirable and glorious."[6] Owen goes so far as to say that "the glory of Jesus Christ consists in grace." This is so for several reasons. First, "Because in this internal grace consists *the reparation of the image of God*." Though created in the image of God, "we left this image, and became as like the devil as if we had been begotten by him." Grace, specifically the grace poured into the human nature of Christ and flowing from the head to the members, "doth repair and renew this image of God" (9:483).

> It is grace that makes a representation of God unto us; and therefore doth Christ's glory consist in grace.... "We behold the glory of God in the face of Jesus Christ." How is that? Why, in that abounding grace that was in Christ there is made such a representation of God, that there we may see his likeness. It is the human nature of Christ that makes the great representation of God, because he hath all that which is the image and likeness of God—namely, grace in the fullness of it—in him. (9:483)

In a later chapter we will observe the impact of this representation of the glory of God in the face of Christ Jesus. It is necessary to point out here, however, the clear emphasis placed upon the human nature as the medium of this representation.

Furthermore, this grace *inclines the heart* of Christ unto all that goodness and kindness that he hath showed unto us. Whence was it that Jesus Christ loved us so as to lay down his life for us? Whence does he continue to have compassion on us, even when we were ignorant, and wandered out of the way? It is from that abounding, unspeakable, heavenly love that was in his heart and soul, that inclined him to it.... There was that abundance in Christ that inclined him to do all this good for us,—to live, to die, to intercede for us. (9:483)

This grace with which Christ is filled makes him the great "example and pattern" for the believer (9:483).

The Incarnate Deity

As might be expected, Owen's declarations of the deity of Christ are richly accompanied with applications for the spiritual life of the reader. Owen's comments concerning the "endless, bottomless, boundless grace and compassion" of "our husband, as he is the God of Zion," are worth quoting in full, both as an illustration of this point, and an example of his rhetoric not always seen in more polemical treatises:

It is not the grace of a *creature*, nor all the grace that can possibly at once dwell in a created nature, that will serve our turn. We are too indigent to be suited with such a supply. There was a fullness of grace in the human nature of Christ,—he received not "the Spirit by measure," John iii. 34; a fullness like that of light in the sun, or of water in the sea (I speak not in respect of communication, but sufficiency); a fullness incomparably *above the measure of angels:* yet it was not properly an infinite fullness,—it was a created, and therefore a limited fullness. If it could be conceived as separated from the Deity, surely so many thirsty, guilty souls, as every day drink deep and large draughts of grace and mercy from him would (if I may so speak) sink him to the very bottom; nay, it could afford no supply at all, but only in a moral way. But when the conduit of his humanity is inseparably united to the infinite, inexhaustible fountain of the Deity, who can look into the depths thereof? If, now, there be grace enough for sinners in an all-sufficient God, it is in Christ; and, indeed, in any other there cannot be enough....

And on this ground it is that if all the world should ...set themselves to drink free grace, mercy, and pardon, drawing water continually from the wells of salvation;...they would not be able to sink the grace of the promise one hair's breadth. There is enough for millions of worlds, if they were; because it flows into it from an infinite, bottomless fountain. (2:61-62)

Similarly, Christ's love is eternal, free, unchangeable, and fruitful because of his divine nature:

The love of Christ in his human nature towards his is exceeding, intense, tender, precious, compassionate, abundantly heightened by a sense of our miseries, feeling of our wants, experience of our temptations; all flowing from that rich stock of grace, pity, and compassion, which, on purpose of our good and supply, was bestowed on him: but yet this love, as such, cannot be infinite nor eternal, nor from itself absolutely unchangeable. Were it no more, though not to be paralleled nor fathomed, yet our Saviour could not say of it, as he doth, "As the Father hath loved me, so have I loved you," John xv. 9. His love could not be compared with and equalled unto the divine love of the Father, in those properties of eternity, fruitfulness, and unchangeableness, which are the chief anchors of the soul, rolling itself on the bosom of Christ. (2:62)

Though not exclusively so (as observed above), the dignity of Christ's person which makes him "fairer than the children of men," (Ps. 45:2), consists in the glory of his divine nature.

"The Life Was Manifested, And We Have Seen It"

It should not be surprising if Owen fails to provide a view of the earthly life of Christ which appeals to the critic who demands that Christology must begin "from below" as this is not Owen's perspective. He would no doubt view such a requirement as a carnal preoccupation with knowing Christ "after the flesh," rather than "after the Spirit" (2 Cor. 5:16, NIV reads "from a worldly point of view"). Nevertheless, Owen shows a great interest in Christ's earthly life. His interests are summarized in his comments upon the way the life of Christ enforces the necessity for a life of holiness in the believer:

> The Lord Christ, coming into the world as the mediator between God and man, wrought and accomplished a mighty work amongst us; and what he did may be referred to three heads:— 1. The *life* which he *led*. 2. The *doctrine* which he *taught*; and, 3. The *death* which he *underwent*. Concerning all these, there ever was a great contest in the world, and it is yet continued. (3:648)

After mentioning the slanderous opposition rendered by ancient pagans and Jews, the practical opposition of "carnal gospellers, and all idolatrous, superstitious worshippers," who deny their profession by their lives, and those "of late risen amongst us...who esteem all that is spoken concerning him to be a mere fable," Owen asserts,

> In opposition hereunto, the Lord Christ calls all his true disciples to bear witness and testimony unto the holiness of his life, the wisdom and purity of his doctrine, the efficacy of his death to expiate sin,... with the power of his whole mediation to renew the image of God in us, to restore us unto his favour, and to bring us unto the enjoyment of him. This he calls all his disciples to avow unto and express in the world; and by their so doing is he glorified (and no otherwise) in a peculiar manner. (3:648-49)

With regard to Owen's general approach to Christ's earthly life the following should be kept in mind. First, Owen emphasizes the importance of Christ's life as an example. This is perfectly consistent with his emphasis on the imputation of Christ's obedience to us, and his alarm at Socinian and Latitudinarian moralizing. Except for the obedience which was uniquely required of Christ as the mediator of the covenant, the life Christ lived for us was the life of obedience which was due to God by us. As the perfect and archetypal man, Christ provided an example of what was due to God from all men. Owen stresses Christ's example as a major reason for the necessity of a holy life:

> We are obliged to profess that the *life of Christ* is our example. This, in the first place, are we called unto, and every Christian doth virtually make that profession. No man takes that holy name upon him, but the first thing he signifies thereby is, that he makes the life of Christ his pattern, which it is his duty to express in his own; and he who takes up Christianity on any other terms doth woefully deceive his own soul.... How may we bear testimony unto the holiness of his life against the blasphemies of the world and the unbelief of the most, who have no regard thereunto? Can this be any otherwise done but by holiness of heart and life, by conformity to God in our souls, and living unto God in fruitful obedience? Can men devise a more effectual expedient to cast reproach upon him than to live in sin, to follow divers lusts and pleasures, to prefer the world and present things before eternity, and, in the meantime, to profess that the life of Christ is their example, as all unholy professors and Christians do? Is not this to bear witness with the world against him, that indeed his life was unholy? Surely it is high time for such persons to leave the name of Christians or the life of sin. It is, therefore, in conformity alone to him, in the holiness we are pressing after, that we can give him any glory on account of his life being our example. (3:649)

Second, the life of Christ, when viewed through the eye of faith, manifests fully the doctrine of the person of Christ revealed in the Scriptures. The true "historical Jesus"—that is, the one who actually lived and walked the roads of Galilee—is, for Owen, the Christ of faith. This is not because Owen lived in a pre-critical period but because he understood the Scriptures as teaching that even Christ's contemporaries did not know him, except for those who like John and Peter were enabled by the Spirit to "behold his glory," and were inwardly taught that he was "the Christ, the son of the living God."

Thirdly, one's interest in the life of Christ is not solely to be determined by the number of commentaries one has written on the four gospels, as Knappen implies (1939, 376). It is true, Owen does not preach many sermons based upon texts from the four gospels;[7] however, he makes some reference to most of the gospel pericopes. When the occasion came to illustrate or to prove a point by a reference to the gospels, the reference usually seems to appear naturally, as if the event is familiar and its significance perceived through study and meditation.

The Work of the Holy Spirit in the Life of Christ

Interestingly, the greatest information available on Owen's view of the earthly life of Christ comes from his treatise on the Holy Spirit. The work of the Holy Spirit in the life of Christ receives considerable attention from Owen, because 1) the Holy Spirit is given to assist Jesus Christ in his role as the mediator of the covenant, and 2) because Christ is the archetype and fountain of the work of the Holy Spirit for the new humanity.

In the life of Christ the Holy Spirit "carried on that work whose foundation he had laid" in the creation and sanctification of Christ's human nature in the womb of the virgin.[8] Consequently, from beginning to end, the life of Christ will manifest true human life together with the powerful influence of the Holy Spirit and Christ's dependence upon the Spirit. This is particularly true of the Savior's ministry. Owen first emphasizes that, as a man,

> Christ exercised all grace by the rational faculties and powers of his soul, his understanding, will, and affections; for he acted grace as a man, "made of a woman, made under the law."... Being a perfect man, his rational soul was in him the immediate principle of all his moral operations even as ours are in us. (3:169)

Growth in Wisdom and Knowledge
Consequently, as indicated in Luke 2:40, Christ grew in wisdom and knowledge.

> Now, in the improvement and exercise of these faculties and powers of his soul, he had and made a progress after the manner of other men.... In their increase, enlargement, and exercise, there was required a progression in grace also; and this he had continually by the Holy Ghost.... As the faculties of his mind were enlarged by degrees and strengthened, so the Holy Spirit filled them up with grace for actual obedience. (3:169)

Owen observes that "The human nature of Christ was capable of having new objects proposed to its mind and understanding, whereof before it had a simple *nescience.*" This, Owen emphasized, is "an inseparable adjunct of human nature as such." Therefore, the human soul of Christ was not omniscient. Against the accusation that any ignorance in Christ's human nature would have constituted him morally deficient, Owen answers that this would only be the case if he were ignorant of that which he "ought to know," and insists that in this nature is "nothing inconsistent with the highest holiness and purity of nature" (3:170). "In the representation, then, of things anew to the human nature of Christ, the wisdom and knowledge of it was *objectively increased*, and in new trials and temptations he *experimentally* learned the new exercise of grace" (3:170).

This experimental learning of the exercise of grace is Owen's way of expressing what took place as Jesus "learned obedience by the things that he suffered" (Heb. 5:8). This passage raises three questions for Owen concerning this obedience: 1) its nature, 2) what is meant by his having "learned" it, and 3) "by what *means* he did so." This "obedience," he explains, means "'an obediential compliance with the commands of another,' when we hear, and thereby know them" (21:523). With this in mind, Owen first describes the obedience which marked the general course of Christ's life, noting that "every thing he did was not only *materially holy*, but *formally obediential*." That is, they were not only holy because good, but obediential because done out of regard for the commands of another. The obedience referred to in the text, however, is Christ's "peculiar obedience…in dying, and in all things that tended immediately thereunto" (21:523).

Secondly, Christ is said to have "learned *obedience*"; which Owen distinguishes from learning "to obey," and describes as having a "three-fold sense." We learn obedience *materially* when we learn our duty. We learn it *formally* when we are "guided, instructed, directed, helped, in the acts and acting of the obedience required." Owen denies that Christ learned obedience in either of these senses since he had a perfect comprehension of the duty he had undertaken and because "he had a fullness of grace always in him and with him, inclining, directing, guiding, and enabling him unto all acts of obedience that were required of him. Being always full of grace, truth, and wisdom, he was never at a loss for what he had to do, nor wanted any thing of a perfect readiness of mind for its performance" (21:523).

While the second of these denials seems reasonable, given the fullness of grace in Christ's human nature, it seems Owen's denial that Christ materially learned obedience is inconsistent with what he had said earlier. Why might Christ's duty not be among the things represented anew to his human nature? Though he could have avoided inconsistency here (cf. Murray, 1977, 151-57), his remarks seem to be due to a concern to focus upon the person of the mediator—not directing his attention to what the human nature of Christ learned *per se*, but upon the obedience of the mediator—who with a full comprehension of the duty lying upon him entered into it; and who, having accomplished that duty has, in that human nature, obtained that which he did not have before, but will ever have afterwards: a feeling of what it is to suffer in obedience. This is the third sense Owen gives for what it is to learn obedience:

> an experience of it in its exercise.... And it was one especial kind of obedience that is here intended, as was declared before, namely, a submission to undergo great, hard, and terrible things, accompanied with patience and quiet endurance under them, and faith for deliverance from them. This he could have no experience of, but by suffering the things he was to undergo, and the exercise of the graces mentioned therein. Thus learned he obedience, or experienced in himself what difficulty it is attended withal, especially in cases like his own. (21:524)

The means of learning obedience were "through the things that he suffered" (Heb. 5:8; 21:525). To learn from the things we experience it is required that they "are improved unto a good end." This Christ did through "the exercise of those graces of humility, self-denial, meekness, patience, faith, which were habitually resident in his holy nature, but were not capable of the peculiar exercise intended but by reason of his sufferings." To this Owen adds that "there was somewhat peculiar in that obedience which the Son of God is said to learn from his own sufferings, namely, what it is for a *sinless person* to suffer for sinners, "the just for the unjust" (21:525).

Gifts of the Spirit
"The Holy Spirit, in a peculiar manner, anointed him with all those *extraordinary powers and gifts* which were necessary for the exercise and discharge of his office on earth" (3:171). These gifts, according to Isaiah 61:1, were intended for the exercise of his *prophetic office*, "the office which he principally attended unto here in the world, as that whereby he instructed men in the nature and use of his other offices" (3:171). Owen distinguishes the "Spirit that was upon him" from his incarnation, from "his being 'anointed to preach' which contains the communication of the gifts of that Spirit unto him" (3:171-72). The "collation" of these gifts took place at his baptism, as is evident from the "visible pledge" made by the appearance of the Holy Spirit as a dove, from the fact that he now "wholly *gave himself up* unto his work, and from the explicit scriptural description of him as "full of the Holy Ghost" (3:171-74; cf. Goodwin, 1863, 6:11-12).

Christ's Baptism
In addition to what has already been mentioned, Owen makes few comments concerning the baptism of Christ, beyond stating that it was part of his mediatorial obedience. For example,

> He was to observe all ordinances and institutions of the worship of God, not for any need he had in his own person of the especial ends and significations of some of them; yet as he was our sponsor, surety, and mediator, standing in our stead in all that he so did, he was to yield obedience unto them, that so he might "fulfill all righteousness," Matt. iii. 15. So was he circumcised, so was he baptized, both which had respect unto sin, though absolutely free from all sin

in his own person; and that because he was free from no obedience unto any command of God. (6:465)

His remarks upon the Holy Spirit's descent in the form of a dove are suggested to him by Severinus' Syrian ritual of baptism. Owen says,

> in the assumption of this form there may be some respect unto the dove that brought tidings to Noah of the ceasing of the flood of waters, and of the ending of the wrath of God, who thereon said that he would curse the earth no more, Gen. viii. 11, 21, for herein also was there a significant representation of him who visited poor, lost mankind in their cursed condition, and proclaimed peace unto them that would return to God by him, the great peace-maker, Eph. ii. 14-17. And this work he immediately engaged into on the resting of this dove upon him. (3:75-76; cf. Ambrose 1855, 230-34)

The Miracles of Christ

Owen says, "It was in an especial manner by the power of the Holy Spirit he wrought those great and *miraculous works* whereby his ministry was attested and confirmed" (3:174). Commenting on Luke 11:20, Owen says when Christ performed miracles it was by the "finger of God" which is the

> infinite divine power of God. But the power of God acted in an especial manner by the Holy Spirit, as is expressly declared in the other evangelist, Matt. xii. 28; and, therefore, on the ascription of his mighty works unto Beelzebub, the prince of devils, he lets the Jews know that therein they blasphemed the Holy Spirit, whose works indeed they were. (3:174)

Owen views this work of the Spirit as his testimony to Christ as the Son of God, "necessary unto the conviction of the Jews, to whom he was sent, John x. 37, 38" (3:174; cf. Goodwin, 6:12-13).

Guided and Comforted by the Spirit

By the Holy Spirit, Owen adds, Christ was "*guided, directed, comforted, supported*, in the whole course of his ministry, temptations, obedience, and sufferings" (3:174). To illustrate this Owen points to Christ's temptation in the wilderness where it is affirmed that the Spirit "driveth him." This *direction*, Owen says, was a "guiding and rational conduct," by the Holy Spirit, and "a high and strong impression of the Holy Spirit on his mind" (3:174-75). Christ also received *assistance* from the Spirit to make a "perfect conquest" over the devil in all of his temptations. At their conclusion Christ "returned in the power of the Spirit" (Luke 4:14), that is, he was "powerfully enabled by the Holy Spirit unto the discharge of his work." This was how Christ entered upon his ministry: "And as he thus began his ministry in the power of the Spirit, so, having received him not by measure, he continually on all occasions put forth his wisdom, power, grace, and knowledge, to the astonishment of all, and the stopping of the mouths of his adversaries, shutting them up in their rage and unbelief" (3:175).

The Temptations of Christ [9]

Christ "suffered being tempted," which is to say, he suffered in his temptations. Christ's temptations receive Owen's attention in his remarks upon Hebrews 2:17-18, where he correctly observes that "'temptations,' are things in themselves of an indifferent nature," without any moral evil in them. Rather, temptation "compriseth any thing, state, or condition whereby a man may be tried, exercised, or tempted." Christ, Owen says, suffered four general types of temptation: First, he mentions,

> His state and condition in the world. He was poor, despised, persecuted, reproached, especially from the beginning unto the end of his public ministry. Herein lay one continued temptation; that is, a trial

of his obedience by all manner of hardships....In this temptation he suffered hunger, poverty, weariness, sorrow, reproach, shame, contempt; wherewith his holy soul was deeply affected. And he underwent it cheerfully, because it was to be the condition of them whose preservation and salvation of them as their high priest he had undertaken." (20:478)

This is the point of the text, that Christ, having suffered temptation is "able to succor them that are tempted." Secondly, Owen continues,

> Whilst he was in this state and condition, innumerable particular temptations befell him, under all which he suffered: —[1.] Temptations from his relations in the flesh, being disregarded and disbelieved by them,—which deeply affected his compassionate heart with sorrow; [2.] From his followers, being forsaken by them upon his preaching the mysteries of the gospel; [3.] From his chosen disciples, all of whom left him, one denied him, and one betrayed him; [4.] From the anguish of his mother, when "a sword pierced through her soul" in his sufferings; [5.] From his enemies of all sorts;—all which are at large related in the Gospel: from all which his sufferings were inexpressible. (20:478)

Thirdly, Christ suffered in an extraordinary way by temptations from Satan:

> Satan had a principal hand in the temptations wherein he suffered. He set upon him in the entrance of his ministry, immediately in his own person, and followed him in the whole course of it by the instruments that he set on work. He had also a season, an hour of darkness, allowed unto him, when he was to try his utmost strength and policy against him; under which assault from him he suffered, as was foretold from the foundation of the world, the bruising of his heel, or the temporal ruin of all his concernments. (20:478)

Fourthly, and worst of all, he suffered God's desertion of him on the cross: "As this was most mysterious, so his sufferings under it were his greatest perplexity, Ps. xxii. 1, 2, Heb. v. 7" (20:478).

Christ *suffered* in all of these temptations: "He had the heart of a man, the affections of a man, and that in the highest degree of *sense and tenderness*. Whatever sufferings the soul of a man may be brought under, by...any afflictive passions within or impressions of force from without, he underwent, he felt it all" (20:484-85). His suffering, in fact, was not less, but greater, than that of other men. As Owen explains,

> Because he was in the favour of God, and in the assurance of the indissolubility of the union of his person, we are apt to think that what came upon him was so overbalanced by the blessedness of his relation unto God as not to cause any great trouble unto him. But we mistake when we so conceive. No sorrows were like to his, no sufferings like unto his. He fortified not himself against them but as they were merely penal; he made bare his breast unto their strokes, and laid open his soul that they might soak into the inmost parts of it, Isa. l. 6. All those reliefs and diversions of this life which we may make use of to alleviate our sorrows and sufferings he utterly abandoned. He left nothing, in the whole nature of sorrow or suffering, that he tasted not and made experience of. Indeed, in all his sufferings and temptations he was supported with the thoughts of the glory that was set before him; but our thoughts of his present glory should not divert us from the contemplation of his past real sufferings. All the advantage that he had above us by the excellency of his person, was only that the sorrows of his heart were enlarged thereby, and he was made capable of greater enduring without sin. (20:484-85)

Again, it is interesting to observe how Owen's description of the life of Christ contrasts with Eusden's remarks concerning the Puritans' neglect of the *via cruces* [way of the cross]. Consider the following remarks by Owen:

> Thus we find him at all times full of this compassion and pity towards all the sons of men, yea, the worst of his enemies, expressing itself by sighs and tears, intimating the deep compassion of his heart. And this made him as it were even forget his own miseries in his greatest distress; for when, seeing the daughters of Jerusalem mourn for him, as he was going to his cross, he minds them of that which his compassionate heart was fixed on, even their approaching misery and ruin, Luke xxiii. 28. (20:470)[10]

The Death of Christ

The central focus of our meditations for the Lord's Supper is the sufferings of Christ, which Owen divides into the sufferings of his soul, his body, and *"his person* in the dissolution of his human nature, soul and body, by death itself" (9:586). The sufferings of Christ's soul are *"Privative,*...in the desertion and dereliction of God his Father; and...*positive,* in the emission of the sense of God's wrath and the curse of the law on his soul" (9:587). In what sense was he deserted by God? Owen explains that Christ was forsaken of God *"as to all influence of comfort and all evidence* of love from God the Father (who is the fountain of love and comfort), administered by the Holy Ghost" (9:587). Regarding the supposed despondency of Christ in the garden and on the cross, Owen answers,

> In this difficult inquiry two things are to be stated:— first, in reference *to his person,* That it was impossible Christ should have the indissolubility of his personal union utterly hid from him. He knew the union of his human nature unto the Son of God could not be utterly dissolved,—that could not be utterly hid from him; so that there could not be de-

spair, properly so called, in Christ. And secondly, this is certain also, That the *contract* he had with the Father, and the promises he had given him of being successful, could never utterly be hid from him. So that his faith, either as to his person or cause, could not possibly be utterly ruined. (9:533)

By "despair, properly so called," Owen understands the "*total want of the evidence of faith* as to acceptance with God; and *a resolution in the soul to seek no farther after it*, and not to wait for it from that fountain." Such despair is sinful; Christ's was not, in that he did not cease to wait upon God (9:587).

Both positive and privative sufferings are evident in Owen's description of causes of the "severe and terrible conflict" in Christ's human nature, which was due to four things:

> First. From the view which he was exalted to take of *the nature of the curse that was then upon him*. For the curse was upon him, Gal. iii. 13,... Give me leave to say, Jesus Christ saw more into the nature of the curse of God for sin than all the damned in hell are able to see; which caused a dreadful conflict in his human soul upon that prospect.

> Secondly. It arose from hence, that *the comforting influences of the union with the divine nature were restrained*. Jesus Christ was in himself "a man of sorrows, and acquainted with grief;" but yet, all the while, there were the influences of light and glory from the divine nature to the human, by virtue of their union;—and now they are restrained, and instead of that, was horrible darkness, and trembling, and the curse, and sin, and Satan, round about him; all presenting themselves unto him: which gave occasion to that part of his prayer, Ps. xxii. 12-21, "Deliver my soul from the sword; my darling from the power of the dog. Save me from the lion's mouth," etc. There was the sword in the curse of the

law, and the dog and the lion, or Satan, as it were, gaping upon him, as if ready to devour him; for it was the hour and power of darkness, dread and terror. Besides, there were cruel men, which he compares to "the bulls of Bashan," which rent him. This caused that terrible conflict.

Thirdly. It was from the *penal desertion of God*. That he was under a penal desertion from God is plain: "My God, my God, why hast thou forsaken me?" And when I say so, I know little of what I say;—I mean, what it is to be under such penal desertion. For the great punishment of hell, is an everlasting penal desertion from God.

Fourthly. It was from the *unspeakable extremity of the things that he suffered;*—not merely as to the things themselves which outwardly fell upon his body, but as unto that "sword of God which was awakened against him," and which had pierced him to the very soul. The advantage which he had in his sufferings by his divine union, was that which supported and bore him up under that weight, which would have sunk any mere creature to nothing. His heart was enlarged to receive in those pains, that dread and terror, that otherwise he could not have received. (9:533-34)

In one of the sacramental discourses, Owen says, "I am afraid we do not consider enough" the bodily sufferings of Christ, adding, "Some poor souls are apt to consider *nothing* but the sufferings of his body; and some do not *enough* consider them" (9:588). In none of his sacramental discourses does Owen dwell as much on the bodily and mental (i.e., in addition to the ways just mentioned) sufferings of Christ as in the *Vindiciae Evangelicae* (12:485-96).

Christ truly suffered. This suffering extended to the suffering of death: Christ must "taste of death," that is, "so die as to experience the sorrows, bitterness, and penalties of death" (20:358). This "tasting" of death means he is *"really to die,"* and that "there was *bitterness* in the death he underwent." "It compriseth," continues Owen, "somewhat more than merely to die, it expresseth also to find out and experience what is in death," particularly, "death, as threatened to sinners" (20:359).

Before leaving the subject of the death of Christ, especially in view of Owen's comments concerning the "sword of God" and the "penal desertion" of Christ, it is important to observe Owen's comments upon the Father's actual attitude toward the Son as he was bearing the guilt of our sins. Against the idea that the Father must consequently "hate" Christ, Owen replies that "sin inherent renders the soul polluted, abominable, and the only object of *divine aversation*; but for him who was perfectly innocent..., to take upon him the guilt of other sins, thereby to comply with and accomplish the design of God for the manifestation of his glory and infinite wisdom, grace, goodness, mercy, and righteousness, unto the certain expiation and destruction of sin,—nothing could render him more glorious and lovely in the sight of God or man." Only if "hate" were understood as "a will of punishing...where sin is imputed," would the expression be allowable (5:203-204).

Conclusion

We have peered with Owen into the great "mystery of godliness" of the manifestation of God in flesh: a mystery, indeed, of unfathomable depths, far beyond the bounds of reverent speculation; but a mystery revealed, and, consequently, "incessantly" to be adored. The principal objects of our admiration in this mystery are 1) the wisdom and power of God displayed in the *enhypostatic* union of perfect human nature with God the Son, 2) the condescension of the Son to assume that nature, with the life that attends it in a fallen world, and 3) the wonderful manner in which Christ, as the God-man (*theanthropos*), was, and forever remains, an all-sufficient Savior for sinners.

In the next chapter we will examine Owen's exposition of another aspect of this great "mystery of godliness," Christ's reception into glory (1 Tim. 3:16).

---

[1] Arndt and Gingrich give "robbery" as the primary meaning of ἁρπάγμοσ, but then argue that this meaning is "next to impossible in Phil. 2:6...the state of being equal w. God cannot be equated w. the act of robbery." However, as it is a not un-Pauline figure of speech to express a positive by the denial of the negative, it is arguable that such is what we have here. Equality with God was Christ's true quality, with its all of its honors and privileges rightfully his. These, in becoming incarnate, he temporarily "laid aside" for the enrichment and advancement of poor sinners, thereby providing the ultimate model for denial of one's rights for another's good.

[2] Richard Sibbes elaborates: "When she assented to the word, presently Christ was conceived; her faith and her womb conceived together. When her heart did conceive the truth of the promise, and yielded assent thereunto, her womb conceived at the same time also" (1862-64, 7:110).

[3] Owen is aware that "many learned men" think Nestorius was "condemned undeservedly"; his comments are directed against the "doctrine condemned at Ephesus and Chalcedon as the doctrine of Nestorius" (1:12). His remarks here reflect the traditional view of Nestorius. For a more recent and objective analysis of Nestorius' position see Kelly 1976, 310-17. The validity of Owen's Christological concerns *as applied to the opinions of his contemporaries* is unaffected by the accuracy of his knowledge of the Nestorian struggle.

[4] In 1654, Parliament called a committee to draft a list of articles defining the fundamental doctrines of Christianity in order to establish a standard by which true Christians might be distinguished among all the sects then existing in the Commonwealth. The eleventh of the sixteen articles, worded by Owen, states, "That this same Jesus Christ being the only God and Man in One Person remains for ever a distinct Person from all saints and angels notwithstanding their union and communion with Him." The threat to Christianity which was presented in this form from Quakerism or from seventeenth-century forms of "spirit-Christology" was perceived to be so significant as to require this specific assertion in a very limited statement

of fundamentals. Bunyan's *Light for Them That Sit in Darkness* (1853, 1:393-436), addresses the incarnation as part of a more general work on the person and work of Christ, while his *Some Gospel Truths Opened* and *Vindication of Gospel Truths* (Bunyan 1853, 2:129-214) are polemical works, expounding the importance of the incarnation against the "spirit-Christology" of his day. On the incarnation see also Manton (1870, 1:476-94).

[5] A "*suppositum*" is a "self-existent or self-subsistent thing" (Muller, 1985, 291).

[6] This fullness of grace in Christ is the principal thing in which the saints have communion with him (2:47). See 2:46-78 for another extended exposition of this, drawn principally, but not exclusively, from the Song of Solomon.

[7] Thomas Manton's collected works include 170 sermons from texts in the four gospels. For other expositions of portions of Christ's life see, for example, Hutcheson's *Commentary on the Gospel of John;* Goodwin, 1863, 5:196-271. *Looking Unto Jesus*, by Isaac Ambrose, directs the reader in meditating upon Christ as his grace and character is manifested in many of the events of his earthly life (Ambrose 1855, 165-413). Also, on Christ's entire state of humiliation, his incarnation, life, and death see chapters 18-38 of Flavel's *Fountain of Life* (1820, 1:223-485).

[8] On the role of the Holy Spirit in the incarnation and earthly life of Christ, see Charnock's comments in his *Discourse of God's being the Author of Reconciliation* (1684, 289-98), and Goodwin's *The Work of the Holy Ghost in Our Salvation* (1863, 6:10-13).

[9] See Thomas Manton's sermons on *The Temptation of Christ* (1870, 1:258-336).

[10] See John Howe's, "The Redeemer's Tears Wept Over Lost Souls," (1836, 1:435-53). On the incarnation and the sufferings of Christ see also Thomas Brooks (1861-67, 5;164-218). It should be borne in mind that it is common, when expounding the death of Christ, to place it in the broader context of the full doctrine of the work of redemption, with appropriate references to the covenant of redemption, the incarnation, what was accomplished, and the use. See, for example, James Durham's seventy-two sermons on Isaiah 53, entitled *Christ Crucified, or the Marrow of the Gospel* (1723).

CHAPTER
12

"He Ascended into Heaven"

One great matter of debate between Lutheran and Reformed theologians was over the nature of Christ's exaltation. Recent studies have shown that many of the leading participants in these debates were not the "dry as dust" theologians they were reputed to have been, and that the issue was not a mere academic squabble; rather, the debate was often waged by sincere men contending for what each believed to be a vital principle of the faith (Wagner 1960, 146; Davis 1982, 130; Preus 1970, 29-30). Owen, while deploring curious and arid speculation, believed that the truth pertaining to Christ's exaltation was a crucial part of the gospel, upon which the ordinary Christian ought to exercise himself much in meditation (1:235-36).

The work to be accomplished by Christ in the exercise of his mediatorial offices was the recapitulation of all things unto the glory of God in the removal of the enmity between God and fallen mankind, and in the destruction of the enemies of God and the church.[1]

> In the gradual accomplishment of this work—according as the church of the elect is brought forth in successive generations...he is to continue unto the end and consummation of all things.... He will not cease his work whilst there is one of his elect to be

saved, or one enemy to be subdued. He shall not faint nor give over until he hath sent forth judgment unto victory. (1:236)[2]

This is the work of the exalted Christ: to continue in the exercise of his mediatorial office until he has "put down all rule and authority and power," and all his enemies are under his feet.

The Triune Nature of the Resurrection and Exaltation of Christ

As with all of God's external works, the resurrection of Christ is an act of the Triune God, with each person "equally concerned in their operation" but distinctly involved in some aspect of the work. The resurrection is attributed to the Father "on account of his authority and the declaration therein of Christ's perfect accomplishment of the work committed unto him" (3:181). In Acts 2, Peter says that God raised up Jesus, "having loosed the pains of death," which Owen explains as equivalent to the "cords" of death, or the "power it had to bind the Lord Christ for a season under it" (3:181).

> These God loosed, when, the law being fully satisfied, the sentence of it was taken off, and the Lord Christ was acquitted from its whole charge. This was the act of God the Father, as the supreme rector and judge of all. Hence he is said to "raise him from the dead," as the judge by his order delivereth an acquitted prisoner or one who hath answered the law. (3:181-82)

The Son also is said to have raised himself up (John 2:19; 10:18). Owen does not say very much about this, though he does emphasize it against Biddle's catechism where it is denied in the interest of denying Christ's deity (12:560; 3:182).

Owen ascribes a "peculiar efficacy" to the working of the Holy Spirit in the "reuniting of his most holy soul and body" (3:182). Along with Romans 8:11, which plainly asserts this, Owen appeals to Romans 1:4 ("according to the Spirit of holiness"), to demonstrate this point.[3]

The Glorification of Christ's Human Nature

Owen simplifies the doctrine of Christ's glorification somewhat by distinguishing between the two natures, commenting upon the person and peculiarly emphasizing the mediatorial offices. Of a real "addition of glory," the person of the Son as to his divine nature, is incapable of any exaltation.

> The person of Christ, as to his divine nature, was always *on the throne*, and is incapable of the exaltation here mentioned, of sitting down at the right hand of it. Although "he came down from heaven," although "he descended into the lower parts of the earth," although he was exposed unto all miseries, was "obedient unto death, the death of the cross," wherein "God redeemed his church with his own blood," yet did he all this in the human nature that he assumed. His divine person can no more really leave the throne of majesty than cease to be.... In his divine nature he was still on the throne of majesty; for this being an inseparable property of divine authority, he could never really forego it. (23:11)

The divine nature itself, Owen explains,

> is capable of no real exaltation by an *addition of glory*, but only by the way of *manifestation*. So God absolutely is often in the Scriptures said to be "exalted;"—that is, he is so when he himself, by any acts of grace or providence, makes the eternal glory of his power, his holiness, or any other property of his nature, manifest and conspicuous; or when others ascribe unto him the glory and praise that are his due. (23:11)

However, this does not prevent there being an "exaltation

or manifestation of glory peculiar and proper unto the person of Christ," that is, the person of the Son, "distinct from the persons of the Father and the Holy Spirit." If the manifestation of glory is the exaltation of God, then the person of the Son received a glorification peculiar to himself, since he alone had "cast a veil over his eternal glory, so as that it appeared not in its own native lustre.... But after his resurrection his glory was unveiled, and made conspicuous, even when he was 'declared to be the Son of God with power'" (23:11). The glory of the divine nature was eclipsed, but the eclipse being past, "it shines forth in its infinite lustre and beauty," the "infinite, uncreated glories of the divine nature, manifesting themselves in his person" (1:344).

Is there no *real* exaltation? Indeed there is: "It is the human nature of Christ, or Christ in his human nature, or with respect unto it, that is *capable of this real exaltation, by a real addition of glory*" (21:613). Notice that he maintains the emphasis upon the hypostatic union: it is not merely the human nature of Christ, but Christ in his human nature that is exalted. It is a true exaltation:

> It is not the manifestation of his glory with respect unto his human nature, but the real collation of glory on him after his ascension, that is intended. This the whole Scripture testifieth unto, namely, a real communication of glory unto Christ by the Father, after his ascension, which he had not before. (23:12)

Concerning the glory of this exaltation Owen makes the following observations. First it is not

> *absolutely infinite and essentially divine glory*. This cannot be communicated unto any. A creature, as was the human nature of Christ, cannot be made God, by an essential communication of divine properties unto it. Neither are they so communicable, nor is that a capable subject of their inhesion. (23:12)

Owen is very critical of the Lutheran doctrine of the

communicatio idiomatum. Rather than glorifying the human nature, a *communicatio* such as the Lutherans propose destroys it. "To affix unto the human nature divine properties,...is to deprive it of its own" (1:238). It is also to deprive the church of a principal article of its faith: the same body which was conceived by the Holy Ghost, which bare our sins, which lay in the grave,

> without any alteration as unto its substance, essence, or integral parts, and not another body, of an ethereal, heavenly structure, wherein is nothing of flesh, blood, or bones, by which he so frequently testified the faithfulness of God in his incarnation, is still that temple wherein God dwells, and wherein he administers in the holy place not made with hands. The body which was pierced is that which all eyes shall see, and no other. (1:238-39)

The same might be said for his "rational soul" (1:344).

Owen explains that "this exaltation and glory of Christ in his human nature is not only absolutely above, but also of another kind, than the utmost of what any other *created being* either hath, or is capable of" (23:12). By comparison to the glorification of the saints the glory of Christ's human nature is of a completely different kind. First, it has an *eternal subsistence* in the person of the Son of God. "This is, and shall be, eternally peculiar unto him, in distinction from, and exaltation above, the whole creation of God, angels and men" (1:239). The human nature naturally had this glory from the moment of conception, but "as unto the demonstration of it, 'he emptied himself.'" In other words, even the human nature possessed glory which was hidden and then manifested, in kind and in degree. Furthermore, as a result of this, "*the union of the human nature of Christ unto God*, and the communications of God unto it, are of another kind than those of the blessed saints" (1:240). By virtue of this hypostatic union, "the human nature of Christ, in his divine person and together with it, is the object of *all adoration* and worship, Rev. v. 13" (1:241). In a manner unique to him, by his human nature, the "holy glorious properties" of God are "made evident unto all the holy ones that are about the throne" (1:241).

In other respects the glorification of Christ's human nature excels that of the saints in degree. First, "the glory of his body is the example and pattern of what they shall be conformed unto," hence, his has preeminence (1:246). In his thoughts on the exaltation of Christ, Owen continues to emphasize the role of Christ as the pattern for the elect. Just as the Holy Spirit was peculiarly involved in the formation of the "head of the new creation," in a similar manner the Holy Spirit accomplishes the glorification of the great prototype of glorified saints.

> It was the Holy Spirit that *glorified*, the human nature [of Christ], and made it every way meet for its eternal residence at the right hand of God, and a pattern of the glorification of the bodies of them that believe on him. He who first made his nature *holy*, now made it *glorious*. And as we are made conformable unto him in our souls here, his image being renewed in us by the Spirit, so he is in his body, now glorified by the effectual operation of the same Spirit, the exemplar and pattern of that glory which in our mortal bodies we shall receive by the same Spirit; for "when he shall appear, we shall be like him," 1 John iii. 2, seeing he will "change our vile bodies, that they may be fashioned like unto his glorious body, according to the working whereby he is able even to subdue all things unto himself," Phil. iii. 21. (3:183)

Christ's soul, likewise, shall "appear more excellent than what we are capable of." He had the Holy Spirit "without measure" in this world, but the "inward beauty" arising from this grace was relatively hidden to men, being "veiled" on his side, and dimly observed from the "darkness which was on their minds."

> The grace that was in Christ in this world is the same with that which is in him now in heaven. The nature of it was not changed when he ceased to be *viator*, but is only brought into a more glorious exercise now he is *comprehensor*. And all his graces are now made manifest, the veil being taken from them, and light communicated to discern them. (1:246)

In all of these respects Christ has a glory which belongs to his *person*, and as his human nature since its creation eternally subsists in the person of the Son of God, this glory shall never diminish, not even at the end of his mediatorial reign. The principal subject of Owen's meditations, however, is the glory of Christ's mediatorial office.

The Mediatorial Exaltation of Christ

The primary focus of Owen's meditations upon the glory of the exalted Christ concentrates upon the glory which is his as the *mediator*.[4] The reader will remember that for Owen the covenant of redemption included the promise of exaltation. We might expect to find the doctrine developed with regard to the mediatorial *office* of Christ, and so it is. Owen explains that Christ, though always "clothed with all his offices," exercises his offices, sometimes distinctly, and sometimes together. In his exaltation, his passing "through the heavens," Christ "puts forth the power" of two of his offices "at the same time, and in the same manner, though with different respects" (21:407). "His ascension, as unto change of place, from earth to heaven, and as unto the outward manner of it, was one and the same, and at once accomplished; but as unto the end of it, which is the exercise of all his offices, it had various respects, various prefigurations, and is distinctly proposed unto us with reference unto them" (1:247). For example, Christ's ascension was *"triumphant,* as he was a *King*" ascending to his throne, and "sitting down on the right hand of the Majesty on high," and it was "*gracious*, as he was a Priest," entering "through the veil into the holy place not made with hands" (1:247; 21:407). These also show that Christ was not passive in the exaltation; it was an exercise of his official power.

"He passed through the heavens"
Owen identifies three things which set out the "greatness and glory" of Christ's ascension: his passage through the heavens, his reception into glory, and the exaltation consisting of his being seated at God's right hand.

The first of these is the "passage itself," concerning which Owen makes four observations. First, he notes Christ's "*entrance* into it, or the time and place when and where he began his triumphant entry into heaven." Commenting upon Acts 1:9-12 he says,

> It was forty days after he was alive, "after his passion." As he went forty days in the wilderness to be tempted of the devil before he entered on his ministry, so he continued forty days in the world triumphing over him after he had finished his ministry. But the chief reason hereof was, that whereas his apostles, who were to be the eye-witnesses of his resurrection, could not bear his continual presence with them, he might have opportunity to show himself unto them by "many infallible signs and tokens," Acts i. 3. (21:407)

Following a general description of the Mount of Olives, he supplies an interpretation of its significance for the ascension, together with an observation concerning the effect of the ascension on the disciples:

> This was the mountain unto which the glory of the LORD went up," when it left the temple and city of Jerusalem, Ezek. xi. 23. And so did He now who was "the brightness of his glory, and the express image

of his person." With him the glory of God utterly departed from the temple and city, or the worship and people. Here he was taken up; and his disciples were...earnestly, carefully, with love, diligence, and delight, looking on whilst these things were doing. Those who had not long before seen him hanging on the cross between two thieves, bleeding and dying, now saw him gloriously and triumphantly taken up into heaven. From their eyes a cloud received him. Elijah was taken up, before, alive into heaven,...but it was with fire and in a whirlwind, with dread and terror,...but here, when his disciples were fully instructed, and were now no longer to live by sense, but by faith, whilst they earnestly and steadily looked on him as he ascended, a cloud draws the curtain, placidly interposing between him and their sight, who were not able as yet to look on what was doing within that veil. (21:408)

Second, Owen calls this event "the time and day of *heaven's triumph*," which he explains in terms of the biblical motif of the holy war between God and his enemies. In doing so he employs the image of Christ as the Captain of Salvation.

Ever since the apostasy of angels and men by sin, there had been an enmity and war between heaven and earth, pleaded by the interest of heaven in the earth here below. God had sent forth his champion, the Captain of salvation, typed out of old by Joshua, and David, and all those worthies which were employed to vanquish the enemies of the church in their especial stations. He had now finished his work, having fully conquered the first apostate, the great enemy of God, and spoiled him of his power. And he was now entering into that glory which he had left for a season to engage in the difficult and perilous service of subduing all the adversaries of God. And now was all heaven prepared for his triumphant reception. As when a great conqueror of old returned from a far country, where he had subdued the enemies of his people and brought home the leaders of them captives, all the citizens went forth with applauses and shouts of joy to meet him,—to which custom our apostle alludeth in this matter, Col. ii. 5; so was it with the glorious inhabitants of heaven upon the return of this victorious Captain of salvation. (21:408)

The next two observations are drawn largely from Psalm 68. Commenting on verses 17 and 18, he had earlier said,

The most glorious appearance of God upon the earth, under the Old Testament, was that on Mount Sinai, in the giving of the law. And as his presence was there attended with all his glorious angels, so, when, upon the finishing of that work, he returned or ascended into heaven, it was in the way of a triumph with all that royal attendance. And this prefigured the ascent of Christ into heaven, upon his fulfilling of the law, all that was required in it, or signified by it. He ascended triumphantly after he had given the law, as a figure of his triumphant ascent after he had fulfilled it. (1:247-48)

From this same passage of Scripture Owen observes, third, that the glory of Christ's ascension is remarkable because of his "*attendants*." In one of many references to the event, he describes Christ's angelic escort:

As when he descended on old upon the earth at the giving of the law on mount Sinai, he was attended with the heavenly host, who ministerially wrought all those glorious and dreadful effects which were wrought on the mount, Exod. xix.; so now in his ascension he was attended with the angels of God, who were as the chariots in his triumph, that carried and bore up the human nature, and waited on him, ready to do his will and manifest his glory.... With them, then, and by their ministry, he "passed through the heavens;" a sight too glorious for mortal eyes to behold. (21:409)

Fourth, from the same psalm Owen observes "the *disposal of his enemies*." In his ascension Christ "led captivity captive" (Ps. 68:18, Eph. 4:8). Owen identifies this "captivity" as "the authors of all bondage, of all captivity in sin and misery." This is further affirmed in Paul's account of the spoiling of principalities and powers (Col. 2:15), when Christ made a "'show of them openly' in his triumph," as illustrated by a Roman procession (21:409-10).

"Received up into glory"
Christ's "actual reception into the especial presence of God, at the end of his passage, adds to the manifestation of his greatness and glory" (21:410). Owen notes that Christ was "received gloriously into the highest heaven, the habitation of the blessed" (21:410). This is not the "aspectable heavens which we behold," since he passed "through them,...into the place of the residence of God in glory and majesty,...the palace of this King of saints and nations" (1:248). Here Christ received "refreshment, after all the travail of his soul." Further, Owen ties in the biblical motif of the heavenly spouse: "Then was the time of the espousals of his church, the day of the gladness of his heart." The effect of this upon the heavenly community is also noteworthy:

> There is joy in heaven upon the returning and repentance of one sinner; and what was there when He that causes them to return, and saves all that do so, was received into his glory? No heart can conceive, much less can any tongue express, the glorious reception of the human nature of Christ in heaven. (21:410)

"Seated at the right hand of the Majesty on high"
Christ was enthroned at the right hand of the majesty on high, which signifies his enthronement in the place of

honor and glory, the "ensign of rule and judgment" (21:410). Owen explains this as a possible allusion to the practice of the Sanhedrin:

> He who presided in it was called אב דין, "The father of judgment," or, "Father of the house of judgment," and sat at the right hand of the..."prince" of the Sanhedrin, next unto him unto whom belonged the execution of the sentence of the court. Of this *ab din* mention is made in the Targum...agreeable to that, "The Father judgeth no man, but hath committed all judgment unto the Son." (20:119)

The meaning of the metaphor is that "the Son, as mediator" is "made partaker of the greatest glory that God hath to bestow in heaven," that is, "that glory and honour which is *bestowed on him by the Father*, after and upon the sacrifice of himself for the expiation of sin (20:119). Owen reminds us that the important phrase is not so much the right hand of God, which indicates God's power, but Christ's act of *sitting* at it, indicating his "eminency of glory." Christ possesses

> *majesty and glory* inexpressible;—all that can be given of God in heaven. God on his throne is God in the full manifestation of his own majesty and glory; on his right hand sits the Mediator, yea, so as that he also is "in the midst of the throne," Rev. v. 6. How little can our weak understandings apprehend of this majesty! (20:120)

One important aspect of this exaltation is the "*security* of Christ from all his adversaries and all sufferings for the future" so that "the fruit of the church, being secured from the rage and persecution of Satan, is said to be "caught up unto God, and to his throne, Rev. xii. 5" (20:119-20).

Another result of the exaltation coming after the humiliation of Christ is the "assured pledge of the final glory and blessedness of all that believe in him, whatever difficulties and dangers they may be exercised withal in the way." As Owen emphasizes, "He is not crowned with honour and glory merely for himself, but that he may be a captain of salvation, and bring others unto a participation of his glory" (20:373).

As noted earlier, Christ's ascension may also be considered to be "gracious," as it is the ascent of the High Priest. This is the ascent referred to by Christ in John 20, as Owen explains:

> His design herein was not the taking on him the exercise of his power, kingdom, and glorious rule; but the acting with God on the behalf of his disciples. "I go," saith he, "to my Father, and to your Father; to my God, and to your God,"—not his God and Father with respect unto eternal generation, but as he was their God and Father also. And he was so, as he was their God and Father in the same covenant with himself; wherein he was to procure of God all good things for them.... With this design in his ascension, and the effects of it, did he often comfort and refresh the hearts of his disciples, when they were ready to faint on the apprehensions of his leaving of them here below, John xiv. 1, 2, xvi. 5-7. (1:249)

This ascent was typified by the solemn ascent of the high priest up the stairs of the temple, on the Day of Atonement. In particular, in his comments on Hebrews 4:14 ("we have a great high priest, that is passed into [Owen translates it "through"] the heavens"), Owen notes three stages of his ascension typified by the high priest: first, the priest departed out of the sight of the people; second, he "*passed through the second veil* of the tabernacle, which received him and hid him by the closing of the curtains from the sight of all"; and third, "in the place wither he thus went were the *especial pledges* of the covenant of God, Lev. xvi. 2" (21:393-96). Owen also distinguishes this ascent from the royal ascent in calling it "*joyful*" though not triumphant. The most eminent type was the day of jubilee, the "great type of the spiritual deliverance of the church," for in the ascension of Christ, "proclamation was made in the Gospel, of mercy, pardon, peace, joy, and everlasting refreshments, unto all that were distressed by sin, with a communication of righteousness unto them, to the eternal glory of God" (1:250). In this regard Christ ascended into heaven as it was "the sanctuary above," the place of the throne of grace, the mercy-seat, where he would carry out the work of intercession.

In this manner Owen describes the twofold ascent of Christ as king and priest:

> He ascended triumphantly into heaven, as Solomon ascended into his glorious throne of judgment described 1 Kings x. 18-20. As David was the type of his conquest over all the enemies of his church, so was Solomon of his glorious reign. The types were multiplied because of their imperfection.... But he ascended graciously, as the high priest went into the holy place; not to rule all things gloriously with mighty power, not to use his *sword* and his *sceptre*—but to appear as *an high priest, in a garment down to the foot, and a golden girdle about his paps*, Rev. i. 13,—as in a tabernacle or temple, before a throne of grace. His sitting down at the right hand of the Majesty on high adds to the glory of his priestly office, but belongs not unto the execution of it. So it was prophesied of him, that he should be "a priest upon his throne," Zech. vi. 13. (1:250-51)

The exaltation "gives glory unto his office," as it is a "manifest.... evidence of the *absolute perfection of his oblation*;" as "*by his glorious power he makes all things subservient unto the ends of his mediation*"; and as, being in heaven in the exercise of the office of a priest he is "able to render the *persons and duties of believers* accepted in the sight of God" (23:13).

Does Christ ascend as a Prophet? Owen does not say

so. Rather he says that when Christ ascended, the great promise he made unto his disciples (as they were to be preachers of the gospel, and in them unto all that should succeed them in that office) was that he would "send the Holy Spirit unto them," to teach and guide them, to lead them into all truth—to declare unto them the mysteries of the will, grace, and love of God, for the use of the whole church. This he promised to do, and did, in the discharge of his prophetical office. And although his giving "gifts unto men" was an act of his kingly power, yet it was for the end of his prophetical office (1:251).

One point which Owen emphasizes is that the life of Christ in heaven, while it is a "state of the highest glory," is also a "*state of office-power*, work and duty" in love and care carrying out the office of the mediator.[5]

Christ as Forerunner
In addition to the foregoing, Owen makes some interesting comments upon Christ's role as a "forerunner." Since this principally respects his entrance into heaven, it is best considered in this context. The phrase is found in Hebrews 6:20. According to Owen's commentary on the passage the author aims to "give new assurance unto the efficacy and prevalency of the hope fixed on the promises, as it enters in unto that within the veil; namely, because Christ, our high priest, is there" (22:286). Hope is steadfast and sure because it passes through the heavens and fixes on God upon the throne of grace, on Christ as the high priest, and on "the counsel of peace being between them both." The author's argument, as Owen correctly recognized, is that the hope of believers is not fixed upon the types on earth, but upon the heavenly reality.

The forerunner is "Jesus." Owen observes the practice of the apostolic preachers in so identifying him: they stressed the fact that the very same Jesus who was crucified was the one exalted. Owen's conclusion from this is apparently directed against the Quakers of his time, but it seems equally applicable to anyone emphasizing the "Christ spirit" rather than the person of Jesus: "they testified hereby that they were not ashamed of his cross, so they laid in security for faith against all those fond imaginations which have been since vented, that Christ in heaven and in us is somewhat else than that Jesus who was crucified on the earth" (22:287).[6] What does he mean by "forerunner"? The word refers to one who "in an affair of public concern makes speed by himself unto the place whereunto the affair belongs, to give an account of it, and to dispose of all things needful and suited unto the disposal of the affair that he reports" (22:288). Christ is a forerunner, but he is more; "he is the person in whose hand lieth the whole affair and its conduct. And he was himself the forerunner because of the greatness of the matter he had in hand, not manageable by any other." The Old Testament priest by contrast was not a forerunner; he entered the holy place *instead of*, but not at the *head of* the people. As Owen observes,

> We have, then herein another instance of the excellency of our high priest and his office. When he entered into the holy place, he did it not merely for himself, but to go before, to lead and conduct the whole church into the same glory. (22:288)

As a forerunner, Christ performs three acts. First, he *carries tidings* of his victory. He announces that he has "*discharged his original engagement* for the salvation of believers under the old testament on the faith whereof they were accepted with God and saved." He also declares "the *redemption of all the elect* that were to follow him in their several generations. This is triumphantly declared in heaven, Ps. xlvii. 5-7, lxvii. 18, 24-26" (22:288, 289). Secondly, he *prepares the way* for the saints. The saints enter the heavenly sanctuary in two ways. In the present they enter by faith and prayer, enjoying an entrance into the presence of God unknown to the believers under the old covenant.

> We have an entrance into heaven even whilst we are here on the earth. An entrance is made for our faith, for our hope, for our prayer. Wherever they enter, our souls do enter and are present. And this entrance we make daily, and that with boldness and assurance, on account of our forerunner. (22:289)

He also prepares the way for their "future entrance into glory," preparing mansions for us (John 14:2-3), and "us for those mansions, suiting grace and glory unto each other" (22:289).

Thirdly, this forerunner takes "*possession.*" Having obtained eternal redemption and an everlasting inheritance for his elect, he enters heaven "in their name, to take possession of, and to reserve it in the heavens for them." This is evident from the Scripture's teaching concerning his entering "within the veil," or heaven itself. This triumphant entrance into heaven was given with respect to what he had accomplished upon the earth, for which it received God's "blessed approbation." Further, it was given with respect to the work of his mediation which yet remained. "Hence it is that he is not said absolutely to enter into his glory, but to enter as a priest, as through a veil, as into the holy place; where he continues as our forerunner in the exercise of that office, as the apostle declares in the close of the verse, 'Made an high priest for ever after the order of Melchisedec'" (22:289, 290).

Owen's application of this text to believers is a typical example of the Puritan "use." It is given here to provide a small example of Owen's interest in the earthly life of the Lord as well as providing additional evidence of his Christocentric view of the Christian life. First, we are encouraged by the security given by this doctrine:

> Now the Lord Jesus being thus entered into heaven as our forerunner, gives us manifold security of our

entrance thither also in the appointed season.—This he assures us of, John xiv. 3, 19. For, 1. He *passed through all the storms of trials*, temptations, persecutions, and death itself, that we are exposed unto, and yet is landed safely in eternal glory. His anchor was trust and hope in all his storms, Heb. ii. 13; Isa. l. 7-9. And it was tried to the utmost, Ps. xxii. 8-10. It preserved him in them all; and will be no less faithful unto the whole church. As he hath thus gone before us, he is able to succour us, and hath given us in himself a pledge of success. 2. He is *now where our hope is fixed*, namely within the veil, where he takes care of it, and will preserve it unto the end. (22:290)

Secondly, we are directed to our duty:

Again; if the Lord Christ be entered into heaven as our forerunner, it is our duty to be following him with all the speed we can.—And it is required hereunto, 1. That we be willing to follow him in the way wherein he went, as well as unto the place whither he is gone. And the way he went was, (1.) The way of obedience, Heb. v. 8, 9; (2.) The way of suffering, Heb. xii. 2. Holiness and the cross are the two essential parts of the way whereby our forerunner entered into glory. 2. That we burden not ourselves with any thing that will retard us, Heb. xii. 1. (22:290)

Finally, we are reminded that these things apply to the entire church:

And we may see whereon the security of the church doth depend, as to the trials and storms which it undergoes in this world.—He that can consider the opposition that is made unto it in the world;...cannot but admire whence it is that it is preserved one moment from destruction. (22:290)

We see that, while bringing out the peculiar nuances of this image, Owen avoids the modern error of concluding that its existence somehow diminishes the significance of the doctrine of penal substitution (i.e., by providing an *al-*

ternative image). In fact, just the opposite is true, as the immediate context of the passage makes clear: the forerunner is "an high priest for ever after the order of Melchisedec" (Heb. 6:20).

Conclusion

With this fact we are reminded once more of an important feature of Owen's Christology. Rather than viewing the work of Christ in terms of a variety of equally valid but independent images, Owen approaches the various roles and actions of Christ as distinguishable aspects of the one great comprehensive work of the Mediator. This enables him to incorporate the diversity of biblical images in a manner which reflects the unity of the Scripture in its witness to Christ's redemptive action. This unity encompasses the two states of Christ, as we have seen in the last two chapters. Before the incarnation, during the state of humiliation, and in the state of glory, the Son has exercised the office of Mediator. We turn now to a more detailed examination of Christ's offices of Prophet, Priest, and King, where we will again witness Owen's understanding of the necessary relation between the manifold activities of Christ and his glorious person.

---

[1] See Manton (1870, 1:464-75; 10:191-95).

[2] See Richard Sibbes's exposition of Matt. 12:20, in "The Bruised Reed and Smoking Flax" (Sibbes, 1862-64, 1:77-99).

[3] Romans 1:4 would better serve to support Owen's next point than this one. John Murray comments, "The only conclusion is that Christ is now by reason of the resurrection so endowed with and in control of the Holy Spirit that, without any confusion of the distinct persons, Christ is identified with the Spirit and is called 'the Lord of the Spirit' (II Cor. 3:18). Thus, when we come back to the expression 'according to the Spirit of holiness,' our inference is that it refers to that stage of pneumatic endowment upon which Jesus entered through his resurrection.... The thought of verse 4 would then be that the lordship in which he was installed by the resurrection is one all-pervasively conditioned by pneumatic powers" (1997, 11).

[4] See Manton (1870, 10:126-39; 270-75).
[5] See Goodwin's *The Heart of Christ in Heaven Toward Sinners On Earth* (1863, 4:95-150).
[6] This was another of the sixteen doctrines deemed fundamental by the Commonwealth divines in committee.

CHAPTER
13

"A Priest Forever"

The Importance of the Doctrine of Christ's Priesthood
While Owen expounds each of the three offices of Christ, he gives a priority to the priesthood. He shows this, for example, in the conclusion he draws from the fact that the first *personal type* of Christ was Melchisedek, a priest. God was teaching, he says,

> that the foundation of all that the Lord Christ had to do in and for the church was laid in his priestly office, whereby he made atonement and reconciliation for sin. Every thing else that he doth is built on the supposition hereof... an interest in the effects of the priestly office of Christ is that which in the first place we ought to look after. This being attained, we shall be willing to be taught and ruled by him, and not else. (22:310)

The doctrine's importance is also evident from the labor duly required in understanding it, if we would go "on to perfection" (19:5). Indeed, it is with respect primarily to this doctrine that Owen says, "It is an evidence of a thriving and healthy state of soul, to have an appetite unto the deepest mysteries of the gospel." Conversely, "the case of that people is deplorable and dangerous whose teachers are not able to carry them on in the knowledge of the mysteries of the gospel" (21:602; 22:13).

This explains why Owen devoted his most exhaustive labors to that most plentiful of resources for the doctrine of Christ's priesthood, the epistle to the Hebrews (cf. 19: 3-8). Of this epistle's exposition of Christ's priesthood Owen writes, "The Holy Ghost reserved it unto this as its proper place, where, upon the consideration of the institutions of the old testament and their removal out of the church, it might be duly represented, as that which gave an end unto them in their accomplishment, and *life* unto those ordinances of evangelical worship which were to succeed in their room" (19:3-4). Only in the book of Hebrews is Christ specifically called a "priest" and said to have taken that *office*. Here we find the clearest New Testament teaching on his oblation and intercession (19:4).

As with Christ's *person*, the doctrine of Christ's priesthood "hath in all ages,...been either directly opposed or variously corrupted; for it contains the principal foundation of the faith and consolation of the church" (19:5). Its greatest opponents have been the papacy and the Socinians—the former, by the substitution of another order of priesthood; the latter, by the substitution of another view of the work of a priest. Owen adds, "there are others also, pretending unto more sobriety than those before mentioned, who do yet think that these doctrines concerning the offices and mediation of Christ are if not unintelligible by us, yet not of any great necessity to be insisted on; for of that esteem are the mysteries of the gospel grown to be with some, with many among us" (19:6). Again, we see evidence of Owen's concern for the decline of interest in the mysteries, a concern that moves him to write as well for the "edification of those that are sober and godly" (19:6).

The Origin and Nature of the Priesthood of Christ
The origin of the priesthood of Christ is an important consideration in determining its nature. Ultimately, it lies

in the hidden counsels of God, made known through "several degrees of divine revelation...until he brought them to their complement in the external exhibition of his Son" (19:15). Significantly, the explanation of this provides the setting of Owen's definitive treatment of the doctrine of the decree.

Owen is particularly concerned to demonstrate that the office of priesthood did not pertain to the state of innocence. The "proper" duty of the priest is to offer sacrifices for other men. The offering of bloody sacrifices is for making atonement. Hence, God did not ordain the priesthood or sacrifice under the law of creation (19:16, 17). In the state of uncorrupted nature there would have been need of some to act in God's stead, e.g., parents, but there was no need of anyone to act toward God on behalf of men (ὑπὲρ ἀνθρώπων, τὰ πρὸς τὸν Θεόν), as the Scripture says every priest does (Heb. 5:1).

In particular, with regard to the *nature* and *purpose* of the priest's sacrifices under the Old Testament, Owen shows that the sacrifice consisted of "a slain or killed offering," concluding that,

> there neither is nor can be any sacrifice, properly so called, but what is made by killing or slaying of the thing sacrificed; and the offerings of inanimate things under the law, as of flour or wine, or the fruits of the earth, were improperly so called, in allusion unto or by virtue of their conjunction with them that were properly so.... All such sacrifices must respect sin, and an atonement to be made for it. There never was, nor ever can be, any other end of the effusion of blood in the service of God. (19:20)

For several other similar reasons Owen concludes that "the supposition of the entrance of sin, and what ensued thereon in the curse of the law, lie at the foundation of the designation of the priesthood and sacrifice of Christ" (19:20-41).

This interest in the origin of the priesthood was motivated by the question of its nature. According to the Socinians, Christ was called a high priest "improperly and metaphorically" by allusion to an activity of the Old Testament priests, namely, his appearing in the heavenly holy place where he "received power from God to help, and relieve, and assist the church" (19:140). In support of this they argued that his priesthood is "of the same nature with his kingly office, both of them consisting in a power, ability, authority, and readiness, to do good unto the church," and that he entered upon his priesthood upon his ascension, when he was given this power and authority (19:140). The "object of the acts of the priesthood of Christ is firstly and principally *man*, yea, it is only so, none of them having God for their object, no more than the acts of his kingly power have" (19:140). The offering of sacrifice is noticeably absent.

Owen firmly rejects their assertion that Christ is a priest only metaphorically: "He unto whom all things whatever *properly belonging unto a priest* are ascribed, and to whom belongs the description of a priest in all things essential unto him,… is a high priest properly so called" (19:141). Jesus has these qualifications. He has the *name* of priest given to him, "frequently," and meets the description of a high priest given in Hebrews 5:1, as truly as Aaron does. The argument of Hebrews 7:11-16 rests upon the change of a priesthood, from an Aaronic to a Melchisedecian, and upon the latter as being a true, even a superior priesthood (19:141).

Against the assertion that mankind is the object of Christ's work as a priest, Owen clearly demonstrates that just as the acts of the Old Testament priests had God as their object, "those of Christ did so also, or there is no similitude or analogy between these things; which to affirm is to overthrow both the old testament and the new" (19:145, 146). Their "principal duty" was to offer sacrifices of atonement for sin, as Owen is able to show. As to the "nature, use, and end of atonement," Owen says it was "to avert the anger of God due to sin, and to pacify him that the sinner might be pardoned." Of the word "atonement," Owen explains,

> This is the importance of the word, and this was the end of those sacrifices whereby atonement was made. The word is sometimes used where no sacrifice was implied, but is never used in any other sense than that declared.... A person guilty of sin, convicted in his own conscience, condemned by the sentence of the law, by God's allowance and appointment brought a clean beast, assigned in general for that use, and, bringing it to the altar, confessed over it his sin and guilt, laying them legally upon it, so delivering it up into the hands of the priest, by whom it was slain, and the blood poured out, as suffering under the guilt laid upon it; wherein, with some other ensuing acts, it was offered to God to make atonement for the sin committed and confessed. Thus was blood given unto the people to make atonement for their souls, because the life of the beast was in the blood, which was destroyed in the shedding thereof, Lev. xvii. 11. (19:147)

To the Socinian confusion of the priestly and kingly offices of Christ, Owen counters that the three mediatorial offices Christ exercises towards the church are "distinct among themselves." To the extent that there is an "affinity between them," he argues, "the kingly and prophetical do make a nearer pass unto each other than either of them do unto the sacerdotal…; for the nature of these two offices requireth that the object of their exercise be men" (19:148-49). Moreover, "This would render the whole instruction intended for the church in the Aaronical priesthood and sacrifices useless and impertinent," and "the accommodation of it unto the priesthood of Christ by our apostle would be altogether vain" (19:150).

That God is the object of Christ's priestly office is also evident "from the nature of *sacerdotal acts and duties*," namely, his oblation and intercession. Our author rightly asserts, "The actual help and aid which he gives us"—which to Socinians was the only reason Christ was called a priest—"is the fruit and effect of these sacerdotal actings" (19:150).

In this argument for the Godward activity of the priestly office, one may find what is perhaps Owen's most comprehensive definition of Christ's priesthood:

> The priesthood of Christ is "the power, office, and duty, whereby he makes an interposition between God and us,—that is, with God on our behalf." And there are two general ends of this interposition,... (1.) "*Averruncatio mali*," the removal of all sorts of evil from us, every thing that did or might befall us in a way of evil, hurt, damage or punishment, on the account of our sins and apostasy from God. (2.) "*Acquisitio boni*," the procuring and obtaining for us every thing that is good, with respect unto our reconciliation to God, peace with him, and the enjoyment of him. And these are intended in the general acts of his office; for,—first, his oblation principally and firstly respects the making atonement for sin, and the turning away of the wrath that was due unto us as sinners; wherein he was Jesus, the deliverer, who saves us from the wrath to come. And this is all that is included in the nature of oblation as absolutely considered. But as the oblation of Christ was founded on the covenant before described, it was not only *satisfactory*, but *meritorious*; that is, by the sacrifice of himself he did not only turn away the wrath which was due unto us, but also obtained for us "eternal redemption," with all the grace and glory thereunto belonging. (19:151-52)

His concluding comment in this definition of the priesthood of Christ expresses one of his principal arguments against all semi-Pelagian forms of salvation:

> There remains nothing to be done on our behalf, after the once offering of himself, whereby he "perfected for ever them that are sanctified," but only the actual application of these good things unto us, or our actual instating in the possession of them. Hereunto is his intercession, the second duty of his priestly office, designed; the especial nature whereof must be elsewhere declared and vindicated. (19:152)

Christ's Qualifications and Excellencies as a High Priest
The nature of Christ's priesthood dictates its necessary qualifications. This is perhaps most neatly expressed in Owen's comments upon Hebrews 7:26, "For such an high priest became us, who is holy, harmless, undefiled, separate from sinners, and made higher than the heavens." The passage alludes to a condition requiring "such a high priest." In summary, he must be someone who,

> (1.) Could *make atonement* for our sins, or perfectly expiate them; (2.) *Purge our consciences* from dead works, that we might serve the living God, or sanctify us throughout by his blood; (3.) *Procure acceptance* with God for us, or purchase eternal redemption; (4.) *Administer supplies* of the Spirit of grace unto us, to enable us to live unto God in all duties of faith, worship, and obedience; (5.) *Give us assistance and consolation in* our trials, temptations, and sufferings, with pity and compassion; (6.) *Preserve us by power* from all ruining sins and dangers; (7.) Be in a *continual readiness* to receive us in all our addresses to him; (8.) To *bestow upon us the reward of eternal life.* Unless we have a high priest that can do all these things for us, we cannot be "saved to the uttermost." Such a high priest we stood in need of, and such a one it became the wisdom of God to give

unto us. And God, in infinite wisdom, love and grace, gave us such a high priest as, in the qualifications of his person, the glory of his condition, and the discharge of his office, was every way suited to deliver us from the state of apostasy, sin, and misery, and to bring us unto himself, through a perfect salvation. (22:548)

A high priest without these abilities could not answer the purposes of God for the priesthood.

"Holy, harmless, undefiled, separate from sinners"
To say Owen's doctrine of the person of Christ assumes the background for his exposition of Christ's qualification for the priesthood would be a great understatement, but obviously no surprise: to meet the qualifications for the priesthood was the purpose of his incarnation. We have already seen that Christ was holy. Owen says, "This holiness of nature was needful unto him who was to answer for the ungodliness of our nature, and to take it away" (22:554). As holiness respects his nature, "'harmless' respects his life" (22:554.). As he was "harmless" he "did no evil in himself"; as "undefiled" he "contracted none from any thing else" (22:555). In his exposition of Christ's being "separate from sinners," Owen says, in brief, Christ "was not separate from them as unto *community of nature;*... He was not, therefore, really separate from sinners as they were *flesh*, but as they were *sinful flesh*" (22:556). Nor was he "separate from sinners as to the *duties of outward conversation.*" At this, Owen accuses ancient and modern hermits of forsaking the example of Christ who "conversed freely with all sorts of persons.... to call sinners to repentance, and to set before their eyes an example of holiness" (22:557). Rather, he was separate from them "in *sin*, in its *nature*, causes, and effects. Whatever of that sort he underwent was upon our account, and not his own" (22:558).

This "absolute holiness and spotless innocency," Owen

says, had several consequences. First, as it was for our sakes, it reveals his "pure, unmixed love and grace" (21:473). Secondly, it "had a signal influence into the efficacy of his sacrifice," there being in his oblation "the highest sufferings and the most absolute innocency, knit together by an act of most inexpressible obedience" (21:473).

"Like his brethren"
In relating the incarnation and earthly life of Christ to his priestly office, Owen explains, "He was made man, that he might be a high priest; he suffered being tempted, that he might be merciful and faithful" (20:468). This connection between the incarnation and high priestly office of Christ is clearly asserted in Hebrews 2:17-18, where an explanation is given for the humiliation described earlier in the chapter. He is "made like unto his brethren in all things (κατὰ πάντα)," in order that he might "make reconciliation for the sins of the people." This objective necessitates an important and reasonable qualification to "all things": "The proposition is of the nature of them that are...universal, but not universally to be understood." That is, κατὰ πάντα "respects only all those things which are necessary unto the end assigned (20:466). For instance, and very importantly, it was not necessary for him to be made like unto his brethren *in their sin*, in order for him to carry out the duty of a priest in their behalf, but he must be like them in several other respects.

First, he was made like unto them "in the essence of human nature, a rational spiritual soul, and a mortal body, quickened by its union there withal," but "that he should take this nature upon him by natural generation, after the manner of the brethren, this was not necessary;—yea, so to have done would not have furthered the end of his priesthood, but have enervated the *efficacy* of it, and have rendered him incapable of being such a priest as he was to be," since it would have rendered his nature defiled, contrary to Hebrews 7:26. With explicitness rare even in Reformed theologians, Owen ties the doctrine of *enhypostasia* ("in-personality," *supra* pp. 273-76) to the office of priesthood, saying,

> Again, it was not necessary that this human nature should have its individuation from itself, and a particular subsistence in and by itself;—yea, this also would have overthrown his priesthood; for whereas the efficacy thereof depends on the excellency of the divine nature, this could not have given its influence thereunto, had not the human nature been taken into the same personal subsistence with itself. Only, as we said, that he should have a human nature, truly and really as the brethren, and therein be like unto them, this was necessary, that he might be an offering priest, and have of his own to offer unto God (20:467).

Secondly, it was necessary that "in and with his human nature he should take upon him all the properties and affections of it, that so he might be made like unto the brethren" (20:467). After a denial of the Lutheran doctrine of ubiquity, Owen emphasizes that Christ's soul is not "*freed* from the affections which are connatural to a human rational soul, as love, joy, fear, sorrow, shame, and the like; nor was his body to be free from being obnoxious unto hunger, thirst, cold, pain, death itself"; that he is "like unto us in temptation," and that his sufferings were in common "with them that the brethren under went" (20:467, 468). On the other hand, for the carrying out of his office there was no need for him to have the "irregular perturbations" of his brethren which pertain to their sinful natures.

Explaining this, Owen says that Christ must be like us in temptations in order that he might "succour them that are tempted." However,

> herein also some difference may be observed be-

tween him and us; for the most of our temptations arise from within us, from our own unbelief and lusts. Again, in those that are from without, there is somewhat in us to take part with them, which always makes us fail in our duty of resistance, and ofttimes leads to further miscarriages. But from these things he was absolutely free; for as he had no inward disposition or inclination unto the least evil, being perfect in all graces and all their operations at all times, so when the prince of this world came unto him, he had no part in him,—nothing to close with his suggestions or to entertain his terrors. (20:468)

To these observations Owen adds that Christ's sufferings

were of the same kind with them that the brethren underwent, or ought so to have done; yet they had far different effects on him from what they would have had on them. For whereas he was perfectly innocent and perfectly righteous, no way deserving of those sinful consequents which attend the utmost sufferings under the curse of the law by sinners themselves. (20:468)

It has been sufficiently emphasized already that Christ must partake of human nature. However, this necessity means that, strictly speaking, a certain reservation must be had with respect to the idea that Christ was a priest *before* his incarnation: "although the benefits of the priesthood of Christ were communicated unto all believers from the foundation of the world," by virtue of the covenant of redemption, "yet he was not actually, nor could be a high priest, until he was clothed with flesh, and made partaker of the nature of the children." If this were the case with the high priest in general, it is even more evident in the case of Christ, whose sacrifice as high priest was his own body (20:469).

Why was Christ subject to infirmities, sufferings, and temptations? Owen makes the interesting assertion that while Christ's incarnation and his obedience to God were "all that was required of him as to his being a high priest," the "estate and condition of the brethren" required something more. "Their sorrows, tenderness, weakness, miseries, disconsolations, are such, that if there be not a contemperation of his sublime holiness, and absolute perfection in fulfilling of all righteousness, with some qualifications inclining him to condescension, pity, compassion, and tender sense of their condition, whatever might be the issue of their safety in the life to come, their comfort in this life would be in continual hazard" (20:469).[1]

Two attributes of this great high priest arise out of his thus sharing in human life: his mercifulness and faithfulness. There is in Christ a peculiar mercifulness: "Mercy in God is but a naked simple apprehension of misery, made effective by an act of his holy will to relieve," but "mercy in Christ is a compassion, a condolency, and hath a moving of pity and sorrow joined with it." This mercy is a grace of the Spirit produced in the human nature to an "incomparable" degree. But in this description of the high priest, it is not "this mercifulness in general that the apostle intends; but he considers it as excited, provoked, and drawn forth by his own temptations and sufferings. He suffered and was tempted, that he might be merciful, not absolutely, but a merciful high priest" (20:470). He is also "faithful." This indicates "his exact, constant, careful consideration of all the concernments of the brethren, under their temptations and sufferings. This he is excited unto by his own experience of what it is to serve God in such a condition" (20:470).

The consequence of Christ's suffering temptation, and of his being a merciful and faithful high priest is that he is "able to succour them that are tempted" (Heb. 2:18). This ability coming from his suffering is a "moral power, and not a natural one," not the "power of the hand, but...a power of heart and will, an ability in readiness of mind"

(20:480). Owen explains the working of this power in the following way:

> [1.] He had a particular experience thereby of the weakness, sorrows, and miseries of human nature under the assaults of temptations; he tried it, felt it, and will never forget it.
>
> [2.] His heart is hereby inclined to compassion, and acquainted with what it is that will afford relief. In his throne of eternal peace and glory, he sees his poor brethren labouring in that storm with so much travail of soul himself passed through, and is intimately affected with their condition....
>
> [3.] This compassion moves and excites him unto their relief and succour. (20:480; see 20:479; 21:403)

The knowledge of this mercy and compassion in Christ is a great encouragement to believers to come to him as their high priest. He will give them strength, consolation, and deliverance through his promises, the Spirit, and his providence (20:481). It is their duty to cry unto him, and him alone, in time of temptation, for, as Owen announces, he is "sufficient" to help them:

> He hath a sufficiency of care, wisdom, and faithfulness, to observe and know the seasons wherein succour is necessary unto us; a sufficiency of *tenderness*, mercy and compassion, to excite him thereunto; a sufficiency of *power* to afford succour that shall be effectual; a sufficiency of *acceptation* at the throne of grace, to prevail with God for suitable supplies and succour. He is every way "able to succour them that are tempted." To him be praise and glory for evermore! (20:486)

Call and Inauguration to Priestly Office

Christ's call may be considered in a number of ways.[2] First, Owen says, it "consisted in that eternal covenant which was between the Father and him concerning his undertaking the work of our recovery and salvation" (19:152). He distinguishes between that call's "designation," as "it is expressed in the words of God the Father to him, "Thou art my Son, this day have I begotten thee," and its "manifestation," consisting in the *protoevangelion* of Genesis 3:15 (19:152, 153). In his "actual inauguration into it, and susception of it," Christ was

> vested with all his offices from his conception and nativity. There was no time wherein he was, as to his human nature, and was not the king, priest, and prophet of his church; for he received all his offices by the unction of the Spirit, when God "anointed him with the oil of gladness above his fellows." And this was done fundamentally in his incarnation, when he was conceived and sanctified by the Holy Spirit, communicated unto him not by measure. And so he was born "Christ the Lord," Luke ii. 11. He was born one anointed by the Holy Ghost, Lord, and consequently priest and prophet,—all which offices were communicated by unction. Together with those graces, gifts, and abilities, which were necessary to their discharge, right, title, and authority for their exercise in their proper seasons were conveyed unto him thereby. And in these two doth all office and power consist. (19:153)

Owen lists three things that "concurred unto the inauguration of the Lord Christ unto this office": "His *real unction* by the Holy Ghost with an all-fulness of gifts and graces, at his incarnation" (19:154); reception of a "*declarative unction* at his baptism, when the Spirit descended upon him, and filled him with power for the exercise of all the gifts and graces he had received for the discharge of his whole office" (19:154); and finally,

> an *especial dedication* to the actual performance of the duties of this office. And this was his own act, which he had power for from God. This himself expres-

seth, John xvii. 19, ... " I sanctify," that is, I consecrate or dedicate, "myself." (19:154)

As Owen explains this last remark, Christ consecrated himself to be "the sacrificer" of himself as the sacrifice (19:154).

> The seventeenth chapter of John is identified as the beginning and entrance of the exercise of his priestly office. Whatever he did after this unto the moment of his death belonged principally thereunto. Sundry things, I confess, fell in occasionally afterwards, wherein he acted his prophetical office in bearing witness unto the truth; but the scope of all his ensuing actions and passions respect his priestly office only: for although his sacrifice, precisely considered, consisted in his actual offering of himself on the cross, yet his sacerdotal actings with reference unto it are not to be confined thereunto (19:154). One notable exercise of the priestly office is Christ's intercessory prayer offered in this same chapter of John. (11:367-69)

The Acts of the Priesthood of Christ

Incarnation

Owen mentions three aspects of the work of redemption which are "peculiarly ascribed to the person of the Son." The first, his incarnation, has already been observed. However, it is appropriate at this point to emphasize the relation between the incarnation and the Old Testament priesthood. While the Aaronic priesthood may be seen as typifying that of Christ, it must also be remembered that Christ's priesthood is God's provision "to supply the defect and insufficiency of legal sacrifices." It is this perspective which we find in Owen's exposition of Hebrews 10:5-10. The sacrifices of the Old Testament were not capable of bringing about the "perfect, real expiation of sin, and the justification, sanctification, and eternal salvation of the church, with that perfect state of spiritual worship which was ordained for it in this world" (23:454). They were to show that "without a sacrifice there could be no atonement made for sin;" but *those* sacrifices of themselves were incapable of making this atonement. The apostle expresses the words of the psalmist in the "antithesis": "Sacrifice and offering thou wouldst not, but a body hast thou prepared." According to Owen,

> As sacrifices were that which he *would not* unto this end, so this preparation of the body of Christ was that which he would, which he delighted in and was well pleased withal. So the whole work of Christ and the effects of it are expressly referred unto this will of God, verses 9, 10. (23:457)

This passage also asserts that the incarnation provided the *means* of Christ's willing obedience.

At this point it would be well to consider in detail Owen's exposition of Christ's obedience which is in view here. Owen's best discussion of the obedience of Christ is found in his treatise *The Doctrine of Justification by Faith* (5:5-400).[3] Having demonstrated that the "original, immutable law of God" must be established, that "all mankind have by sin fallen under the penalty threatened unto the transgression of this law," and, that there is no way our personal righteousness can suffice to establish or fulfill the law, Owen directs his readers to the "perfect obedience and righteousness of Christ," who, according to the apostle Paul, is "the end of the law for righteousness unto all that do believe" (5:240-50). Owen's point here is that much disputed one that the righteousness by which we are justified is the *active* righteousness of Christ, imputed to believers.[4]

What is the "active righteousness" of Christ? This is generally considered his obedience to the law rendered during his life, distinguished from the "passive righteousness" of his sacrificial death (or, more correctly, all the sufferings of Christ endured during the state of humiliation). However, Owen recognized that this latter righteousness was inadequately described as "passive." As he explains, "the sufferings of Christ, as they were purely penal, are imperfectly called his passive righteousness; for all righteousness is either in *habit* or in *action*, whereof suffering is neither; nor is any man righteous, or so esteemed from what he suffereth" (5:253-54).

It is Christ's "whole obedience to God, in all that he did and suffered for the church" (5:209). Owen argues that "if it were necessary that the Lord Christ, as our surety, should undergo the penalty of the law for us, or in our stead, because we have all sinned, then it was necessary also that, as our surety, he should yield obedience unto the preceptive part of the law for us also; and if the imputation of the former," that is, the penalty, "be needful for us unto our justification before God, then is the imputation of the latter," i.e., the preceptive part, "also necessary unto the same end and purpose" (5:251).

Socinians and others had objected to the imputation of Christ's obedience on three grounds: First, it was "impossible," since his obedience was performed for himself, as a man under the law, and hence could obtain justification for none but himself (5:252). To the contrary, Owen argues, "*the Lord Christ fulfilled the whole law for us.*" It is necessary to remember the importance of the doctrine of Christ's *person*, and its relation to his mediatorial office:

> The obedience we treat of was the obedience of Christ the mediator: but the obedience of Christ, as "the mediator of the covenant," was the obedience of his person; for "God redeemed his church with his own blood," Acts xx. 28. It was performed in the human nature; but the person of Christ was he that performed it. (5:255)

To clarify this point Owen employs two terms which were first introduced by the fathers and revived in the contemporary Reformed and Lutheran Christological debate over the *communicatio idiomatum*, i.e., the relation of the proper qualities of Christ's two natures to his person (Muller, 1985, 72-75).

> As in the person of a man, some of his acts, as to the immediate principle of operation, are acts of the body, and some are so of the soul; yet, in their performance and accomplishment, are they the acts of the person: so the acts of Christ in his mediation, as to their ἐνεργήματα [power], or immediate operation, were the actings of his distinct natures,—some of the divine and some of the human, immediately; but as unto their ἀποτελέσματα [accomplishment], and the perfecting efficacy of them, they were the acts of his whole person,—his acts who was that person, and whose power of operation was a property of his person. (5:255)

By distinguishing between the natures as to their ἐνεργήματα, and relating the ἀποτελέσματα, i.e., the "accomplishment" of the work to the whole person in his mediatorial office, Owen illustrates the Reformed position.

Having made this distinction, Owen proceeds to explain how the obedience of Christ was consequently not for himself but for us. "The Son of God," argues Owen,

> was never absolutely made ὑπὸ νόμον,—"under the law,"—nor could be formally obliged thereby.... Wherefore, the obedience whereof we treat, being not the obedience of the *human nature abstractedly*, however performed in and by the human nature; but the *obedience of the person of the Son of God*, however the human nature was subject to the law...it was not for himself, nor could be for himself; because his whole person was not obliged thereunto. It is therefore a fond thing, to compare the obedience of Christ with that of any other man, whose whole person is under the law. For although that may not be for

himself and others...yet this may, yea, must be for others, and not for himself. (5:255-56)

As Christ's obedience was not owed by himself, neither was it designed for himself, but for us. Again, Owen points to the motive of the incarnation:

> Now, the susception of our nature was a voluntary act of his own, with reference unto some end and purpose; and that which was the end of the assumption of our nature was, in like manner, the end of all that he did therein. Now, it was for us, and not for himself, that he assumed our nature; nor was any thing added unto him thereby. Wherefore, in the issue of his work, he proposeth this only unto himself, that he may be "glorified with that glory which he had with the Father before the world was," by the removal of that veil which was put upon it in his exinanition. But that it was for us that he assumed our nature, is the foundation of Christian religion, as it is asserted by the apostle, Heb. ii. 14; Phil. ii. 5-8. (5:257)

Second, the Socinians had further argued that the active obedience of Christ was a necessary qualification for the mediator, and was therefore rendered for himself. Owen denied this on the ground that "the Lord Christ was every way meet for the whole work of mediation, by the ineffable union of the human nature with the divine, which exalted it in dignity, honor, and worth, above any thing of all things that ensued thereon" (5:258). Because of this union with the person of the Son of God the human nature of Christ "had a right unto, and might have immediately been admitted into, the highest glory whereof it was capable, without any antecedent obedience unto the law" (5:258, 259; cf. Heppe 1950, 460). Hence, what Christ did as mediator did not qualify him to be a mediator; the qualification arose from the hypostatic union. The motive of that union, as emphasized above, was to fulfill the obligations upon the surety of the covenant. Apart from this consideration Christ needed no obedience for himself.

But was not Christ exalted as a reward for his obedience? Not exactly:

> The actual possession of this glory was, in the ordination of God, to be consequential unto his obeying and suffering, not for himself, but for us. But as unto the right and capacity of the human nature in itself, all the glory whereof it was capable was due unto it from the instant of its union; for it was therein exalted above the condition that any creature is capable of by mere creation. (5:259)

Owen distinguishes the "foundation of the divine glory of Christ," which was the hypostatic union, from the "way of his actual possession of that part of his glory which consists in his mediatory power and authority over all," which was his obedience (5:259). His obedience was necessary while he was a *"viator,"* [traveler] under the law according to his human nature by and during an "especial dispensation," as the surety of his people. As a surety, Christ is a "public person." "But what a public person doth as a public person,—that is, as a representative of others,... whatever may be his own concernment therein, he doth it not for himself but for others" (5:260, 261; cf. Heppe, 1950, 461-63).

This still leaves open the objection that Christ, as a creature according to his human nature, is "subject unto the *law of creation*," that law which necessarily rests upon every rational creature's obligation to love and serve God. To this Owen agrees, but it will not serve the purpose of the Socinians, as he is able to demonstrate (5:261-62).

As our surety Christ answered both the obedience the law required and the penalty that it threatened. Since no one suggested that he answered the penalty for himself, Owen wondered that anyone could think he "yielded obedience unto it for himself only. The whole harmony of the work of his mediation would be disordered by such a supposition" (5:259, 260). It should be remembered that the reason for this emphasis upon Christ's obedience unto God *for* us is that this is the foundation of the imputation of that same righteousness *to* us.

It was further objected that since the death of Christ obtained the pardon of our sins, and that this pardon made us completely righteous, the imputation of Christ's righteousness was "useless." The problem with this argument lies in the minor premise; that "he who is pardoned his sins of omission and commission, is esteemed to have done all that is required of him." This is mistaken on several grounds. First, "in the pardon of sin, neither God nor man doth judge that he who hath sinned hath not sinned." Rather, "he is looked upon as an innocent man, as unto the punishment that was due unto him; but no man thinks that he is made righteous thereby, or is esteemed not to have done that which really he hath done" (5:263). Pardon, Owen assures us, "only removeth guilt, which is the respect of sin unto punishment, ensuing on the sanction of the law" (5:264). Secondly, it wrongly assumes that "the law, in case of sin, doth not oblige unto punishment and obedience both." However, the law has both precepts and sanctions. Man, though a sinner under the sanctions of the broken law, remains under the government of God's precepts, and every "disobedience...casteth us afresh and farther under its power of obliging unto punishment" (5:265). As pardon frees us "only from the obligation unto punishment, there is moreover, required unto our justification an obedience unto what the law requireth" (5:266). Christ's death, as punishment, perfectly answers the demand of the curse of the law, but it does not, as punishment, constitute obedience to the law, for "passion, as passion, is not obedience,—though there may be obedience in suffering, as there was in that of Christ unto the height" (5:266). Thirdly, the argument erroneously supposes "*pardon of sin gives title unto eternal blessedness in the enjoyment of God*" (5:266). As Owen explains,

> These things, I confess, are inseparably connected in the ordinance, appointment, and covenant of God. Whosoever has his sins pardoned is accepted with God, has right unto eternal blessedness. These things are inseparable; but they are not one and the same. And by reason of their inseparable relation are they so put together by the apostle, Romans 4:6-8,... It is the imputation of righteousness that gives right unto blessedness; but pardon of sin is inseparable from it, and an effect of it, both being opposed unto justification by works, or an internal righteousness of our own. But it is one thing to be freed from being liable unto eternal death, and another to have right and title unto a blessed and eternal life. (5:267)

The obedience and sufferings of Christ make up that "whole" which is "imputed unto every one that doth believe" (5:270).

Oblation

The second act of Christ's priesthood was oblation, which Owen defines as "that act or duty of his sacerdotal office whereby he offered himself, his soul and body, or his whole human nature, an expiatory sacrifice to God in his death and blood-shedding, to make atonement for the sins of mankind, and to purchase for them eternal redemption" (19:195). By putting it in terms of Christ's *offering*, and not merely Christ's suffering, Owen not only retains the biblical emphasis upon the atonement as Christ's action, but also the biblical association of his action with the work of the high priest.

What is the relationship of Christ's oblation to his obedience? First, the oblation was an act of willing obedience,

> without which it would not have been of any value (for if the will of Christ had not been in it, it could

never have purged our sins), therefore, in that regard, I refer it to his actions.... He might have been cruciated on the part of God; but his death could not have been an oblation and offering had not his will concurred. "But he loved me," saith the apostle, "and gave himself for me," Gal. ii. 20. Now that alone deserves the name of a gift which is from a free and willing mind, as Christ's was when "he loved us, and gave himself for us an offering and a sacrifice to God for a sweet-smelling savour." Eph. v. 2. He does it cheerfully. (10:175-76)

Secondly, Christ's oblation was a life-long act. It was not merely

the particular offering of himself upon the cross an offering to his Father, as the Lamb of God without spot or blemish, when he bare our sins or carried them up with him in his own body on the tree, which was the sum and complement of his oblation and that wherein it did chiefly consist; but also his whole humiliation, or state of emptying himself, whether by yielding voluntary obedience unto the law, as being made under it, that he might be the end thereof to them that believe, Rom. x. 4, or by his subjection to the curse of the law, in the antecedent misery and suffering of life, as well as by submitting to ... the death of the cross: for no action of his as mediator is to be excluded from a concurrence to make up the whole means in this work. (10:80; cf. 10:176)

Christ's priestly work, therefore, is especially to be understood in terms of his making a sacrifice: "If he be a priest, he must have a sacrifice; the very nature of his employment requires it" (12:421).

A Sacrifice to God

"The person *designing, appointing, and instituting* this sacrifice, is God the Father, as in grace contriving the great work of the salvation of the elect" (12:432). Owen explains,

> He to whom it was offered was God, God *essentially considered*, with his glorious property of justice, which was to be atoned: "He gave himself an offering and a sacrifice to God for a sweet-smelling savour," Eph. v. 2; that is, to atone him, being provoked. (12:432)

This distinction answers the objection, "If Christ were God himself, how could he offer himself unto God" (23:302)? If Christ had but one nature, this would be a pertinent objection, but having two natures, "so infinitely distinct as they are, both acting under such distinct capacities as they did, there is nothing unbecoming this mystery of God, that the one of them might be offered unto the other" (23:303). Furthermore, "the Son did not formally offer himself to himself, but unto God, as acting supreme rule, government, and judgment, in the person of the Father" (23:303).

The sacrifice made by Christ must have certain peculiar properties. For a number of reasons it must be a sacrifice none of the priests before had offered (12:421). First, those sacrifices were instituted by the law, but the law was incapable of providing a satisfactory sacrifice since "it had a shadow of good things to come, and not the very image of the things" themselves (12:422). Moreover, the sacrifice under the law could not "make perfect; that is, it could not perfectly atone God, and so take away their sins that the conscience should no more be troubled or tormented with the guilt of sin" (12:422-24). Secondly, "those sacrifices had been *disallowed* as to the end of taking away sin and bringing sinners to God" (12:424). Against the objection that that was the purpose of their appointment, Owen answers,

> They were never appointed of God to accomplish that end by any real worth and efficacy of their own, but merely to typify, prefigure, and point out, him and that which did the work which they repre-

sented; and so served, as the apostle speaks, "until the time of reformation," Heb. ix. 10. They served the use of that people in the under-age condition wherein God was pleased to keep them (12:425).

Describing this further he says, "Absolutely, the sacrifices of the law expiated no sin, and so were they rested in by the Jews; typically, they expiated all, and so Paul [Acts 13:38, 39] calls them from them to the antitype (the thing typified), now actually exhibited (12:428).

Moreover, God had clearly rejected them to that end, as indicated in Psalm 40:6, 7 and Hebrews 10:5-9. In short, "Look to what end Christ had a body fitted and prepared, for and to that end, and the compassing of it, are all sacrifices rejected of God" (12:425).

Christ's Sacrifice of Himself

Previously we observed that Christ must take human nature in order to be a high priest, at this point we will look at Owen's exposition of the incarnation as it pertains to *what* Christ offered as a sacrifice, namely, his human nature (12:430-31). This is precisely what the author of Hebrews intended in his exposition of Psalm 40:6.

> Plainly, כָּרָה signifies not only, in its first sense, to "dig," but also to "prepare"; and is so rendered by the LXX. Now, whereas the original expresseth only the ears, which are the organ by which we hear and become obedient (whence to hear is sometimes as much as to be obedient), it mentions the ears synecdochically for the whole body, which God so prepared for obedience to himself; and that which the original expressed synecdochically, the LXX, and after them the apostle, rendered more plainly and fully, naming the whole body wherein he obeyed, when the ears were only expressed, whereby he learned obedience. (12:429)

The sacrifice made by Christ is expressed in three

ways. First, "It is said to be of the *body* and *blood* of Christ, Heb. x. 10." As Owen says, "The offering of the body of Jesus and the blood of Christ is said to purge us from our sins, that is, by the sacrifice of it, and in his blood we have redemption, Eph. i. 7, 1 John i. 7; and by his own blood did he enter into the holy place, Heb. ix. 12, and most expressly chap. xii. 12" (12:430). It is also referred to his soul, as in Isaiah 53:10. However, as Owen observes, "It is most frequently said to be *himself* that was offered,... his whole human nature;... body and soul as a propitiatory sacrifice to God, a sacrifice for atonement and expiation" (12:430).

What does the Scripture mean when it says that Christ offered himself? Owen answers, "'He,' in the first place, as it is spoken of the sacrificer, denotes the person of Christ, and both natures therein," acting jointly and distinctly. Referring to Hebrews 9:14 ("Through the eternal Spirit he offered himself to God"), Owen explains, "His eternal Spirit or Deity" (in 23:304, he says "the divine nature acting in the person of the Son"), "was the principal agent, offering" (12:430). Elsewhere, with a little more clarity, he says, "it was an act of his *entire person*, wherein he discharged the office of a priest"; his person being the priest, his divine nature giving "*dignity*, worth, and efficacy unto the sacrifice of himself," and his human nature being the sacrifice (23:304).

"As in all acts of his mediation," Owen says, "the divine person of the Son, the eternal Spirit acting in him, acted in love and condescension" (20:304). "The *free will* of his human nature was in it also," he adds, explaining that the expression, "Lo, I come to do thy will," "sets out the readiness of the human will of Christ." This is "evident," Owen says, "from that exposition which is given of it, Ps. xl. 8, 'Yea, thy law is within my heart,' or 'in the midst of my bowels;'—'Thy law, the law of the mediator, that I am to undertake, it is in the midst of my heart;' which is an expression of the greatest readiness and willingness possible" (12:431).⁵ Thus, "wherever there is mention of Christ's offering himself, it relates principally to the person, God-man, who offered (12:430). "He then, that offers is our mediator, God and man in one person; and the offering is the act of the person" (12:431).

Secondly, he sacrificed "himself." Owen explains that a sacrifice is "a religious oblation, wherein something by the ministry of a priest, appointed of God thereunto, is dedicated to God, and destroyed as to what it was, for the ends and purposes of spiritual worship whereunto it is instituted" (12:431). How was the human nature of Christ offered as such a sacrifice? Owen says,

> Now, the person of Christ was not dissolved, but the union of his natures continued, even then when the human nature was in itself destroyed by the separation of soul and body. It was the soul and body of Christ that was sacrificed, his body being killed and his soul separated; so that at that season it was destroyed as to what it was, though it was impossible he should be detained by death. (12:431)

Owen adds that this sacrifice was "by the eternal Spirit," which

> is here opposed to the *material altar* as well as unto the fire. The altar was that whereon the sacrifice was laid, which bore it up in its oblation and ascension. But the eternal Spirit of Christ was the altar whereon he offered himself. This supported and bore it up under its sufferings, whereon it was presented unto God as an acceptable sacrifice. Wherefore this reading of the words gives a sense that is true and proper unto the matter of. (23:305)

At this point it is necessary to consider an important question concerning the interpretation of Hebrews 9:14. Owen says that the word "by" used here denotes the "principal efficient cause in that work" (23:303). Is the "eternal Spirit" referred to in the text the Holy Spirit, or the Divine nature of Christ? Owen answers,

> The truth is, both these concurred in, and were absolutely necessary unto the offering of Christ. The acting of his own eternal Spirit was so, as unto the *efficacy* and *effect*; and the acting of the Holy Ghost in him was so, as unto the *manner* of it. (23:304)

The previous remarks assume the former of these positions. How, then, might Christ be said to offer himself by the Holy Spirit? Owen's answer reflects his thoughts concerning the work of the Holy Spirit in filling the human nature of Christ with all grace requisite for the exercise of his mediatorial office (*supra*, chap. 11). Hence, in the offering of himself, he made a "free, voluntary, oblation and sacrifice" by the graces of "love and compassion," "zeal unto the glory of God," "holy submission unto the will of God," and "faith and trust in God" (23:305). Moreover, the fire upon the altar in the Old Testament was a type of the Holy Spirit (12:432). Owen believed that both sides of this issue reflect the truth. In his earlier works he inclined toward the position that the text referred to the Holy Spirit (12:432; 3:176-80), while in the Hebrews commentary he leans the opposite way because it is more appropriate to the context. The reasons given in his treatise on the Holy Spirit are essentially the same as those presented later; apparently only his evaluation of the significance of each had changed.

Concerning the altar on which this sacrifice was offered, Owen disagrees with those who identify it as the cross.

> Christ himself is said to be an altar, Heb. xiii. 10; and he is said to sanctify himself to be an offering or a sacrifice, John xvii. 19. So that, indeed, the deity of Christ, that supported, bore up, and sanctified the human nature as offered, was the altar, and the cross was but an instrument of the cruelty of man,

that taketh place in the death of Christ as it was a penalty, but hath no place in it as a sacrifice. (12:432-33; cf. 24:438-42)

This was a sacrifice of propitiation, typified by the sacrifices of the Old Testament. Owen mentions several aspects of the Old Testament sacrifices which constitute "types and resemblances of what was afterwards to be done by Christ himself," which consequently shed light upon Christ's priestly activity. "First," he says, "there was required thereunto the *adduction* of the...beast to be sacrificed, unto the priest," which "made it a 'corban,' a gift brought, sacred, dedicated to God." Christ's offering answers to several typical aspects of this adduction but Owen's exposition of this can be noted here only briefly (cf. 19:155).

Christ accomplished this adduction "in all those sacred actions of his which were previously preparatory unto his death" (19:157). Owen mentions four ways in which this was done. The first was Christ's going up to Jerusalem to the Passover. That this was for the purpose of making the great sacrifice is clear from Luke 18:31-33, and Matthew 20:17-19. Christ's rebuke of Peter's well-intended attempt to dissuade him makes this quite clear:

> Peter, considering only the outward part of his sufferings, with the shame and scandal wherewith it was attended, would have prevailed with him to have avoided it; which he knew was in his power to do. But withal, which he knew not, he dissuaded him from going to offer himself unto God, for which cause principally he came into the world, and so fell under this sacred rebuke; for this great and weighty work of obedience was so fully implanted in the heart of Christ, that he could not bear with any thing that had the appearance of a diversion from it. With such intention, freedom, willingness, and readiness of mind, did he go to offer himself, accord-

ing to the will of God; which gave life, virtue, and merit, unto his oblation. (19:157)

Second, Christ's "going into the garden the night before his suffering" was "as it were the bringing of himself to the door of the tabernacle to offer himself unto God, or to make his soul an offering for sin, according to the will of God" (19:157). Third,

> he offered up unto God prayers and supplications; which, because they had respect unto his sacrifice, are reckoned by our apostle as sacerdotal acts, Heb. v. 7.... And herein did our Saviour actually give himself unto God to be a sacrifice; which was to be done by expressions of his obedience, and supplications for that issue thereof which was promised unto him." (19:157)

Fourth,

> his propassion or foresuffering in the garden, in the anguish of his soul, the agony of his mind, and bloody sweat belongs hereunto. Hereon, indeed, succeeded an external shame, which was necessary for the leading and bringing of him "as a lamb to the slaughter," Isa. liii. 7, but his own mind and will it was that brought him to be a sacrifice to God. The offering himself was his own act, from first to last, and is constantly ascribed unto him. (19:157-58)

Following adduction there took place "*mactation*" or the actual slaying of the offering. As Owen explains,

> (1.) Herein the intention of the sacrificer and sacrificed, in that solemn *formula* which was understood in all expiatory sacrifices, '*Quod in ejus caput sit*,' [let it be upon his head] was effected or accomplished.... so the especial rite of confessing sin over the head of the scape-goat, thereby laying it on him, yea, and the command that he who brought his sin or trespass-offering should therewithal confess his own guilt, do make it evident.

"A Priest Forever"

(2.) It was the blood whereby atonement was made, and that as it was the life of the creature; and the reason why it was given to make atonement was because the life was in it. Wherefore that act whereby the blood of the creature was so taken away as that thereby the life of it was destroyed, was the principal thing in the sacrifice itself. (19:156)

After the mactation, Owen says, came the *"burning of the sacrifice,* or in some cases the principal parts of it, on the altar."* Owen's emphasis that this completes the sacrifice is due to the Socinian restriction of the sacrifice to the ceremony of sprinkling, thereby separating Christ's death from his priestly activity, restricting the latter to what took place after his resurrection. In reply Owen asserts that this sprinkling "was the only way whereby the perpetual efficacy of the blood of Christ in heaven, which was shed on the earth, might be represented" (19:156).

The Nature of the Sacrifice, or Oblation of Christ

The end and effect of the sacrifice of Christ was "atonement or reconciliation," that is, the full restoration of sinners to God. A number of key biblical words and motifs enter into Owen's exposition of the work of Christ. These must now be considered.

- Price

The sacrifice of Christ was a "price." Since this point was denied by Biddle, its full significance missed by the Arminians, and the appreciation of it is so important to true piety, Owen deals with it often (sometimes at great length) in his polemical and practical works.[6]

Owen defines this price in terms of 1 Peter 1:18-19.

It is the blood of Christ which in this business hath that use which silver and gold have in the redeeming of captives; and paid it is into the hand of him by whose power and authority the captive is detained,... And himself tells us what kind of a price it is that is so paid; it is *lutron*, Matt. xx. 28, "he came to lay down his life λύτρον ἀντὶ πολλῶν [ransom price for many]" which, for its more evidence and clearness, is called *antilutron*, 1 Tim. ii. 6, "a price of redemption" for the delivery of another. (12:419)

In order to demonstrate this, Owen undertakes a study of λύτρον and related words. Most importantly, in accordance with the covenant of redemption, through his obedience unto death, Christ obtained the deliverance of his people from all the consequences of the fall, and secured them unto himself. In reply to the teaching that, as in the case of Moses (Acts 7:35), redemption may not involve the payment of a price but only deliverance, Owen objects, "Shall we say, because that word is used improperly in one place, where no price could be paid, where God plainly says it was not done by a price but by power, therefore it must be so used in those places where there is express mention of a price, both the matter of it and its formality as a price, and speaketh not a word of doing it any other way but by the payment of a price?" (12:419).

- Satisfaction[7]

The price which Christ paid was a satisfaction for sin. Owen explains that satisfaction is a legal term for a "full compensation of the creditor from the debtor" (10:265; see pp. 265-88). It may be made by paying the "very thing" owed to the debtor, or by the payment of "so much, although in another kind,... which, by the creditor's acceptation stands in the lieu of it; but by virtue of an act of favour." Owen says for Christ to make satisfaction for sins "it is required only that he undergo the punishment due to them, for that is the satisfaction required where sin is the debt" (10:266). In making this satisfaction Christ did "that which God, who was offended, was more delighted and pleased withal, than he was displeased and offended with all the sins of all those that he suffered and offered himself for." This surely made it a "complete satisfaction" (10:267).

The question is, which of these two kinds of satisfaction did Christ make; a payment of the very thing ("*solutio ejusdem*"), or the payment of "so much" ("*solutio tantidem*"). Hugo Grotius built his famous doctrine of the atonement upon the latter opinion. If Christ paid the very thing, argued Grotius, the sinner would consequently be freed from his obligation, and there would be no room for pardon. It has been alleged that the former opinion is a legalistic denial of God's gracious pardon for sin. Owen grants the first inference, and denies the second. Yes, Christ did "actually, or *ipso facto*, deliver us from the curse," but this hardly means the deliverance from bondage is any less gratuitous for the sinner. Owen's justification for this assertion is very important, not only for the Christological debate, but for Christian piety and assurance. He says,

> God's gracious pardoning of sin compriseth the whole dispensation of grace towards us in Christ, whereof there are two parts:— *First*, The laying of our sin on Christ, or making him to be sin for us; which was merely and purely an act of free grace, which he did for his own sake. *Secondly*, The gracious imputation of the righteousness of Christ to us, or making us the righteous ness of God in him; which is no less of grace and mercy, and that because the very merit of Christ himself hath its foundation in a free compact and covenant. However, that remission, grace, and pardon, which is in God for sinners, is not opposed to Christ's merits, but ours. He pardoneth all to us; but he spared not his only Son, he bated him not one farthing. The freedom, then, of pardon hath not its foundation in any defect of the merit or satisfaction of Christ, but in three other things:—*First*, The will of God freely

appointing this satisfaction of Christ, John iii. 16; Rom. v. 8; 1 John iv. 9. *Secondly*, in a gracious acceptation of that decreed satisfaction in our steads; for so many, no more. *Thirdly*, in a free application of the death of Christ unto us.

Remission, then, excludes not a full satisfaction by the solution of the very thing in the obligation, but only the solution or satisfaction by him to whom pardon and remission are granted. (10:268-69)

The question remains, what did Christ pay in making satisfaction for our sin. Owen explains: "It was a full, valuable compensation, made to the justice of God, for all the sins of all them for whom he made satisfaction, by undergoing the same punishment which, by reason of the obligation that was upon them, they themselves were bound to undergo" (10:269). Since this, for sinners, would be eternity in hell, we might wonder how Christ could be said to have, in Toplady's words, "to the utmost farthing paid, whate'er thy people owed." Owen explains that by "the same" he means "essentially the same in weight and pressure, though not in all accidents of duration and the like" (10:269-70). Christ suffered the penalty of sin which was death. Explaining further, he says,

It is true, this death may be considered either in respect of its essence...which is called the 'pains of hell,' which Christ underwent,... or of its attendancies, as duration and the like, which he could not undergo, Ps. xvi. 8-11, Acts ii. 24-28. so that whereas eternal death may be considered two ways, either as such *in potentia* [potentially], and in its own nature, or as actually, so our Saviour underwent it not in the latter, but first sense, Heb. ii. 9, 14, which by the dignity of his person,...which raises the estimation of punishment, is *aequipotent* [of equal efficacy] to the other. There is a sameness in Christ's sufferings with that in the obligation in respect of essence, and equivalency in respect of attendancies. (10:448)[8]

- Merit

In addition to making satisfaction for sin, Christ, by virtue of the covenant of redemption, merited all good for his elect.

> All these hath our Savior by his death merited and purchased for all them for whom he died; that is, so procured them of his Father that they ought, in respect of that merit, according to the equity of justice, to be bestowed on them for whom they were so purchased and procured. (10:287-88)

Though the word "merit" is lacking in the Scriptures, "the thing itself" is there, as Owen argues from the various ways the Bible speaks of Christ's "meritorious procuring," purchasing, or otherwise obtaining God's "good things" for us by his death. In this respect, "merit" and "price" are closely related ideas (see, e.g., 12:78; 7:553). Owen classifies these good things as "privative," referring to the deliverance of his people from all and every kind of evils; and as "positive," the securing to them of everything needed to bring them into the enjoyment of everlasting salvation, conformed to the image of Christ (10:287-88; see 7:553; 10:465-68; 11:301-302).

- Reconciliation

The objective of this propitiatory work was that God and men, who were formerly in a state of enmity, might be reconciled. Owen disproves the Abelardian and Socinian claim that the proper act of Christ is the exertion of a converting influence upon fearful and unbelieving men. Like Luther before him, however, Owen retains that influence as a necessary aspect of reconciliation. He begins with a clarification of the terminology:

> By "reconciling God," we intend the making of such atonement as whereby his wrath or anger, in all the effects of it, is turned away. Though we use not the expression of "reconciling God to us," but of "recon-

ciling us to God," by the taking away or removal of his wrath and anger, or the making reconciliation with God for sin, yet, as to reconcile God intends the appeasing of the justice and anger of God, so that whereas before we were obnoxious to his displeasure, enmity, hatred, and wrath, thereby and on that account, we come to be accepted with him, we say Christ died to reconcile God to us. (12:414)

In a sense it may be said that Christ by his death "brought God to us," namely, in "*the procurement of the grace and favour of God towards us*, and his loving presence to be with us" (12:414). However, there is also a human side to this reconciliation. "Reconciliation as it stands on our part, is our *conversion* unto God, our deliverance from all that enmity and opposition unto God which are in us by nature; and this also we say is the effect and fruit of the death of Christ" (12:414). Thus,

"Our bringing unto God" mentioned 1 Pet. iii. 18, is of a larger and more comprehensive signification than that our reconciliation, containing the whole effect of the death of Christ, in the removal of every hinderance and the collation of every thing necessarily required to the perfect and complete accomplishment of the work of our salvation; and so contains no less the reconciliation of God to us than ours to him, and is not proper to make up one member of the division there instituted, being a general expression of them both,

and, "without them both the work of reconciliation is by no means complete" (12:414).

As proof, Owen argues that "if in the Scripture it is expressly and frequently affirmed, that, *antecedently* to the consideration of the death of Christ and the effects thereof, there is not only a *real enmity* on our part against God, but also a *law enmity* on the part of God against us, and that both of these are removed by virtue of the death of Christ, then the reconciliation of God to us and our reconciliation to God are both of them one entire effect of the death of Christ" (12:415). Owen convincingly demonstrates from the Scriptures that both of these types of enmity in fact existed, concluding that "there being, then, a mutual enmity between God and us, though not of the same kind (it being physical on our part, and legal or moral on the part of God): Christ, our mediator, making up peace and friendship between us doth not only reconcile us to God by his Spirit, but God also to us by his blood" (12:415). One Scripture Owen expounds in support of this point is 2 Corinthians 5:18-20, which speaks of reconciliation "*in both the senses insisted on;*—of us to God, verse 20, where the apostle saith the end of the ministry is to reconcile us to God, to prevail with us to lay down our enmity against him and opposition to him; of God to us, verse 19,... which... is evinced from the exegetical expression immediately following" (12:416).[9]

Intercession
In addition to oblation, Christ carries out the "second duty of the priestly office," intercession.[10] "Without this," Owen says, Christ's oblation "would not profit us; if he had done no more he could not have been a priest" (23:32-34).

Intercession, according to Owen, "is of two sorts:—(1.) *Formal* and *oral*; (2.) *Virtual* and *real*" (19:196). The first sort, formal and oral, takes place

> when any one, by words, arguments, supplications, with humble earnestness in their use, prevails with another for any good thing that is in his power to be bestowed on himself or others. Of this nature was the intercession of Christ whilst he was on the earth. He dealt with God, by prayers, and supplications,... with respect unto himself in the work he had undertaken, but principally for the church of his elect, Heb. v. 7; John xvii. (19:197)

Owen distinguishes this formal supplication by Christ "suited unto the state wherein he was"—i.e., the state of humiliation, from the "virtual or real intercession" now made by the glorified Christ. The formal supplication was grounded upon an oblation yet to be completed;

> But now, in heaven, the state and condition of Christ admitting of no oral or formal supplications, and the ground, reason, or argument of his intercession, being finished and past, his intercession, as the means of the actual impetration of grace and glory, consists in the real presentation of his offering and sacrifice for the procuring of the actual communication of the fruits thereof unto them for whom he so offered himself. The whole matter of words, prayers, and supplications, yea, of internal conceptions of the mind formed into prayers, is but accidental unto intercession, attending the state and condition of him that intercedes. The real entire nature of it consists in the presentation of such things as may prevail in the way or motive or procuring cause with respect unto the things interceded for. And such do we affirm the intercession of Christ as our high priest in heaven to be. (19:197)

This intercession of Christ is an *"appearing for us* in heaven in the presence of God, a demonstration of his sacred body, wherein for us he suffered" (10:184). In passing, it is interesting to compare this concept of Christ's intercession with that expressed in Charles Wesley's hymn which begins, "Arise my soul arise." Wesley wrote:

> Five bleeding wounds he bears,
> Received on Calvary;
> They pour effectual prayers,
> They strongly plead for me;
> Forgive him, O forgive, they cry,
> Nor let that ransomed sinner die!

"A Priest Forever"

This is but poetically to express Owen's more technical description:

> In this his appearance *he presents himself unto God as a Lamb that had been slain*, Rev. v. 6. He is now alive, and lives forever. But there must, as unto efficacy in this appearance, be a representation of his sacrifice, his suffering, his death, his blood,—of himself as a Lamb slain and offered unto God. And this was to be so in answer unto the blood of the expiatory sacrifice which the high priest carried into the holy place. For he was himself both the priest and the sacrifice, the offerer and the lamb. And as that blood was sprinkled before the ark and the mercy-seat, to apply the atonement made unto all the sacred pledges of God's presence and good-will; so from this representation of the offering of Christ, of himself as "a Lamb that had been slain," in this his appearance before God, doth all the application of its benefits unto the church proceed. (23:384)

One of Owen's principal objections against the general ransom which Wesley was to champion in the following century was just this matter of Christ's "effectual prayers" made by these "five bleeding wounds." The wounds themselves, as marks of Christ's satisfaction of divine justice, plead against any further punishment for sin. Moreover, as they were received in fulfillment of the covenant, they also, according to that covenant, effectually plead for the application of that redemption in regenerating, converting, sanctifying, and preserving the heirs of salvation.

As he had emphasized that Christ's oblation consisted of more than his crucifixion, Owen also asserts that his intercession included not only

> that heavenly appearance of his in the most holy place for the applying unto us all good things purchased and procured by his oblation; but also every act of his exaltation conducing thereunto, from his

resurrection to his "sitting down at the right hand of the Majesty on high, angels, and principalities, and powers, being made subject unto him." Of all which his resurrection, being the basis, as it were, and the foundation of the rest..., is especially to be considered, as that to which a great part of the effect is often ascribed; for "he was delivered for our offences, and was raised again for our justification," Rom. iv. 25;—where, and in such other places, by his resurrection the whole following dispensation and the perpetual intercession of Christ for us in heaven is intended. (10:180)

Further, Owen emphasizes that this appearance of our high priest in heaven is *for us*. "It is as it were the appearance of an advocate, a law in the behalf of others" (23:384).

The Relation Between Oblation and Intercession
The connection between Christ's oblation and his intercession is extremely important to Owen's understanding of the work of Christ, comprising an essential stone in the foundation of Christian assurance, and a crucial point of conflict with every form of universal redemption. This relation is evident from a number of scriptural observations. There is a picture of this, for instance, in the action of the high priest (19:195-96; cf. 10:176). In fact, Christ's intercession has always been associated with his oblation, as Owen reminds us in the following remarks:

> Now, his intercession before his actual oblation in the fulness of time being nothing but a presenting of the engagement that was upon him for the work in due time to be accomplished, certainly that which follows it is nothing but a presenting of what according to that engagement is fulfilled; so that it is nothing but a continuation of his oblation in postulating by remembrance and declaration of it, those things which by it were procured. (10:184-85)

In Charles Wesley's hymn referred to earlier it is asserted that Christ's blood "atoned for all our race, and sprinkles now the throne of grace." Owen certainly would have objected that the poet had failed duly to consider the relation that exists between Christ's oblation and his intercession; arguing that

> though the *oblation* and *intercession* of Jesus Christ are distinct acts in themselves, and have distinct immediate products and issues assigned oftimes unto them..., yet they are not in any respect or regard to be divided or separated, as that the one should have any respect to any persons or any thing which the other also doth not in its kind equally respect. But there is this manifold union between them:—
>
> First, In that they are both alike intended for the obtaining and accomplishing the same entire and complete end proposed,—to wit, the effectual bringing of many sons to glory, for the praise of God's grace;...
>
> Secondly, That what persons soever the one respecteth, in the good things it obtaineth, the same, all, and none else, doth the other respect, in applying the good things so obtained;...
>
> Thirdly, That the *oblation* of Christ is, as it were, the foundation of his intercession, inasmuch as by the oblation was procured every thing that, by virtue of his intercession, is bestowed; and that because the sole end why Christ procured any thing by his death was that it might be applied to them for whom it was procured. (10:181; cf. Kendall 1979, 14-17)

So important is this idea to Owen that he devotes two entire chapters of *The Death of Death* to its demonstration. In the first he proves "the oblation and intercession of Christ to be one entire means with the same personal object." First, Owen shows the, "perpetual union which the Scripture maketh" of oblation and intercession, "so manifesting those things to be most inseparable which are looked upon as the distinct fruits and effects of them" (10:182). For example, Owen directs our attention to the descriptions of Christ's work found in Isaiah 53, and in Romans 4 and 8 (10:182).

Secondly, Owen points to the union of these as two indispensable "acts of the same sacerdotal office" incumbent upon every "faithful priest." From 1 John 2:1-2, Owen insists, "He must be an *advocate* to intercede, as well as offer a propitiatory sacrifice, if he will be such a merciful *high priest* over the house of God as that the children should be encouraged to go to God by him" (10:182).[11]

Next Owen expounds this link as present in Hebrews 9:11-13, adding,

> I cannot but demand of those who oppose us about the death of Christ whether they will sustain that he intercedeth for all or no;—if not, they make him but half a priest; if they will, they must be necessitated either to defend this error, that all shall be saved, or own this blasphemy, that Christ is not heard of his Father, nor can prevail in his intercession, which yet the saints on earth are sure to do when they make their supplications according to the will of God, Rom. viii. 27, 1 John v. 14. Besides that, of our Saviour it is expressly said that the Father always heareth him, John xi. 42; and if that were true when he was yet in the way, in the days of his flesh, and had not finished the great work he was sent about, how much more then now, when having done the will and finished the work of God, he is set down on the right hand of the Majesty on high, desiring and requesting the accomplishing of the promises that were made unto him upon his undertaking this work! (10:184)

The fact that the intercession is *real* rather than vocal is a further argument to the "inseparable conjunction between" intercession and oblation. As he puts it, "if the *oblation* and death of Christ procured and obtained that every good thing should be bestowed which is actually conferred by the intervening of his *intercession*, then they have both of them the same aim, and are both means tending to one and the same end." For proof Owen appeals to the covenant of redemption as the, "ground and foundation of our Saviour's *intercession*." His intercession is based upon a promise, for example, Psalm 2:8, "Ask of me, and I will give thee the heathen for thine inheritance." Consequently, Owen argues,

> ... these promises being nothing but an engagement to bestow and actually collate upon them for whom he suffered all those good things which his death and *oblation* did merit and purchase, it cannot be but that he intercedeth for all for whom he died, that his death procured all and every thing which upon his *intercession* is bestowed; and until they are bestowed, it hath not its full fruits and effects. (10:185; 23:203-204)

Effects of Christ's Sacerdotal Activity

The "immediate" effects of the Priesthood of Christ (i.e., towards God) are "atonement and reconciliation." Owen says, "Without a supposition of these all other things are rendered useless" (3:629). The "mediate" effects, on the other hand, are those experienced by us on account of the former. These are divided into "*moral*, as our *justification and pardon of sin*," and "*real*, in our *sanctification and holiness*" (3:629).

Forgiveness and Justification

It may already be apparent, and should shortly appear quite certain, that this doctrine of the priesthood excludes both legalism and antinomianism by seeing Christ as the one in whom the law is fulfilled for our justification, and the one by whose grace the righteousness of the law is fulfilled in us (Rom. 8:1-4).

Forgiveness, "flows from the cross, and springs out of the grace of Christ." Commenting on Isaiah 53:11, Owen says,

> Of the justification of sinners, absolution or pardon is the first part. This ariseth from Christ's bearing their iniquities.... Our redemption in his blood is our forgiveness: not that we are all actually pardoned in the blood of his cross, for thereunto must be added gospel condonation,... but thereby it is procured, the grant of pardon is therein sealed, and security given that it shall in due time be made out unto us. (6:405)

Just as we saw that intercession is the pleading of covenant kept by Christ, so forgiveness is the granting of what was procured by Christ's blood. The connection is firm: "Our redemption is our forgiveness, as the cause contains the effect" (6:405). The reason for this is that "*in his blood the promised pardon is ratified and confirmed*, so that nothing is wanting to our complete forgiveness but our pleading the promise by faith in him." Since his death, Christ's covenant has become a testament, "so ratified in his blood that mercy and forgiveness of sin is irrevocably confirmed unto us therein" (6:406). This is likewise confirmed by his resurrection, as the head of his body, the church, Christ has "received an acquitment," a "discharge" for them all. Moreover, interestingly (but not surprisingly, given what Owen says about the role of Christ as mediator), forgiveness has been placed by the Father into the hand of Christ, so that "all forgiveness is now at his disposal, and he pardoneth whom he will, even all that are given unto him of the Father, not casting out any that come to God by him" (6:406).

Cleansing

Christ performs a two-fold cleansing of his people. Owen

notes that cleansing in the Scripture denotes "to purge by expiation or atonement" or "*real actual purification*" such as the spiritual purification accomplished through sanctifying grace" (20:110). The first of these, referred to in Hebrews 1:3, was accomplished "by himself" in his death, and is a "thing already past and perfected" (20:110). This, Owen emphasizes, answers to the type of the purgations performed by the Old Testament priests when they made expiatory sacrifices:

> This purging, then, of our sins, which the apostle declareth to have been effected before the ascension of Christ and his sitting down at the right hand of God, consisteth not in the actual sanctification and purification of believers by the Spirit, in the application of the blood of Christ unto them, but in the atonement made by him in the sacrifice of himself, that our sins should not be imputed unto us. And therefore is he said to purge our sins, and not to purge us from our sins. And wherever sins, not sinners, are made the object of any mediatory act of Christ, that act immediately respecteth God, and not the sinner, and intends the removal of sin, so as that it should not be imputed. (20:111)

In addition to this, however, and flowing out of the virtue of it, is the "actual" purification of believers "by the application of the blood of Christ to them." Owen calls the blood of Christ the "*meritorious* procuring, and so the effective cause, that *immediately purgeth* us from our sins, by an especial application of it unto our souls by the Holy Ghost" (3:438). This is the cleansing typified by the Old Testament ceremonies of purification such as the cleansing of the leprous and defiled.

Owen's exposition of the way the blood of Christ works in the process of sanctification is extraordinary, even in an age noted for its emphasis upon the doctrine of sanctification. By the "blood of Christ" Owen understands the "blood of his *sacrifice*, with the power, virtue, and efficacy thereof" (3:440). The blood of the sacrifice was offered to make atonement and "*sprinkled* on other things for their purging and sanctification." The blood thus sprinkled was effectual, legally speaking, for the removal of guilt and defilement. "Every one, therefore, who at any time hath an especial actual interest in the blood of Christ, as sacrificed, hath as real a purification from the defilement of sin as he had typically who stood by the priest and had blood or water sprinkled on him" (3:440-41). As these sacrifices were done continually for the "daily incursions of secret and unknown sins," and yearly for "all their known and great sins," and upon other occasions for the occasional "miscarriage or surprisal," so the blood of Christ is effectual for the continuous cleansing of our sins and purification of our persons.

This purification takes place in two ways: by the removal from the sinner of "loathsomeness in the sight of God" due to his sins; and by the removal of "shame out of the conscience," so that the believer may have "boldness in the presence of God" (3:442).[12]

Preservation
Another benefit of the oblation and intercession of Christ is the preservation of the saints. Christ, Owen says, "intercedes for the preservation of believers in the love and favour of his Father to the end" (11:365, see 365-79). In fact, this is especially the intent of Christ's intercession. Against the opinions of the Arminian John Goodwin, Owen argues that Christ's intercession is not in order that believing and persevering sinners might be saved, since by the "law of the gospel" they must be. Rather, he intercedes in order that those for whom he offered an oblation might actually be delivered from guilt and abide in peace with God.

The content of Christ's heavenly intercession is suggested in the "preface" to it found in John 17, where the mediator pleads his perfect compliance with the Father's will in order that the power of God's "name" might be engaged for the preservation of his believers "in the love and favour of God, by their continuance in believing, and preservation from the power of temptations and oppositions arising against their perseverance in communion with God" (11:367-69).

The priesthood of Christ holds out a great encouragement to perseverance in the faith. Not only may we be subjectively strengthened by the knowledge that he pities believers in their trials, but he also provides actual help for our faith, our obedience, and our profession (21:403, 404).

The Beneficiaries of the Priesthood of Christ

R. S. Franks undertakes the analysis of Owen's *The Death of Death* with the assumption that the "idea of absolute predestination...dominated the greatest of the Puritan theologians, John Owen," and that Owen's treatise on the doctrine of the work of Christ "is entirely consecrated to the complete subjugation of the doctrine" of Christ's work "to this idea" (Franks 1962, 460). Franks failed to do Owen justice on two counts. First, he has failed to answer Owen's proof of the premise which Franks would so eagerly revise. Second, he has erred in suggesting that Owen's doctrine of the atonement is distorted by being subjugated to the doctrine of predestination. The preceding discussion cannot adequately convey the force of Owen's logic, but it should be sufficient to show that while Owen's doctrine of the work of Christ supports a Calvinist doctrine of predestination, it is not "dominated" by it. It is apparent throughout that Owen believes the Bible's own description of the atonement is universally incompatible with a universal redemption.

In addition to this positive description of the work of

redemption, it was necessary for Owen to answer the pleas and objections of the advocates of a "general ransom." It would be unfair to Owen to suggest that the strength of his case, argued at such length and with such force, could be communicated in the remainder of this chapter. The following description, given merely to acquaint the reader with a portion of Owen's argument, is made in violation of Owen's own very justifiable dictum regarding the study of his treatise: "If thou art, as many in this pretending age, a *sign or title gazer*, and comest into books as Cato into the theatre, to go out again,—thou hast had thy entertainment; farewell!" (10:149). Nevertheless, we should take notice of his "titles."

The first argument against universal redemption is based upon the doctrine of the covenant of grace. This covenant was "established, ratified, and confirmed in and by the death of Christ; that was the testament whereof he was the testator, which was ratified in his death, and whence his blood is called 'The blood of the new testament,' Matt. xxvi. 28." Its effects cannot be "extended beyond the compass of this covenant," which was "not made universally with all, but particularly only with some, and therefore those alone were intended in the benefits of the death of Christ" (10:236). The new covenant, furthermore, must be distinguished from the old. In the old covenant God required the fulfilling of the condition prescribed, but in the new, "he promiseth to effect in them himself with whom the covenant is made" (10:236).

Next, Owen argues that it is not consistent with the love and wisdom of God to send Christ to die for those who by his own providence shall never be told of the condition for enjoying its benefits (10:238-40). This is certainly no argument against the need of evangelism, and it would be unjust to make it one. In fact, Owen draws the opposite conclusion, as he argues in "A Vision of Unchangeable, Free Mercy." In that sermon he says "there is a right in the gospel, and a fitness in that gracious dispensation to be made known to all people in the world." This right rests upon the new covenant and the

> infinite value and worth of the blood of Christ, giving fulness and fitness to the promises founded thereon to be propounded to all mankind; for through his blood remission of sins is preached to whosoever believes on him, Acts x. 43,—"to every creature," Mark xvi. 15. God would have a price of that infinite value for sin laid down, as might justly give advantage to proclaim a pardon infinitely to all that will come in and accept of it,— there being in it no defect at all (though intentionally a ransom for some), but that by it the world might know that he had done whatsoever the Father commanded him, John xiv. 31. (8:20)

The providential management of the spread and success of the gospel (as described in the same sermon) is a fact, nevertheless, which argues against the idea of a ransom made for those who by God's own determination shall not receive the gospel.

Third, Owen argues that if Christ died for all it was either *absolutely*, or upon some condition by them to be fulfilled. If absolutely, then all must be saved. If conditionally, then Christ procured the condition or he did not. If it is upon a condition procured, then this condition must be made known. If men are able to perform this condition, Owen asks, are they able to meet it by the power of their free will? Scripture clearly answers that they are not. If it is "wrought within them by the free grace of God," Owen argues,

> then when God gave his son to die for them, to procure eternal redemption for them all, upon condition that they did believe, he either purposed to work faith in them all by his grace, that they might believe, or he did not? If he did, why doth not

> he actually perform it,...Why do not all believe? If he did not purpose to bestow faith on them all,... then the sum of it comes to this: That God gave Christ to die for all men, but upon this condition, that they perform that which of themselves without him they cannot perform, and purposed that for his part he would not accomplish it in them. (10:240-41)

Given the premise of man's inability due to sin and the necessity of regenerating grace, Owen's conclusion is denied with the greatest difficulty (cf. 10:114-29; 3:242-337).

Fourth, Owen argues,

> If all mankind be...distinguished into two sorts and conditions, severally and distinctly described and set forth in the Scripture, and Christ be peculiarly affirmed to die for one of these sorts, and nowhere for them of the other, then did he not die for all: for of the one sort he dies for all and every one, and of the other for no one at all. (10:243)

Of course, it is easy to demonstrate that the Scripture makes such a distinction. "Now," he asks, "Christ is said expressly and punctually to die for them on the one side:... Whence we may surely conclude that Christ died not for all and every one (10:243-45).

It is the second of these conclusions which comes under attack by modern Arminians (eg., Miethe, 1989, 73). It is argued that such assertions of Christ dying for his "sheep," for "us," etc. merely assert that he died for the group in view and have no relevance to a hypothetical people not in the group ("non-sheep" for instance). Against this Owen argues,

> is it not, without any forced interpretation, in common sense, and according to the usual course of speaking, to distinguish men into two such opposite conditions as elect and reprobate, sheep and goats, and then affirm that he died for his elect, [is it not] equivalent to this, he died for his elect only? Is not

"A Priest Forever"

the sense as clearly restrained as if that restrictive term had been added? Or is that term always added in the Scripture in every indefinite assertion, which yet must of necessity be limited and restrained as if it were expressly added? (10:245)

In his fifth argument, Owen challenges the claim that the Scripture makes the assertion that Christ died *for all men*: "That is not to be asserted...which the Scripture doth not anywhere go before us in, but the Scripture nowhere saith Christ died for all men, much less for all and every man (between which two there is a wide difference...): therefore this is not to be asserted" (10:245-46). Owen undertakes an extensive examination of the passages pleaded in favor of this claim (10:316-403).

Owen's next argument is based upon the biblical relation between Christ and those for whom he died as a "sponsor" and as a mediator.

> For whom Christ died he died as a *sponsor*, in their stead, as is apparent, Rom. v. 6-8,... Now, if he died as the sponsor or surety of them for whom he died, in their stead, then these two things at least will follow:—First, That he freed them from that anger, and wrath, and guilt of death, which he underwent for them, that they should in and for him be all reconciled, and be freed from the bondage wherein they are by reason of death; for no other reason...can be assigned why Christ should undergo any thing in another's stead, but that the other might be freed from undergoing that which he underwent for him. (10:246)

He continues,

> Christ made satisfaction for the sins of all and every man, if he died for them; for the reason he underwent death for us as a surety was, to make satisfaction to God's justice for our sins, so to redeem us to himself.... But Christ hath not satisfied

> the justice of God for all the sins of all and every man. (10:247)

This definition of the atonement as a satisfaction by a substitute was the premise, which Franks sought to eliminate (the logic of Owen's argument being irrefutable).

Owen also directs attention to Christ's role as the mediator.

> For whom Christ died, for them he is a *mediator*: which is apparent; for the oblation or offering of Christ, which he made of himself unto God, in the shedding of his blood, was one of the chiefest acts of his mediation. But he is not a mediator for all and everyone; which is also is no less evident, because as mediator he is the priest of them for whom he is a mediator. Now to a priest it belongs, as was declared before, to sacrifice and intercede, to procure good things, and to apply them to those for whom they are procured;...which, confessedly, Christ doth not for all. (10:249)

"If the blood of Jesus Christ doth *wash*...and *sanctify* them for whom it was shed, or for whom he was a sacrifice," Owen reasons, "then certainly he died,...only for them that in the event are *washed*...and *sanctified*" (10:250). Christ blood is "effectual for all those ends of washing," as is evident from the types. According to Hebrews 9:13f., the type was effectual for the cleansing of the flesh (i.e., it "legally sanctified them for whom it was a sacrifice") but the antitype for the real sanctification of all for whom it was made. This efficacy, moreover, is explicitly affirmed of the death of Christ (10:250-58).

Owen's next set of arguments is based upon the nature of redemption and reconciliation. We have already viewed his treatment of these themes earlier in the present chapter, so at this point we will merely observe their place in his argument. Since redemption is delivery upon the payment of a ransom, "when a ransom is paid for the liberty of a prisoner, is it not all the justice in the world that he should have and enjoy the liberty so purchased for him by a valuable consideration" (10:260-61). The Arminian objection that it is necessary that the captive agree to the release arises from a failure to see the full extent of that captivity. The sinner's unbelief, his "refusal" of the ransom, is actually a manifestation of his captivity, which is not physical but legal (as far as God is concerned), and spiritual (in the captivity of his mind and heart to sin and Satan). Christ's redemptive work restores the sinner into God's favor, and delivers him from captivity to sin and Satan.

As noted already, Christ makes twofold reconciliation: of God to us, and of us to God. "All those to whom he hath reconciled God, he doth also reconcile to God: for unless both be effected, it cannot be said to be a perfect reconciliation; for how can it be if peace be made only on one side?" (10:261). Since reconciliation is the "renewing of friendship *between parties* before at variance," and "all differences removed in respect of any former grudge and ill will," then it follows, "if one be well pleased with the other, and that other continue…unappeased and implacable, there is no reconciliation" (10:262). The biblical doctrine of reconciliation is incompatible with universal redemption because, first, God is not reconciled to all; secondly, "all are not reconciled to God," as Owen observes.

> That reconciliation which is the renewing of lost friendship, the slaying of enmity, the making up of peace, the appeasing of God, and turning away of his wrath, attended with the non imputation of iniquities; and on our part, conversion to God by faith and repentance; this, I say, being that reconciliation which is the effect of the death and blood of Christ, it cannot be asserted in reference to any, nor Christ said to die for any other, but only those concerning whom all the properties of it, and acts wherein it

doth consist, may be truly affirmed; which, whether they may be all men or not let all men judge. (10:264)

The next arguments are based upon the principle of satisfaction to divine justice: "Christ by his death made *satisfaction* to the justice of God for their sins for whom he died, so that they might go free" (10:265).

> Now, that which is aimed at in the payment of this price is, the deliverance of those from the evil wherewith they were oppressed for whom the price is paid; it being in this spiritual redemption as it is in corporal and civil, only with the alteration of some circumstances, as the nature of the thing enforceth. This the Holy Spirit manifesteth by comparing the "blood of Christ " in this work of redemption with "silver and gold," and such other things as are the intervening ransom in civil redemption, 1 Pet. i. 18, 19. (10:259)

The Use of the Priesthood of Christ

The excellencies of the priesthood of Christ resulting from the dignity of his person and the perfection of his acts, result in a wide variety of practical applications for the faith and worship of Christians. Some measure of this may be suggested by the fact that Owen's "Summary of Doctrinal and Practical Observations" drawn from his exposition of Hebrews extends to eighty pages in the Goold edition! Many of these practical observations naturally concern the priestly office. One very important question relative to the extent of the atonement is the "free offer" of the gospel, but this will be discussed in the next chapter where, we believe, Owen would say it belongs.

---

[1] See David Clarkson's *Christ Touched With the Feeling of Our Infirmities* (1696, 639-91).

[2] For a detailed exposition of the call of Christ to the office of priest see Owen's exposition of Hebrews 5:4-6 (21: 475-96).

[3] On justification and the obedience of Christ, see also Anthony

Burgesse's sermons "On The Imputation of the Righteousness of Christ Both Active and Passive" in *The True Doctrine* (1654, 284-456); Bunyan's *Justification by an Imputed Righteousness* (1853, 1:301-34); John Brown of Wamphrey, *The Life of Justification Opened* (1695).

[4] Medieval scholastics distinguished between the active and passive righteousness in Christ, arguing that the (active) righteousness of his life was not imputed to others, but was necessary for himself in order that the (passive) obedience of his death might be applied to others. Reformed theology argued that both the active and passive obedience of Christ was imputed to believers, and that this imputed obedience (i.e., righteousness) is the formal ground of justification. Since the beginning of the Reformation the question of the formal ground of justification was seen as crucial by Protestants, as is clear in their rejection of Cardinal Contarini's mediating position at the Regensberg colloquy, the doctrine of justification fixed by the Council of Trent and advanced by Cardinal Bellarmine, and Osiander's doctrine of justification through participation in the righteousness of God through Christ. C. F. Allison shows that the question of the formal cause of justification "basically divided Anglicanism from the teaching of the Council of Trent, and...determined the direction of a new school of thought that arose during the Civil War in England, a school neither 'orthodox' Anglican nor Tridentine" (Allison, 1966, x). Allison has in mind various Neonomians (e.g., Baxter), Arminians (e.g., John Goodwin), and Latitudinarians (e.g., Fowler, Stillingfleet, and Jeremy Taylor). Allison's work in regard to this issue in seventeenth century England is most helpful in identifying and properly evaluating this theological movement.

[5] See Stephen Charnock, *A Discourse on the Voluntariness of Christ's Death* (1684, 874-83).

[6] Against Socinianism see especially, 5:52; 12:78, 419-33, 508-31; 23:333. Against Arminianism, see 10:230-32, 255-61, 265-88, 295-97. Against Socinianism, Arminianism, and the opinions of Richard Baxter, see *Of the Death of Christ, the Price He Paid and the Purchase He Made*, (10:430-79). For Owen's application of this concept to the Christian life, see 2:165-97; 6:641-48; 4:409-10; 7:553; 8:20, 298; 23:281-84. See also Manton (1870, 1:417-26) and Flavel, (1820, 1:176-97).

[7] See Burgesse (1654, 49-111), Manton (1870, 1:417-26) and Flavel (1820, 1:176-97).

[8] The question of how the temporal sufferings can be accepted for the eternal punishment of sinners is also handled by Anthony Burgesse (1654, 73-74), Manton (1870, 13:182).

[9] For more on the sacrifice of Christ see Charnock's *A Discourse of Christ our Passover* (1684, 846-73); also David Clarkson's *Christ's Sacrifice* (1696, 913-25), and his *Christ Dying for Sinners* (1696, 925-39).

[10] See Goodwin (4:56-150), Charnock, *A Discourse on Christ's Interces-*

sion (1684:1109-54), Manton (1870, 10:241-54), Clarkson (1697, 987-1004), Ambrose (1855, 557-601), and Flavel (1820, 165-75).

[11] In *The Work of Jesus Christ as an Advocate*, John Bunyan emphatically distinguishes between the priesthood and advocacy of Christ (1853, 169-70). Christ is a priest for all his elect, but an advocate only for sinning believers. On the other hand, in *Christ a Complete Savior*, an exposition of Hebrews 7:29, Bunyan describes Christ as a high priest, interceding for the uncalled elect and also for believers (1853, 203-39).

[12] See Stephen Charnock's *Discourse on the Cleansing Virtue of Christ's Blood* (1684, 1183-1211). Charnock says Christ's blood cleanses us "universally" from sin: from the "sense" of it, "the stirrings of it," and God's "condemnation and punishment" of it. The effect of this cleansing "shall appear perfect at the last at the final Sentence" (1195-97). Like most Puritan sermons of this type, it includes a sweeping summary of the main themes of the gospel, with application, thus demonstrating the systematic and pastoral way the Puritans approached particular aspects of the person and work of Christ.

CHAPTER
14

"He who Speaks from Heaven"

The Relation of Christ's Person to His Office

The theme of Christ's revelatory role appears quite early in Owen's major Christological works, filling chapters 5-7 of the *Christologia*, chapter 2 of *The Glory of Christ*, and thirty-eight pages of *Communion with God*. This is not surprising in view of its importance: "What may be known of God," (i.e., the subject of theology),

> is,—his nature and existence, with the holy counsels of his will. A representation of them unto us is the foundation of all religion, and the means of our conformity unto him—wherein our present duty and future blessedness do consist. (1:65)

One of the crucial differences between the Reformed and Socinian Christologies concerned the relation of Christ's person to his office. The prophetic office was the chief interest of the Socinians, who subsumed the whole work of Christ's mediation under it (12:348). That is, Christ came into the world (i.e., into public life) to teach obedience to God and bring to light the promise of the resurrection. In reply, Owen taught that "those who deny his divine person, though they pretend to attend unto him as the teacher of the church, do yet learn no truth from him but embrace pernicious errors in the stead thereof" (1:95). In contrast to this failing of the Socinians, rightly regarding the person of Christ will

> ingenerate in us all those holy qualifications that are necessary to enable us to know the mind and will of God. For hence do reverence, humility, faith, delight, and assurance, arise and flow; without whose continual exercise, in vain shall men hope to learn the will of God by the utmost of their endeavors. And the want of these things is the cause of much of that lifeless, unsanctified knowledge of the doctrine of the Gospel which is amongst many. They learn not the truth from Christ, so as to expect all teachings from his divine power. Hence they never come to know it, either in its native beauty drawing the soul into the love and delight of what they know, or in its transforming efficacy changing the mind into its own image and likeness. (1:96)

Its Necessity for the Knowledge of God

Several factors render this role of the mediator absolutely necessary.[1] The first of these is the incomprehensibility of God:

> His nature being immense, and all his holy properties essentially infinite, no creature can directly or perfectly comprehend them, or any of them. He must be infinite that can perfectly comprehend that which is infinite; wherefore God is perfectly known unto himself only—but as for us, how little a portion is heard of him! (1:65)

An additional cause is his invisibility. While this is usually attributed to his being a spirit, Owen reminds us that God's invisibility is also due to his immensity, and that, though "'no man hath seen God at any time; the only-begotten Son, who is in the bosom of the Father, he hath declared him:' John i. 18" (1:65). Moreover, "All the rational conceptions of the minds of men are swallowed up and lost, when they would exercise themselves directly on that which is absolutely immense, eternal, infinite" (1:66). As Owen explains, even in the glorified state we will be incapable of "seeing" the divine essence for its immensity: the beatific vision will be "through Christ Jesus, who shall for ever be the medium of communication between God and the church" (1:413-14).

With regard to the divine essence we must travel the *via negativa*. That is, "What *we deny* of God, we know in some measure—but what we *affirm we know not; we only declare what we believe* and adore" (1:65). Our knowledge of God is "ingenerated in us and regulated, under the conduct of divine revelation, by reflections of his glory on other things, and representations of his divine excellencies in the effects of them" (1:67). However, there is a tremendous distance between the infinite uncreated excellency of God and the finite reflection of that excellency made by the creature; moreover, the reflections themselves are beyond our comprehension (1:67). In the works of creation and providence God has "placed many characters of his divine excellencies," but they are "unto us obscure and not clearly legible without the light of revelation"; they do not "represent God as the complete object of all our affections,...in that way whereby he may be glorified, and we may be brought unto the everlasting fruition of him" (1:68-69).

Not even a "mere external doctrinal revelation of the divine nature," such as the Holy Scripture, brings us to this end. Owen does not hereby diminish the necessity or authority of the Bible, but points out that the purpose of Scripture is to "declare and describe" the representation of the divine nature made to us by Christ (1:69).

"God himself hath declared that, in his own way," (as opposed to the way of idolatrous human invention), "a near representation of himself which would span the infinite distance between God and man was needful"—a representation he designed to accomplish in the person of Christ. This, Owen explains, would require:

> (1.) That all the properties of the divine nature—the knowledge whereof is necessary unto our present obedience and future blessedness—be expressed in it, and manifested unto us.
>
> (2.) That there be, therein, the nearest approach of the divine nature made unto us, whereof it is capable, and which we can receive. And both these are found in the person of Christ and therein alone. (1:69)

In the consideration of this subject it may be helpful to keep in mind that Christ is the revealer by what he is and by what he does, as well as by the words he says. That is, he is the revealer and the revelation. As such, the relation of his office to his person is crucial.

The basis for his revelatory role is his being the "image of the invisible God" (Col. 1:15). It is the invisibility of God which makes this image indispensable, "For he intends not only the absolute invisibility of his essence, but his being unknown unto us in himself" (1:70). In chapter six we saw how Christ is the "essential image" of the Father with respect to his divine person. With respect to his divine nature he is not the image of the Father, for, as Owen explains, "he and the Father are one; and one and the same thing cannot be the image of itself, in that wherein it is one" (1:71). (The Son is *autotheos* according to his nature, of the Father according to his person.) With respect to his divine person as Son of the Father, he is the essential image of the Father. "In his incarnation," Owen adds,

> the Son was made the representative image of God unto us—as he was, in his person, the essential image of the Father, by eternal generation. The invisible God—whose nature and divine excellencies our understandings can make no approach unto—doth in him represent, exhibit, or make present unto

our faith and spiritual sense, both himself and all the glorious excellencies of his nature. (1:72)

In the person of Christ as God incarnate there is "a blessed representation made unto us of all the holy properties of the nature of God—of his wisdom, his power, his goodness, grace, and love, his righteousness, truth, and holiness, his mercy and patience" (1:70). Owen is thinking here of the glory of God seen in the face of Jesus Christ, where we see "the most incomprehensible approach of the divine nature made unto ours, such as all the imaginations of men did ever infinitely fall short of," and the "nearest approach of the Divine Being unto us that the nature of the thing is capable of" (1:70; cf. 20:93-97). More specifically, Christ is called the "wisdom of God," Owen notes correctly, "as he is *crucified*...; that is, all that wisdom which God layeth forth for the discovery and manifesting of himself and for the saving of sinners" (2:79). Again, we see the Christocentric nature of the foundation of Puritan theology: in this representation we "see, know, and learn all the divine excellencies—so as to live unto God and be directed unto the enjoyment of him" (1:72).

This raises an important question, the answer to which (in view of Owen's zealous defense of, and reverence for, the text of Scripture) should illustrate Owen's skill at avoiding the dangers of substituting the Bible for Christ on the one hand, or, on the other, diminishing Scripture's divine authority:

> It may be said, that the Scripture itself is sufficient for this end of the declaration of God unto us, so that there is no need of any other representation of him; and [that] these things serve only to turn the minds of men from learning the mind and will of God therein, to seek for all in the person of Christ. But the true end of proposing these things is, to draw men unto the diligent study of the Scripture,

wherein alone they are revealed and declared. And in its proper use, and unto its proper end, it is perfect and most sufficient. It is λόγοσ τοῦ θεοῦ —"the word of God;" howbeit it is not λόγος οὐσιώδεσ, the internal, essential Word of God—but λόγοσ προπηορικὸσ, the external word spoken by him. It is not, therefore, nor can be, the image of God, either essential or representative; but is the revelation and declaration of it unto us, without which we can know nothing of it. (1:74; see 2:287-91)

A Representation Which Glorifies God

There are four ways in which this representation of the glory of God in the face of Christ glorifies God and directs the saints in their duty. First, by it, "the glory of God's wisdom is exalted, and the pride of the imaginations of men is proportionably debased" (1:75). This is because it represents a divine rebuke at their apostasy in making for themselves representations of the glory of God. Moreover, this is why Owen sees any subsequent use of images in the Christian church to be so evil: "as the way that God in infinite wisdom found out for the representation of himself unto us, was the only means of recovery from the first apostasy—the way found out by men, unto the same end, was the great means of casting the generality of mankind unto the farthest degree of a new apostasy from God whereof our nature is capable" (1:76).

Second, this revelation of God produces a knowledge "far more clear, certain, steady, effectual, and operative, than we can attain in and by all other ways of revelation." The reason for this, Owen explains, is

> not only because there is a more full and extensive revelation made of God, his counsels and his will, in Christ and the Gospel, than in all the works of creation and providence; but because this revelation and representation of God is received by *faith alone*,

the other by reason only: and it is faith that is the principle of spiritual light and life in us. What is received thereby is operative and effectual, unto all the ends of the life of God. (1:76-77)

Owen's application of this to the new rational divinity is striking but consistent: "There is not the meanest believer but,—in the real exercise of faith in Christ—hath more glorious apprehensions of God, his wisdom, goodness, and grace, of all his glorious excellencies, than the most learned and wise in the world can attain unto, in the exercise of reason on the proper objects of it" (1:77). His judgment upon the ethics of the new moralism is quite similar, for generally the same reasons, as will be seen below.

Third, Owen adds, "it is the highest degeneracy from the mystery of the Christian religion, for men to satisfy themselves in natural discoveries of the Divine Being and excellencies, without an acquaintance with that perfect declaration and representation of them which is made in the person of Christ" (1:77). Owen explains the seventeenth-century apostasy from Christ as originating in the greater esteem given to natural revelation above that made in the person of Christ: "For when the proper *use* of it is despised, on what grounds can the *notion* of it be long retained?" (1:78).

Fourth, Owen concludes, the reason for the wickedness of his times, the reason why religion was so "barren and fruitless in the world," is that

> it is the knowledge of "God in Christ" alone that is effectually powerful to work the souls of men into a conformity unto him. Those alone who behold the glory of God in the face of Jesus Christ are changed into the same image, from glory to glory. (1:79)

"I am the Truth"
Having shown that Christ is the *"essential image of the Fa-*

ther," and the "*representative* image of him unto us," Owen proceeds to show the relation of "spiritual supernatural truth" to the person of Christ. Divine truth consists of "that which is essentially so," being God himself; and "that which is so declaratively," or the "counsel of his will." In regard to the first of these, we have already seen Owen's description of Christ as the "image of God." In regard to the later, Owen directs our attention to the counsels of God as

> the next spring and cause—as also the subject-matter or substance—of all truth.... Of them all the person of Christ is the sacred repository and treasury.... All their efficacy and use depend on their relation unto him. He is the centre and circumference of all the lines of truth—that is, which is divine, spiritual, and supernatural. And the beauty of it is presented unto us only in *his* face or person. We see it not, we know it not, but as God shines into our hearts to give us the knowledge of it therein: 2 Cor. iv. 6. (1:79-80)

Christ is the truth:

> He is so *essentially*—as he is one with the Father, the God of truth:... He is so *efficiently*—as by him alone it is fully and effectually declared;... He is so *substantially*—in opposition unto the types and shadows of the Old Testament;... He is so *subjectively*—for all divine truth relating to the saving knowledge of God, is treasured up in him. (1:80)

In the exposition of the relation of divine truth to the person of Christ Owen focuses upon its glory, its content, and its evidence. Its glory consists in its light, and "no truth whatever brings any spiritual light unto the mind, but by virtue" of its relation to Christ (1:80). It would seem that all truth would convey light, but Owen argues that, as Christ is the "true light," truth separated from him cannot do so. He does not say it is not truth, since many doctrinal truths might be known, but unless they are known in their relation to Christ they do not enlighten the mind (1:81). Truth's glory also consists in its "*efficacy* or power" to renovate the soul:

> Wherefore, as professors of the truth, if separated from Christ as unto real union, are withering branches—so truths professed, if doctrinally separated from him, or their respect unto him, have no living power or efficacy in the souls of men. When Christ is formed in the heart by them, when he dwelleth plentifully in the soul through their operation, then and not else, do they put forth their proper power and efficacy. (1:81)

The content of Christ's revelation, in summary, consists "either of the grace and love of God unto us, or [of] our duty, obedience, and gratitude unto him" (1:82). None of these can be rightly understood, however, "but in the exercise of faith on Christ himself" (1:82). It is noteworthy, in view of the frequent allegations against the Bible's literal authority by sixteenth-century spiritual Anabaptists, seventeenth-century Quakers, and twentieth-century advocates of neo-orthodoxy, that Owen says Christ "is the life and soul of all such truths—without which, they, as they are written in the Word, are but a dead letter, and that of such a character as is illegible unto us, as unto any real discovery of the grace and love of God" (1:82). This is noteworthy in that to Owen this requirement presents no obstacle to a firm insistence upon the divine authority of the written word. The written word is not a dead letter because it is *written*—rather, because the truths contained in the word are incapable of being understood without regard to Christ, "in, by, and from whom alone...they are proposed to us, that we are made partakers of them" (1:82).

The evidence of divine truth is also centered upon and derived from Christ. We rightly believe the doctrine of the resurrection, for example, because Christ arose from the dead (1:82). Owen says "all other truths whatever" have this evidence, which he brings out in his descriptions of Christ's revelation of God's righteousness, patience, wisdom, sufficiency, and faithfulness (e.g., 2:81-94); also in the goodness of obedience and the evil of sin (e.g., 1:211-13; 2:94-103); and, through Christ's example, in the doctrine of the Christian life of faith and prayer (20:430; 24:241).

"God Has Spoken"

One of the more significant differences between the Old Testament and the New is the agents of their revelation. This is the burden of the author in the opening chapter of the epistle to the Hebrews. The first reason given that the Hebrews should persevere in their profession of the gospel rather than return to Judaism is that the "immediate author" of it is "the promised Messiah, the Son of God." This is expounded at length in the first two chapters of Hebrews. Owen's exposition of this text is a major source of his teaching upon the prophetic office of Christ.

The "principal efficient cause" of the revelation of both Mosaic law and gospel was God, who spoke of old in the prophets and, in the last days, in the Son. Owen explains that "God" as used in verse 1 is used hypostatically, not substantially, to denote the divine nature as subsisting in the person of the Father.

> So that God, even the Father, by the way of eminency, was the peculiar author of both law and gospel;... And this observation is made necessary from hence, even because he immediately assigns divine properties and excellencies unto another person, evidently distinguished from him whom he intends to denote by the name God in this place; which he could not do did that name primarily express, as here used by him, the divine nature

absolutely, but only as it is subsisting in the person of the Father. (20:7)

Owen expounds this text from the same economic perspective we have observed so often. Though the Son and Spirit were partakers with the Father in the eternal counsel,

> yet the rise and spring of this mystery was in the Father; for the *order of acting* in the blessed Trinity follows the *order of subsistence*. As the Father, therefore, is the fountain of the Trinity as to subsistence, so also as to operation. He "hath life in himself;" and "he giveth to the Son to have life in himself," John v. 26. And he doth it by communicating unto him his subsistence by eternal generation. And thence saith the Son, "As my Father worketh, so I work," verse 17. And what he seeth the Father do, that doeth the Son likewise, verse 19; not by imitation, or repetition of the like works, but in the same works in order of nature the will and Wisdom of the Father doth proceed. So also is it in respect of the Holy Ghost, whose order of subsistence denotes that of his operation. (20:34-35)

Divine revelation is not only originally from the Father, but its aim is the "accomplishment of the *purpose of the Father*, or that eternal purpose of the will of God which is by the way of eminency ascribed unto the Father: Eph. 1. 8, 9." This is the rationale for the declaration of the mind and will of God by the Son and his apostles: that the elect might come to know the mystery of the gospel. Furthermore, since in the covenant of redemption the Father had promised the elect as an inheritance to the Son, it "became peculiarly the care and work of the Father" to effectually call the elect unto faith in Christ through the revelation of his will "concerning their obedience and salvation" (20:36). Owen is on firm biblical ground here, and makes his point with emphasis and clarity. "Eternal life is with the Father." The Son declares the Father and "speaks nothing but what he heard from and was taught by the Father." The gospel is the gospel of the Father.

Again, effectual calling "doth peculiarly belong unto the Father, which he accomplisheth by his Spirit, 2 Cor. iii. 18, iv. 6." From this Owen concludes that "though all declarations of God and his will, from the foundation of the world, were made by the Son, the second person of the Trinity, and his Spirit speaking in the prophets, 1 Pet. i. 11, 12, yet as it was not by him immediately, no more was it absolutely so, but as the great angel and messenger of the covenant, by the will and appointment of the Father" (20:36; cf. 2:15-16).

This feature of divine revelation is especially significant for the Christian. First, it emphasizes the *authority* of the Word. Interestingly, though not uncharacteristically, Owen emphasizes the *paternal* aspect of the Father's authority. That is, we ought to submit to the authority of this revelation because God is the

> Father of the whole family, from whom Christ himself receives all his power and authority as mediator, Matt. xxviii. 18;... The very name and title of Father carries authority along with it, Mal. i. 6. And in the disposal of the church, in respect of this paternal power, doth the Son affirm that the Father is greater than he, John xiv. 28; and he runs up the contempt of the word, in the preaching of it by his messengers, into a contempt of this authority of the Father: "He that refuseth you refuseth me: he that refuseth me refuseth him that sent me." (20:37)

Secondly, this revelation is an act of paternal *love*: "In the economy of the blessed Trinity about the work of our salvation, that which is eminently and in an especial manner ascribed unto the Father is love" (20:37), as Owen expounds at length in his *Communion with God* (2:17-21). In the exercise of this attribute God reveals his mind and will in infinite love and condescension (20:37). Thirdly, it is an act of *care*:

> The great care of the church is in and on the Father. He is the husbandman that takes care of the vine and vineyard,... And hence our Saviour, who had a delegated care of his people, commends them to the Father, John xvii., as to whom the care of them did principally and originally belong. Care is proper to a father as such; to God as a father. Care is inseparable from paternal love. And this also is to be considered in the revelation of the will of God. (20:38)

The Progressive Character of Divine Revelation

Christ's theanthropic person is absolutely necessary to his prophetic office because of the duration of that office. His prophetic office transcends the period of his earthly ministry to include the whole history of the church from the beginning of the world, wherever it may be found. This was necessary in view of the pastoral care which Christ assumed in the covenant of redemption: "The Son of God having from the foundation of the world undertaken the care and salvation of the church, he it was who immediately dealt with it in things which concerned its instruction and edification" (20:23).

This office of prophet *before the incarnation* was discharged in four ways. First, it was by "personal appearances in the likeness of human nature, in the shape of a man, as an indication of his future incarnation." Owen regards these appearances as not simply occasions of prophetic utterance, but as *representations* of Christ's glory to Old Testament believers. That is, Christ is not only the revealer, but also a revelation on these occasions. With regard to their application to the prophetic office Owen says,

> Those peculiar appearances of the person of the Son for the instruction of believers, are a full demonstration that the care and work of it were committed to

him in a peculiar manner. And I am not without thoughts, although I see some difficulty in it, that the whole Old Testament, wherein God perpetually treats with men by an assumption of human affections unto himself, so to draw us with the chords of a man, proceeded from the person of the Son, in a preparation for, and prospect of, his future incarnation. (1:89)

Secondly, it was accompanied by the ministry of angels:

By the ministry of angels upon his undertaking to be the mediator for the church with God, the angels were in a peculiar manner put into dependence on him, even as he became a new and immediate head unto the whole creation.... Hence the whole ministry of angels was subordinate unto him; and whatever instruction was thereby given unto the church in the mind and will of God it was immediately from him, as the great prophet of the church. (1:89)

Thirdly, Christ sent the Holy Spirit to "inspire, act, and guide the prophets, by whom God would reveal himself." For this Owen draws on 1 Peter 1:11-12, explaining that "it was the Spirit of Christ that was in them that spake by them, that revealed the things which concerned the redemption and salvation of the church." He also draws on 1 Peter 3:19-20, using the most likely interpretation of that traditionally difficult text, saying, "By this Spirit he himself preached unto those that were disobedient in the days of Noah (i.e., preached to them before the flood), who are now in prison for their disobedience.... For he was so the prophet of the church always as to tender manifold instructions unto the perishing, unbelieving world" (1:89-90).

The fourth way is "by the ministry of holy men, acted and moved by his Spirit." By this he seems to mean those Old Testament instruments of divine revelation who did not fill the prophetic office.

"He who Speaks from Heaven"

This emphasis upon Christ's pre-incarnate exercise of his office also bears witness to the unity of the covenant of grace; a unity which is broken if it is denied. Hence, he argues,

> To confine the offices of Christ, as unto their virtue, power and efficacy, unto the times of the Gospel only, is utterly to evacuate the first promise, with the covenant of grace founded thereon. And their minds are secretly influenced by a disbelief of his divine person, who suppose that the respect of the church unto Christ, in faith, love, trust, and instruction, commenceth from the date of his incarnation. (1:90)

There are, of course, differences of major importance between the former and the New Testament revelation, as the first chapter of Hebrews makes clear. First, the former prophecy was made "of old," by the prophets. The contrast with "these last days" is very significant, since it represents a restoration, a *predicted* restoration, of the spirit of prophecy after a period of four hundred years of silence. Owen had already demonstrated that if Christ is not the fulfillment of those prophecies concerning the Messiah they have no chance of fulfillment. Owen disagrees with most expositors who understand "the last days" to mean the times of the gospel in general. Holding instead that the phrase points to the last days of the "Judaical church-state," Owen emphasizes the redemptive-historical significance of the author's language: We must listen to Christ; his revelation at this time brings in a new covenant, a new covenant which supersedes the old, rendering it obsolete, bringing about the destruction of that church state institution which existed by, and for, the old.

A further contrast is in the manner of that revelation. "In opposition to this *gradual revelation* of the mind and will of God under the old testament, the apostle intimates that now by Jesus, the Messiah, the Lord hath at once begun and finished the whole revelation of his will"

(20:20). Like Calvin, Owen sees Hebrews 1:1-2 as highlighting the perfection of the revelation made by God incarnate: "he hath given out the knowledge of the mind of God in different degrees and measures; that which was most perfect being for many reasons reserved unto the times of the Gospel; the sum whereof is, that God designed him unto a pre-eminence above all in his own personal ministry" (1:90). The contrast demonstrates the greatness of this final revelation by the Son, in that

> He who is infinitely good and compassionate, did from the beginning give some relief in this woeful state, by such parcels of divine revelations as he thought meet to communicate unto them by the prophets of old—such as they were able to receive. By them he set up a light shining in a dark place, as the light of stars in the night. But it was the rising of the Sun of righteousness alone that dispelled the darkness that was on the earth, the thick darkness that was on the people, bringing life and immortality to light by the Gospel. The divine person of the Son of God, in whom were hid all the treasures of wisdom and knowledge, who is in the bosom of the Father, hath now made known all things unto the church, giving us the perfect idea and certainty of all sacred truth, and the full assurance of things invisible and eternal. (1:93-94)

Like Calvin, Owen understands this to mean that since the period of the New Testament, "no new revelation is to be expected, to the end of the world. Nothing shall be added unto nor altered in the worship of God any more. God will not do it; men that attempt it, do it on the price of their souls" (20:20).

Though tersely expressed here, this understanding of the closing of the canon with the proclamation of the new covenant by Christ and his apostles, alongside of the conviction that worship was a covenantal activity, is a predominant theme in Reformed theology, and at the heart of the debate between Anglicanism and Puritanism.

The revelation is further contrasted in the manner of its bestowal. It was given "in divers manners" to the prophets, i.e., through "dreams, visions, inspirations, voices, angels," etc., but immediately in the Son, "by His preaching the gospel who was anointed with the Spirit without measure" (20:20). This "immediacy" is apparently more "immediate" than the former, as Owen explains:

> There is a difference between the Son of God revealing the will of God in his *divine person* to the prophets, of which we have spoken, and the Son of God as *incarnate* revealing the will of God immediately to the church. This is the difference here insisted on by the apostle. Under the old testament the Son of God, in his divine person, instructed the prophets in the will of God, and gave them that Spirit on whose divine inspiration their infallibility did depend, 1 Pet. i. 11; but now, in the revelation of the gospel, taking his own humanity, or our nature hypostatically united unto him, in the room of all the *"internuncii,"* or prophetical messengers he had made use of, he taught it immediately himself. (20:23)

The Knowledge of the Great Prophet of the Church

> The full comprehension of the mind and will of God, of the whole divine counsel concerning his glory in the sanctification and salvation of the church, could not at once reside in the mind of any mere creature. Yet was this necessary unto him who was to be the prophet of the church; that is, the fountain of truth, life, and knowledge unto it. (1:91)

In contrast to Christ, no man, not even Moses had seen God at any time, which is to say, says Owen, ever "had a perfect comprehension of his counsels, his mind and will, as they were to be declared unto the church." The Son, however, has perfect comprehension. First, Owen explains,

> Jesus Christ in his divine nature, as he was the divine Word and Wisdom of the Father, not by a voluntary communication but eternal generation, had an omnisciency of the whole nature and will of God, as the Father himself hath, because the same with that of the Father, their will and wisdom being the same. This is the blessed συμπεριχώρησις,[2] or in-being of each person, the one in the other by virtue of their same nature. Thus, as God, he hath an absolute omniscience. (20:30)

To this knowledge of "in-being" may be added the knowledge of *counsel*. The Son knew the whole divine counsel concerning the redemption of the church "by virtue of his own personal transactions with the Father," in the covenant of redemption (20:30). Thus, His lying in the bosom of the Father (John 1:18) indicates not only "his being his eternal delight and love, but also as one acquainted with all his secret counsels—as his fellow and participant of all his bosom thoughts" (1:91). According to the divine nature, this knowledge of the Son is not diminished in the incarnation. The one who is in the bosom of the Father is the incarnate Word, as Owen is well aware.

Owen's exposition of John 3:11-13 bears out his application of the person of Christ to his prophetic office. The "heavenly things" that Nicodemus is slow to understand are "the deep counsels of the will of God above." Christ's comments answer the question of how he possesses knowledge of these things: "We speak that we do know, and testify that we have seen." Owen explains:

> Hereof he gives an account in these words. Wherefore the ascending into heaven, which he denies unto all men whatever...is an entrance into all the divine heavenly counsels of God; no man either hath or ever had a full comprehension of these

heavenly things but he himself alone. And unto him it is ascribed on a double account: first, That he came down from heaven; secondly, That when he did so, he yet still continued in heaven: which two properties give us such a description of the person of Christ as declare him a full possessor of all the counsels of God. He descended from heaven in his incarnation, whereby he became the Son of man; and he is and was then in heaven in the essence and glory of his divine nature.... He who, being always in heaven in the glory and essence of his divine nature, came down from heaven, not locally, by a mutation of his residence, but by dispensation in the assumption of our nature into personal union with himself—he alone is meet and able to be the prophet of the church in the revelation of the heavenly mysteries of the counsels of the will of God. (1:92-93)

Owen emphasizes that "the Lord Christ discharged his office and work of revealing the will of the Father in and by his human nature,...for although the person of Christ, God and man, was our mediator,...yet his human nature was that wherein he discharged the duties of his office and the *'principium quod'* [primary agent] of all his mediatory actings" (20:30). Owen did not attribute omniscience to the human nature of Christ, but by virtue of the union with the Son of God it was "radically filled with all that perfection of habitual grace and wisdom which was or could be necessary to the discharge of that whole duty which he owed unto God" (20:30). Through this He was, "furnished with all that wisdom and knowledge which the human nature was capable of, both as to *principle* and *exercise*, in the condition wherein it was, without destroying its finite being and variety of conditions from the womb" (20:28).

Owen asserts, however, that *this* wisdom is not "that whereby God so revealed his mind unto him as thereby to be said to speak to us in him," since it arises by virtue of the union of the human nature and the person of the Son. Hebrews 1:1, on the other hand, assigns this revelation to the *Father* who is speaking in the (incarnate) Son. Hebrews clearly identifies the source of the revelation as the Father (20:28). The "foundation" and manner of God's speaking in the Son, therefore, was not by the speaking of the Divine nature of the Son, but of the Father speaking by the Holy Spirit. Owen is arguing that as the mediator, born a man under the law, Christ had a "peculiar endowment with the Spirit, without and beyond the bounds of all comprehensible measures, that he was to receive as the great prophet of the church, in whom the Father would speak and give out the last revelation of himself" (20:30). It was a "communication of the Spirit unto it without measure," which according to Isaiah 11:2-3 was "the spirit of wisdom and understanding, the spirit of counsel and might, the spirit of knowledge and of the fear of the Lord," or put otherwise, "an understanding peculiar unto himself; as above that of all creatures, so beneath the essential omniscience of the divine nature" (1:93). In contrast to the prophet's knowledge of the truths of divine revelation, Christ was granted not a "transient irradiation by them, but a permanency and constant abode of them with him in their fullness, all 'treasures of wisdom and knowledge' being hid in him, Col. ii. 3, as their home and proper abiding place; which made him of 'quick understanding in the fear of the Lord,' Isa. xi. 3" (20:31).

From the permanency and quickness of Christ's knowledge, Owen turns to consider its *extent*. It was "altogether a comprehension of the whole will and mind of God, as to whatever he would have revealed of himself, with the mystery of our salvation, and all that obedience and worship which in this world he would require of his church," including "all the mysteries of the counsel between the Father and the eternal Word for the salvation of the elect, with all the way whereby it was to be accomplished,

"He who Speaks from Heaven"

through his own blood," and "all the bounds, the whole extent of that worship which his church was to render unto God, with the assistance of the Spirit that was to be afforded unto them for that end and purpose" (20:31-32).

Owen thus has no difficulty in affirming that there were some things that Christ did not know "as a man." His ignorance of the date of his second coming is a well-known example. "But," says Owen, "he is the prophet of the church in his whole entire person, and revealed the counsel of God, as he was in heaven in the bosom of the Father" (1:93). As to his human nature, "the Spirit of God dwelling in him, in all the fulness of his graces and gifts, gave him an understanding peculiar to himself" (1:93). This was that gift of wisdom which amazed the doctors in the temple when he was twelve, and which increased with his maturity. In the face of adoptionist opponents Owen does not hesitate to assert that at his baptism Christ received

> the full communication of this Spirit, with special reference unto the discharge of his public office, with the visible pledge of it in the Holy Ghost descending on him in the shape of a dove..., Matt. iii. 16; when also he received his first public testimony from heaven, verse 17; which, when again repeated, received the additional command of hearing him, Matt. xvii. 5,—designing the prophet that was to be heard on pain of utter extermination, Deut. xviii. 18, 19. And therefore he was thereupon said to be..."full of the Holy Ghost," and sealed to this work by the sign foretold of God, John i. 33. (20:30-31)

"Three things," says Owen, "are necessary, that we may have the benefit and comfort of divine light or truth," and we cannot really have assurance of these, and thus derive this benefit and comfort, but "in the exercise of faith on his divine person, which is the eternal spring from whence this [prophetical] office derives all life and efficacy" (1:94, 95). It must be *full*; we cannot rest given the possibility that some necessary point of knowledge may remain unknown, therefore it must be fully revealed. Likewise it must be *infallible*, for its contents are "heavenly, eternal mysteries, transcending the reach of human reason," requiring the "absolute infallibility of the revealer" to "bring the mind of man to assurance and acquiescency." This infallibility is a necessary foundation of Christian piety since it "gives the soul assured rest and peace in the belief of things which 'eye hath not seen, nor ear heard, nor can enter into the heart of man to conceive.' Upon the assurance of this truth alone can it with joy prefer things invisible and eternal above all present satisfactions and desires" (1:94). Thirdly, it must be *authoritative*. When Owen says that the benefit of divine truth depends upon the authority "from whence it doth proceed," he does not mean merely the intrinsic objective authority it has as the word of God. It certainly means that much, but something more is required if it is to be beneficial to us, and this also pertained to the office of Christ.

> It was requisite unto the office of this great prophet of the church, and the discharge thereof, that he should have power and authority to send the Holy Spirit to make his revelations of divine truth effectual unto the minds of men. For the church which he was to instruct, was not only in darkness, by reason of ignorance and want of objective light or divine revelations, but was incapacitated to receive spiritual things in a due manner when revealed. Wherefore, it was the work of this prophet, not only external directive light, but also to irradiate and illuminate our minds, so that we might savingly apprehend them. (1:95)

The *Great* Prophet

Much of the foregoing finds a more vivid expression in Owen's comments on Hebrews 3:1, where he describes the greatness of the "apostle...of our profession." First, it was the greatness "of *grace, love, and condescension.*" We have already noted the greatness of the condescension in connection with his priestly office, but there was also a greatness of condescension in God to

> send a message unto... poor, perishing rebels, an embassy to treat with them about peace and reconciliation. But this now is so great a thing,... that sinners know not how to believe it. And indeed, who is fit to testify it unto them? Objections that arise against it are able to shake the credit and reputation of any angel in heaven. Wherefore God commits this message unto his Son, his only Son, makes him his apostle, sends him with these tidings, that they may be believed and accepted.... If the sealed book of prophecies concerning the judgment of God in the Revelation, was of so great concernment that.... no creature "was able to open it, or look thereon," ... until the Lamb himself undertook it, ... how much less was any creature meet or worthy to open the eternal secret counsels of the bosom of the Father, concerning the whole work of his love and grace, but the Son only! The grace of this message was too great for sinners to receive, without the immediate attestation of the Son of God. (20:504-505)

Second, "there is a *greatness in the work* itself that is incumbent on the apostle of God, which required that the Son of God should be engaged therein." This arises from the fact that he is "perfectly to represent *the person of the Father unto us.*" Other messengers, i.e., the prophets, were forerunners to "give notice of the coming of this great apostle or ambassador of God." Moses, although a "special legate," nevertheless came far short of making this perfect representation of the Father. Only he who was the "brightness of his glory, and the express image of his person," "the image of the invisible God," could do this. In this manner we behold "the glory of God in the face of

Jesus Christ" (20:504-506). This apostle must not only perfectly represent the *person* of the Father, he must also be "intimately *acquainted with all the secret counsels of God* that lay hid in his infinite wisdom and will from all eternity" (20:506). This knowledge must be

> always abiding with him, that at all times and on all occasions he might be able to declare the mind and will of God. It was not enough that originally, as he was God, he knew all things of God, but also as he was sent, as he was the apostle of God, the counsel of God was constantly to abide with him. This is another thing; for the wisdom and knowledge of Christ as mediator, to be acted in the human nature, was distinct from his knowledge as he was in himself God over all, blessed for ever. And without this none could have been a meet apostle from God unto sinners; for how else should he reveal the will of God unto them according unto all emergencies and occasions? (20:506-507)

Owen emphasizes that others, such as Paul, might "know so much of the mind of God as to declare unto others the whole of their duty," but only Christ had a "full, *habitual comprehension* of the whole mind of God," resident in him, "answering all occasions and emergencies, and that originally and immediately" (20:507). The "nature of the work required *that the ambassador of God to sinners should be able to make his message to be believed and received by them*" (20:508).

Third, the greatness of this ambassadorship is seen in the "end of it," which was to "proclaim and establish peace between God and man" after he had made it (20:508-509).

The Doctrine of the Great Prophet

In his work on the Holy Spirit Owen divides the doctrine taught by Christ into two parts:

1. The *revelation* of God in his *name and love*, in the

mystery of his *grace*, and *goodness*, and *truth*, by his *promises*, that we may *believe* in him. 2. The *revelation* of God in his *will* and *commands*, that we may *obey* him. (3:631)

His opinions regarding the first of these may be known by what has been covered to this point. His remarks in this work regarding the preceptive part of Christ's doctrine are particularly interesting as addressing the "Carolingian moral theology."

First, he describes Christ's ministry to the Jews as consisting in "the declarations, exposition, and vindication, that he gave unto the church of all *divine precepts* for obedience which had been given before" (6:631). As Owen explains, the church by the end of the Old Testament era had "grown corrupt," and had misapplied the promises and precepts of the law. "Our blessed Saviour applies himself, in the discharge of his prophetical office, with respect unto the end of the command, which is our holy obedience, . . . in the declaration of its excellency and efficacy" (3:631-32). This consisted in preaching the "*inward spiritual nature of the law*," and the "*true sense of its commands*, their nature, signification, and extent" (3:632). Owen concludes,

> The full revelation of the mind and will of God, in the perfection and spirituality of the command, was reserved for Christ in the discharge of his office; and he gave it unto us that we might have a perfect and complete rule of holiness. This, therefore, was the *immediate end* of this work or duty of the office of Christ; and when we answer it not, we reject that great prophet which God hath sent; to which excision is so severely threatened. (3:632)

To this personal ministry exercised during his earthly ministry Owen adds the "ministry of the apostles, as divinely inspired by him,... in the *revelation of those duties of holiness*, which although they had a general *foundation* in the *law*, and the *equity* of them was therein established, yet could they never have been known to be duties in their *especial nature*, incumbent on us and necessary unto us, but by his teachings and instructions" (3:632).

In both respects, Christ gave a clear revelation of our obedience toward God. Owen describes Christ's doctrine of obedience in respect to three outstanding characteristics which, as he develops them, reveal the great difference between Christian and humanist ethics. First, he says, Christ's doctrine of obedience "*reacheth the heart itself*, with all its *inmost* and *secret actings*, and that in the *first place*"; which "requires the *renovation* of our *whole souls*, in all their faculties, motions, and actings, into the image of God" (3:633). Secondly, "It is *extensive*,... a *perfect rule* of holiness and obedience." Thirdly, Owen points to its "*clearness, perspicuity*, and *evidence* of divine truth and authority in all" (3:633). With considerable force, Owen demonstrates that with respect to content, manner, and authority, the efforts of contemporary humanists in their moralizing fall far short of the teaching of Christ (3:633-37).

In another context Owen summarizes "all true wisdom and knowledge" as consisting in "the *knowledge of God*, his nature, properties, and works"; "the *knowledge of ourselves*"; and "skill to walk in *communion with God*": none of which is "to any purpose to be obtained,...but only in and by the Lord Christ" (2:80). We have observed this with regard to the knowledge of God, but what does Christ teach us concerning ourselves? This Owen summarizes in terms of "sin, of righteousness, and of judgment to come." Again, this revelation consists in what Christ verbally taught, and in what must be inferred from the facts of his mediation (2:79-111). Apart from these, all man's learning will disappoint him (2:111-17).

The "Free Offer of the Gospel"

Perhaps the greatest difficulty with respect to the Reformed doctrine of the extent of the atonement was its supposed impediment to the work of evangelism. The otherwise strictly Calvinist John Bunyan said that for this reason he would not preach that Christ died only for the elect (Bunyan 1863, 2:348-49). Conversely, there were others who maintained that a logical application of the principles of Calvinism meant that the promise or offer of Christ should be limited to sinners demonstrating some evidence of being among the elect. The question, "Can a Christ who died to secure the salvation of a certain elect people be freely and sincerely offered to sinners," had already received a clear, affirmative, and official answer: the Canons of Dordt plainly asserted that the promise of everlasting life through faith in Christ "ought to be declared and published to all nations, and to all persons promiscuously and without distinction, to whom God out of his good pleasure sends the gospel," and,

> As many as are called by the gospel are unfeignedly called. For God hath most earnestly and truly shown in his Word, what is pleasing to him, namely, that those who are called should come to him. He, moreover, seriously promises eternal life, and rest, to as many as shall come to him, and believe on him. (Head II, Article 5; Head III/IV, Article 8)

The Westminster Assembly, in its *Sum of Saving Knowledge*, had likewise asserted four Scripture-based "Warrants and Special Motives to believe": 1) The invitations of God, 2) his "earnest request" that sinners be reconciled to God, 3) the "awful command" of God for faith and repentance, and 4) the assurances of life for believers, and "certification of destruction, in case they obey not." Owen is in perfect accord with these principles. It is interesting to observe his method of dealing with the several problems associated with this issue.

What is the gospel? The Arminians taught that a sinner is to believe that Christ died for him in particular, and so to come to him. The proposition that "Christ has died for me, has made atonement for me" thus becomes the object of faith. Owen rejects this as contrary to the scriptural pattern:

> We invite not men as all men, no man as one of all men, but all men as sinners; and we know that Christ died for sinners. But is this the first thing that we are, in the dispensation of the gospel, to propose to the soul of a sinner under the law, that Christ died for him in particular? Is that the beginning of our message unto him? Were not this a ready way to induce him to conclude, "Let me, then, continue in sin, that grace may abound?"—No; but this is in order of nature our first work, even that which we have had in hand; this is the "beginning of the gospel of Jesus Christ;" this is "the voice of one crying in the wilderness, Prepare ye the way of the Lord:"—"There is a way of reconciliation provided. 'God is in Christ reconciling the world to himself.' There is a way of acceptance; there is forgiveness with him to be obtained.... This was the ministry of the Baptist, and they who received it not "rejected the counsel of God" concerning their salvation, Luke 7:10, and so perished in their sins. This is the sum of the blessed invitation given by Wisdom, Proverbs 9:1-5. And here men stumble, fall, and perish, Proverbs 1:29, 30. (6:523)

Owen makes the same point in *The Death of Death*: the warrant for faith is the gospel message that there is full salvation in Christ for sinners. Since it is not revealed that Christ died for him in particular, the belief that Christ died for him in particular cannot be the biblical warrant for faith in Christ. Owen insists,

> If the gospel should now be preached to the Turks and the Indians, and they should reject it, certainly they should be damned for not believing that which they were, upon the preaching of it, bound to believe. Now, what is this? that Christ died for every

"He who Speaks from Heaven" 413

one of them in particular? No, doubtless; but this, "There is none other name under heaven given among men, whereby we must be saved," but only by the name of Christ, made known to us in the gospel, Acts 4:12. [They would be damned] for rejecting the counsel and wisdom of God to save sinners by the blood of Jesus; for not believing the necessity of a Redeemer, and that Jesus of Nazareth was that Redeemer, — according to his own word to the Jews, "If ye believe not that I am he, ye shall die in your sins;" as, indeed, the peculiar infidelity of that people was their not believing him to be their Messiah, whom they saw to be declared to be the Son of God with power. The not believing these things would be the soul-damning infidelity of such obstinate refusers to come in upon the call of the gospel, and not a refusing to believe that Christ died for every one of them in particular; which could not, by the rule of the gospel, be proposed unto them, and which they never come so far as to question or esteem. (10:406)

The assurance that Christ died for anyone in particular comes after, as the result of coming to Christ in faith. As Owen explains, the truths which are to be believed by one coming to Christ for salvation have a sequential order to them, like the rungs of a ladder. One must believe that the gospel is true that declares Christ to be God's way of salvation; secondly, that this salvation is by faith alone, and that one personally needs the Christ offered in the gospel. In the belief of these principles, one makes

> a serious full recumbency and rolling of the soul upon Christ in the promise of the gospel, as an all-sufficient Savior, able to deliver and save to the utmost them that come to God by him; ready, able, and willing, through the preciousness of his blood and sufficiency of his ransom, to save every soul that shall freely give up themselves unto him for

that end, amongst whom he is resolved to be. And in doing of all this, there is none called on by the gospel once to inquire after the purpose and intention of God concerning the particular object of the death of Christ, every one being fully assured that his death shall be profitable to them that believe in him and obey him. (10:407-408)

When sinners are commanded to "believe on the name of Jesus Christ," Owen argues, it is not to believe that "he died for my sins,' but "to rest upon him for salvation, as Isaiah 50:11."[3] He continues,

> Neither is the testimony of God, to which we ought to set our seal that it is true, any other but this, "He that hath the Son hath life, but he that hath not the Son of God hath not life," 1 John 5:12; which reprobates disbelieving, do what in them lies to make God a liar, and are justly condemned for it. He that desireth to see more of this argument, let him consult, if he please, Piscator, Perkins, Twisse, Synod of Dort, Du Moulin, Baronius, Rutherford, Spanheim, Amesius, others, etc. (10:409)[4]

Like many other Reformed theologians of the period, Owen taught much concerning the ordinary course of events in the conversion of sinners, including preparatory works of the Spirit such as conviction of sin through the work of the Law. These normally antecedent works, however, must not be confused with *warrants* for coming to Christ.[5] As Owen argues,

> When did God give the great promise of Christ to Adam? Was it when he was sorrowing, repenting, qualifying his soul? No; but when he was flying, hiding, and had no thoughts but of separation from God. God calls him forth, and at once tells him what he had deserved, pronounces the curse, and gives him the blessing.... From the very place of sin Christ raiseth up the soul. So Isaiah 46:12, "Hearken to me, ye stout-hearted, that are far from righteousness."

"He who Speaks from Heaven"

> Here are two notable qualifications, stout-heartedness, and remoteness from righteousness. What saith God to them? Verse 13, He discourses to them of mercy and salvation; and, Isaiah 55:1, "Buy," saith he, "wine and milk." "Yea, but I have nothing to buy withal, and these things require a price." Indeed, so they do; but take them "without money, and without price." (9:48-49)

"But," someone will say, "he calls on them only who are 'thirsty.'" "True," says Owen, "but it is a thirst of indigency and total want, not a thirst of spiritual desires; for in whomsoever that is, they have already tasted of this wine and milk, and are blessed, Matthew 5." Though motivated by a desire to clear an obstacle from the path to Christ for doubting, troubled sinners, Owen's point opposes the "hyper-Calvinism" that was then making its presence felt in the Reformed churches.

> Nay, we may go one step farther. Proverbs 9:4, 5, Christ invites them to his bread and wine who have no heart. This, commonly, is the last objection that an unbelieving heart makes against itself,—it hath no mind to Christ. Indeed he hath no heart for Christ. "But yet," saith Christ, "thou shalt not thus go off,—I will not admit of this excuse; you that have no heart, 'turn in hither.'" (9:49)

If the sinner's warrant and obligation to repent and believe the gospel is not the persuasion that Christ died for him in particular, nor an awareness of a prior work of grace, what is it? It is the authority of the great prophet of God, revealing the good will of God toward sinners, bringing them gracious terms of peace, exhorting, pleading, and commanding their acceptance (6:515-37).[6] In his sermon "The Strength of Faith: Sermon II" (9:37-53) Owen argues that the sinner should consider,

> His condescension to entreat us that it may be so, — that he may exercise pity, pardon, goodness, kind-

ness, mercy towards us. He is so full, that he is, as it were, pained until he can get us to himself, that he may communicate of his love unto us. "We pray you," says the apostle, "in Christ's stead, as if God by us did beseech you." What to do? what is he so earnest about? what would God have of us? Some great thing, some difficult service assuredly. "No," says he, "but, 'be reconciled to God,'" 2 Corinthians 5:20. Says God, "O ye sons of men, 'why will ye die?' I beseech you, be friends with me; let us agree;—accept of the atonement. I have love for you; take mercy, take pardon; do not destroy your own souls." "This is the rest wherewith ye may cause the weary to rest; and this is the refreshing," Isaiah 28:12. Remember how the Scripture abounds with exhortations and entreaties to this purpose. (9:41)

Owen presses the point further with a quotation from Ezekiel 33:11:

"Now, 'as I live, saith the Lord,' I would not the death of a sinner,"...Methinks this should put an end to all strife. We have his promise and oath, Hebrews 6:18, and what would we have more? He is of an infinite loving and tender nature; he entreats us to come to him, and swears we shall not suffer by our so doing. Innumerable other instances of the like kind might be given, to evidence the actings of God towards us to be suitable to his name and nature, before insisted on. (9:41)

In another place Owen explains at length how the terms proposed by God for sinners are "equal, holy, righteous, yea, pleasant and easy," (6:524) concluding,

This way is free and open for and unto sinners. He that fled to the city of refuge might well have many perplexed thoughts, whether he should find the gates of it opened unto him or no, and whether the avenger of blood might not overtake and slay him whilst he was calling for entrance. Or if the gates were always open, yet some crimes excluded men thence, Numbers 35:16. It is not so here, Acts 13:38, 39.

This is the voice of God, even the Father: "Come," saith he, "to the marriage, for all things are prepared,"—no fear of want of entertainment, Matthew 22:4; whence the preachers of the gospel are said in his stead to beseech men to be reconciled, 2 Corinthians 5:20. And It is the voice of the Son: "Whosoever," saith he, "cometh to God by me, 'I will in no wise cast out,' John 6:37. Whoever he be that comes shall assuredly find entertainment. The same is his call and invitation in other places, as Matthew 11:28; John 7:37. And This is the voice of the Spirit, and of the church, and of all believers: Revelation 22:17, "The Spirit and the bride say, Come. And let him that heareth say, Come. And let him that is athirst come. And whosoever will, let him take the water of life freely." All center in this, that sinners may come freely to the grace of the gospel. (6:529)

To which he adds, "It is the known voice of the gospel itself, as Isaiah 55:1-3; Proverbs 9:1-5," and "It is the voice of all the saints in heaven and earth, who have been made partakers of forgiveness; they all testify that they received it freely" (6:529).

Finally, someone will object, "If the doctrines of God's sovereignty and man's inability are true, then how can men be blamed for their unbelief?" The freeness and fullness of the gospel *offer* removes this excuse and obliges the sinner to repentance and faith under penalty of destruction. As Owen argues,

> Some, indeed, endeavor to abuse this concurrent testimony of God and man. What is spoken of the freedom of the grace of God, they would wrest to the power of the will of man; but the riches and freedom of God's mercy do not in the least interfere with the efficacy of his grace. Though he proclaim pardon in the blood of Christ indefinitely, according

> to the fullness and excellency of it, yet he giveth out his quickening grace to enable men to receive it as he pleaseth; for he hath mercy on whom he will have mercy. But this lies in the thing itself; the way is opened and prepared, and it is not because men cannot enter, but because they will not, that they do not enter. (6:529)

This is a most important distinction: the "thing itself," i.e., pardon in the blood of Christ, and the "way," which is believing the divine testimony concerning Christ, and trusting oneself unto him. There is nothing in the nature of the gospel that prevents the sinner from coming to Christ, and nothing that can excuse their not coming, as the words which follow make clear:

> As our Savior Christ tells the Pharisees, "Ye therefore hear not God's word, because ye are not of God," John 8:47, 6:44; so he doth, "Ye will not come to me that ye might have life," John 5:40. In the neglect and inadvertency of the most excusable, there is a positive act of their will put forth in the refusing of Christ and grace by him; and this is done by men under the preaching of the gospel every day. There is nothing that at the last day will tend more immediately to the advancement of the glory of God, in the inexcusableness of them who obey not the gospel, than this, that terms of peace, in the blessed way of forgiveness, were freely tendered unto them. Some that hear or read this word may perhaps have lived long under the dispensation of the word of grace, and yet it may be have never once seriously pondered on this way of coming to God by forgiveness through the blood of Christ, but think that going to heaven is a thing of course, that men need not much trouble themselves about. Do they know what they have done? Hitherto, all their days, they have positively refused the salvation that hath been freely tendered unto them in Jesus Christ. Not they, they will say; they never had

such a thought, nor would for all this world. But be it known unto you, inasmuch as you have not effectually received him, you have refused him; and whether your day and season be past or no, the Lord only knows. (6:529-30)

"Hear Ye Him!"

The greatness of the messenger and his message results in a great obligation upon the hearer to take heed. Although Owen emphasizes this in a number of contexts, it is, perhaps, most forcefully expressed in his comments upon Hebrews 12:25-27, where the author of Hebrews cautions his readers to "see that ye refuse not him that speaketh."

> And this command hath respect unto the *double solemn charge given of God* unto the church; the first on the closing of the law, and the other as the beginning and foundation of the gospel. The first, given to prepare the church for their duty in its proper season, is recorded, Deut. xviii. 18, 19, "I will raise them up a Prophet from among their brethren, like unto thee, and will put my words in his mouth; and he shall speak unto them all that I shall command him. And it shall come to pass, that whosoever will not hearken unto my words, which he shall speak in my name, I will require it of him;"—which words are applied to the Lord Christ, Acts iii. 22, vii. 37. This the apostle now minds them of: 'Take heed that ye hear him; for if not, God will require it of you in your utter destruction.' The other charge to this purpose was given immediately from heaven, as the foundation of the gospel, Matt. xvii. 5, "Behold a voice out of the cloud, which said, This is my beloved Son, in whom I am well pleased; hear ye him;"—which voice the apostle Peter tells us came "from the excellent glory" of the person of the Father," 2 Pet. I. 17, 18. (24:354-55)

As an "enforcement of this duty," the apostle argues from the "consideration of the Person" who now "speaks from heaven," by pointing to the duty that lay upon those who heard him speak "upon earth." Owen argues convincingly that the contrast is not between two persons speaking, but between speaking on earth and speaking from heaven. It was the Son of God, that is, "the divine nature acting itself in a peculiar manner in the person of the Son," that spake upon the earth in the giving of the law upon Sinai: "What is purely divine was proper to his person, and what was of condescension belonged unto him in a way of office, as he was the angel of the covenant, in whom was the name of God" (24:356).

How can Christ be said to be speaking from heaven by contrast to his speaking on earth at Sinai? Owen's answer to this question is simply a summary of all the excellencies which pertain to the exalted Christ who now speaks to us from heaven: his "full *comprehension* of all heavenly mysteries;... his infinite *condescension* in his incarnation and susception of the *office* of mediator,... called his coming down from heaven.... His sovereign heavenly *authority* in the discharge of his office.... His glorious ascension into heaven...his *sending the Holy Ghost* from heaven to confirm his doctrine," and "his opening heaven, and all the treasures of it, 'bringing life and immortality to light by the gospel,' in comparison whereof the things of the law are called 'earthly things'" (24:358-59).

Once more we see Owen's sense of the importance of Christ's person to his office and the impact of redemptive history upon our understanding of that office: the incarnation, and then, distinctly, the ascension have real significance: men now have a revelation of the mind and will of God which is not only true, but full and powerful to the saving of his elect, and sufficient for the condemnation of those who neglect "so great salvation." The importance of Christ's person and state will also appear with respect to the office of king.

---

[1] Other Puritan sources for the doctrine of the office of Christ as Prophet and its relation to the person of Christ include Manton (1870, 10:139-69), Goodwin (1863, 5:525-49), and Flavel. Flavel has two chapters on the prophetic office in *The Fountain of Life*, the first of these dealing with Christ role as the only source of knowledge of the Father, the second dealing with Christ as the author of illumination, or the opening of the mind to receive the revelation given (1820, 1:181-142).

[2] For a discussion of "*perichoresis*" or "in-being" see Macleod (1998, 140-42).

[3] He probably intends Isaiah 50:10, "Who *is* among you that feareth the LORD, that obeyeth the voice of his servant, that walketh *in* darkness, and hath no light? let him trust in the name of the LORD, and stay upon his God...."

[4] Some possible references: William Twisse, *The Riches of God's Love* (1653); Pierre Du Moulin, *The Anatomy of Arminianism* (1620); Samuel Rutherford, *Christ Dying and Drawing Sinners Unto Himself* (1647).

[5] Of considerable help in this regard is "Part I" of Goodwin's treatise on *The Object and Acts of Justifying Faith* (Goodwin 1863, 8:3-255). See also Robert Traill (1810, 3:107-21).

[6] Many examples of this kind of preaching might be found among the Puritans. See, for example, *Christ's Gracious Invitations to Sinners*, by Owen's successor, David Clarkson (1696, 438-92). See also the instructions to preachers in "How Christ is to be Proposed," given by Robert Bolton in his *Instructions for a Right Comforting of Afflicted Consciences* (1641, 184-94).

CHAPTER
15

"Thy Throne, O God"

There is a peculiar glory in the kingly office of Jesus Christ, that we should daily exercise our thoughts about. The comfort, joy, and refreshment of believers, in this world, lie in the kingly power of Christ.

There is a peculiar glory in the kingdom of Christ, that we ought much, for our relief, to meditate upon. If we could behold the internal and external workings of Christ; what he hath done, what he will do,—how that certainly he will save every believer, how that certainly he will destroy every enemy,—how infallible in his grace, and never-failing in his vengeance;—we should then see a peculiar glory in his kingdom. (9:475)

As for his exaltation at his ascension, it was not by any investiture in any new office, but by an admission to the execution of that part of his work of mediatorship which did remain, in a full and glorious manner, the whole concernment of his humiliation being past. In the meantime, doubtless, he was a king when the Lord of glory was crucified, 1 Cor. ii. 8. (12:373)

The Divine Heir

In the *Exposition of the Epistle to the Hebrews* Owen makes an extended digression to describe the Kingdom of

Christ, beginning with the assertion that this kingdom is his as an inheritance. The kingship of Christ is mediatorial; though dependent upon his divine nature it is Christ in the *unity* of his theanthropic person who is made "heir of all things." As Owen explains,

> The Son, as God, hath a *natural dominion* over all. To this he can be no more appointed than he can be to be God. On what account he hath his divine nature, on the same he hath all the attributes of it, with all things that necessarily on any supposition attend it, as supreme dominion doth. Nor doth this denotation of him respect merely the human nature; for although the Lord Christ performed all the acts of his mediatory office in and by the human nature, yet he did them not as man, but as God and man in one person. John i. 14, Acts xx. 28. And therefore unto him, as such, do the privileges belong that he is vested with on the account of his being mediator. Nothing, indeed, can be added unto him as God, but there may be to him *who is God*, in respect of his condescension to discharge an office in another nature which he did assume. (20:40-41)

This is a very important distinction, missed by antitrinitarians who argue that since the most high God cannot be appointed an heir by another, and the Son of God is appointed heir of all things, the Son of God is therefore not the most high God. Referring to Genesis 14:19, Owen explains that "most high God" is used "with reference to his sovereign and supreme exaltation over all his creatures," i.e., as he is the "possessor of heaven and earth." It is not used of God in the sense of comparing him to another who might be called the "high" God (20:41).

The word "heir" may be used for a "possessor, a trustee, and a legatary," and not only one who comes to this position through the death of another. (20:41). Thus the Son is not heir by the death of the Father, but by appointment from him.

> Neither is the title and right given to the Son as mediator the same with that of God absolutely considered. This is eternal, natural, co-existent with the being of all things; that new, created by grant and donation, by whose erection and establishment the other is not at all impeached. For whereas it is affirmed that "the Father judgeth no man, but hath committed all judgement unto the Son," John v. 22, 27, 30, it respects not title and rule, but actual administration. (20:41-42)

"Heir" indicates three things concerning Christ. The first is *title, dominion, or lordship*. "The heir is the lord of that which he is heir unto." Owen correctly observes this principle in the biblical notion of the "first-born" [בְּכוֹר, πρωτότοκον], and applies it to that text of Scripture which is a favorite of Arians, Colossians 1:15.

> And in this sense Christ is called בְּכוֹר, "the first-born," Ps. lxxxix. 28, "I will give him to be my first-born, higher than" (or "and high above") "the kings of the earth;" "*princeps, dominus, caput familiae*,"—"the prince, lord, and head of the family," that hath right to the inheritance, and distributes portions to others. Hence בְּכוֹר, is used for everything that excelleth, and hath the pre-eminence in its own kind, Job xxvii. 11; Isa. xiv. 30; Ezek. xlvii. 12. So Col. i. 15. (20:42)[1]

The second is *possession*, so "Christ is made actual possessor of that which he hath title unto." Owen here makes the distinction between God's absolute possession of heaven and earth and Christ's possession "by grant." However, it is not such a possession by grant that it might have been given to another. Approving the comments of Chrysostom and Theophylact on the text, Owen emphasizes that "there was a suitableness that he that was the Son should thus be heir," and that,

> it was agreeable and consonant that he who was eternally μονογενής [only begotten], and had on that account an absolute dominion over all with his Father, becoming πρωτότοκος ἐν πολλοῖς ἀδεγφοῖς, Romans 8:29, "the first-born amongst many brethren," should have a delegated heirship of all, and be given to be "the head over all to the church," Ephesians i. 22. (20:42)

Thirdly, as already noted, Owen emphasizes that Christ has this "title and possession by *grant* from the Father."

The way in which Christ came to his inheritance was by appointment (Heb. 1:2). Owen holds that the word ἔθηκε, translated as "appointed" in the Authorized Version, has a twofold significance. It may mean "those special acts whereby he came into the full possession of his heirship," that is, "the glorious investiture of the Lord Christ in the full actual possession of his kingdom after his resurrection, with the manifestation of it in his ascension, and token of its stability in his sitting at the right hand of God" (20:44-45). Regarding this "investiture" and "manifestation," Owen distinguishes the resurrection and ascension thus:

> The *grant* was made to him upon his resurrection, Matt. xxviii. 18, and therein fully declared unto others, Rom. i. 4; Acts xiii. 33: as there was of Solomon's being king, when he was proclaimed by Benaiah, Zadok, and Nathan, 1 Kings i. 31-34. The *solemnization* of it was in his ascension, Ps. lxviii. 17, 18, Eph. iv. 8-10; and typed by Solomon's riding on David's mule unto his throne,... All was *sealed and ratified* when he took possession of his throne at the right hand of the Father; by all which he was made and declared to be Lord and Christ, Acts ii. 36, iv. 11, v. 30, 31. (20:45; italics mine)

The significance of the resurrection and ascension for Owen's redemptive-historical understanding of Christology may be illustrated from the words which directly follow. He says,

> Such weight doth the Scripture lay upon this glorious investiture of Christ in his inheritance, that it speaks of his whole power as then first granted unto him, Rom. xiv. 9; Phil. ii. 7-10; and the reason of it is, because he had then actually performed that work and duty upon the consideration whereof that power and authority were eternally designed and originally granted unto him. God's actual committing all power over all things and persons in heaven and earth, to be exerted and managed for the ends of his mediation, declaring this act, grant, and delegation by his resurrection, ascension, and sitting at his right hand, is that which this word [ἔθηκε] denotes. (20:45)

This is the proper and intended significance of *etheke* in Hebrews 1:2.

In addition to this more specific understanding of the appointment of Christ to this inheritance in his resurrection and ascension, Owen says the term may be extended to include other "preparatory acts that long preceded them, especially if we shall take it to be of the same importance with ἔθετο in the second aoristus." These would include "the eternal purpose of God," the "covenant that was of old between the Father and Son," the "promises made unto him in his types," the "promises left upon record in the Old Testament for his supportment and assurance of success," and the "solemn proclamation of him to be the great heir and lord of all, at his first coming into the world, Luke ii. 11, 30-32." The "grant of dominion" to the Messiah is "intimated" in the protoevangelion, "confirmed in the renewal of that promise to Abraham," and "fully revealed unto David" (20:46-47). Owen emphasizes that "it is the consummation of all these," which is meant in Hebrews 1:2, but by now it should be clear that these others, especially the first two, possess great significance as certain appointments to his inheritance.

The Extent of Christ's Dominion

According to the Scriptures, the object of this inheritance is "all things absolutely." God has subjected all things unto Christ (1 Cor. 15:27), who is said to be "God over all" in Romans 9:5. Referring to the book of Hebrews, Owen says, "This sense suits the apostle's argument," by providing a twofold reason for their perseverance in the gospel. That it means "all things absolutely" is strongly indicated by the phrase which follows in Hebrews 1:2, "by whom also he made the worlds." That is, "He made all, and it was meet he should be Lord of all" (20:43). Furthermore, this understanding "answers the promise of it unto Abraham, which was that he should be 'heir of the world,' Rom. iv. 13, namely, in his seed," and the promise given to Christ himself in Psalm 2:8 (20:43).

The most fundamental argument is drawn from the doctrines of creation and fall. Man had been created as God's "heir, vicegerent, and substitute in the earth." The angels "made up another branch of God's providential kingdom," independent of man and together with man dependent upon God. When man fell, "the whole subordination of all things unto him, and by him unto God, was lost, and all creatures returned to an immediate absolute dependence on the government of God, without any respect to the authority and sovereignty delegated unto man." The fall of a portion of the angels showed that the remainder of the heavenly creation was fallible also. The entire creation hereby shown to be unstable:

> one branch of the kingdom of God, under the administration of man, or allotted to his service, being cast out of that order wherein he had placed it, and

> the other in an open possibility of being so also,—it seemed good to the Lord, in his infinite wisdom, to erect one kingdom out of these two disordered members of his first dominion, and to appoint one common heir, head, ruler, and lord to them both. And this was the Son, as the apostle tells us, Eph. 1. 10: "He gathered together in one all things in Christ, both which are in heaven, and which are on earth; even in him." He designed ἀνακεφαλαιώσασθαι, "to bring all into one head" and rule in him. . . . as Chrysostom well intimates on the place, it is as if he had said, . . . "He appointed one head to them all," angels and men, with whatsoever in the first constitution of the divine government was subordinate unto them. (20:44)

Having demonstrated that the inheritance which Christ receives is "all things absolutely," Owen proceeds to describe this universal dominion in more detail. It includes all "persons" and all "things." "Persons," i.e., "rational subsistences," include the good and evil angels together with elect and reprobate men.

King of Angels
As the author of the epistle to the Hebrews makes clear, Christ has a pre-eminence above the angels, being "preferred above them." This pre-eminence refers to his *office*, to which he has been admitted, but rests upon his "nature and existence" (20:125). Owen's redemptive-historical insight into Christology appears in his disagreement with those who attribute this exaltation to the time of his incarnation (e.g., the Lutherans), or to the time of his baptism. He reasons,

> It must . . . be the time of his *resurrection*, ascension, and exaltation at the right hand of God, which ensued thereon, that is designed as the season wherein he was made more excellent than the angels, as evidently appears from the text and context:

for,—[1.] that was the time,... when he was gloriously vested with that *all power* in heaven and earth which was of old designed unto him and prepared for him. [2.] The *order* also of the apostle's discourse leads us to fix on this season: "After he had by himself purged our sins, he sat down," etc.: "being made so much more excellent;" that is, therein and then he was so made. [3.] The *testimony* in the first place produced by the apostle in the confirmation of his assertion is elsewhere,...applied by himself unto his resurrection and the glory that ensued, and consequently they are also in this place intended. [4.] This *preference* of the Lord Christ above the angels is plainly included in that grant of all power made unto him, Matt. xxviii. 18; expounded Eph. i. 21, 22. [5.] The testimony used by the apostle in the first place is the word that God spake unto his King, when he set him upon his holy hill of Zion, Ps. ii. 6-8; which typically expresseth his glorious instalment in his heavenly kingdom. (20:125-26)

Demonstrating once more the consistency of the doctrine of two natures with the data of Scripture, Owen concludes:

> The Lord Christ, then, who in respect of his divine nature was always infinitely and incomparably himself more excellent than all the angels, after his humiliation in the assumption of the human nature, with the sufferings and temptations that he underwent, upon his resurrection was exalted into a condition of glory, power, authority, excellency, and intrusted with power over them, as our apostle here informs us. (20:126)

Christ's lordship over the angels is "universal and absolute." They are put into subjection unto Christ, "in a way of grant of privilege and honour unto him," and they are commanded to *"adore and worship him,*—the highest act of obedience and most absolute subjection" (20:50-51). The worship of the angels was always his, of course, by his divine nature, but they are specifically commanded to worship him by virtue of his dignity as the exalted Messiah, the dignity of the "first-begotten."

Further, the angels *"attend his throne."* Owen refers to the worship of Christ described in Isaiah 6:1-2. That this is Christ is clear from John 12:39-41. To this Owen adds several less familiar examples of angelic attendance unto the throne of Christ. For instance, when Christ spoke with the church in the wilderness, "that is, on Mount Sinai,... the angels attending him as on chariots, ready to receive his commands, were 'twenty thousand, even thousands of angels.'" When He walks among the golden candlesticks, the angels are "also present in church assemblies, as attending their Lord and Master." When he returns in judgment they will be in attendance also (20:50-51).

Of considerable importance to Owen is the "original right and equity" of the grant of this authority over angels unto Christ. "The radical, fundamental equity of this grant lies in his divine nature, and his creation of angels, over whom as mediator he is made Lord." This is evident in Hebrews 1:2, where his being appointed heir is followed by "by whom also he made the worlds." Owen quite rightly asserts that this reason is "particularly applicable to every part of his inheritance, and is especially pleaded in reference unto angels: Col. i. 15, 16," where it is plain that "His creation of those heavenly powers is the foundation of his heirship of lordship over them" (20:51).

The second foundation for this grant of authority lies in the "*establishment* in the condition of their creation, which by his interposition to recover what was lost by sin, and to preserve the untainted part of the creation from ruin, they did receive" (20:52). As noted earlier, following the fall of some of their number the stability of the remainder was in question; they were not yet *established* as to their state.

"Thy Throne, O God"   431

Their confirmation,—which also was attended with that exaltation which they received by their new relation unto God in and through him,—they received by his means, God gathering up all things to a consistency and permanency in him, Eph. i. 10. And hence also it became equal that the rule and power over them should be committed unto him, by whom, although they were not, like us, recovered from ruin, yet they were preserved from all danger of it. So that in their subjection unto him consists their principal honour and all their safety. (20:52-53)

The "ends" of His mediatorial lordship over the angels are also notable. First, it constituted *"an addition unto that glory that was set before him* in his undertaking to redeem sinners...and the sovereignty over them is granted him as a part of his reward, Phil. ii. 8-11; Eph. i. 20, 21" (20:53). Secondly,

...God hereby *gathers up his whole family,...* into one body under one head.... Before this the angels had no immediate created head; for themselves are called..."gods," Ps. xcvii. 7; 1 Cor. viii. 5. Whoever is the head must be..., the "God of gods," or "Lord of lords,"—which Christ alone is; and in him, or under him as a head, is the whole family of God united. (20:53)

Thirdly, Christ may "with an absolute sovereignty, use and dispose of all things," including angelic ministers, "to the benefit and advantage of the church" (20:53).

"The Lamb has Conquered"

The Lordship of Christ over the *evil* angels is of a quite different nature, though nonetheless real. Though they do not belong to him as his possession as heir, and he is not "a king and head unto them," they are under his dominion as their Lord and judge. As with the good angels, Owen describes the right and ends of this authority of

Christ. Again, his right of dominion has both an ontological basis in his divine nature, and a mediatorial basis. As Owen explains:

> He made these angels also, and therefore, as God, hath an absolute dominion over them. The creatures cannot cast off the dominion of the Creator by rebellion. Though they may lose their moral relation unto God, as obedient creatures, yet their natural, as creatures, cannot be dissolved. (20:54)

As with the good angels, "this dominion of Christ over fallen angels as God makes the grant of rule over them to him as mediator just and equal" (20:54).

However, "the immediate and peculiar foundation of his right unto rule over fallen angels, rendering the special grant of it equal and righteous, is lawful conquest" (20:54). This is part of the Old Testament expectation of the Messiah given in the first promise, and confirmed in the New by the apostle Paul in Colossians 2:15, which Owen interprets thus:

> "He spoiled principalities and powers,"—divested fallen angels of all that title they had got to the world, by the sin of man; "triumphing over them," as captives to be disposed of at his pleasure. He "stilled," or made to cease as to his power, this "enemy," ...and "self-avenger," Ps. viii. 2; "leading captivity captive," Ps. lxviii. 18; "breaking in pieces the head over the large earth," Ps. cx. 6; "binding the strong man and spoiling his goods." (20:54)

Without entertaining the unscriptural ideas of a ransom paid to the devil, or of a swindling of the devil, Owen does not fail to set forth the important biblical teaching concerning Christ the conqueror (*Christus victor*). However, Owen is free from the error of presenting *Christus victor* as an alternative theory to atonement by substitution. This is because Christ's sacrifice *for* us is his means of destroying Satan's power *over* us.

"Thy Throne, O God"

> The fourfold power of Satan in reference unto death, before mentioned, was all founded in sin. The obligation of the sinner unto death was that which gave him all his power. The taking away, then, of that obligation must needs be the dissolution of his power. The foundation being removed, all that is built upon it must needs fall to the ground. Now this, in reference unto the children for whom he died, was done in the death of Christ,—*virtually* in his death itself, actually in the application of it unto them. When the sinner ceaseth to be obnoxious unto death, the power of Satan ceaseth also. (20:450)

To each aspect of the fourfold power of Satan over sinners, Owen presents us with a corresponding destruction of that power by Christ, with each resulting from the substitutionary death of Christ.

> The first branch of his power consisted in the bringing of sin into the world. This is dissolved by Christ's "taking away the sin of the world," John i. 29; which he did as "the Lamb of God," by the sacrifice of himself in his death, typified by the paschal lamb and all other sacrifices of old. Again, his power consisted in his rule in the world, as cast under sin and death. From this he was cast out, John xii. 31, in the death of Christ. When contending with him for the continuance of his sovereignty, he was conquered, the ground whereon he stood, even the guilt of sin, being taken away from under him, and this title defeated. And actually believers are translated from under his rule, from the power of darkness, into the kingdom of light and of the Son of God. (20:450-51)

As believers understand these objective realities they obtain further deliverance from Satan's influence over them, as Owen points out:

> Nor can he longer make use of death as penal, as threatened in the curse of the law, to terrify and af-

fright the consciences of men: for "being justified by faith" in the death of Christ, "they have peace with God," Rom. v. 1. Christ making peace between God and us by the blood of his cross, Eph. ii. 14, 15, 2 Cor. v. 19-21. the weapons of this part of his power are wrested out of his hand, seeing death hath no power to terrify the conscience, but as it expresseth the curse of God. And lastly, his final execution of the sentence of death upon sinners is utterly taken out of his hand by the death of Christ, inasmuch as they for whom he died shall never undergo death penally. And thus was Satan, as to his power over death, fully destroyed by the death of Christ. (20:451)

In this manner God "ordered things so, that this death of Christ should pull out that pin which kept together the whole fabric of sin and Satan,—that, like Samson, he should in his death pull down the palace of Satan about his ears, and that in dying he should conquer and subdue all things unto himself" (20:452). As C. S. Lewis later wrote of a "deeper magic" which destroyed Narnia's witch in her attempt at Aslan's destruction, Owen writes that "Satan laid his claim unto the person of Christ; but coming to put it in execution, he met with that great and hidden power in him which he knew not, and was utterly conquered" (20:453).

Christ has entered into conflict with the evil angels and has prevailed. They are consequently "subjected unto him as to their present actings and future condition." By their "actings" Owen means that Christ, "suffers them, in his holiness and wisdom, to act in temptations, seductions, persecutions," but "he bounds and limits their rage, malice, actings," and "orders and disposes the events of them to his own holy and righteous ends." They are his unwilling instruments in his providential government of mankind. This subjection is unto his own glory, for the church's safety, for the "exercise" of the saints to their "eternal advantage," and for the "exercising of his wrath and vengeance upon his stubborn enemies, whom these slaves and vassals to his righteous power seduce, blind, harden, provoke, ruin and destroy" (20:55). Their "future condition" is subject to Christ also, as he "keeps them under chains for the judgement of the last day, when, for the full manifestation of his dominion over them, he will cause the meanest of his servants to set their feet on the necks of these conquered kings, and to join with himself in sentencing them unto eternal ruin, 1 Cor. vi. 3; which they shall be cast into by him, Rev. xix. 20" (20:55).

Jesus' exercise of authority over the demons in the coming of the kingdom of God, as seen in the exorcism accounts, are deliberate demonstrations of the presence of the kingdom of God in the person of the Messiah and therefore have no small significance in the life of Christ. In view of the claim that the Puritans were uninterested in the earthly life of Christ, it is noteworthy that Owen has a similar understanding of the significance of these events: "The Scripture of the New Testament is full of instances as to his executing his power and authority over evil angels; they take up a good part of the historical books of it" (20:54).

King of Saints
As with all other persons and things, the foundation of the authority of Christ over the elect is his divine nature in which he is their creator and Lord. Besides this, he has been granted by the Father a lordship over them on account of his mediatorial office. The elect were given to the Son from eternity in the covenant of redemption. As John 17:2 indicates, "of the πάσης σαρκός 'all flesh' over which the Son had authority, there was a particular πᾶν ὃ δέδωκε [all which you gave], "a universality of them whom the Father gave him, in an especial manner" (20:56). They were given to him to save. This grant, adds

Owen, "is strengthened by *redemption*, purchase, and acquisition." Owen is on firm biblical ground when he says, "This was the condition of the former grant, Isa. liii. 10-12, which was made good by him; so that his lordship is frequently asserted on this very account, 1 Cor. vi. 20; 1 Pet. i. 18, 19; 1 Tim. ii. 6; John x. 15; Eph. v. 25-27; Rev. v. 9; John xi. 51, 52" (20:56).

It is noteworthy that here—and not only in his exposition of the priesthood of Christ—the mediatorial lordship of Christ over and his possession of the saints is the fruit of the "covenant of the mediator." It proceeds "from his *especial and greatest love*,... Being accompanied with a *purchase* for them which they shall certainly enjoy, and that of grace and glory" (20:56). The relation between the covenant of redemption, the death of Christ, and the power exerted in the calling of the elect, is emphasized by Owen who reminds the reader that "the controversy about the death of Christ is not primarily about its extent, but its efficacy and fruits in respect of them for whom he died" (20:56).

The elect are divided into the called and uncalled. The first are those who have actually been effectually called to faith and union with Christ. Owen emphasizes the completeness of the authority of Christ over them thus:

> He stands towards them in *all relations* of authority: is their father, master, elder brother, teacher, king, lord, ruler, judge, husband; ruling in them by his Spirit and grace, over them by his laws in his word, preserving them by his power, chastening them in his care and love, feeding them out of his stores, trying them and delivering them in his wisdom, bearing with their miscarriages in his patience, and taking them for his portion, lot, and inheritance, in his providence; raising them at the last day, taking them to himself in glory, and every way avouching

them to be his, and himself to be their Lord and Master. (20:57)

The uncalled also abide under the lordship of Christ, belonging "unto his lot, care and rule." They are his "other sheep" (John 10:16), "by grant and purchase, though not yet really so by grace and holiness" (20:57). Over both called and uncalled elect, Christ's power is "universal, unlimited, absolute and exclusive of all other power over them, as unto the things peculiarly belonging unto his kingdom" (20:57).[2]

The Potter with Power over the Clay
The dominion of Christ over the entire race must naturally include the reprobate (i.e., the non-elect), and that upon two grounds. First, by virtue of Christ's "*interposition*, upon the entrance of sin, against the immediate execution of the curse due unto it; as befell the angels," the world received a "dispensation" of "forebearance and patience," and of "goodness and mercy" (20:57). Here we find Owen grounding the doctrine of "common grace" in the covenant made for the salvation of God's elect by Christ, while denying the reprobate any real interest in that covenant as such:

> That God, who spared not the angels when they sinned, but immediately cast them into chains of darkness, should place sinners of the race of Adam under a dispensation of forbearance and goodness,—that he should spare them with much longsuffering during their pilgrimage on the earth, and fill their hearts with food and gladness, with all those fruits of kindness which the womb of his providence is still bringing forth for their benefit and advantage,—is thus far on the account of the Lord Christ, that though these things, as relating unto reprobates, are no part of his especial purchase as mediator of the everlasting covenant of grace, yet

they are a necessary consequent of his interposition against the immediate execution of the whole curse upon the first entrance of sin, and of his undertaking for his elect. (20:57-58)

The second ground of Christ's dominion over the reprobate is his conquest over them; they comprise his enemies destined to be made his footstool. This resulting dominion is "sovereign and absolute." It is also "judiciary," exercised over them in regard to their sins, "even in this world, before he gloriously exerts it in their eternal ruin." How does he exercise it in this world?

> He enlightens them by those heavenly sparks of truth and reason which he leaves unextinguished in their minds, John i. 9.... [He] strives with them by his Spirit, Gen. vi. 3; secretly exciting their consciences to rebuke, bridle, yoke, afflict, and cruciate them, Rom. ii. 14, 15. And,... on some of them he acts by the power and authority of his word; whereby he quickens their consciences, galls their minds, aggravates their sins, hardens their hearts, and judges their souls, Ps. xlv.; Isa. vi.... He exerciseth rule and dominion over them in providential dispensations,... by all which he makes way for the glory of his final judgement of them. (20:58)

In these remarks we learn that those "common operations" of the Spirit, which are unaccompanied with the grace of regeneration, are, in the case of the reprobate, tokens of Christ's judgment upon their sin. The Puritan teaching concerning non-salvific operations of the Holy Spirit has been regarded as a manifestation of their move away from Calvin's Christocentricism. In the context of Christ's exercise of his kingly office we find a description of the Holy Spirit's work upon the reprobate which is reminiscent of Calvin's teaching. The ends of this dominion are the same as those for the dominion over evil angels: Christ's glory and the good of the church (20:58).

"Over all principalities and power"

Christ has become the heir of "all things," not merely the rational creatures mentioned already. In his exposition of Christ's kingdom Owen categorizes the remainder of Christ's dominion as all things spiritual, ecclesiastical, political, and natural. This is a most significant indication of the Christocentricity of Owen's thought: everything conceivably connected with life, and most notably those things of the greatest concern to a Puritan, is quite explicitly acknowledged to be subject to Christ's mediatorial dominion.

Spiritual things include the grace and gifts which come to his elect in the present age, and the glory of the age to come. Included in this category of "grace" are all the divine works which constitute the subjects of Owen's many notable treatises in Puritan practical divinity: pardon of sin, regeneration, sanctification, preservation, adoption, and the privileges which flow from it.

> All these, with all those admirable and inexpressible mercies that they branch themselves into,—giving deliverance unto sinners from evil temporal and eternal, raising them to communion with God here, and to the enjoyment of him for ever hereafter,—are called grace, and do belong to the lordship of Christ, as he is heir, lord, and possessor of them all. All the stores of this grace and mercy that are in heaven for sinners are given into his hand, and resigned up to his sovereign disposal. (20:59-60)

In addition to grace, Christ as the mediatorial king also has the sovereign disposal of "gifts," natural and spiritual. In his emphasis upon natural gifts and his assertion of Christ's rule over the natural world, Owen makes a valid, though unheeded, point for a truly reformed apologetic which challenged rather than granted the presuppositions of the new deism. It is in this regard that we see Owen's understanding of common grace as it acts in the human mind. Explaining Christ's lordship over it, Owen says:

> (1.) In that the *very use of men's reason* and their natural faculties, as to any good or purpose, is continued unto them upon the account of his interposition, bringing the world thereby under a dispensation of patience and forbearance, as was declared, John i. 9. (2.) He is endued with power and authority to use them, in whose hand soever they lie, whether of his friends or enemies, to the especial ends of his glory, in doing good unto his church. And indeed, in the efficacy of his Spirit and power upon the gifts of the minds of men, exciting, ordering, disposing, enabling them unto various actings and operations, by and with them; controlling, overruling, entangling each other and themselves in whom they are by them; his wisdom and care in the rule, government, chastisement, and deliverance of his church, are most conspicuous. (20:63)

The subject of spiritual gifts is handled at length in *A Discourse of Spiritual Gifts* under the general subject of the work of the Spirit. Nonetheless, they are appropriately handled under the Kingdom of Christ for a number of reasons. First, these spiritual gifts are

> that without which the church cannot subsist in the world, nor can believers be useful unto one another and the rest of mankind unto the glory of Christ.... They are the "powers of the world to come;" those effectual operations of the power of Christ whereby his kingdom was erected and is preserved. (4:420-21)

As Owen explains it, they are peculiarly associated with the New Covenant and constitute much of that which distinguishes evangelical worship from that under the Old Covenant. Without them, the worship and institutions of the New Testament, despite their being "accommodated unto that administration of grace and truth which came by Jesus Christ,... must lose their whole glory, force, and efficacy" (4:421). Furthermore, it is Christ that gives the gifts.

The gifts are particularly discussed under the kingdom of Christ, however, because they are given to him upon his ascension, an "investiture," which "he had as a fruit of his suffering, as a part of his purchase," making up a "choice portion of his lordship and kingdom" (20:64-65). Interpreting Paul's reference to Psalm 68:18 (Eph. 4:8), Owen says,

> whereas it is foretold in the psalm that Christ should *receive gifts,*—that is, *to give them unto men,* as that expression is expounded by the apostle,—so he did this by *receiving of the Spirit,* the proper cause and immediate author of them all as Peter declares, Acts ii. 33, "Therefore being by the right hand of God exalted, and having received of the Father the promise of the Holy Ghost, he hath shed forth this, which ye now see and hear," speaking of the miraculous gifts conferred on the apostles at the day of Pentecost; for these gifts are from Christ, not as God absolutely, but as mediator, in which capacity he received all from the Father in a way of free donation. Thus, therefore, he received the *Spirit* as the author of all *spiritual gifts.* (4:422)

These gifts are given to advance the interests of the kingdom. In this regard Owen mentions in particular the propagation of the gospel, the edification of the church, and the glorification of God (20:64; 4:426). Owen emphasizes that no other means are effective for these ends, while these spiritual gifts are "the slings and stones before which the Goliaths of the earth and hell did fall" (20:65; cf. 4:427).

In addition to grace and gifts below, Christ's kingdom also includes "all spiritual eternal things," that is, "glory." Owen says that as Christ is the Lord of Glory and Judge of all, he will give glory to his followers as a reward. To this end he has purchased this glory, taken possession of it, and become the *"forerunner* of those on whom he will bestow it" (20:67).

• Ecclesiastical

Christ exercises his dominion in what Owen calls *"ecclesiastical things*, or things that concern church institutions, rule, and power" (20:67). He is its *only* Lord, whether one is talking of the Old Testament or the Christian administration. Owen observes that there was "a church-state ever since God created man on the earth," which had Christ as its Lord. Owen describes four ways in which Christ exercised his lordship over the Old Testament church-state: "In and by its *institution* and erection"; "by prescribing a *complete rule* and form of worship and obedience unto it, being erected"; "by way of *reformation*, when it was collapsed and decayed"; and "by way of *amotion*, or taking down what he himself had set up" (20:67-68).

He is the Lord of the New Testament church: he erects it upon the foundation of himself, gives it its *"laws and rules* of worship and obedience," and everlastingly abides as its *"head, ruler, king, and governor"* (20:68). This, Owen says, "is his proper kingdom, on which all other parts of his dominion do depend: for he is given to be 'head over all things to the church'" (20:68).

• Political

In addition to his rule in the church, Owen says that Christ is "Lord also of *political things"*; that is, the non-ecclesiastical governments of the earth. Again, this cannot be summarized better than by quoting Owen:

> He alone is the *absolute potentate*; the highest on the earth are in a subordination unto him. That, 1. He was *designed unto*, Ps. lxxxix. 27. And accordingly he is, 2. made Lord of lords, and King of kings, Rev.

xvii. 14,... And, 3. He exerciseth dominion answerable unto his title, Rev. vi. 14-17,... And, 4. Hath hence right to send his gospel into all nations in the world, attended with the worship by him prescribed, Matt. xxviii. 19,... which none of the rulers or governors of the world have any right to refuse or oppose; nor can so do, but upon their utmost peril. And 5. All kingdoms shall at length be brought into a professed subjection to him and his gospel, and have all their rule disposed of unto the interest of his church and saints, Dan. vii. 27. (20:68)

The political impact of Christ's reign over the nations is expounded in a number of sermons preached to Parliament. Even when addressing that august assembly, Owen was first an ambassador of Christ, commissioned to display the glories of his Lord, compelling all men, even "judges and rulers," to "kiss the Son, and own his scepter, and advance his ways." His post-millennialism is reflected in a sermon entitled "The Shaking and Translating of Heaven and Earth," in which he says, "The Lord Jesus Christ, by his mighty power, in these latter days, as anti-Christian tyranny draws to its period, will so far shake and translate the political heights, governments, and strength of the nations, as shall serve for the full bringing in of his own peaceable kingdom;—the nations so shaken becoming thereby a quiet habitation for the people of the Most High" (8:260). This shaking of this anti-Christian kingdom will be

> transacted with so much obscurity and darkness, Christ not openly appearing unto carnal eyes, that though 'many shall be purified, and made white, and tried, yet the wicked shall do wickedly: and none of the wicked shall understand; but the wise shall understand,' Dan. xii. 10. There shall be no such demonstration of the presence of Christ as to open the eyes of hardened men; but at length, having suffered the poor, deceived wretches to drink of

> the cup prepared for them, he appears himself gloriously, Rev. xix. 13, in a more eminent manner than ever before, to the total destruction of the residue of opposers. And that this will be the utmost close of that dispensation wherein now he walketh, I no way doubt. (8:263)

There are four reasons for this shaking: first, that the martyrs may be avenged; second, that Christ might "frame such a power as may best conduce to the carrying on of his own kingdom among the sons of men"; third, because the "present power of the nations stands in direct opposition to the bringing in of the kingdom of Christ"; and fourth, that the saints, seeing this shaking "may be raised up to the laying hold of that durable kingdom that shall not be removed" (8:263, 264, 266, 268). The second of these reasons is necessary from the fact that the present kingdoms are so "framed to the interest of Antichrist" that "no digging or mining, but an earthquake, will cast up the foundation-stones thereof" (8:266).

The third reason was particularly significant at the time, and no doubt made a favorable impression upon the sympathetic Parliamentary leader, Oliver Cromwell, present in the congregation. Like the majority of English Puritans, Owen believed the latter day conversion of the Jews was a necessary preamble to the bringing in of the kingdom of Christ. The nations, in the form of the "Turkish power" and of the "Romish Babylon," presented a real obstacle to this; hence they must be removed. There was also a moral obstacle which Cromwell was deeply concerned to remove: the idolatry of the Gentile worshipers. A second prerequisite to the coming of the kingdom is the "tremendous total destruction of Babylon, the man of sin, and all his adherents, that are not obedient to the heavenly call" (8:267). Pull down the powers of the world, those pillars of the temple of Antichrist, and it will be shaken to the ground.

However, Owen makes it clear that there is no "carnal" advantage in this shaking of the nation, and exhorts his hearers to make straight paths for the coming Lord. First, they are told,

> Give the Lord Jesus a throne in your hearts, or it will not at all be to your advantage that he hath a throne and kingdom in the world.... Oh, that it were the will of God to put an end to all that pretended holiness, hypocritical humiliation, self-interested religion, that have been among us, whereby we have flattered God with our lips, whilst our hearts have been far from him! Oh, that it might be the glory of this assembly, above all the assemblies of the world, that every ruler in it might be a sincere subject in the kingdom of the Lord Jesus!... Oh, that I could nourish this one contention in your honourable assembly, that you might strive who should excel in setting up the Lord Jesus in your hearts! (8:277)

Owen is careful to remind the Parliament that unless this kingdom of "righteousness, peace, and joy in the Holy Ghost," is within them, to the exclusion of "pharisaical, rigid, supercilious affectation," the Day of the Lord will be "darkness to you, and not light." The purpose of God in this shaking is that he might revenge their opposition to the kingdom of his dear Son, and that he might remove every hindrance to it.

• Natural Things

Finally, in keeping with what was said above in chapter eight, Christ is the sovereign lord of the physical world, as he demonstrated in his earthly life as recorded in the gospel (20:68-9).

The Character of the Kingdom: "A Scepter of Righteousness"

Owen remarks that in Hebrews 1:8 "scepter" denotes the actual administration of rule, both the laws of the kingdom and the efficacy of the government itself. Christ's scepter is the "means whereby Christ carrieth on his kingdom"; which Owen understood as his "Word and Spirit, with a *subserviency of power* in the works of his providence, to make way for the progress of his word to avenge its contempt" (20:183). Owen explains that Christ's power is

> wholly clothed with the word; thereby it is conveyed to the souls of men; therein is "the hiding of his power," Hab. iii. 4. Though it seems weak, and is despised, yet it is accompanied with the hidden power of Christ, which will not fail of its end, 1 Cor. i. 18. And the word preached is not otherwise to be considered, but as that which is the conveyance of divine power to the souls of men. And every impression that it makes on the heart is an effect of the power of Christ. (21:367)

This is a scepter of righteousness because, recalling Owen's definition of righteousness in God,

> all the laws of his gospel are righteous, holy, just, full of benignity and truth, Tit. ii. 11, 12. And all his administrations of grace, mercy, justice, rewards, and punishments, according to the rules, promises, and threats of it, in the conversion, pardon, sanctification, trials, afflictions, chastisements, and preservation of his elect; in the convincing, hardening, and destruction of his enemies; are all righteous, holy, unblameable, and good. (20:184)

The righteousness of Christ's kingdom arises from the "*habitual frame of the heart of Christ* in his regal administrations" (20:184).

"An Everlasting Kingdom"

The throne of Christ is said to be "for ever and ever"—that is, Owen explains, "in opposition unto the frail, mutable Kingdoms of the earth." "It shall neither decay of itself, nor fall through the opposition of its enemies: for he must reign until all his enemies are made his footstool, I Cor. xv. 24-27" (20:183). The "eternity, stability, and unchangeableness" of Christ's kingdom arise from his divine nature (20:191).

First Corinthians 15:24, however, indicates that Christ's mediatorial reign is not, as such, absolutely eternal. There is no difficulty in affirming the "perpetuity" of Christ's kingdom and his giving up that kingdom to the Father: "It is enough that it continue until all the *ends of rule* be perfectly accomplished" (20:183). By "ends of rule" Owen refers to the salvation of the church and the conquest of the enemies unto the glory of God. With regard to the church's dependence upon Christ's mediatorial office, however, Owen maintains, "there are some things which belong unto the essence of that state which shall continue unto all eternity." Though the Scripture is addressing the mediatorial kingdom, the things to which Owen refers pertain to Christ's mediatorial office in general, and not solely to the kingly office.

Consistent with the Christocentric emphasis we have observed so far, Owen says,

> 1st, I do believe that the person of Christ, in and by his human nature, shall be for ever the *immediate head of the whole glorified creation*. God having gathered all things unto a head in him, the knot or centre of that collection shall never be dissolved. We shall never lose our relation unto him, nor he his unto us.
>
> 2ndly, I do therefore also believe, that he shall be the *means and way of communication* between God and his glorified saints for ever. What are, what will be, the glorious communications of God unto his saints for ever, in life, light, power, joy, rest, and ineffable satisfaction, (as all must be from him unto eternity,) I shall not now inquire. But…they shall be all made in and through the person of the Son, and the

human nature therein. That tabernacle shall never be folded up, never be laid aside as useless. (1:271)

Conclusion

In our survey of Owen's teaching on the kingdom of Christ two things particularly stand out. First, Owen is careful to expound the kingdom of Christ as his *mediatorial* kingdom, over which he rules in the unity of his person. As with the offices of prophet and priest, there is a notable interest in the significance of redemptive history. That is, Owen takes seriously the change that was made by the advent of Christ without diminishing the importance of his eternal work as the mediator between God and man, i.e., in the Old Testament, and in the eternal state. Second, we see the extent of this kingdom. Nothing is outside of it, nothing can be neutral to it, and nothing can resist it. Owen can only conclude his most general exposition of it by exclaiming, "How small a portion of his glorious power are we able to comprehend or declare!" (20:69). Finally, we have seen yet another example of the systematic character of Owen's thinking, bringing together Christ's wonderful works as prophet priest and king as the works of one Christ, undertaking the salvation of his people unto the glory of God.

Having said this, and before leaving this study of the three mediatory offices of Christ, it should be observed that, while Owen employed the model of the three offices for his exposition of the work of Christ, he did not restrict himself to the use of these names. In a footnote to his catechism question, *"How many are the offices of Jesus Christ,"* he observes, "In the exercise of these offices, Christ is also the sole head, husband, and first-born of the church" (1:480). The first of these receives considerable attention in his doctrine of the church, the subject of our next chapter.

[1] The reference is to Psalm 89:28 in the Hebrew text, 89:27 in KJV.
[2] See Flavel's expositions, "The Kingly Office of Christ, as Executed Upon the Souls of the Redeemed," and "The Kingly Office of Christ, as Providentially Executed for the Redeemed," in *The Fountain of Life*. (1820, 1:198-222). The latter includes teaching on the rule of Christ over all things.

CHAPTER 16

A Christ-Centered Church

While the definition of the word "Puritan" remains a matter of some debate, there is no doubt that ecclesiastical issues were close to the heart of every Puritan preacher. Despite the fact that in creed and sermon the doctrine of the church was incessantly expounded in terms of the covenant and of grace and the doctrines of Christ's threefold office, historians of the period have not paid much attention to the strong Christocentric nature of the Puritan doctrine of the church. A full exposition of John Owen's ecclesiology is beyond our present purpose, which is merely to demonstrate that Owen's views of the church's nature, composition, authority, mission, ministry, and worship have strong and direct ties to Christology.[1]

The Nature of the Church

In the writings of John Owen one can find the following definitions of the church. The first is a definition of God's house, his Zion:

> By the church of Christ I understand, primarily, the whole multitude of them who antecedently are chosen of his Father, and given unto him; consequently, are redeemed, called, and justified in his blood;— the church which he loved, and gave himself for,

'that he might sanctify and cleanse it with the washing of water by the word; that he might present it to himself a glorious church, not having spot, or wrinkle, or any such thing; but that it should be holy, and without blemish,' Eph. v. 26, 27. And, secondarily, also every holy assembly of mount Zion, whereunto the Lord Christ is made beauty and glory,—every particular church of his saints, inasmuch as they partake of the nature of the whole being purchased by his blood, Acts xx. 28. (8:286)

The second definition is in his *Inquiry of Evangelical Churches*:

The name of the church under the New Testament is capable of a threefold application... (1.) For the catholic invisible church, or society of elect believers in the whole world, really related by faith in him unto the Lord Jesus Christ as their mystical head; (2.) for the whole number of visible professors in the whole world, who, by baptism, and the outward profession of the gospel, and obedience unto Christ, are distinguished from the rest of the world: and,— (3.) For such a state as wherein the worship of God is to be celebrated in the way and manner by him appointed, and which is to be ruled by the power which he gives it, and according to the discipline which he hath ordained. (15:233)

From these two definitions it is apparent that the church, whether invisible or visible, universal or particular, derives its nature and existence from its relation to Christ. The elect, who as yet are uncalled are the church in the purpose of God, for they are the object of the redemptive acts of Christ, but they are not properly and practically called the church until they are called and sanctified unto God from the world by the Spirit. This sanctification is into union with Christ in visible, particular churches, or "holy assemblies." It is vitally important to remember that the word "church" is used both for the body of true believers and for the society of professors and practitioners and their children. Though the two are not identical, Christ is related to the church in each case.

The church exists in visible structured societies, and must do so, since man was created to act in society, and the "principle end" of living in society is the glory and worship of God. To create a holy worshipping society, God revealed his will to Adam in innocence, and, after the fall, with a specific view toward the coming of Christ, to Adam's descendants. Owen often calls such a society a "church-state" to signify all the various ecclesiastical structures since creation: households of patriarchs, the nation which covenanted together at Sinai, and the particular local church of the New Testament era (a "gospel," or "evangelical, church-state"). By any definition, it centers on Christ.

The Church's Lord
With characteristic precision, Owen emphasizes that the origin of the "evangelical church-state" is "directly, immediately, and solely" Jesus Christ (15:234). "Christ alone," Owen says, "is the author, institutor, and appointer, in a way of authority and legislation, of the gospel church-state, its order, rule, and worship, with all things constantly and perpetually belonging thereunto, or necessary to be observed therein" (15:244; cf. 15:232-33). Visible, particular churches are "the ordinance and institution of Christ" (15:22).

Christ: Author of the "Gospel church-state"
From principles we have observed in previous chapters, Owen supplies three reasons why Christ is "meet" to be the author of the "gospel church-state." The first is Christ's threefold "right and title to dispose of all men, in all their spiritual and eternal concernments" (15:235), which right he has by the 1) "*donation* from the Father," 2) "by virtue of

purchase," and 3) "by *right of conquest.*" This conquest was both over his enemies (who had held his church captive), and over his church, who were enemies to him in their minds and needing to be conquered "by his word, his Spirit, and his grace" (15:235-36).

Secondly, along with right and title to the persons of the church, Christ also has authority with respect to rules, etc., established for the church's privileges and duty. This authority, is "enclosed unto him, so that no other can have any interest in it," making him "the only 'lawgiver' of the church" (15:237). This authority is "immediately" from Christ, and delegated to the apostles: "For as he took it on himself as his own work to build his church, and that upon himself as its foundation, so he employed his apostles to act under him and from him, in the carrying on that work unto perfection" (15:234). The apostles "received revelations of what did belong unto this church-state, and what was to be prescribed therein." Owen emphasized that although the apostles did advise and exercise authority, they never attempted to "invent, contrive, institute, or appoint any thing in the church and its state, which they had not by immediate revelation from Christ," whose authority "acted in them and by them" in the church (15:234). When they had no immediate revelation from Christ they ruled "only by a due application unto present occasions" of the revelation they had received (15:235). Further, as apostles, "Christ sent them, as his Father sent him; and he was so sent of the Father as that he did 'stand and feed in the strength of the LORD, in the majesty of the name of the LORD his God,' Mic. v. 4. So did they feed the sheep of Christ in his strength, and in the authority of his name" (15:235). It will soon become apparent how this principle has a special significance for the Puritan pastor.

Thirdly, to his understanding of the church, Owen makes application of the *faithfulness* of Christ. Christ, as mediator, has been given power over the church by the Father:

> Hence, it follows, that in the execution of it he hath respect unto the mind and will of God, as unto what he would have done and ordered, with respect whereunto this power was committed unto him. And here his faithfulness takes place, exerted in the revelation of the whole mind of God in this matter, instituting, appointing, and commanding all that God would have so ordained, and nothing else. And what can *any man do that cometh after the King?* (15:242)

The Church's Life, Glory, and Stability

We may obtain a good view of Owen's thoughts concerning the relation of Christ and the church by looking at his exposition of the principal scriptural images of the church as Christ's building, body, and bride.

The Son Over His House

The building motif is explained at length in a sermon entitled "The Branch of the Lord the Beauty of Zion: or, The Glory of the Church in its Relation Unto Christ." Owen identifies the architects and builders as principally the Spirit, and secondarily and instrumentally the prophets and apostles.

The house is a living house. "Christ, the foundation, is a living stone, and they that are built upon him are living stones. Hence they are said to grow together into a house" (8:288). It is a strong house because of the foundation which as a living rock is "continually communicating strength unto every stone in the building, that it may be enabled to abide in him" (8:289). It is a glorious house: "glorious in respect of inward glory, brought unto it of God in the face of Jesus Christ, being beautiful through the comeliness that he puts upon it," i.e., by the justification and sanctification of its members who, "partaking of His nature, are very glorious therein" (8:289). The incarnation brings glory to the church: "he being 'the branch of the Lord and fruit of the earth,' is made beauty and glory, excellency and comeliness, thereunto, Isa. iv. 2" (8:289). It is also glorious in respect of its "outward structure," that is, in the "peculiar assemblies thereof"—local churches where the administration of Christ's glorious ordinances are carried out. "The glory of the ordinances of the gospel is their vigor and purity. There is nothing so glorious as our King on his throne, Christ in his court, this house reigning in the administration of his ordinances" (8:290). The great significance of this for Puritan ecclesiology will appear in the discussion of Owen's doctrine of worship. Thirdly, "it is glorious in respect of the exaltation it hath above and the triumph over all its opposers" (8:290).

The members of the church comprise a spiritual temple. Jesus Christ stands in a twofold relation unto this temple: 1) in respect of its "fabric and building," and 2) in respect of its state and condition. Explaining its "fabric and building," Owen says that Christ is its foundation, its ark, its altar, and its candlestick.

The Church's Foundation
Christ is its foundation, "the foundation of the apostles and prophets," which they laid by their preaching of the gospel (8:291, 286-87). Three things required to a foundation are "eminently seen in the Lord Christ, in reference to this house": it must be "first laid," it is "hidden," and it "bears up the entire weight of the building."

How was he "first laid"? Christ was the first laid in the purpose of God: "God purposing to build his elect into a holy temple, purposed that Jesus Christ should be the foundation" (8:291-93). He was first in respect of outward manifestation: in the first gospel of Genesis 3:15, "God first manifests and declares him, before he laid one stone in this building" (8:292). Further, "in the order of nature, Christ must be first laid in the heart of every individual stone before they are laid up in this building." He is first "in respect of every particular assembly and little sanctuary of mount Zion": as every congregational minister knew, men must first give themselves up to Christ in faith before they give themselves up to one another in a church covenant. Otherwise, such churches would "prove pinnacles of Babel, not towers of Zion" (8:292).

The foundation that holds up the building is also hidden from view. The significance of this fact in mid-seventeenth-century England had not always been apparent to Owen, as he explains:

> Men looking upon the church do find that it is a fair fabric indeed, but cannot imagine how it should stand. A few supporters it seemeth to have in the world, like crouching antics under the windows, that make some show of under-propping it:—here you have a magistrate, there an army, or so. Think the men of the world, "Can we but remove these props, the whole would quickly topple to the ground." Yes, so foolish have I been myself, and so void of understanding before the Lord, as to take a view of some goodly appearing props of this building, and to think, How shall the house be preserved if these should be removed?... when, lo! suddenly some have been manifested to be pargeted posts, and the very best to be held up by the house, and not to hold it up. On this account the men of the world think it no great matter to demolish the spiritual church of Christ to the ground:—they encourage one another to the work, never thinking of the foundation that lies hidden, against which they dash themselves all to pieces. I say, then, Christ, as the foundation of this house, is hidden to the men of the world,—they see it not, they believe it not. There is nothing more remote from their ap-

prehension than that Christ should be at the bottom of them and their ways, whom they so much despise. (8:292-93)

Owen goes on to describe the relation of Christ to the church in terms of this building's furniture.

The Furniture of the Temple
Christ is the ark of the house of God, containing "in himself the new covenant; it is made with him originally, established in him irreversibly, —made out through him in all the grace of it faithfully" (8:294). He is also its altar. In fact, Christ is two altars: the altar of sacrifice, and the altar of incense (8:294), signifying Christ's atonement and intercession. In this context Owen reminds us that all the living stones of this house are priests to offer sacrifice on these altars. That is, by him, as priests, they may draw near to the holy place, where they have a share and participation in all the sacrifices that are offered upon or by him (8:295). Christ is the candlestick. Drawing upon Zechariah's description of the candlestick, Owen says that Christ alone, "is this candlestick, and all the light which this house hath it is from him" (8:295). The candlestick gives light to the house in two ways: by "doctrinal revelation" and by "real communication," which were described above under the work of Christ as prophet.

Owner
Owen adds five ways in which Christ relates to the house's "state and condition": He is its owner, builder, watchman, "inhabiter," and avenger. Christ is the owner, by right of inheritance, purchase, and conquest. With respect to Christ's purchase of the church, Owen offers us another biblical nuance to his doctrine of the atonement as a price:

> When he should come to take possession of this house, he finds that it is mortgaged, and that a great

debt lies upon it; which he must pay to the utmost farthing, if he ever intend to have it.... Jesus Christ being the heir, the right of redemption belonged unto him. It was not for his honour that it should lie unredeemed. Full well he knew that if he did not, the whole creation was too beggarly to make this purchase.... He likes the house, and will have it to dwell in, whatever it cost him. "Here," saith he, "shall be my habitation, and my dwelling for ever, " Ps. cxxxii. "Know ye not," saith the apostle, "that ye are the temple of the Spirit of Christ?" Well, and how come we so to be? "Ye are bought with a price," 1 Cor. vi. 19 (8:297-98).[2]

Christ's third title to the house is his conquest: "An unjust usurper had taken possession of this house, and kept it in bondage;—Satan had seized on it, and brought it, through the wrath of God, under his power" (8:298). As we saw earlier, Christ's victory over Satan has its cosmic and personal dimensions. In this context, Owen combines them thus:

> Christ bound the strong man, and then spoiled his goods, Matt. xii. 29. All that darkness, unbelief, sin, and hardness, that he had stuffed this house withal, Christ spoils and scatters them all away. And to make his conquest complete, he triumphs over his enemy, and like a mighty conqueror, makes an open show of him, to his everlasting shame, Col. ii. 15,... and by this means strengthens his title to his inheritance. (8:298)

To these three reasons for ownership, Owen adds that it is his house by the "donation of his Father," and by the "actual possession he takes of it by his Spirit" (8:299).

Builder

Secondly, this "mystical habitation" of God is *built* by Jesus Christ. This is one principal aspect of the glory of Christ that which sets him above Moses as an authority in

A Christ-Centered Church

the church (see Owen's exegesis of Hebrews 3:5 in the commentary). As described in *The Branch of the Lord*, there is a "twofold building:... Spiritual, of all the stones thereof into one mystical house," and "ecclesiastical, of some particular stones into several tabernacles" (8:300).

Three distinct operations required in Christ's building of the house of God were typified in the building of the tabernacle. The first of these is the "giving out the design, platform, and pattern of it, in its laws, ordinances, and institutions, that it may answer the end whereunto it is designed" (20:542). Owen's sense of redemptive history is evident in his description of how, before the foundation of the world and in each successive operation in history, the Son of God is the principal agent. His remarks, not unique, demonstrate the way the doctrine of the covenant of redemption came to expression in popular exposition.

> The first thing required unto it may be considered two ways:— First as to the delineation or forming of this house in his own eternal mind, as the Son and Wisdom of the Father. He was in the eternal counsels of the Father about the providing and framing of this habitation for himself. God from all eternity had laid the plot and design of this great fabric and all the concernments of it in the idea of his own mind. And there it was hid, even from all the angels in heaven, until its actual rearing, until the event, Eph. iii. 9-11. This design and purpose of his "he purposed in Christ Jesus;" that is, this counsel of God, even of Father and Son, Prov. viii. 31, 32, was to be accomplished in and by him. And this glorious pattern he had in his mind in all ages, and brought with him into the world when he came to put the last hand unto it. This answered the...idea represented to Moses in the mount. He expressed this conception of his mind, when he gave out laws, rules, orders, ordinances, institutions of worship,

the whole pattern of the house, as it was in divers manners and at sundry seasons to be erected. (20:543-4)

As the church was one in all ages, so it had one builder, through whom all of God's dealings with man have taken place. Owen is not troubled by the problem raised by modern dispensationalists over Matthew 16:18 ("Upon this rock," i.e., the rock of faith in his person and work, "I will build my church"). He acknowledges, "the principal instance of this work is in the church of the New Testament, whose foundation in himself and erection on himself he did so expressly and particularly undertake" (20:543). There is no contradiction between this and a unity with the God's Old Testament congregation.

The second operation performed by Christ is the "preparing and fitting of the materials of it," "framing" and "compacting of them together, that they may grow up unto a house" (20:542, 544). Christ accomplishes the first of these through his "giving life unto dead stones; or rather, being life unto them" (8:300). Neither free will nor the strictest religious practice can fit a person for this building: "If the most skillful workmen in the world should go to the pit of nature, by their own strength to hew out stones for this building, they will never, with all their skill and diligence, lay one stone upon it" (8:300-301; 293). Therefore, in a sermon devoted to ecclesiology, Owen counsels the sinner,

> Lay thyself before the Lord Jesus; say to him that thou art in thyself altogether unfit for the great building he hath in hand;—that thou hast often attempted to put thyself upon it, but all in vain:—"Now, Lord Jesus, do thou take me into thine own hand. If thou castest me away, I cannot complain,—I must justify thee in all thy ways; but thou callest things that are not as though they were,—thou turnest dead stones into children of Abraham:

oh, turn my dead into a living stone!" Fear not; he will in no wise cast thee out. (8:302)

These stones have communion with one another in being placed into particular assemblies, in which Christ's "directions" for the building must be strictly observed. For instance, in comparison with the free-will offerings which went into the building of the tabernacle (Ex. 35:4-5), Christ "invites none, receives none, admits of none, but those that willingly offer themselves": those who have been made "willing in the day of his power," willingly "give up themselves to the Lord, and to the officers of his house" (20:544-45).

The construction of the tabernacle by Bezaleel and Aholiab, Owen reminds us, was a work of "art, wisdom, and skill. But the fashioning of the real spiritual house of God by Christ in all ages is a thing full of mysterious wisdom and holiness" (20:545). At this point the metaphors of building and body become mixed (as they do in Scripture, which speaks of "living stones" and a body "edifying itself in love"), but, as Owen observes,

> The sum is, that in Christ, the head of this body, the lord and builder of this house, there is resident a Spirit of life, which by him is communicated to every stone of the house, which gives it life, usefulness, union unto the head or lord of the body or house, as also order and beauty in reference unto the whole; that is, being all alike united unto Christ, and acted in their places and order by one Spirit, they become one house unto God. (20:545; cf. 8:287, 288; 13:246)

Owen describes the uniting of these materials as twofold—first, physical and living; secondly, legal or moral.

> The former is, as was said, by the communication of the same Spirit of life unto them all which is in Christ their head, so that they are all animated and

acted by the same Spirit. The latter is their regular disposition into beautifully-ordered societies, according to the rules and laws of the gospel. (20:545-46)

Each individual stone is built upon him: every promise made unto the church, such as "the gates of hell shall not prevail against it," is made unto each believer (13:126, 246).

Indweller

Thirdly, Christ is the indweller of this house, as typified by the "solemn entrance of the presence of God" into the tabernacle "for its appropriation, dedication, and sanctification unto God" (20:542). Christ indwells the house in three ways: by His Spirit, by His graces, and by His ordinances. In stark contrast to the absent Christ of medieval sacramental thought (Dorner, 1880, 271), Owen joins the Reformers in asserting that Jesus Christ

> doth not build temples merely for graces, created graces; he dwells in them himself,—he dwells in them by his Spirit. And this is a glorious privilege of this house, that Jesus Christ in a mystical and wonderful manner should dwell in it, and every stone of it. Hereby all believers come to be not one personal, but one mystical Christ, 1 Cor. xii. 12. However we are distanced in respect of his human nature, yet mystically we are one,—one body, one mystical Christ, because we have one Spirit dwelling in us and him. (8:304)

While insisting that Christ does not build these temples *merely* for graces, Owen adds that the Lord indeed also dwells in them by his graces, which are the "ornaments of the living stones of this house, to make them meet and fit for such an indweller as the Lord Christ" (8:305). The "great ornaments of his kingly court," however, are his ordinances, by which "he is glorious in all the assemblies of mount Zion" (8:305). This is the way in which the saints hold communion with Christ (8:305-308).

A Christ-Centered Church 463

The Church's Keeper

Christ is the guarantor of the continuance of the gospel church-state, despite certain changes which have occurred in its "outward form and order" from the time of the apostles (15:247-48; 251-61; 15:327-34). The apostolic church was administered by those distinguished from all others by an *immediate* call from Christ, by "extraordinary gifts and power," by "divine inspiration and infallible guidance," and with an "extensive commission, giving them power towards all the world for their conversion, and over all churches for their edification" (15:249). The officers which succeeded the apostles (to the present) are no less appointed to their offices by Christ, mediately to be sure, but by means appointed by Him. Christ is the "great watchman, or keeper of this house," who continually watches over it, to see to its every want and guard it from "the son of violence" (8:302-303). Further, he is "the great avenger of this house, and of all the injuries or wrongs that are done unto it," who "fearfully broke the old Roman-pagan empire," for their persecution of the church, "and will as fearfully destroy the antichristian Roman power [i.e., the papacy] with all its adherents" (8:308).

Owen gives five reasons for the perpetuity of the church. First, "the supreme cause hereof is the Father's grant of a *perpetual* kingdom in this world unto Jesus Christ, the mediator and head of the church" (15:251). This includes the grant of the *"real subjects"* of that kingdom to Christ, a grant that insures that in every age Christ would have "a multitude, that are the true, real, spiritual subjects of his kingdom" (15:251). It also included a grant of *"outward visible profession*, of subjection and obedience unto him, and the observation of his laws," with the effect that "the world and the worst of men therein were to see and know that he hath still a kingdom and multitude of subjects depending on his rule" (15:252). Very significantly, the gathering of particular churches is, likewise, a part of the grant by the Father to the Son, for in them the purposes of the gospel are accomplished (15:252-53). Second, "the continuation of this church-state depends on the promise of Christ himself to preserve and continue it." Thus, Owen reasons, "If the gates of hell do prevail either against the faith of sincere believers, or the catholic profession of that faith, or the expression of that profession in the duties and ordinances to be observed in particular churches, the promise fails and is of no effect" (15:254). Third, the continuation of the gospel church "depends on the word or law of Christ, which gives right and title unto all believers to congregate themselves in such a church state" (15:254). By this Owen emphasizes that Christians have no need of any authority beyond the word of Christ for the gathering of gospel churches; nor, acting upon his authority, will they lack the presence of Christ, "which brings along with it all church power and privileges" (15:254-55). Fourth, Christ has assumed the responsibility of communicating spiritual gifts unto the church, "for the work of the ministry," unto the end of the world. Finally, Christ has by his Spirit and grace implanted into believers a "due sense of their duty," and an "instinct...to associate themselves in holy communion, for the joint and mutual exercise of those graces of the Spirit, which are the same, as unto the essence of them, in them all" (15:256).

The Head of the Body

Many similar points might be made regarding the head-body image.[3] Owen emphasizes that Christ is the "only" head of the church (20:329). This holds true not only for the entire church, "but also unto every individual believer in the church,... and that in both those senses wherein he is a head,—that is, according to the natural and metaphorical use of the word" (20:329-30). First, he is its natural head (13:127). As such he is "the only head of

A Christ-Centered Church

vital influence to the whole church and every member thereof," the source of its life and grace, "for the enlivening strengthening, acting, guiding, and directing," of every believer (20:30). Metaphorically, Christ is the "only head of rule and government unto the whole church and every member thereof" (20:30).[4] Owen urges this against the Episcopal as well as the Roman hierarchy. Submission to church officers is due not upon the authority of the church, but upon that of Christ. Moreover, Christ is "our immediate head." With regard to church officers and ordinances Owen says,

> these belong only unto the way of our dependence, and hinder not but that our dependence is immediate on himself, he being the immediate object of our faith and love. The soul of a believer rests not in any of these things, but only makes use of them to confirm his faith in subjection unto Christ: for all these things are ours, they are appointed for our use, and we are Christ's as he is God's, 1 Cor. iii. 21-23. (20:331)

A Christ-Centered Worship

It is a popular misunderstanding of the simplicity of Puritan worship that it was motivated primarily by a rejection of Romanism. The rejection of the "popish ceremonies" of Rome, however, was motivated by an earnest desire to keep the second commandment, i.e., the "regulative principle" that nothing ought to be done in worship except what stands upon God's revealed will. To introduce forms or ceremonies of human invention is idolatrous. In Owen's exposition, however, not only does the regulative principle have a Christological foundation, but the recognition of this foundation involves much more than the external purification of the church of Roman and Anglican ceremonies.

Owen distinguishes the worship of God into that which is "natural or moral," arising from man's natural relationship to God his creator, and that which is "external," directed by God's express commandment (15:8-9; 15:447-50). These are not two types of worship, each acceptable to God; rather, man's natural relationship to God requires that we worship him according to the manner of his appointment. The substitution of other forms of worship is a violation rather than an acknowledgement of that relation. This is the basic message of the second commandment. This commandment, however, as Owen makes clear, is quite Christocentric in nature. Owen says,

> whereas, ever since the entrance of sin into the world, God had always respect unto the promise of the Lord Christ and his mediation, in whom alone he will be glorified, and faith in whom he aimed to begin and increase in all his worship, he hath suited his institutions of the means thereof to that dispensation of light and knowledge of him which he was pleased at any time to grant. Thus, immediately after the giving of the *promise*, he appointed *sacrifices* for the great means of his worship; as to glorify himself expressly by men's offering unto him of the principal good things which he had given them, so to instruct them in the faith, and confirm them in the expectation of the *great sacrifice* for sin that was to be offered by the promised seed,... Hereunto he nextly added *circumcision*, as an *express sign of the covenant, with the grace of it, which he called* Abraham and his seed unto by Jesus Christ,... And to the same general end and purpose he afterwards superadded the *passover*, with its attendant institutions, Exod. xii. 3-24; and then the whole law of institutions contained in ordinances,... So by sundry degrees he built up that fabric of his *outward worship*, which was suited, in his infinite wisdom, unto his own glory and the edification of his church, until the.... coming of Christ in the flesh, and the work of his mediation. (15:451)

God, who "reserved unto himself the sovereign power of altering, changing or utterly abolishing" any part of his instituted worship, forbade man to do so, but has done so by Christ, "the Lord over his whole house," with the institution of the new covenant and its attendant forms of worship.

Old Testament worship was glorious. The heart of the issue between Anglican and Puritan was, how has the coming of Christ made New Testament worship yet more glorious. Owen's answer is to be found in several treatises, including two sermons on *The Nature and Beauty of Gospel Worship* (9:53-84). Owen opens the first of these by saying that, by his death Christ has fulfilled, and so abolished, the ceremonial law, and the curse of the moral law. Previously, Gentiles had been totally separated from God, and the Jews had "no immediate admission" to God; it was only through the priests, only from a distance, and only through elaborate and burdensome ceremonies, "outward and carnal ordinances, which were mere shadows of what was to come" (9:53-61). Now, through the most costly blood of Christ, through the new and living way which is his flesh, having this glorious ministering high priest, Jews and Gentiles are admitted to the true holy of holies; they have access, they *draw near*, "with reverent boldness," to God their Father (9:61-69). They have this "by the Holy Spirit," enabling them to hear Christ's word, enabling them to approach God "in a spiritual manner, to pray with grace in their hearts," working in them "faith, love, delight, fervency, watchfulness, perseverance," so that they enjoy a "heavenly intercourse" with God (9:69-73). Furthermore, as this worship is performed in the Spirit, so it is, Owen argues, "*in one Spirit*," which constitutes the only true uniformity (9:76). Gospel worship, Owen concludes, "may well be reckoned among the unspeakable privileges that are purchased for us by the blood of Christ" (9:84).

The principal objectives in the institutions of gospel worship are that we 1) "sanctify the name of God," 2) "own and avow our professed subjection to the Lord Jesus Christ," 3) "build up ourselves in our most holy faith," and 4) "testify and confirm our mutual love" (15:455). Each of these (not only the second) has a Christocentric character, as Owen expounds them (15:456-62).

The "due observation of instituted worship" is required of men for the "*honour* of God in this world, the *trial* of our faith and obedience, the *order* and beauty of the church, the *exaltation* of Christ in our professed subjection to him, and the *saving* of our souls in the ways of his appointment" (15:471-72). In each of these areas, Owen emphasizes, the worship of God is ordered with respect to Christ. Consequently, no worship not centered upon Christ can be acceptable to God or good for the souls of men (15:471-76). Moreover, the apostasy of the church "consists principally in false worship and a departure from the institutions of Christ" (15:476).

This is crucial for Owen: all legitimate forms of worship were instituted by Christ. All of these forms, even those which are "founded in the law of nature," are "to be observed principally on the authority of Jesus Christ" (15:478). Owen's reason for this is reminiscent of his description of the formal reason of our faith in God.

> The principal thing we are to aim at, in the whole worship of God, is the discharge of that duty which we owe to Jesus Christ, the king and head of the church:... This we cannot do unless we consider his authority as the formal reason and cause of our observance of all that we do therein; for that he hath annexed unto our doing and observing whatever he hath commanded, and that because he hath commanded us: Matt. xxviii. (15:478)

One of the most important differences between Owen and the Anglican establishment with regard to worship was over its "beauty." The advocates of the Anglican forms emphasized what they called the "beauty of holiness"; by which they meant what would more appropriately be called "the holiness of beauty." That is, the rites and ceremonies of Anglicanism were appropriate, good, and *"holy" because of their appearance*. Owen, by contrast, viewed the simple institutions of gospel worship as *beautiful because they were "holy,"* instituted by God himself as the most appropriate way for believers to "behold the glory of God in the face of Christ Jesus."

Owen's emphasis upon this transforming vision of Christ is so great as to require us to regard it not as one of several reasons given to justify a pre-conceived Puritan position, but as one of Owen's most deeply held convictions concerning the gospel, a conviction based upon his understanding of the history of redemption, and all that it means in terms of God's full manifestation of himself in Christ. Any man-made form, no matter how beautiful, no matter what its reputation for illustrating the glory of Christ, dishonored Christ by inevitably obscuring his true glory. This glory could not be represented with man's arts, but could only be known through the word of the gospel.[5]

Referring to religious rites he argues that the "comeliness and beauty of gospel worship doth not in the least depend upon them nor their observation" (15:468). The most glorious rites were enjoyed by the Old Testament church; yet, as Paul vigorously argues in 2 Corinthians 3:7-11, the worship of the New Testament, "for beauty, glory, and comeliness," is far advanced above that of the Old (15:468-69). From Hebrews 10:19-21, Owen argues that the glory of the New consists "in its relation to God in Christ, with the liberty and boldness of the worshippers to enter into the holy place, unto the throne of grace, under the ministry of their merciful and faithful high priest, being enabled thereunto by the Spirit of adoption and supplications" (15:469). Making an application of this that is typical for Owen, he concludes,

> This is the glory of gospel worship and the beauty of it; whose consideration whilst the minds of men are diverted from, to look for beauty in the outward preparation of ceremonies, they lose the privilege purchased for believers by the blood of Christ. Instead, then, of furthering the beauty and comeliness of gospel worship, they are apt to lead men into a dangerous error and mistake,—namely, that the beauty and excellency of it consists in such things as, upon a due consideration, will appear to be mean and carnal, and far beneath those ceremonies and ordinances of the Old Testament, which yet, in comparison of the worship of the gospel, are called "worldly, carnal, beggarly," and are said to have "no glory." (15:469)

In his most severe critique of the Roman church, Owen focuses upon this feature of their worship. The religion of Rome, he says, "is nothing but a dead image of the gospel, erected in the loss of an experience of its spiritual power, overthrowing its use, with all its ends, being suited to the taste of men, carnal, ignorant, and superstitious" (8:551). The reason for this is that, in the place of the "representation made of Christ and his glory in the gospel," by which "believers have an experience of the power and efficacy of the divine truth contained therein," the Romanists have substituted the "making of *images of him* of wood and stone, or gold and silver, or painting on them" (8:552). Owen says he is not concerned in this treatise with their being the objects of *adoration*, but as they are the way of *representation*, or as he puts it, "set up in the room of the gospel, and for the ends of it, as means of teaching and instruction" (8:553).

This Christological emphasis has been generally overlooked by historians of Puritanism, who focus upon the second commandment as the foundation for the regulative principle in worship but fail to observe the theological basis for the commandment, a foundation well known and important to the Puritans. With Owen it is precisely the new covenantal character of gospel worship, with its doctrine of the presence of Christ filling the temple that makes the addition of artificial means of glory so offensive. "Let men think as meanly as they please of the spiritual worship of God amongst his people, all glory that ever yet appeared in the world was but a bubble to it,—all that God ever instituted before came exceedingly short of it" (8:290).

The Pastoral Ministry
"The Lord Jesus Christ hath faithfully promised to be present with his church unto the end of the world." This presence of Christ is by the Spirit, and is "secured by an everlasting, unchangeable covenant." The great end for which the Spirit is promised is the continuation and preservation of the church, and its conformity unto Jesus Christ. By what means does Christ work by His Spirit to accomplish this great end? The principal means, according to Owen, is the pastoral ministry. Owen's understanding of the office, calling, and work of the church's pastors is also firmly built upon his Christology. The importance of the ministry may be observed in a number of Owenian treatises, most notably his *Discourse of Spiritual Gifts*, and two sermons: "The Ministry a Gift of Christ" and "Ministerial Endowments the Work of the Spirit."

As the resurrection of Christ inaugurated a new order of worship, with the replacement of type and carnal ceremonies with the spiritual enjoyment of divine realities, so a new kind of ministry was needed, and a new kind of ministry was supplied:

> He that enabled the shoulders of the Levites to bear the ark of old, and their arms to slay the sacrifices,

without which natural strength those carnal ordinances could not have been observed..., hath, upon their removal and the institution of the spiritual worship of the gospel, undertaken to supply the administrators of it with spiritual strength and abilities for the discharge of their work. (15:11)

This is the purpose of the gifts of the Spirit. Within this context of spiritual gifts, Owen asserts there is "a gift of Christ which is the foundation and subject of them," namely, the pastoral ministry (4:486). He bases this emphasis on Paul's exposition of the institution of the New Testament ministry in Ephesians 4:7-16. This gift, Owen observes, in both the office *per se*, and also in "the persons to discharge it, is an *eminent, most useful fruit and effect of the mediatory power of Christ*," and "the great fundamental of all church order, power, and worship" (4:487, emphasis mine). The eminence of this gift of ministry is evident from the "grandeur of its introduction" in the exaltation of Christ, and its "original acquisition in the humiliation of Christ" (4:487-88). Owen concludes, the ministry "is a fruit whose root is in the grave of Christ" (4:490; cf., 9:441). Its object is "the body of Christ himself, and its end, the edification of this body, or its increase in faith and obedience, in all the graces and gifts of the Spirit, until it come unto conformity unto him and the enjoyment of him. And a ministry which hath not this object and end is not of the giving or grant of Christ" (4:497).

The officers of the church are instituted by Christ (15:490-530). This fact determines the nature of their offices, their functions, and their character qualifications. Thus, "The especial design of the rule of the church in its government is, to represent the holiness, love, compassion, care, and authority of Christ towards his church" (16:135). Church-rule is a due care and provision that the institutions, laws, commands, and appointments of Jesus Christ be duly observed, and nothing else (16:135). It is enlightening to read Owen's ecclesiastical treatises with these responsibilities in mind. Churches are the schools of Christ for the perfecting of disciples (21:770-71). In the training of disciples, for instance, Owen argues that ministers must teach even the most abstruse and difficult truths of the mysteries of the gospel for the edification of the church (21:551).

The gift *of* the ministry consists of gifts *for* the ministry. Christ gives ministers to the church by appointing first the office, then distributing the requisite spiritual gifts to men to enable them to discharge the office, then by giving power to the church to call and separate these gifted individuals to the work. No church, by ordaining a man, can give him a gift and authority which Christ has not given him. Thus, ordination is not a means of conveying authority from Christ to men, but the local church's acknowledging it in those already possessing it by virtue of Christ's call (4:492-96). It is a fundamental principle of his "congregational" ecclesiology, however, that the Spirit-gifted pastoral ministry (including teaching and ruling elders and the distinct office of "teacher"), as it is the *only* means appointed by Christ, *must be sufficient* for Christ's end of the perfecting of the church. Furthermore, as it is the solemn responsibility of those so gifted to exercise those gifts, it is Christ's command to the church to "set such, in his name and strength, in the way and unto the work that he hath allotted to them" (15:12).

Qualifications and Call to Ministry
This call to the office of pastor, Owen reminds us, must be "according to the mind of Christ." This is because it was Christ who "in his own person and by his own authority, was the author of this office;" who "appointed" it "to abide in the church unto the consummation of all things;" and to bear the "whole weight of the order rule, and edification of his church" (16:51). Even in his treat-

ment of the qualifications of the minister, Owen's eye is on Christ, the "great example and pattern." Owen put it bluntly:

> Our Lord Jesus Christ, being the good Shepherd, whose the sheep are, the Shepherd and Bishop of our souls, the chief Shepherd, did design, in the undertaking and exercise of his pastoral office, to give a type and example unto all those who are to be called unto the same office under him; and if there be not a conformity unto him herein, no man can assure his own conscience or the church of God that he is or can be lawfully called unto this office. (16:49)

Nor is it only in these introductory comments that Owen emphasizes the example of Christ. Each particular qualification is built upon some pastoral virtue of the chief Shepherd: *"furniture with spiritual gifts and abilities* by communication of the Holy Ghost"; *"compassion and love to the flock"*; "a *continual watchfulness over the whole flock*, to keep it, to preserve it, to feed, to lead, and cherish it, to purify and cleanse it, until it be presented unspotted unto God"; *"zeal for the glory of God"*; and conformity to Christ in, and *"some degree of eminency above* others," in being "holy, harmless, undefiled, separate from sinners" (16:49-51). In addition, they must, like Christ in heaven, have a sense of the infirmities of his flock, and "endeavor in an especial manner to succor them that are tempted" (16:85).

Elsewhere, Owen identifies three things that are necessary for the recognition of someone as "a gift given by Christ unto the church": 1) imitation of Christ, 2) representation of Christ, and 3) zeal for Christ. First, the pastor imitates Christ in "meekness, in care, in love, in tenderness towards the whole flock" (9:436-37). Secondly, he represents Christ in his threefold mediatorial office. As king,

> in the rule and conduct of the church; that the church, under our rule and conduct, may be sensible that the government of Christ is spiritual and

holy. What a woeful presentation of Christ is made by men who undertake to rule the church of God with rods and axes, with fire and fagot! Is this to represent the meek and holy King of the church, or rather a devouring tyrant, unto the world? It is our great work, in what interest Christ hath given us in the rule of the church, to represent him as spiritual, as holy, as meek, — as universally tending to edification, and not to destruction. (9:437)

Principally, the minister represents him in his office as prophet,

"to preach the word in season and out of season;"— by all means to carry on the church in the knowledge of God, and of our Lord and Savior Jesus Christ." "I will give them 'pastors that shall feed them with knowledge and understanding.'" Those who take upon themselves to be pastors, and neglect this work of feeding the flock, may, at as cheap a rate, and with equal modesty, renounce Jesus Christ. (9:437)

Furthermore he represents Christ in the "imitable part of his sacerdotal office; which is, to make continual prayers and intercession for the church,—and that church, in particular, whereunto we belong" (9:437). Thirdly, he must have zeal for Christ: "He that comes as an ambassador from Christ, in Christ's stead, will have zeal for all the concerns of Christ in the church; for his worship, for the purity of his ordinances, for the conversion of souls, and for the building up of the saints" (9:438).

Its origin in the death and resurrection of Christ, its equipment with the Christ-bestowed gift of the Holy Spirit, its "end" in preaching "that peace to mankind which was made by the death of Christ," and its role in the transformation of saints into Christ's image make the pastoral office an eminent and glorious gift. Indeed, "There is a greater glory in giving a minister to a poor congregation, than there is in the installment and enthroning of all the popes, and cardinals, and metropolitans, that ever were in the world: let their glory be what it will, Christ is upon his theater of glory in the communication of this office and these officers" (9:439).

The Non-Conformist and Congregationalist

We have seen the basis for Owen's non-conformity: his conviction that Christ is the sole, ultimate, and immediate authority on the structure, authority, teaching, and worship in the church, the sole and all-sufficient source of the church's spiritual life and glory. Nothing beyond what Christ gives is needed, anything beyond what Christ warrants is disallowed. Owen was not only a Non-Conformist, however, he was also a Congregationalist. This was because of his conviction that Christ had not only given all that was sufficient to the church, but had given it the local congregation. To fully appreciate the Christocentric nature of Owen's Congregationalism it would be helpful to consider one more description of the "visible church-state which Christ hath instituted under the New Testament." He describes its subjects, and the ends of Christ for the church as,

> an especial society or congregation of professed believers, joined together according unto his mind, with their officers, guides, or rulers, whom he hath appointed, which do or may meet together for the celebration of all the ordinances of divine worship, the professing and authoritatively proposing the doctrine of the gospel, with the exercise of the discipline prescribed by himself, unto their own mutual edification, with the glory of Christ, in the preservation and propagation of his kingdom in the world. (15:262)

"Unto such a church," a particular congregation of covenanting visible saints, meeting together to observe Christ's ordinances and keep his commands, with his guides and rulers, "and every one of them," Owen argues, "belong of right all the privileges, promises, and power that Christ doth give and grant unto the church in this world" (15:262).

Congregational churches "alone," he concludes, "have a "suitableness and sufficiency unto all the ends for which the Lord Christ appointed such churches" (15:302; cf. 252f, 267-69, 479-86), such as "mutual love among all Christians" (15:302-306), preservation of true doctrine (15:306-308), propagation of the gospel (15:308-309), and evangelical discipline (15:358-59). Owen is persuaded that, since Christ has given both authority and power to the local assembly, all that is biblically necessary for accomplishing the ends of Christ in the world are manageably-sized gathered church of visible saints, under the scriptural leadership of congregationally-called officers. If this is all that is necessary, then it is biblically unwarranted for anyone, even the local assembly itself, to deprive such congregations of the liberty which Christ has given them (15:313-19).

For these ends of Christ, Christians were required to join particular churches. "It is the duty of every one who professeth faith in Christ Jesus, and takes due care of his own eternal salvation, voluntarily and by his own choice to join himself unto some particular congregation of Christ's institution, for his own spiritual edification, and the right discharge of his commands" (15:320; cf. 15:486-89). Church membership is necessary if believers are to carry out the duties, ordinances, worship, mission, perfection, preservation, and discipline which Christ has commanded (13:176). "It is an obediential act unto the commands of Christ; whereunto is required subjection of conscience unto his authority, faith in his promises, as also a respect unto an appearance before his judgment-throne at the last day" (15:322).

The requirements for admission into the church reflect the same Christocentric emphasis we have seen throughout Owen's work. Generally, Owen's position is this: "We desire no more to constitute church-members, and we can desire no less, than what, in the judgment of charity, may comply with the union that is between Christ the head and the church" (16:20). This will mean a life consistent with a living union with Christ by his Spirit, and a profession of knowledge of Christ, and faith in him. With respect to this latter requirement, Owen says, "They must be such as do make an open profession of the subjection of their souls and consciences unto the authority of Christ in the gospel, and their readiness to yield obedience unto all his commands" (16:14). This will require "a competent knowledge of the doctrines and mystery of the gospel, *especially concerning the person and offices of Christ*" (16:15, emphasis mine; see also 16:24). As he says elsewhere, without knowledge of the mysteries of the gospel,

> no privilege of the gospel can be profitably made use of, nor any duty of it rightly performed, so saving light is of the essence of conversion, and doth inseparably accompany it: 2 Corinthians 4:6, "God, who commanded the light to shine out of darkness, hath shined in our hearts, to give the light of the knowledge of the glory of God in the face of Jesus Christ." Where this is wanting, it is impossible for any person to evidence that he is delivered from that blindness, darkness, and ignorance, which all men are under the power of in the state of nature. Such a measure, then, of light and knowledge, as whereby men are enabled to apprehend aright of the person and offices of Christ, of the nature of his meditation, the benefits thereof, and the obedience that he requires at the hands of his disciples, is expected in them who desire to be admitted into the fellowship of the church. (15:526)

It will also require their professed subjection to Christ's authority, "conviction and confession of sin, with the way of deliverance by Jesus Christ" (16:16). They must also be "willing to give up themselves unto the rule of Christ in the church, and a subjection unto all his ordinances and institutions therein" (16:24; 16:24, 26-33, 36).

In his *Inquiry Concerning Evangelical Churches*, Owen answers the question what kind of particular churches Christ's disciples ought to join. The first among several disqualifying features is the rejection or corruption of "any fundamental article of faith"; a fundamental error being one against the foundation, such as those of the Socinians (15:335). Rather, it "must be such a church as wherein all the fundamental truths of the gospel are believed, owned, and professed, without controversy, and those not borne withal by whom they are denied or opposed" otherwise "it doth not hold the Head, it is not built on the foundation of the prophets and apostles" (15:339). Secondly, "it must be a church as wherein the divine worship instituted or approved by Christ himself is diligently observed, without any addition made thereunto" (15:340). Thirdly, "it is required that the ministry of a church...is not defective in any of those things which, according to the rule of the gospel, are fundamental thereunto" (15:341), including, fourthly, "gospel discipline" (15:343). It is interesting to observe Owen's insistence upon both the necessity of adherence in fundamental doctrines, ministry, and discipline; and the liberty of judgment in the choice of an edifying church (15:334-44; 16:21-22).

Conclusion

Owen's ecclesiastical treatises and sermons constitute a great portion of his labors in the cause of Christ, much more than this short survey could adequately expound. Nevertheless, the objective of this chapter was to illustrate that Owen's ecclesiology was informed and motivated by his understanding of the relationship between the church and Christ. We have seen the Christological basis for the nature, character, structure, worship, ministry, and life of the church. In the next chapter, we will examine more carefully and on a more particular and personal level what Owen taught concerning the Christian's life.

---

[1] In addition to the references cited in this chapter, see the following pages: Vol. 8:20, 28, 38-39, 95-96, 283-309, 560-63; Vol. 9: 53-84, 271-95, 307-20, 431-62; Vol. 13:112-13, 123, 126-27, 137, 179, 246; Vol. 15:7, 8, 10-12, 44-46, 58-59, 73-106, 109, 119, 121, 143-44, 164-65, 179, 212-22, 227-49, 251-61, 302, 328-32, 339-40, 343, 473, 478-79, 481, 490-530; Vol. 16:14-16, 20, 24, 26-33, 36, 49-53, 85, 87, 90, 133-35, 190; Vol. 20:30, 329-31, 542-46; Vol. 21:235, 551, 570-71, 584-85; Vol. 22:149, 172.

[2] See Edward Reynolds', *The Lord's Property in His Redeemed People* (1679, 1009-1018).

[3] See Manton (1870, 1:453-63)

[4] Owen's use of "head" as "source" is based upon such Scripture texts as Ephesians 4:16 and Colossians 2:19. It is obvious from the remainder of his discussion that Owen does not see any contradiction between head as source of life and head as authority (cf. Grudem 1991, p. 434).

[5] See John LaShell (1985, 178-214) for a discussion of this feature of Puritan thought.

CHAPTER 17

"To Live Is Christ"

> The glory, life, and power of Christian religion, as Christian religion, and as seated in the souls of men, with all the acts and duties which properly belong thereunto, and are, therefore, peculiarly Christian, and all the benefits and privileges we receive by it, or by virtue of it, with the whole of the honour and glory that arise unto God thereby, have all of them their formal nature and reason from their relation unto the person of Christ; nor is he a Christian who is otherwise minded. (1:104)

John Owen on the Christian Life is the title of a full study of the subject of this chapter written by Sinclair Ferguson (1987). It is not the purpose of this chapter to repeat or condense the material contained in that work, and the reader should consult it for a more comprehensive view. This chapter is designed to demonstrate the extent and the manner of Owen's application of his Christology to his doctrine of the Christian life. It will become clear that Owen's doctrine of the Christian life is explicitly, extensively, and intensively established upon the foundation of his Christology. In *Christologia*, Owen says,

> The respect which we have in all acts of religion unto the person of Christ may be reduced unto these four heads: I. Honour. II. Obedience. III. Conformity. IV.

The use we make of him, for the attaining and receiving of all Gospel privileges—all grace and glory. And hereunto the whole of our religion, as it is Christian or evangelical, may be reduced. (1:104)

Significantly, a full twenty percent of Owen's *Christologia* is devoted to the exposition of the first three of these heads, while the subjects comprising the fourth head, Owen asserts, are handled in other discourses "and that with respect unto the end here designed." This means Owen's famous discourses on justification, sanctification, and perseverance (to mention some major categories) are all expositions of the "use" we make of Christ (1:177-78).[1]

Honor

First, Owen says, the "person of Christ is the *object of divine honour and worship*," as he is the bearer of all of the "essential infinite excellencies" of the divine nature (1:104). The reason is explicitly stated in John 5:23: it "is the will of the Father that all men should honour the Son, even as they honour the Father" (1:105). Owen explains that in this text we are commanded to honor him "*distinctly as the Son*" (1:106). We are *commanded* so lest any conceive that the honor was not due him. The honor due is the *same* honor which is due the Father, and to be given in "the *same manner*" (1:106). The want of this "great fundamental principle of our religion," among so many persons was a matter of great concern for Owen: "To honour the Son as we ought to honour the Father, is that which makes us Christians, and which nothing else will so do" (1:107).

Adoration

Owen identifies two duties of honor to Christ: adoration and invocation. As illustrated by the heavenly worship of the lamb (Rev. 5:6-14), the object of this adoration is Christ, "distinctly from the Father and jointly with him,...

as having fulfilled the work of his mediation" (1:108). In the same text we see the motives for this distinct honoring of the Son, namely, "the unspeakable benefits which we receive by his mediation." Moreover, we see the nature of this honor to consist in solemn prostration, the ascription to him of divine honor and glory, and the singing of songs of praise (1:109).

Invocation

The invocation of Christ consists in "an *ascription* of all divine properties and excellencies unto him whom we invocate," and also "a *representation* of our wills, affections, and desires of our souls, unto him on whom we call, with an expectation of being heard and relieved, by virtue of his infinitely divine excellencies" (1:110). In this regard we have the example of Christ himself, who, when he was dying, committed his soul to the Father. Owen argues that, on the principle of honoring the Son as the Father, we might do the same unto the Son. Likewise, the martyr Stephen gave

> divine honour unto Christ in the especial invocation of his name, in the highest instances that can be conceived. In his first request, wherein he committed his departing soul into his hands, he ascribed unto him divine omniscience, omnipresence, love, and power; and in the latter, for his enemies, divine authority and mercy, to be exercised in the pardon of sin. In his example is the rule established for the especial invocation for the effects of divine power and mercy. (1:110)

As an additional argument Owen mentions the apostolic description of the church, being "all that call upon the name of our Lord Jesus Christ, both their Lord and ours" (1:110-11; 1 Cor. 1:2).

As with adoration, the object of this invocation is Christ, as one having all of the perfections of the divine nature. For motivation, Owen points to "all that the Lord Christ hath done for us, and all the principles of love, grace, compassion, and power from whence what he hath so done did proceed" (1:111-12). Owen refutes the Socinian assertion that it is lawful, but not a duty, to call upon Christ, by pointing out that "prayer without an ascription of divine excellencies...is but vain babbling, that hath nothing of true prayer in it; and to make such ascriptions unto him who by nature is not God, is idolatrous" (1:112).

The unique place of Christ as both God and mediator introduces a number of problems associated with this invocation, which Owen addresses with characteristic skill. We are taught by him to "call on God under the name and notion of a father...by and in the name of the Son, Jesus Christ, through the aid of the Holy Ghost" (1:112). Owen calls this "ordinary solemn evangelical invocation." If we are ordinarily to call upon God *through Christ*, how or when are we to call upon Christ himself? Owen answers that in evangelical devotion there are specific occasions when the invocation of Christ is "most acceptable"—the reason being his special relation to us as the mediator. For instance, in "times of great distresses in conscience through temptations and desertions" it is appropriate to call upon Christ because he was tempted, etc. Also appropriate are "times of *gracious discoveries* either of the glory of Christ in *himself*, or of his *love* unto us" (1:114). Because our relationship to him is personal and dynamic, and not merely formal and static, there are times when we experience or "sense" his love more than others. In those times we will want to make returns of invocation, praise, and love to him; and at all times we ought to "dispose our hearts" to it (1:114-16). Thirdly, in *"times of persecution for his Name's sake, and for the profession of the gospel,"* the saints will have their thoughts on Christ's "person, love, grace, and authority," as well as the "especial concernment" he has in their condition. "In these circumstances, it is impossible for them who are under the conduct of his Spirit, not to make *especial applications* continually unto him" for the grace and help they need (1:116-17). Fourthly, invocation of Christ is due *"when we have a due apprehension of the eminent actings of any grace in Christ Jesus,* and withal a deep and abiding sense of our own want of the same grace." Here Owen instructs us in one of several uses to be made of Christ's example: "When they have a view of the glory of any grace as it was exercised in Christ, and withal a sense of their own defect and want therein—conformity unto him being their design—they cannot but apply themselves unto him in solemn invocation, for a farther communication of that grace unto them, from his stores and fullness" (1:117-18). Finally, Owen mentions the "time of death, whether natural, or violent for his sake" (1:118).

Another question which arises concerns the propriety of praying for Christ to intercede for us. Owen rejects this activity, explaining that, not only have we no scriptural precedent for it, but it demonstrates a failure to properly regard the basis for our invocation of Christ at all, which is his divine person. As Owen explains:

> Had the Son of God never been incarnate, he had been the object of all divine worship. And could there have been a mediator between God and us who was not God also, he could never have been the object of any divine worship or invocation. Wherefore Christ the Mediator, God and man in one person, is in all things to be honoured, even as we honour the Father; but it is as he is God, equal with the Father, and not as Mediator—in which respect he is inferior unto him. With respect unto his divine person, we ask immediately of himself in our supplications;—as he is Mediator—we ask of the Father in his name. (1:119)

If this is the case with respect to Christ, the theanthropic mediator, one can easily understand Owen's vigorous rejection of the invocation of the saints.

Admiration

Perhaps the response most frequently cited by Owen to the revelation of the person and work of Christ is "admiration." Not developed in any particular section of *Christologia* nor *The Glory of Christ*, the admiration of Christ's person and of the wisdom, power, and grace of God displayed in its "constitution" (i.e., "the assumption... of the human nature into personal subsistence with the Son of God") was one of Owen's principal objectives in both works (1:15-17; 45-53; 275; 277).

Contrary to the opinion that "the incarnation for the Puritans was not a mystery in which man should lose himself" (Eusden 1968, 20), Owen was so overwhelmed by it that he was forced to confess,

> We *speak* of these things in a poor, low, broken manner,—we *teach* them as they are revealed in the Scripture,—we labor by faith to adhere unto them as revealed; but when we come into a steady, direct view and consideration of the *thing itself*, our minds fail, our hearts tremble, and we can find no rest but in a holy admiration of what we cannot comprehend. Here we are at a loss, and know that we shall be so whilst we are in this world; but all the ineffable fruits and benefits of this truth are communicated unto them that do believe. (1:330)

These articles of faith, the incarnation and other doctrines of the gospel, were not merely propositions to be held in the mind, but motives for admiration. Consider the following:

> Might we here stay to contemplate and admire, in our dim and dawning light, in our weakness, according to the meanness of our apprehensions of

> the reflections of it in the glass of the gospel, the eternity of this contrivance; the transactions between Father and Son about it; the retrievement of the lost glory of God by sin, and ruined creation in it; the security of the holiness, righteousness, veracity, and vindictive justice of God, provided for in it; with the abundant overflowings of grace, goodness, love, mercy, and patience, that are the life of it; we might manifest that there is enough in this fountain to render the streams flowing from it great and glorious. And yet, alas! what a little, what a small portion of its glory, excellency, beauty, riches, is it that we are able in this world to attain unto! (20:304; see 6:66-67)

Again, "The soul being, as it were, ravished with that view which it hath of the glorious excellencies of God in Christ, hath no way to express its affections but by admiration" (3:586). This admiration might begin with a contemplation of the excellencies of Christ in his care for the church, or the grace that was in his teaching, in his compassion and perseverance in his sufferings and death.

> Should we go to speak now of the love of Christ, on the one side, it is an ocean,—we cannot fathom it. The best act of our souls towards Christ's love is *admiration*, astonishing admiration, till the heart is quite overwhelmed with it,—till our thoughts and understandings are, as it were, lost; the soul is taken out of itself, and laid in the dust as nothing, to be swallowed up in a holy contemplation of the unspeakable, inconceivable love of Jesus Christ. (9:468)

The soul would look in awe on the condescension of the Son in the incarnation, and lose itself in wonder of the mystery of the miracle of the hypostatic union. They admire its foundation in the divine counsels (1:59-60), the divine attributes which it manifests, (1:178-205), and it "will be the object of holy adoration and admiration unto eternity" (1:205). Christ is and ever will be "admired in them that believe."

Owen saw this admiration as a characteristic, essential, necessary, and profitable activity for all the saints. He says, for instance,

> Wherefore, according to our apprehension and admiration of the wisdom of God in the constitution of this way of salvation is our faith, and no otherwise; where that does not appear unto us, where our minds are not affected with it, there is no faith at all. (5:412)

It would appear from this that admiration of Christ is "of the essence of faith." Moreover, it is a principal part of sanctification:

> For as contemplation is an act of faith with respect unto our measure of comprehension, so is admiration with respect unto what exceeds it. And what way soever faith acts itself on Christ, it will bring in advantage and refreshment to the soul. And we are never nearer Christ than when we find ourselves lost in a holy amazement at his unspeakable love. And, indeed, his love herein, that "although he were a Son," the eternal Son of God, yet he would condescend unto the condition before described for our deliverance and salvation, is that which fills the souls of believers with admiration, not only in this world, but unto eternity. (20:654)

Again,

> The spiritual *intense fixation of the mind*, by contemplation on God in Christ, until the soul be as it were swallowed up in admiration and delight, and being brought unto an utter loss, through the infiniteness of those excellencies which it doth admire and adore, it returns again into its own abasements, out of a sense of its infinite distance from what it would absolutely and eternally embrace, and, withal, the inexpressible rest and satisfaction which the will and affections receive in their approaches unto the

eternal Fountain of goodness, are things to be aimed at in prayer, and which, through the riches of divine condescension, are frequently enjoyed. The soul is hereby raised and ravished, not into ecstasies or unaccountable raptures, not acted into motions above the power of its own understanding and will; but in all the faculties and affections of it, through the effectual workings of the Spirit of grace and the lively impressions of divine love, with intimations of the relations and kindness of God, is filled with rest, in "joy unspeakable and full of glory." (4:329-30)

"But faith which is truly divine, is never more in its proper exercise—doth never more elevate the soul into conformity unto God—than when it acts in the contemplation and admiration of the most incomprehensible mysteries which are proposed unto it by divine revelation," the highest mystery, having the greatest effect in this regard, being the constitution of the person of Christ (1:50-51). Conversely, "those whose minds are not delighted in the admiration of, and acquiescency in, things incomprehensible, such as is this constitution of the person of Christ...do not much prepare themselves for that vision of these things in glory, wherein our blessedness doth consist" (1:52).

Faith in Christ
"The principle and spring of the assignation of divine honor to Christ, in both the branches if it," that is, in adoration and invocation, "is faith in him" (1:120).[2] Owen emphasizes that "it is the person of Christ which is the first and principal object of that faith wherewith we are required to believe in him; and that so to do, is not only to assent unto the truth of the doctrine revealed by him, but also to place our trust and confidence in him for mercy, relief, and protection—for righteousness, life, and salvation—for a blessed resurrection and eternal reward" (1:127).

Among many Scriptures cited as proof of this personal faith in Christ, Owen's explanations of two of them (John 14:1, and Gal. 2:20) particularly stand out. In John 14, the same faith is required in Christ as in the Father, that is, *faith in his person* (1:128). In Galatians 2, Paul asserts that the "faith of the Son of God," is the cause of spiritual life. "Of this faith," Owen says, "the Son of God is both the author and the object; the latter whereof is here principally intended" (1:129). Two additional arguments for faith in the person of Christ accrue from the duty to call upon him, and from our baptism into his name:

> For we are therein given up unto universal spiritual subjection of soul unto him, and dependence on him.... Faith in Christ is that grace whereby the church is united unto him—incorporated into one mystical body with him. It is thereby that he dwells in them, and they in him. (1:129-30)

Having shown that faith is in the person of Christ, Owen proceeds to expound the way this faith becomes the foundation for divine honor unto him. This is evident from the consideration of Christ's *person*, and his work, that is, "in the discharge of the office of mediation" (1:130).

First, the person of Christ is the "*absolute* and *ultimate* object of our faith" because of his "being partaker of the nature of God" (1:130). The divine nature is the "proper formal object," that is, that which gives the believer a "reason, ground and warranty" to believe on him, while the "entire person" is faith's immediate object: "In placing our faith on him we consider him as God and man in one and the same person. We believe in him because he is God; but we believe in him as he is God and man in one person" (1:131).[3] It is this latter consideration which distinguishes faith in Christ, from faith in the Father or the Holy Spirit. Faith in Christ is also distinguished by its peculiar motives, which are the works of his mediation (1:131).

"This faith in the person of Christ is the spring and

fountain of our spiritual life.... In and by the actings hereof it is preserved, increased, and strengthened" (1:132). The importance of this for Owen is evident when one compares a catalogue of his published works with the following brief summary of particular aspects of the Christian life which are dependent upon this faith in Christ:

> "For he is our life," Col. iii. 4; and all supplies of it are derived from him, by the actings of faith in him. We receive the forgiveness of sins, and an inheritance among them that are our peace with God maintained.... All strength for the mortification of sin, for the conquest of temptations—all our increase and growth in grace—depend on the constant actings of this faith in him. (1:132)

Second, "faith is acted on Christ under the formal notion of *mediator between God and man*" with respect to "all the acts of his office" (1:133). In this regard Christ is the immediate, though "not the ultimate object of our faith, wherein it rests, but God through him" (1:133). Of justifying faith Owen says that faith is not in Christ alone as a priest or prophet or king, but "principally respects his person for all those ends for which he is the ordinance of God" (5:116). In faith we receive *him*, and he is not to be considered but as vested with all his offices, although "formally justifying faith respecteth Christ in his priestly office alone" (5:117-23).

As this comment suggests, Owen taught a variety of ways in which faith is exercised upon Christ. For example, Hebrews 12:2 speaks of our "looking unto Jesus." This text combines two uses of the person of Christ. Owen says that the apostle "proposeth his person in the first place, as the object of our faith, from whom we might expect aid and assistance for conformity unto himself, in that wherein he is proposed as our example" (24:237). Christ in this text is a suitable object for our faith by virtue of his name, Jesus, which "minds us of him as a Saviour and a sufferer," and his office as he is faith's author and finisher. As Owen explains, "So is he the 'author' or beginner of our faith, in the *efficacious working* of it in our hearts by his Spirit; and 'the finisher' of it in all its *effects*, in liberty, peace, and joy, and all the fruits of it in obedience: for 'without him we can do nothing'" (24:238).

Faith, Owen says, gives "subsistence…unto the death of Christ in the soul" (21:248). Consequently, genuine faith in Christ crucified will act toward the mortification of sin.

The exercise of faith upon Christ in his mediatorial office figures prominently in Owen's sacramental discourses where we observe the act of faith as it is exercised in the sacrament of the Lord's Supper. These will be examined in our discussion of "Communion with Christ."

Obedience to Christ

After honor to Christ, Owen looks upon obedience to Christ as "the second part of our religious regard unto the person of Christ" (1:134). The subject of obedience to Christ was very volatile in the middle of the seventeenth century. Familists and other antinomians were denouncing any obedience to the law as opposed to Christ; Romanists and latitudinarian moralists were urging obedience to Christ as the ground of justification; Neonomians were turning faith into the new law of obedience to Christ, creating a *tertium quid* between these two. In the midst of this dispute, Owen observed that "obedience itself is on all hands generally neglected." Therefore, he undertook the exposition of the saint's obedience to Christ.

With regard to the moral precepts of the Old Testament, Christ neither gave any new law, nor abrogated any. In the gospel, "only the duties of the moral and eternal law are plainly declared in the doctrine of it, enforced in its motives, and directed as to their manner and end" (1:135). The Old Testament institutions of worship, on the other hand were abolished and replaced by a "new law of worship, consisting in several institutions and ordinances of worship" pertaining to the new covenant (1:135-36). The crucial point for Owen is that obedience to Christ respects both of these: the moral law which he confirmed, and the new law of evangelical worship (1:136; 21:131).

Owen provides a number of further considerations which emphasize the relation of Christology to his ethics. First, he says, obedience to Christ consists not in merely doing what he requires, but in doing them "from an express subjection of our souls and consciences unto him." Second, the formal reason of obedience unto him is his deity. If he is not God by nature then religious obedience to him is idolatry. Third, there is a peculiar respect unto him in all moral obedience as Mediator (1:136). By the authority vested in him as the head of the church and mediator of the new covenant they are peculiarly "his commands," and therefore respect must be had unto him in all our obedience unto them. Thus moralists deceive themselves, who speak of the performance of the moral law (the law of creation, laws of nature):

> Although the law hath never lost, nor ever can lose, its original power of obliging us unto universal obedience, as we are reasonable creatures; yet is our obedience unto it as Christians... immediately influenced by its confirmation unto the Evangelical Church in the hand of our Mediator. For... God hath given unto the Lord Christ all power in his name to require this obedience from all that receive the Gospel. (1:137)

As we have seen already with regard to the Father's part in Christ's mediatory office "all judgment upon and concerning this obedience is committed unto him by the Father" (1:138). As the moral law has a peculiar relationship to Christ (cf. 3:633-41), so also has the *"law of evangelical worship"* (1:136, 138-39). In all respects Owen would insist, it is "a vain thing to pretend love to Christ and keep not his commandments" (21:133). Love to Christ, as we will see, is indispensable to the due observance of his commandments (1:148-49).

Love to Christ

One of Owen's principal motives in life, and one which he felt constrained to emphasize against the deistical tendencies in his generation was love to Christ; specifically, love to his person. "There is, and ought to be, in all believers, a divine gracious love unto the person of Christ, immediately fixed on him, whereby they are excited unto, and acted in, all their obedience unto his authority" (1:140).

Characteristics of Love to Christ

This love must be genuine, a fruit of faith, and based upon a true understanding of him, rather than arising from a false representation or a heretical notion. "There cannot be true evangelical love unto a false Christ, such as these imaginations do fancy" (1:141). It must be regulated by the Scripture.

Owen provides a number of reasons for this all-consuming love to Christ. First, he says that "*The person of Christ is the principal object of the love of God*, and of the whole creation as participant in his image." Secondly, Owen observes that the angels, partaking of that image are always "upheld by love to the person of Christ" (1:147-48). Interestingly, it is "love proceeding from sight" of Christ which is the "life of the church above" (1:147). Similarly, love "proceeding from faith" is the life, joy, and glory of the church below" (1:148).

Man was created with the capacity to love in order that love to God "might be an instrument of our adherence unto him" (1:150). Owen says, "Not only our persons in their nature and being, but in all their powers and faculties, were fitted and prepared unto this end, of living unto God, and coming unto the enjoyment of him" (1:151). The object of this love is the divine goodness, particularly "as comprehensive of...mercy, grace, and bounty"; however, since the entrance of sin, "our love can find no amiableness in any goodness—no...satisfaction in any—but what is effectual in that grace and mercy by Christ" (1:151-52). This has the highest significance:

> God is love, of a nature infinitely good and gracious, so as to be the only object of all divine love. But this love can no way be known, or be so manifested unto us, as that we may and ought to love him, but by his love in Christ, his sending of him and loving us in him. Before this, without this we do not, we cannot love God. (1:152)

Owen expounds this love as including the "*desire of union*," as "*assimilation*," "*complacency*, and...*benevolence*," "*friendship*...accompanied by *spiritual boldness*" (1:152-56). In every respect Christ is central, as manifesting the divine goodness and love of God and as the object of the love of the saints. He is so "as he was incarnate.... That single effect of infinite wisdom and grace, in the union of the divine and human natures in the one person of the Son of God, renders him the object of this love in a peculiar manner" (1:156-57).

The "end" of the Bible's description of Christ's excellencies is to "ingenerate" love to Christ in us and to "excite it unto its due exercise" (1:157). Owen asserts, "It is evident unto all whose eyes are opened to discern these things, that there is no property of the divine nature which is peculiarly amiable—such as are goodness, grace, love, and bounty, with infinite power and holiness—but it is represented and proposed unto us in the person of the Son of God, to this end, that we should love him above all, and cleave unto him" (1:158). The same is true concerning the scriptural description of his human nature, of his love, his work, and his benefits. In all these respects, "invisible to the eyes of flesh," Christ is "altogether lovely" (1:157-61; 2:71-78; 9:462-89).

Owen emphasizes the role of scriptural revelation in this activity. Other means, such as the creation of mental or material images of him are disqualified, not only because forbidden, but as unable to truly represent the loveliness of Christ (1:159-61). Significantly, however, despite his vigorous protest against superstitious means in the love of Christ, Owen is even more critical of his contemporaries who "abhor these *idols*, and when they have so done, commit *sacrilege*" by denying love to Christ as a distinct act of obedience. Against this deistical tendency Owen asserts, "The most superstitious love unto Christ—that is, love acted in ways tainted with superstition—is better than none at all" (1:160).

Motives and Means to This Love
Owen says the motives for our love to Christ are too many, great, and "diffused through the whole dispensation of God" to be "fully expressed"; the "studying," "collecting," and "the meditation on them and improvement of them, are among the principal duties of our whole lives" (1:162-63). Briefly they consist of "all the acts of his mediatory office, with all the fruits of them," (i.e., "Christ and his benefits"), and that which was the "*spring and fountain* of those acts," which was his own love unto us (1:163-69).

Conformity to Christ and Following His Example
From faith, which "will cast the soul into the form or frame of the thing believed," and love, which "worketh an assimilation," there is produced that change in us which makes up the goal of our redemption, namely, conformity to Christ. By "conformity unto Christ and following his example," Owen expresses two aspects of the same thing. In conformity to Christ he is especially look-

ing at Christ's inward character: "Internal conformity unto his habitual grace and holiness is the fundamental design of a Christian life" (169-70). In the following of his example this inward conformity of character finds expression in Christian behavior.

"The Fundamental Design of a Christian Life"
As we saw earlier, it was the design of God to glorify himself in the salvation of that nature which had sinned in Adam. That nature had not only incurred guilt, but had suffered the "loss," or ruin, of the image of God. For our redemption, this image must be restored: "God, in the human nature of Christ, did perfectly renew that blessed image of his on our nature which we lost in Adam" (1:170). Christ's own human nature was not renewed, it being perfect and "filled with all grace" from its creation, but by its being so created God provided "an example of what he would by the same grace renew us unto, and what we ought in a way of duty to labor after" (1:170).[4] Owen shows clearly how the Scripture presents Christ as the "prototype" of God's workmanship in the renewal of fallen man. In particular, Christ is the "pattern of our graces" and "of our glory also" (1:171-72). Furthermore, this image of God is shown to us in the gospel (it being "utterly impossible we should have any just comprehension of it" otherwise). In the gospel, through the life of Christ manifesting the *imago dei* in his human nature, we "behold as in a glass the glory of the Lord, and are changed into the same image." This, Owen says, is the reason we are given the Holy Spirit: to take away the veil from our hearts, to "unite us unto him, and make us like him" (1:172). Again, the "infinite perfections of God" are represented to us in the gospel of Christ, the image of the invisible God, and only in him are they suitably represented unto us for our imitation (1:173).

If we are to be like Jesus Christ, two things are required. The first is a *"spiritual light,* to discern the beauty, glory, and amiableness of grace in Christ" and "every grace in him" (1:173). As Owen explains,

> If we are not able to discern an excellency in meekness and lowliness of heart, (as they are things generally despised,) how shall we sincerely endeavour after conformity unto Christ in them? The like may be said for all his other gracious qualifications. His zeal, his patience, his self-denial, his readiness for the cross, his love unto his enemies, his benignity to all mankind, his faith and fervency in prayer, his love to God, his compassion towards the souls of men, his unweariedness in doing good, his purity, his universal holiness;—unless we have a spiritual light to discern the glory and amiableness of them all, as they were in him, we speak in vain of any design for conformity unto him. (1:178)[5]

We also need a love to those graces such as is created by that spiritual light, otherwise we will not seriously endeavor after conformity to him.

In *The Grace and Duty of Being Spiritually Minded*, Owen gives many practical directions which would equally supply as directions for our "labour for this conformity," to Christ. In *Christologia*, he briefly summarizes his directions under the two heads of *"opposition unto all sin,* in the root, principle, and most secret springs of it, or original cleavings unto our nature," and the *"due improvement of all continual growth in every grace"* (1:174-75). In short, all that he had ever written on the subject of sanctification is assumed under the heading of the grace and duty of being conformed unto the image of Christ, just where it is found in the Pauline epistles.

"Following the Example of Christ"
"Following the example of Christ in all duties towards God and men, in his whole conversation on the earth" is

enjoined throughout Owen's works. In *Christologia*, Owen says the subject requires a to be "handled distinctly and at large by itself; which, if God will, may be done in due time" (1:175). Unhappily, this was never accomplished in a separate treatise, though many examples appear in the commentary on Hebrews. Owen mentions that "his meekness, lowliness of mind, condescension unto all sorts of persons—his love and kindness unto mankind—his readiness to do good unto all, with patience and forbearance—are continually set before us in his example." He explains that in these respects, Christ was "the great representative of the divine goodness unto us;" providing an example which, if we follow we "more express the virtues and excellencies of Christ than thousands can do with the most magnificent works of piety or charity, where this frame is wanting." On the other hand, if we neglect it we "crucify him afresh" (1:175-76). Owen says that Christ's disciples are also to follow his example in his "self-denial, readiness for the cross, with patience in sufferings," (1:176). They are to "consider him" in time of trouble, by making a "just estimate between him and us in our sufferings" and remembering the "event of his suffering," which was his being "set down at the right hand of God" (24:242-44; cf. 22:559-60; 21:113). Upon reading Owen's description of Christ's example as "the pole-star of the church in all its storms; the guide and comfort, support and encouragement of" those undergoing "persecution for righteousness sake" (21:176), one can easily believe he is listening to one who knows whereof he speaks.

Communion with Christ
In his treatise *On Communion With God*, Owen defines "communion" as "mutual communication...bottomed upon some union," and describes our communion with God as "his communication of himself unto us, with our

returnal unto him of that which he requireth and accepteth, flowing from that union which in Jesus Christ we have with him" (2:8). In chapter 7, attention was drawn to our federal union with Christ. Because of this union, we are brought into a "real" organic union with him through the operation of the Holy Spirit. This is our "subsisting in him," as branches in the vine (21:145; 145-152). With respect to Christ, their communion chiefly consists in "grace": "This, then is that which we are peculiarly to eye in the Lord Jesus to receive it from him, even grace, gospel-grace, revealed in or exhibited by the gospel" (2:47). Owen refers to two general kinds of grace received from Christ. The first he calls "personal grace," or the grace of Christ's "*personal presence and comliness*," and the second he calls "purchased grace" consisting of the "*free favour and acceptance*," by God, and of the "*fruits of the Spirit*, sanctifying and renewing our natures" (2:47-48).

Communion in Christ's Personal Grace
By Christ's personal grace Owen refers specifically to the "graces of the person of Christ as he is vested with the office of mediation,—his spiritual eminency, comeliness, and beauty, as appointed and anointed by the Father unto the great work of bring home all his elect unto his bosom" (2:48). We have already considered Owen's description of these excellencies in his exposition of the Person of Christ. Owen says we hold communion with Christ in his personal grace by "*conjugal relation*. He is married unto us, and we unto him; which spiritual relation is attended with suitable conjugal affections" (2:54). Their communion consists, first, in a "*mutual resignation of themselves one to the other*," as bridegroom and bride. Thus, Christ first "gives himself to the soul, *with all his excellencies*, righteousness, preciousness, graces, and eminencies, to be its Saviour, head, and husband, for ever to dwell with it in this holy relation" (2:56). That is,

The Lord Jesus Christ, fitted and prepared, by the accomplishment and furniture of his person as mediator, and the large purchase of grace and glory which he hath made, to be a husband to his saints, his church, tenders himself in the promises of the gospel to them in all his desirableness; convinces them of his good-will towards them, and his all-sufficiency for a supply of their wants; and upon their consent to accept of him,—which is all he requires or expects at their hands,—he engageth himself in a marriage covenant to be theirs for ever. (2:57)

The saints, in response, make a *"free, willing consent* to receive, embrace, and submit unto the Lord Jesus, as their husband, Lord, and Saviour,—to abide with him, subject their souls unto him, and to be ruled by him for ever (2:58). This *"self resignation* of the soul" to Christ, Owen explains, consists in the *"liking* of Christ, for his *excellency,* ... far above all other beloveds whatever, preferring him in the judgment and mind above them all," and the "accepting of Christ by the will, as its only husband, Lord, and Saviour" (2:58). As the Lord's initial tender of himself unto the saints is followed by consequent donations of himself unto them, so the saints, following their initial union with Christ have "consequential...renewed acts of consent all their days." It is these consequential acts of consent which Owen especially denotes by "communion" with Christ (2:58).

In typically Puritan fashion, Owen makes an extended "pathetic" exposition of Christ's excellencies in order, as he says, "to strengthen our hearts in the resignation...of ourselves unto the Lord Christ as our husband, as also to make way for the stirring of us up to...consequential conjugal affections" (2:59). These have already been considered at some length (though not without loss of effect through being removed from this context).

What, then, are the "mutual consequential affections"

of our union with Christ by which our communion with him is "carried on"? According to their different parts in this relation, Christ and the saints carry on their communion in different but, it would seem, related and, reciprocal ways. Thus, Owen says,

> Now the love of Christ, wherewith he follows his saints, consists in these four things:—I. Delight. II. Valuation. III. Pity, or compassion. IV. Bounty. The love, also, of the saints unto Christ may be referred to these four heads:—Delight; Valuation; Chastity; Duty. (2:118)

Owen's heart so obviously "burns within him" as he expounds the delight of Christ in his saints, that it is difficult not to catch some of his spark. For example:

> Now, Christ delights exceedingly in his saints: "As the bridegroom rejoiceth over the bride, so shall thy God rejoice over thee," Isa. lxii. 5. Hence he calleth the day of his espousals, the day of the "gladness of his heart," Cant. iii. 11. It is known that usually this is the most *unmixed* delight that the sons of men are in their pilgrimage made partakers of. The delight of the bridegroom in the day of his espousals is the height of what an expression of delight can be carried unto. This is in Christ answerable to the relation he takes us into. His heart is glad in us, without sorrow. And every day whilst we live is his *wedding-day*. (2:118)

Referring to one of his favorite scriptural images in describing the love of God to the saints, Owen continues,

> It is said of him, Zeph. iii. 17, "The LORD thy God in the midst of thee" (that is, dwelling amongst us, taking our nature, John i. 14) "is mighty; he will save, he will rejoice over thee with joy; he will rest in his love, he will joy over thee with singing;" which is a full description of delight, in all the parts of it,—joy and exultation, rest and complacence. (2:118)

To illustrate this delight in one particular way ("amongst a thousand") in which it is manifested, Owen points to Christ's way of revealing his "secrets" to the saints, and of enabling them to "reveal the secrets of their hearts to him" (2:119-26). While much of Owen's description of this pertains to the doctrine of revelation and the prophetic office, it is noteworthy that it is here placed in the context of the intercourse of "bosom friends." On the other hand, it is through the exercise of his offices in the giving of the Holy Spirit and in the opening of a "new and living way" that we are enabled to communicate our hearts to him. It is not sufficient that he knows our hearts by way of his omniscience; if we would "walk together as intimate friends," and have "consolation," there must be this exchange (2:121). Owen's description of the delight of the saints in Christ is drawn principally from the Song of Solomon. We have already had occasion to observe his approach to this book as providing a description of the excellencies of Christ and the spiritual "exercises" of the saints.

Owen reflects the view found in many Puritan works that the enjoyment of Christ's love (i.e., the "sense" of Christ's presence and the assurance of his love by various manifestations called the "kisses of his mouth") was something normally to be enjoyed, carefully to be guarded, and, if lost, to be recovered without delay (2:125-32). It is not uncommon, particularly in comments upon the Song of Solomon, to find Owen and others (e.g., Sibbes, Durham, and Rutherford) going beyond the Song in describing the "sweetness" of Christ's "delicacies" and "favours." The Song of Solomon is not so much a source for the doctrine of Christian experience as it is a vivid picture of that communion with Christ which, according to Puritan theology, Christians might expect to enjoy.

Secondly, Christ values his saints, as demonstrated by his incarnation, "exinanition" (i.e., "appearance in the form of a servant"), and death for them. He "prizes" the "meanest, the weakest, the poorest believer on the earth, ...more than all the world besides" (2:136). They, in turn, "value him *above all other things and persons,*" "*above their lives,*" "*above all spiritual excellencies* and all other righteousness whatever" (2:136-39). Christ's valuation of the saints is evident from all that he parted with for their sakes, while their valuation of him is evidenced in their parting with everything "wherein they have delighted or reposed their confidence, *for him and his sake,* that they might enjoy him," and their willingness to "part with all things rather than with him, when they do enjoy him" (2:140).

The third conjugal affection of Christ that Owen identifies is his compassion and pity toward the saints. Again, whereas many of the ways this is exercised have been observed as the acts of Christ's office of priest and king, they are described here as the "pity, tenderness, care, and compassion" of the saints' head and husband, (2:140-46). "In answer to this, I place in the saints chastity unto Christ, in every state and condition" (2:146). This chastity may be observed in the saints' "*affections,*" in their cherishing of the Holy Ghost, "which Christ sends to us, to abide with us in his room and stead," and in "*[keeping] his institutions,* or matter and manner of his worship" (2:146-52). Here we discover a number of Puritanism's principle concerns discussed as questions of chastity to Christ. For instance, any regard for our personal righteousness as unto our justification (even though that personal righteousness is produced by the indwelling Christ) is an adulterous thought, since by it we give Christ's place to another. Indeed, while many conceive of the Puritans as preoccupied with the avoidance of lustful sensual thoughts, Owen's concern is that a man guard his heart, "that nothing creep into its affections to give it peace or establishment before God, but Christ only" (2:148). A further instance concerns an issue of Puritan ecclesiology: the regulative principle. In the previous chapter we observed Owen's Christocentric interest in the regulative principle. At this point it is noteworthy that, for Owen, it is an expression of the chastity of the church when Christians *"will receive nothing, practise nothing, own nothing, in his worship, but what is of his appointment,"* and when they *"readily embrace, receive, and practise every thing that the Lord Christ hath appointed"* (2:150-52).[6]

Fourth, "Christ manifests and evidences his love to his saints in a *way of bounty*,—in that rich, plentiful provision he makes for them." Answerable to this bounty of Christ is the duty of Christians to *"follow after* and practice holiness in the power of it, as it is obedience unto Jesus Christ," and to labor *"to abound in fruits of holiness"* (2:153-54).

Communion in "Purchased *Grace"*
By "purchased grace," Owen intends "all that righteousness and grace which Christ hath procured, or wrought out for us, or doth by any means make us partakers of, or bestows on us for our benefit, by any thing that he hath done or suffered, or by any thing he continueth to do as mediator" (2:154). Owen does not explain the difference between this and the former "personal grace" despite their apparent similarity. It seems best to compare them to Christ's person and his work: personal grace is what Christ shares with his bride by virtue of what he *is*, purchased grace is what Christ shares with his bride by virtue of what he has *done*. The relation of Christ's person to his work explains why there is such a similarity in these two types of grace: we could have no communion with Christ in either without communion in both, but each has its peculiar immediate cause in either his person or his work. This seems evident from the threefold "fountain" of purchased grace in "the *obedience* of his life," "the

suffering of his death," and his "continued *intercession*," which are "all the actions of Christ as mediator" (2:155).

Owen describes the "*nature*" of this grace in terms of three graces "flowing from these heads and fountains," just mentioned:

> (1.) Grace of *justification*, or acceptance with God; which makes a relative change in us, as to state and condition. (2.) Grace of *sanctification*, or holiness before God; which makes a real change in us, as to principle and operation. (3.) Grace of *privilege*; which is mixed. (2:155)

As Christ's role in justification and sanctification has been alluded to already, it is necessary here only to take note of Owen's remarks upon the privileges of the saints.

The "great and innumerable" privileges flowing to the saints "all arise and flow" from the principal grace of adoption through Christ: "Himself was appointed to be the first-born among many brethren, Rom. viii. 29; and his taking us to be brethren, Heb. ii. 11, makes us become the children of God" (2:207). Consequently, the saints have fellowship with Christ, which Owen defines as:

> fellowship in *name*; we are (as he is) sons of God: fellowship in title and right; we are heirs, co-heirs with Christ: fellowship in *likeness* and conformity; we are predestinated to be like the first-born of the family: fellowship in *honour*; he is not ashamed to call us brethren: fellowship in *sufferings*; he *learned* obedience by what he suffered, and every son is to be scourged that is received: fellowship in his *kingdom*; we shall reign with him. (2:222)

The Lord's Supper

Owen brilliantly demonstrates the central motive behind the Reformed doctrine of the Supper: the real, spiritual presence of Christ provides the means for communion with his glorious person. "It is a *universal*, unimpeachable persuasion among all Christians," Owen insists, "that there is a *near, intimate communion with Christ, and participation of him, in the supper of the Lord*" (8:560). In *The Chamber of Imagery*, Owen says:

> The communication of Christ herein, and our participation of him, are expressed in such a manner as to demonstrate them to be peculiar,—such as are not to be obtained in any other way or divine ordinance whatever; not in praying, not in preaching, not in any other exercise of faith on the word or promises. There is in it *an eating and drinking of the body and blood of Christ*, with a spiritual *incorporation* thence ensuing, which are peculiar unto this ordinance. But this special and peculiar communion with Christ, and participation of him, is *spiritual* and *mystical*, by faith,—not carnal or fleshly.... To look for any other communication of Christ, or of his flesh and blood, but what is spiritual, is to contradict him in the interpretation which he gives of his own words. (8:560)

In this treatise against Romanism, he emphasizes the objects and acts of faith for the due observance of the Supper. First, faith "acts itself by *obedience* unto the authority of Christ in this institution" (8:561). The history of Christ's exercise of the threefold office is employed to enforce this. As he puts it,

> the institution of this ordinance was in the close of his ministry or prophetical office on the earth, and in the entrance of the exercise of his priestly office in offering himself a sacrifice unto God for the sins of the church. Between them both, and to render them both effectual unto us, he interposed an act of his kingly office, in the institution of this ordinance;... when his holy heart was in the highest exercise of zeal for the glory of God and compassion for the souls of sinners. Faith hath herein an especial regard unto all these things. (8:561)

Secondly, Owen points to a *"peculiar representation of*

the love and grace of Christ in his death and sufferings," above and beyond that which can be made "by words alone" (8:561). Most impressively, in the light of Owen's emphasis upon the Scriptures and preaching, he proves his point by means of the very same metaphor used in *Christologia* to prove the importance of the incarnation for the knowledge of God:

> As the light, which was first made and diffused unto the whole creation, did suffice to enlighten it in a general way, yet was far more useful, glorious, and conspicuous, when it was reduced and contracted into the body of the sun;—so the truths concerning Christ, as they are diffused through the Scripture, are sufficient for the illumination and instruction of the church; but when, by divine wisdom and institution, they are contracted into this ordinance, their taste and efficacy is more eminent and communicative unto the eyes of our understandings,—that is, our faith,—than as merely proposed by parts and parcels in the word. Hereby faith leads the soul unto a peculiar communion with Christ; which is thereon made partaker of him in an especial manner. (8:561-62)

Thirdly, "Faith, herein, respects "the *peculiar way of the communication and exhibition of Christ unto us, by symbols or sensible outward signs of bread and wine*" (8:562). That is, as opposed to other representations of the sufferings of Christ which are "discernable to sense or reason" (such as the crucifix), this presents Christ and his sufferings to the believer's faith. Significantly, Owen says "it is faith alone that apprehends that *sacramental* union that is between the outward signs and the things signified, by virtue of the divine institution," by which the body and blood of Christ "are really exhibited and communicated unto the souls of believers, as the outward signs are unto their bodily senses,—the signs becoming, thereby, *sacramentally*, unto us what the things signified are in themselves, and are therefore called by their names" (8:562). This Owen calls the "principal use and exercise" of faith in the Supper (8:562).

This leads to the fourth exercise of faith, which is the *"reception of Christ, as his body and blood are tendered and exhibited unto us in the outward signs of them"* (8:569). Faith receives Christ, Owen explains,

> by the gracious *assent* of the mind unto this truth, the choice of him, cleaving and trusting him with the will, heart, and affection, for all the ends of his person and offices, as the mediator between God and man: and in the sacramental mysterious proposal of him, his body and blood,... in this ordinance of worship, faith acts the whole soul in the reception of him unto all the especial ends for which he is exhibited unto us in this way and manner. (8:563)

In another sacramental discourse (9:523-29) Owen distinguishes the general object of faith (the divine veracity) and the special object of *justifying faith* ("Christ in the promises"), from the "special and peculiar object of faith, the *immediate* object of it in this ordinance." He gives a fourfold explanation of this object of faith: the human nature of Christ as the subject wherein mediation and redemption was wrought; his physical nature as distinguished into its integral parts, that is, into body and blood; these parts as *separate*; and as separated by being shed, and by being bruised and broken. Owen apparently realized the possibility that this might be misunderstood:

> You all along know that I do not intend these objects of faith as the ultimate object,—for it is the *person of Christ* that faith rests in,—but those immediate objects that faith is exercised about, to bring it to rest in God. It is exercised about the manner of this separation; that is, the blood of Christ comes to be distinct by being shed, and the body of Christ comes to be separate by being bruised and broken. (9:524)

This faith considers the causes of this separation, which Owen explains in terms of its moving cause, which is the eternal love of God; the procuring cause, which is our sin; and the efficient causes, or the reasons for the separation of Christ's body and blood (i.e., God's justice, his law, and the "instruments" of Christ's suffering—his crucifiers). Finally, "Faith considers in this matter the *end of this separation* of the body and blood of Christ which is thus represented; and that is ultimately and absolutely the glory of God," and subordinately, "to *confirm the covenant*," and the "*strengthening of our faith*" (9:526-27).

Two further discourses are expositions of Galatians 2:20—words which, Owen says, "express as high an acting of faith, I think, as any is in the Scripture" (9:600-606). Here we get a good view of how one acts faith upon Christ in the ordinance of the Lord's Supper. First, it is "*by way of adherence,*—cleaving to, trusting and acquiescing in, God in Christ, as declaring his love, grace, and goodwill in his promises." Without this faith we do not "discern the Lord's body." Secondly, in the ordinance each one by faith ought to make "*special application*" of the promise of Christ as tendered to himself in particular, and that by way of a "particular way of application" (i.e., as the reception of food for spiritual nourishment). In this case, Owen explains that the "*special object* of this special faith" is Christ's "*special love*, in the first place; and...the *special design of the death of Christ in the next place*: 'Who loved me, and gave himself for me'" (9:601). Furthermore, this love is to be considered as "free" and cleansing, and "invincible": "We are to look on this love of Christ as sovereign and free, and with a design of making our souls lovely; so invincible, also, that it broke up the eternal obstacles,—that nothing could stand before it until it had accomplished his whole work and design" (9:602).

Such a dissection of the acts of faith during the partaking of the Supper may seem to introduce a considerable distraction, but it should be borne in mind that this is Owen's way of helping his hearers to "survey the wondrous cross," so to speak, as it is made visible to the eyes of faith in the sacramental meal. In all of these ways, Owen insists, the saints enjoy an *"experience* unto their satisfaction and ineffable joy," of Christ as the "spiritual food of their souls"; whereas men without faith do not enjoy this and so resort to "carnal" ideas of partaking of Christ, such as transubstantiation. Conversely, if submission to that doctrine should ever be forced upon the saints, Owen says, only "a real experience of an *efficacious communication of Christ* unto our souls in this holy ordinance" would preserve the saints from apostasy into that error (8:563-64).

A Christ-Centered Rest

One very interesting feature of Owen's Christocentric Puritan piety has to do with his doctrine of the Sabbath. The observance of the Lord's Day as a day of sacred rest was a hallmark of English Puritanism, as witnessed in the Confessions, but there was also considerable disagreement as to whether or how the day was to be practiced at that time. Owen lists eighteen points of contemporary debate relative to the Sabbath (19:268-71). While the change from the seventh to the first day of the week has always been associated with the coming of Christ, his inauguration of the new covenant, and his resurrection, few have given the Christian "day of sacred rest" the exhaustive analysis it received from Owen.

First, Owen shows that the principle of a day of sacred rest had its origin with the creation of the world (19:286-326). "The reason...of the obligation of the Sabbath is moral," Owen says, but "the determination of the day itself depends on an arbitrary revelation and a law merely positive" (19:332). Moreover, God has established this day to be remembered with respect to some "rest of

God," following a particular occasion of his working (19:333). This rest did not consist of inactivity, so much as "the satisfaction and *complacency* that he took in his works, an effect of his goodness, power and wisdom, disposed in the order and into the ends" of his creating the world (19:334). Such a rest was enjoined upon our first parents, who were to "learn the satisfaction and complacency that God hath in his own work...; that is, to consider the impression of his excellencies upon them, and to glorify him on that account" (19:334). Owen adds that the sabbath rest was "a *pledge* unto man of his rest in and with God" (19:335), and that God had proposed "the way and *means*" for entering into that rest, namely, fidelity to the covenant of works (19:336). Man by sin fell away from the possibility of that rest.

The restoration of this rest is a part of the "renovation of all things by Jesus Christ," promised to the people of God while living under the old covenant:

> The renovation of all things by Jesus Christ is prophesied of and foretold as a new creation of all, even of the heavens and the earth, and all things contained in them,... Hence the state of things to be introduced thereby was under the old testament called "The world to come." (19:404)

Owen quotes approvingly Rabbi Kimchi who interprets the Sabbath day, mentioned in the title of Psalm 92, as "the world to come, which shall be wholly sabbath or rest;...the days of the Messiah" (19:404). In this renovation of all things the old covenant and "all that was peculiar" to it are annulled; "What now remains of them, as to any usefulness in our living to God, doth not abide on the old foundation, but on a new disposition of them, by the renovation of all things in Christ" (19:404; cf. 404-407). The former rest was founded upon God's own rest with regard to the creation. Later, in the "re-creation," represented by the redemption of Israel from Egypt and their entrance into Canaan, another covenant and another rest was enjoined upon the people of God. Owen completes this biblical-theological study of God's rests with a description of the rest which is restored under the new covenant: the rest of God's people which is founded upon God's rest with regard to the new creation by the gospel. The change of day is not an arbitrary decision by the church; it reflects both the change in covenant, and the day on which Christ entered into his rest, "being refreshed in and from his works" (19:408-17). Likewise, the different manner of observation of this day is "suited unto the *spiritual state* of the church under the gospel, delivered from the bondage frame of spirit wherewith it was observed under the law."

Owen's treatment of the Sabbath is impressive because it is so Christocentric. In all the reasons for its observance, its time and manner, it is Christ's day when his people celebrate the new life into which, by him, they have entered.

A Christ-Centered Hope

As his life has been the beholding of Christ by faith, the Christian's hope is to behold him by sight in heaven. This was Christ's prayer for them in John 17:24, a text which Owen refers to frequently. Owen closes his *Meditations on the Glory of Christ* with a lengthy description of this.

First, he emphasizes the "*object*" of this vision "will be *real* and *substantial*. Christ himself, in his own person, with all his glory, shall be continually with us, before us, proposed to us" (1:378). For this reason shall "that corporeal sense" of seeing be restored, and his people shall see him "with the same eyes wherewith they see the tokens and signs of him in the sacrament of the supper" (1:379). "Principally," Owen hastens to add, our vision will be "intellectual," and that in a manner not now known, but "in the immediate beholding of the person of Christ, we shall see a glory in it a thousand times above what here we can conceive" (1:379). We will receive a new "visive power" for this purpose (1:380); a "light of glory" will then "*perfectly transform the soul into the image and likeness of Christ*" (1:383; 410-15). Our minds will be freed from the "clogs of the flesh," "principles of instability and vanity," and distracting temptations; and the "*essential faculties* of our souls" will be transformed that we might "behold and delight in this glory constantly with eternal satisfaction" (1:405-407). To "be ever with him, and see him as he is," Owen says, "is heaven," "blessedness," "eternal rest," and "everlasting refreshment and joy unto our whole souls" (1:385). Such expressions fall in abundance from Owen's pen in the closing sections of *The Glory of Christ*. Until then the saints "breath and pant after" this vision, and look for his appearances to us through the "windows of the ordinances of the gospel" (1:379, 377).

Conclusion

We have seen the pervasive impact of Christology for Owen's doctrine of the Christian life. It is but one demonstration of the error in assuming that Reformed theology is somehow disinterested in the practice of godliness or in spiritual experience. It is equally clear that the allegation cannot be sustained that the Puritans, in stressing the importance of these things, were *ipso facto* less Christocentric than their Continental Protestant forebears. Most importantly, we have surveyed one Puritan pastor's understanding of the pastoral ministry: to "travail" until Christ is "formed" in the hearts and lives of his flock, as they "beholding the glory of the Lord are changed into the same image, from glory to glory."

---

[1] The "use" of Christ, i.e., the appropriation of Christ, by faith, with respect to his office as Mediator, is a common theme in Puritan practical theology. See, for example, John Brown of Wamphray's,

magnificent work of applied Christology, *Christ, the Way, the Truth, and the Life* (Brown, 1839).

² See Thomas Goodwin's lengthy exposition, *Christ Set Forth* (Goodwin 1863, 4:1-91). This work is an entire summary of Christology to prove that Christ is the object of justifying faith and thus to encourage faith in him.

³ For the meaning of "consider," Owen would no doubt agree with Isaac Ambrose: "Consideration is a fixing of our thoughts, a steadfast bending of our minds to some spiritual matter, till it work in the affections and conversation. We may know and yet be inconsiderate of that we do know, but when the intention of our mind and heart is taken up about some one known object and other things are not for the present taken notice of, this is consideration" (*Looking Unto Jesus*, p. 65).

⁴ This union of God's gracious work and our duty (reminiscent of Philippians 2:12-13), is expressed in the title of one of Owen's most famous treatises on the work of sanctification, *The Grace and Duty of Being Spiritually Minded*, where the renewal now under discussion finds a lengthy exposition. Archibald Alexander said this work of Owen's should be read once a year (Alexander, 1864, 93). A comparison between this treatise and Jonathan Edwards' *Religious Affections* would prove to be a very interesting study. Owen's work places great importance upon the affections, understood in many (not all) respects in a similar way to Edwards. Though Edwards quotes from Owen's work on the Holy Spirit, he does not mention *The Grace and Duty*. The meditations of these two great men upon the same subject, it appears, produced two works with much in common; not the least important of which was their emphasis upon the divine glory of Christ as the principal object of spiritual affections (Edwards, 1834, 1:277; Owen, 7:473-74).

⁵ The parallel with Edwards' work on the *Religious Affections* is particularly strong here. Gracious affections, says Edwards, "arise from divine illumination"; "beget and promote the temper of Jesus"; and "have beautiful symmetry and proportion" (Edwards, 1834, 1:281-88; 303-309; 309-12). With regard to their "proportion" Edwards says, "They have the whole image of Christ upon them:... There is every grace in them which is in Christ" (1834, 1:309).

⁶ Just before quoting this passage in full, Cotton Mather wrote that the New England migration was motivated by the "desire to see and seek a reformation of the church according to the Scripture: of which matter I cannot give a briefer, and yet fuller history, than by reciting the memorable words of that great man, Dr. John Owen, who in his golden book of *Communion with God*, thus expresses it:" (Mather, 1852, 1:249). Mather seldom mentions Owen without indicating his great esteem for him.

CHAPTER

18

Conclusion

The principal objective for our study was to provide students of Puritanism, and of historical and systematic theology, with a comprehensive systematic exposition of the Christology of a representative Puritan. John Owen was chosen for this study for two reasons: first, because he has long been considered by many in the Reformed tradition to be one of its greatest theologians; second, because none of the other Puritans considered provided as extensive a store of Christological material from which to draw. We may summarize the results of our study in terms of the three questions raised at the beginning.

What have we learned about Puritan Christology from John Owen? To the extent that Owen is representative of the Puritans, it would seem obvious that the idea advanced by Knappen and others that they were not much interested in Christology must be rejected. We have observed that the knowledge of Christ was the all-surpassing object of Owen's desires, the center of his doctrinal system, and the end, means, and indispensable prerequisite for Christian theology. Examination of the works of several other representative Puritans shows that, in principle, the centrality of Christ in the theological system of John Owen was not unique. In some, such as Sibbes, Goodwin, Manton, Charnock, Flavel, and Bunyan it is obvious, though to varying degrees. In the development of this Christocentric theological *system*, however, Owen was unsurpassed. The lines which he traces from the doctrine of the person of Christ are bold, and long enough to reach every subject of doctrinal inquiry, showing that "by him, all things" [including all doctrinal truths] consist" (Col. 1:17).

In the course of our study, we were able to observe this Christocentricity in several areas. Of particular interest is the place Owen gives to Christ in the decree of election. First, it is apparent that Owen does not structure his theology around the doctrine of election, but, with the exception of *The Display of Arminianism*, handles the doctrine of the decree in the context of teaching the work of Christ. Not only in the choice of context, but also in the details, Christ is central in his exposition of the decree. Thus, he speaks not so often of the decree as of the "counsels" of God, with an emphasis upon the activity of God's eternal Wisdom. Considered as God, Christ is, equally with the Father, the source of the decree. In the execution of that decree, on the other hand, Christ, as the one to become incarnate (*incarnandus*), becomes the surety of those elect in him. Moreover, the execution of the decree is the putting into operation of Christ's "testament," thus securing the gift of objective and effectual redemption in the death of the testator.

Creation and providence consequently become doctrines duly to be treated under the topic of God the Redeemer. Because of the covenant of redemption, these activities belong peculiarly to the person of the Son. As we observed before, however, this is altogether consistent with Owen's strong Trinitarianism. We observed also that redemptive history is centered upon the action of the Son, whose mediatory activity is exercised throughout the Old Testament. Owen's sober, detailed, insightful exegesis of the Old Testament demonstrates not only that it is a Christ-centered book, but also that such a redemptive-historical interpretation of the Old Testament is both warranted and beneficial.

What contributions did Owen make to the doctrine of the person of Christ? In the light of Patristic Christology and of developments in sixteenth-century Reformed theology, it seems that Owen said little concerning the doctrine of Christ's person that had not been said centuries before. Owen's greatest contributions in this regard may be summarized under the categories of comprehension, critique, vindication, exposition, and application. The works of Christian antiquity present a wide range of Christological thought, to which we may add insights arising out of the Lutheran/Reformed and anti-trinitarian struggles of the previous century. It seems that Owen was able to grasp the significance of these insights and to distill these for the benefit of his reader. He is also critical of faulty forms and expressions that confuse rather than give light, and of those persons who set an evil precedent by unedifying speculation into the divine mysteries. Vindication of scriptural testimonies used in the past but now called into question was a great contribution. His exposition of Scripture so as to clearly and convincingly communicate the more complicated, but foundational, principles of the orthodox doctrine of Christ's person was particularly impressive.

Beyond these, it seems Owen's major contributions pertain to the *work* of Christ. Again, Owen moves in the footsteps of his predecessors, but the prints he leaves are his own. This is brilliantly demonstrated in *The Death of Death in the Death of Christ*. Though it was not an absolutely new idea, his powerful demonstration of the *necessity* of the atonement, as given in the *Dissertation on Divine Justice*, may justly be accounted as a major contribution. The same may be said for the manner in which he expounds the doctrine of the Priesthood of Christ in the

Conclusion 519

Hebrews commentary. In addition, he employed a variety of biblical representations of Christ in addition to, and in the interest of, expounding the offices of Prophet, Priest, and King. In this he was not alone: a study of other Puritan's use of other Christological motifs and representations might prove interesting and might better illustrate the Puritan interest in, and exposition of, Christ.

Two features of Owen's work are particularly distinctive. The first is the intensity with which he works across so extensive a range of Christological themes. That is, while one of his contemporaries may develop a particular point at greater length than Owen, none seems to explore so many points as thoroughly. The second feature, alluded to earlier, is the clarity with which he relates the Christian system of doctrine to the person of Christ. That is, it is one thing to say Christian theology ought to be Christocentric, it is quite another to actually understand the entire spectrum of theological *loci* Christocentrically, or to articulate one's theology in a way that manifests this Christocentricity. Owen does this, as we have observed with regard to the knowledge of God, creation, providence, the redemption of man, the mediatorial kingdom, the church, and the Christian life.

How did John Owen address the Christological issues of his day, and what can we learn from him with regard to the current Christological debate? In the vindication and exposition of the doctrine of Christ (and of the doctrine of Scripture which testifies of Christ), Owen stands out as a biblical theologian. While a full exposition of his argument was beyond the limits of this dissertation, we have seen that Owen's exposition of the Trinity, and the Deity and incarnation of Christ was argued cogently from the Scriptures, as interpreted according to his grammatico-historical method. Of course, one may disagree with Owen's exegesis, but, having examined it, one cannot simply brush aside his doctrine of the incarnation as a product of Greek speculation, or his Reformed doctrine of the atonement as Calvinism perverted by Aristotelianism. The strength of Owen's biblical argument is such that opposition to it must be directed against his fundamental presuppositions.

Owen realized the necessity of challenging the presuppositions which continue to lie at the root of modern unbelief in the inspiration and authority of the Scripture. Arguing very powerfully for the Bible's claims for its own inspiration, Owen called his opponents to submit their understanding to the authority of God speaking in the Bible. The alternative developments of Christology during Owen's lifetime and, even more evidently, in the decades following his death, resulted from the acceptance (for many non-theological reasons) of contrary presuppositions, not from greater insights into the teaching of Holy Scripture. It would appear that greater consideration should be given to this question of presuppositions, since it is clear that the rejection of orthodox Christology, despite an occasional reference to the Bible, is built upon a different foundation. This question was inadequately dealt with by Owen's successors. As a consequence, solid exegetical labors in the defense of orthodoxy, such as those of Bishop Waterland, failed to receive the hearing they merited, while works actually less faithful to Scripture, but respecting specious philosophical objections, were widely received.

Owen's profound insight may be gathered by a comparison with several principles advanced by David F. Wells as important in a Christology for today. First, Wells asserts that "the conceptual framework in which Christ must be understood is that of an eschatological 'age to come'" (Wells 1984, 171-72). While Owen and Wells are not precisely on the same track, Owen's discussion of the changes introduced by the coming of Christ points toward an appreciation for an eschatological framework for biblical Christology, though "redemptive-historical" is actually a better description of Owen's approach.

Another principle advocated by Wells was the "inescapable" conclusion that "*some form of enhypostatic union must be employed if justice is to be done to the full range of New Testament teaching*" (1984, 177). Wells correctly points out the need of Leontius' refinement of Cyril's doctrine of *anhypostasia*, a refinement generally ignored by critics of orthodoxy, but, as we observed, a concept of great importance to Owen (though he does not use the term). The concept of *enhypostasia* will help us in at least two ways. First, as Wells and Owen would argue, it enables us to do justice to the New Testament's witness to the person of Christ. No other formulation of the person of Christ has been able to do so. Second, as Wells argues (cf. Hughes 1989, passim) such a conception of the person of Christ is in full accord with the Biblical idea of "human," as the *imago Dei* (Wells 1984, 177-79). The restoration of the image by Christ, the head of the new creation, is a prominent theme in Owen.

As Wells has observed, "The person and work of Christ must constantly be linked, each interpreting the other" (1984, 175). This necessity was emphasized by Luther, and was profoundly influential in the system of Calvin, and, as we have seen, of fundamental importance to the theology of Owen, who excelled in the exposition of the relation of Christ's person to his office. So intimately are these two related that the office cannot be correctly understood apart from the person, nor do we appreciate the glory of God manifested in Jesus apart from the consideration of his work.

Nor can the work of Christ be understood apart from a due sense of the need of man. By a "due sense" we mean that Christology cannot be studied in a detached manner: as Wells expresses it, "To understand Christ aright, we must know something about our own guilt. We must know ourselves to be sinners" (1984, 175). This Lutheran/Calvinistic approach to the knowledge of God (*Institutes* I. 1. i.) is reflected in Owen's emphasis upon the knowledge, the personal "sense," of our state as the result of the fall.

The significance of Owen's work was noted by John Brown of Edinburgh in 1850: "Dr. Owen did good service to the cause of Christianity, two hundred years ago, by showing the pre-eminent place the person of Christ holds in that religion, in opposition to the British rationalists of that age, who had almost lost sight of him in speculation about evidences, and dogmas, and ethics" (Brown, 1850, vi). Brown himself agreed with Owen's emphasis, adding that the "living faith of a living Christ ...lies at the foundation of true Christianity; and the superstructure is composed of that transforming intimate acquaintance with *him*, with *his* person, *his* character, *his* mind, *his* will, which is to be obtained by a careful study of that 'Scripture given by inspiration of God,' which is *his* word—he being at once its author and its subject— under the promised influence of His Spirit—the Spirit of truth and holiness" (Brown, 1850, vi).

Thus, the entirety of the Christian life is understood as centering upon Christ. For this reason, it is the minister's task to teach the "use" of the person of Christ to his flock. For this, however, it is necessary to lay the foundation of the doctrine of Christ's person and his work. We have already noted the central place this activity had in Owen's pastoral ministry. Without a true knowledge of Christ we are not true Christians, and there is nothing true Christians need so much as to grow in their knowledge of Christ. Owen's polemical works against the Socinians and even the Quakers and Arminians were all motivated by the pastoral desire to prevent anything from interfering with the saints' true knowledge of Christ. Owen never saw the vindication of orthodox

Conclusion

views as the end of his work: this was always undertaken in the interest of preserving that doctrinal foundation upon which the superstructure of Christian doctrine and life was to be built. Though it might appear otherwise from the extent of his labors in the vindication of orthodoxy, Owen seems to have believed that the "best defense was a good offence"; that the best strategy for preserving the church from apostasy was not the turning of biblical truths into doctrines coldly to be believed, nor in teaching only a few "simple" doctrines, but in making even the more difficult ones understood in terms of their very significant place in the believer's life.

Finally, it has become clear in the course of this study that the Puritans should be permitted to speak for themselves. Rationalists accused them of "enthusiasm," while Quakers called them "purveyors of the dead letter," who preached only a Christ outside of themselves, believed in with a dead faith, justifying them to live ungodly lives. To whatever degree Owen is representative of the Puritans, it is obvious that these charges are false, reflecting the bias of those on either extreme. Nevertheless, it behooves Christians to heed Owen's example, lest we, through the neglect of living or preaching any part of Christ's gospel, should justify a faulty idea of it.

WORKS CITED

Alexander, J. W. 1864. *Thoughts on Preaching*. Reprint, Edinburgh: The Banner of Truth Trust, 1974.

Allison, C. F. 1966. *The Rise of Moralism: The Proclamation of the Gospel from Hooker to Baxter*. New York: The Seabury Press.

Ambrose, Isaac. 1855. *Looking Unto Jesus: a view of the everlasting gospel, or, The soul's eying of Jesus*. 2 volumes in 1, n.p. Reprint, Harrisonburg: Sprinkle Publications.

Armstrong, Brian. 1969. *Calvinism and the Amyraut Heresy: Protestant Scholasticism and Humanism in Seventeenth Century France*. Madison: The University of Wisconsin Press.

Arndt, William, F. Wilbur Gingrich, Frederick W. Danker, and Walter Bauer. 1979. *A Greek-English Lexicon of the New Testament and Other Early Christian Literature: A Translation and Adaption of the Fourth Revised and Augmented Edition of Walter Bauer's Griechisch-Deutsches Worterbuch Zu Den Schrift En Des Neuen Testaments Und Der Ubrigen Urchristlichen Literatur*. Electronic ed. of the 2nd ed., rev. and augmented. Chicago: University of Chicago Press.

Aulen, Gustav. 1964. *Christus Victor: An Historical Study of the Three Main Types of the Idea of the Atonement*. Translated by A. C. Herbert. New York: Macmillan.

Barclay, Robert. 1692. *Truth Triumphant*. London: n.p.

Bavinck, Herman. 1951. *The Doctrine of God*, translated, edited, and outlined by William Hendriksen. Grand Rapids: Baker Book House.

Baxter, Richard. 1838. *The Practical Works of Richard Baxter*. Vol. 3, "The Saints' Everlasting Rest." London: George Virtue.

Berkouwer, G. C. 1960. *Studies in Dogmatics: Divine Election*. Grand Rapids: Wm. B. Eerdmans.

Bolam, C. Gordon, et al. 1968. *The English Presbyterians: From Elizabethan Puritanism to Modern Unitarianism*. Boston: Beacon Press.

Bolton, Robert. 1641. *The Works of the Reverend, Truly Pious, and Judiciously Learned Robert Bolton*. London: George Miller.

Braithwaite, W. C. 1961. *The Beginnings of Quakerism*, 2d ed. Cambridge: University Press.

Brook, Benjamin. 1813. *The Lives of the Puritans*, in 3 volumes. London: James Black; reprint, Pittsburgh: Soli Deo Gloria, 1994.

Brooks, Thomas. 1861-67. *The Works of Thomas Brooks*, 6 vols., edited by Alexander B. Grossart. Edinburgh: James Nichol; reprint, Edinburgh: The Banner of Truth Trust, 1973.

Brown, John. 1852. *Sayings and Discourses of Christ*, 3 vols., n.p.; reprint, Winona Lake, Ind.: Alpha Publications.

Brown, John (of Wamphray). 1678. *Quakerisme the Path-way to Paganisme, or, A View of the Quaker's Religion*. Edinburgh: John Cairns.

_____. 1834. *Christ: the Way, the Truth, and the Life*. Edinburgh: Robert Ogle.

Bunyan, John. 1853. *The Works of John Bunyan*, 3 vols., ed. George Offer. Glasgow: Blackie & Son.

Burgesse, Anthony. 1654. *The Doctrine of Justification Asserted and Vindicated from the Errours of Many and more especially Papists and Socinians or A Treatise of the Natural Righteousness of God, and the Imputed Righteousness of Christ*. London: Thomas Underhill.

Burroughs, Jeremiah. 1654. *The Saint's Treasury*. London: John Wright.

Burrowes, George. 1853. *A Commentary on the Song of Solomon*, n.p., reprint, London: The Banner of Truth Trust, 1973.

Calvin, John. 1960. *Institutes of the Christian Religion*, in Library of Christian Classics, Vol. 21, ed. John T. McNeill. Philadelphia: Westminster Press, 1960.

_____. 1965. *Calvin's New Testament Commentaries*, 12 vols. eds. David W. Torrance and Thomas F. Torrance, translated by T. H. L. Parker. Grand Rapids: Wm. B. Eerdmans.

Charnock, Stephen. 1684. *The Works of the Late Learned Divine Stephen Charnock, B.D.* Vol. 2. London: Thomas Cockerill.

_____. 1865. *The Complete Works of Stephen Charnock, B.D.* Vol. 4, *The Knowledge of God*. Edinburgh: James Nichol; reprint, Edinburgh: The Banner of Truth Trust, 1985.

Cheynell, Francis. 1643. *The Rise, Growth, and Danger of Socinianisme*. London: Samuel Gellibrand.

_____. 1650. *The Divine Triunity of the Father, Son, and Holy Spirit, or the blessed Doctrine of the three Coessential Subsistents in the eternal Godhead without any confusion or division of the Subsistences, or multiplication of the most single and entire Godhead*. London: Samuel Gellibrand.

Clarkson, David. 1696. *Sermons and Discourses on Several Divine Subjects*. London: Thomas Parkhurst.

Cragg, G. R. 1950. *From Puritanism to the Age of Reason: A Study of Changes in Religious Thought within the Church of England*. n.p.

Cragg, G. R., ed. 1968. *The Cambridge Platonists*. A Library of Protestant Thought. New York: Oxford University Press.

Cunningham, William. 1862. *Historical Theology*, 2 vols., reprint, Edinburgh: The Banner of Truth Trust, 1960.

Davis, D. Clair. 1982. "The Reformed Church of Germany: Calvinists as an Influential Minority." In *John Calvin: His Influence in the Western World*, edited by W. Stanford Reid, 123-38. Grand Rapids: Zondervan.

Dorner, Isaak A. *History of the Development of the Doctrine of the Person of Christ*. 5 vols. Translated by William L. Alexander and D. W. Simon. Edinburgh: T. & T. Clark, 1861-72.

Durham, James. 1753. *Christ Crucifyd: or, the Marrow of the Gospel, Evidently set forth in LXXII Sermons on The Whole 53rd Chapter of Isaiah*. London: Aaron Ward.

_____. 1840. *An Exposition of the Song of Solomon*, n.p. Originally published 1651; reprint of 1840 edition, Edinburgh: The Banner of Truth Trust.

Edwards, Jonathan. 1834. *The Works of Jonathan Edwards*. Edinburgh; reprint, Edinburgh: The Banner of Truth Trust, 1974.

Eeg-Olofsson, Leif. 1954. *The Conception of the Inner Light in Robert Barclay's Theology: A Study in Quakerism*. Lund: C W K Gleerup.

Eusden, John Dykstra. 1968. *Introduction to The Marrow of Theology, by William Ames*. Durham, The Labyrinth Press.

Ferguson, Sinclair B. 1987. *John Owen on the Christian Life*. Edinburgh: The Banner of Truth Trust.

Flavel, John. 1820. *The Works of John Flavel*, 6 vols. London: W. Banes and Son; reprint, Edinburgh: The Banner of Truth Trust, 1968.

Goodwin, Thomas. 1863. *The Works of Thomas Goodwin*, 12 vol. Edinburgh: James Nichol.

Goulder, Michael, ed. 1979 *Incarnation and Myth: The Debate Continues*. Grand Rapids: Wm. B. Eerdmans.

Grudem, Wayne 1991. "The Meaning of Kephale ("Head"): A Response to Recent Studies," in *Recovering Biblical Manhood & Womanhood, A Response to Evangelical Feminism*, edited by John Piper and Wayne Grudem, 425-68. Wheaton: Crossway Books, Counsel on Biblical Manhood and Womanhood.

Gundry, Stanley N. 1984. "John Owen on Authority and Scripture," in *Inerrancy and the Church*, ed. John D. Hanna. Chicago: Moody Press.

Heppe, Heinrich. 1950. *Reformed Dogmatics*. Edited by Ernst Bizer, translated by G. T. Thomson. London: n.p.; reprint, Grand Rapids: Baker Book House, 1978.

Hooker, Richard. 1845. *The Works of that Learned and Judicious Divine, Mr. Richard Hooker: With an Account of His Life and Death by Isaac Walton*, 2 vols., edited by John Keble. New York: D. Appleton & Company.

Howe, John. 1836. *The Works of the Rev. John Howe, M.A.: with Memoirs of His Life, by Edmund Calamy, D.D.*. London: Frederick Westley and A. H. Davis.

Hughes, Philip Edgcumb. 1989. The *True Image: The Origin and Destiny of Man in Christ.* Grand Rapids: Wm. B. Eerdmans.

Hunt, John. 1870. *Religious Thought in England: From the Reformation to the End of the Last Century*, 3 vols., London: Strahan & Co.

Kelly, J. N. D. *Early Christian Doctrines.* San Francisco: Harper & Row, 1960.

Kendall, R. T. 1979. *Calvin and English Calvinism to 1649.* Oxford: University Press.

Knappen, Marshall M. 1939. *Tudor Puritanism.* Chicago: University of Chicago Press.

Lane, A. N. S. 1982. "Christology Beyond Chalcedon." In *Christ the Lord: Studies in Christology Presented to Donald Guthrie*, edited by Harold H. Rowden. Downers Grove: Inter-Varsity Press.

La Shell, John. 1985. "Imaginary Ideas of Christ: A Scottish-American Debate." Westminster Theological Seminary, Ph.D. Dissertation.

Lichtenstein, Aharon. 1962. *Henry More: The Rational Theology of a Cambridge Platonist.* Cambridge: Harvard University Press.

MacLeod, Donald. 1998. *The Person of Christ.* Contours of Christian Theology, Gerald Bray, general editor. Downers Grove: Intervarsity Press.

Manton, Thomas. 1870. *The Complete Works of Thomas Manton*, 22 vols. London: James Nisbet & Co.; reprint, Worthington, PA: Maranatha Publications, n.d.

Mather, Cotton. 1702. *The Great Works of Christ in America*, 2 vols., London: n.p.; reprint, Edinburgh: The Banner of Truth Trust, 1979.

McLachlan, H. John. 1951. *Socinianism in Seventeenth Century England.* Oxford: University Press, 1951.

Meithe, Terry. 1989. "The Universal Power of the Atonement," in The Grace of God, the Will of Man, edited by Clark H. Pinnock. Grand Rapids: Zondervan.

Moulin, Peter (Pierre du Moulin). 1620. *The Anatomy of Arminianism.* London: Nathaniel Newberry.

Muller, Richard A. 1976. "Predestination and Christology in Sixteenth

Century Reformed Theology," Duke University, Ph.D. dissertation.

_____. 1983a. "Incarnation, Immutability and the Case for Classical Theism." *Westminster Theological Journal* 45:22-40.

_____. 1983b. "Christ—The Revelation or the Revealer? Brunner and Reformed Orthodoxy on the Doctrine of the Word of God." *Journal of the Evangelical Theological Society* 26/3: 307-19.

_____. 1985. *Dictionary of Latin and Greek Theological Terms*. Grand Rapids: Baker Book House.

_____. 1986. *Christ and the Decree*. Grand Rapids: Baker Book House.

_____. 2003. *Post-Reformation Reformed Dogmatics*, 4 volumes. Grand Rapids: Baker Book House.

Murray, John. 1977. *Collected Writings of John Murray*. Vol. 2, *Select Lectures in Systematic Theology*. Edinburgh: Banner of Truth.

_____. 1955. *Redemption Accomplished and Applied*. Grand Rapids: Wm. B. Eerdmans.

_____. 1997. *The Epistle to the Romans*. One volume paperback edition, originally published in two vols., 1959 and 1965. Grand Rapids: Wm. B. Eerdmans.

Newman, Paul W. 1987. *A Spirit Christology: Recovering the Biblical Paradigm of Christian Faith*. Lanham: University Press of America.

Nye, Stephen. 1697. *The Grounds and Occasions of the Controversy concerning the Unity of God*. n.p.

Oberman, Heiko. 1970. "The 'Extra' Dimension in the Theology of Calvin." *Journal of Ecclesiastical History* xxi: 43-64.

Owen, John. 1850. *The Works of John Owen, D.D.*, 24 vols., ed. William H. Goold. London and Edinburgh: Johnstone and Hunter.

_____. 1994. *Biblical Theology*. First published as *Theologumena Pantodapa*, in Latin at Oxford in 1661. Translated from the 1850 William H. Goold edition (Volume 17) by Stephen Westcott. Pittsburgh: Soli Deo Gloria Publications, 1994.

Ozment, Stephen. 1980. *The Age of Reform 1250-1550: An Intellectual and Religious History of Late Medieval and Reformation Europe*. New Haven and London: Yale University Press.

Packer, James I. 1974. "Introductory Essay," in John Owen's *The Death of Death in the Death of Christ*. London: The Banner of Truth Trust.

Penn, William. 1825. *The Select Works William Penn*, 3 vols., London: William Phillips; reprint; New York: Kraus Reprint Co., 1971.

Pinnock, Clark H., ed. 1975. *Grace Unlimited*. Minneapolis: Bethany.

Preus, Robert D. 1970. *The Theology of Post-Reformation Lutheranism*. Saint Louis: Concordia.

Reid, J. K. S. 1948. "The Office of Christ in Predestination." *Scottish Journal of Theology* 1:5-19, 131-57.

Reynolds, Edward. 1679. *The Works of the Right Reverend Father in God, Edward Reynolds, Late Lord Bishop of Norwich.* London: Thomas Newcomb, 1679.

Ritschl, Albrecht. 1872. *A Critical History of the Christian Doctrine of Justification and Reconciliation*, translated by John S. Black. Edinburgh: Edmonston and Douglas.

Roberts, James Deotis, Sr. 1968. *From Puritanism to Platonism in Seventeenth Century England.* The Hague: Martinus Nijhoff.

Rutherford, Samuel. 1647. *Christ Dying and Drawing Sinners Unto Himself.* London: Andrew Crooke.

Sibbes, Richard. 1862-64. *The Works of Richard Sibbes*, edited by A. B. Grosart. Edinburgh: James Nichol; reprint, Edinburgh: The Banner of Truth Trust, 1973.

Thompson, Andrew. 1850. "Life of Dr. Owen." Vol. I. *The Works of John Owen, D.D.*, edited by William H. Goold. London and Edinburgh: Johnstone and Hunter; reprint, Edinburgh: The Banner of Truth Trust, 1965.

Toon, Peter. "Growth of a Supralapsarian Christology." *Evangelical Quarterly* 39: 23-29.

Traill, Robert. 1810. *The Works of Robert Traill.* Edinburgh: J. Ogle; reprint, Edinburgh: The Banner of Truth Trust, 1975.

Twisse, William. 1653. *The Riches of God's Love Unto the Vessels of Mercy Consistent with His Absolute Hatred or Reprobation of the Objects of Wrath.* London: Thomas Robinson.

Vines, Richard. 1660. *Christ a Christian's Only Gain.* London: Thomas Johnson.

Vos, Geerhardus. 1956. *The Teaching of the Epistle to the Hebrews*, edited and re-written by Johannes G. Vos. Grand Rapids: Wm. B. Eerdmans.

———. 1980. *Redemptive History and Biblical Interpretation: The Shorter Writings of Geerhardus Vos*, edited by Richard B. Gaffin, Jr. Phillipsburg: Presbyterian and Reformed.

Vose, Godfrey N. 1963. "Profile of a Puritan." State University of Iowa, Ph.D. dissertation.

Wallace, Dewey D., Jr. 1965. "The Life and Thought of John Owen to 1660: A Study of the Significance of Calvinist Theology in English Puritanism." Princeton University, Ph.D. dissertation.

Warfield, Benjamin B. 1956. *Calvin and Augustine*, edited by Samuel G. Craig. Philadelphia: Presbyterian and Reformed.

———. 1970. *The Person and Work of Christ*, edited by Samuel G. Craig. Philadelphia: Presbyterian and Reformed.

———. 1991. *The Works of Benjamin B. Warfield.* Vol. 2, Christology and Criticism. Grand Rapids: Baker Book House.

Watts, Isaac. 1753. *The Works of Isaac Watts.* 6 vols. London: n.p.

Wells, David F. 1984. *The Person of Christ: A Biblical and Historical Analysis of the Incarnation.* Westchester, Ill.: Crossway Books.

Westminster Assembly. 1647 *The Confession of Faith.* Re-issued by The Publications Committee of the Free Presbyterian Church of Scotland, 1976.

Wilbur, Earl Morse. 1952. *A History of Unitarianism In Transylvania, England, and America.* Cambridge: Harvard University Press.

Willey, Basil. 1949. *The Seventeenth Century Background: Studies in the Thought of the Age in Relation to Poetry and Religion.* London: Chatto & Windus.

Willis, E. David. *Calvin's Catholic Christology: The Function of the so-called Extra-Calvinisticum in Calvin's Theology.* Leiden, 1966.

Won, Jonathon. 1989. "Communion With Christ: An Exposition and Comparison of the Doctrine of Union and Communion with Christ in Calvin and the English Puritans." Westminster Theological Seminary, Ph.D. Dissertation.

BIBLIOGRAPHY

I. Owen

A. Primary Literature

Owen, John. *The Death of Death in the Death of Christ: A Treatise in Which the Whole Controversy about Universal Redemption is Fully Discussed*.... Introductory Essay by James I. Packer. London: The Banner of Truth Trust, 1959.

_____. *An Exposition of the Epistle to the Hebrews*. Edited by William H. Goold. 7 vols.; reprinted from vols. 18-24 of the 1850-55 edition of *The Works of John Owen*, Grand Rapids: Baker Book House, 1980.

_____. *The Works of John Owen, D.D.* Edited by Thomas Russell. 21 vols.; London: for Richard Baynes, 1826.

_____. *The Works of John Owen, D.D.* Edited by William H. Goold. 24 vols.; London and Edinburgh: Johnson and Hunter, 1850-55.

_____. *The Works of John Owen, D.D.* Edited by William H. Goold. 16 vols.; London and Edinburgh: Johnson and Hunter, 1850-55; reprint, Edinburgh: The Banner of Truth Trust, 1965.

B. Secondary Literature

Asty, Robert. "Memoirs of the Life of Dr. Owen." In *A Complete Collection of the Sermons of the Reverend and Learned John Owen, D.D.* London: John Clark, 1721.

Baraclough, Peter. *John Owen, 1616-1683*. London: Independent Press, 1961.

Entwistle, T. R. "Some Aspects of John Owen's Doctrine of the Person and Work of Christ." In *Faith and a Good Conscience*. Papers read at the Puritan and Reformed Studies Conference, London, 1962.

Kirby, Reginald. *The Threefold Bond: "Of Communion with God the Father, the Son, and the Holy Ghost."* London: Marshall, Morgan & Scott, n.d.

"The Life of the Late Reverend and Learned John Owen, D.D." In *Seventeen Sermons of the Late Reverend and Learned John Owen, D.D.* London, n.p., 1720.

Lloyd-Jones David M. "John Owen on Schism." In *Diversity and Unity*. Papers read at the Puritan and Reformed Studies Conference, London, 1963.

Moffatt, James. *The Golden Book of John Owen.* London: Hodder and Stoughton, 1904.

_____. *The Life of Dr. Owen.* 1911.

Orme, William. *Memoirs of the Life, Writings, Religious Connections, of John Owen D.D.* London: T. Hamilton, 1820.

"Review of *The Works of John Owen*," edited by William H. Goold. Johnson and Hunter, London and Edinburgh. *Biblical Repository*, 1852.

Rigg, J. M. "Owen, John." *Dictionary of National Biography.* Edited by Leslie Stephen. Vol. XLII. London, 1896. 424-28.

Russell, Thomas, ed. *Memoirs of the Life and Writings of John Owen, D.D.* London: for Richard Baynes, 1826.

Williams, Edward. "Memoirs of the Life of John Owen, D.D." In *An Exposition of the Epistle to the Hebrews.* Boston: Samuel T. Armstrong, 1811.

Wood, Anthony. "Life of John Owen." In *Athanae Oxonienses. An Exact History of all the Writers and Bishops Who Have Had Their Education in the University of Oxford. To Which are Added the Fasti, or Annals of the Said University*, edited by Philip Bliss. London, 1820.

II. Primary Literature: Sixteenth - Eighteenth Centuries

Acontius. *The Devil's Cabinet council discovered.* Translated by John Goodwin, n.p., n.d.

Airay, Henry. *Lectures upon the whole Epistle of St Paul to the Philippians.* London, 1618.

Allen, Richard. *An Antidote against Heresy.* London, 1648.

Alsop, Vincent. *Anti-Sozze.* London, 1675.

Ambrose, Isaac. *Prima, Media, & Ultima: The First, Middle, and Last Things: in Three Treatises.* London, 1650, 1654, 1657.

Ames, William. *The Marrow of Theology.* Translated from the third Latin ed., 1629. Edited by John Eusden. Durham, N.C: The Labyrinth Press, 1968.

Andrewes, Lancelot. *The Works of Lancelot Andrewes.* Vol. 6, 11. (Library of Anglo-Catholic Theology). Edited by James Bliss. Oxford: John Henry Parker, 1852-1860.

Aretus, Benedictus. *A Short history of Valentinus Gentilis the tritheist.* Translated by Robert South. London, 1696.

Arminius, James. *The Works of James Arminius.* 3 vols., translated by William Nichols. London, 1825-1875.

Arnold, Nicholas. *Religio Sociniana refutata.* n.p., 1654.

_____. *Refutatio atheismi Sociniani a Jo. Bidello asserti.* Franeker: 1659.

Bibliography 533

The Articles of the Synod of Dort, and its Rejection of Errors: with the History of Events which made way for that Synod, as published by the Authority of the States-General; and the Documents confirming its decisions. Translated from the Latin, with Notes, Remarks, and References by Thomas Scott. Utica, 1831.

Ashwell, George. *De Socino et Socinianismo dissertatio.* n.p., 1680.

Austin, Benjamin. *Scripture manifestation of the equality of the Father, Sonne, and Holy Ghost, etc.* London, 1650.

Bagshaw, Edward. *Dissertationes duae anti-Socianae;* . . . n.p., 1657.

Ball, John. *A Treatise of the Covenant of Grace: wherein the graduall breakings out of Gospel-grace from Adam to Christ are clearly discovered.* London, 1645.

Barklay, Robert. *An Apology for the True Christian Divinity, Being an Explanation and Vindication of the Principles and doctrines of the People Called Quakers.* Philadelphia. n.d.

Baxter, Richard. *Catholick Theologie: Plain Pure Peaceable: for the Pacification of the Dogmatical Word Warriours.* London, 1675.

_____. *Treatise of Justifying Righteousness.* n.p., 1642.

_____. *Universal Redemption of Mankind by the Lord Jesus Christ.* London, 1694.

Baynes, Paul. *An Entire Commentary upon the Whole Epistle of the Apostle Paul to the Ephesians.* 1618.

Best, Paul. *Mysteries Discovered.* 1647.

Beza, Theodore. *De hypostatica duarum in Christo naturarum unione.* Geneva: 1579.

_____. *Tractationes theologicae.* 3 Vols. Geneva: 1570-1572.

_____. *In Historiam Passionis et Sepulturae Domini Nostri Jesu Christi, Homiliae Theodori Bezae, ex Gallicis latinae factae.* Geneva, 1592

_____. *Testamentum Novum, Sive Novum Foedus Iesu Christi, D.N. Cuius Graeco contestui respondent interpretationes duae: una, vetus: altera, Theodori Bexae, nunc quarto diligenter ab eo recognita.* Geneva, 1589

_____. *Propositions and Principles of Divinity Propounded and Disputed in the University of Geneva . . . under M. Theodore Beza and M. Antionie Favis.* Translated by John Penry. Edinburgh: 1593.

Biddle, John. *Dissertatio de pace, &c., or A Discourse touching the Peace & Concord of the Church. Wherin is eloquently and acutely argued, That not so much a bad Opinion, as a bad Life, excludes a Christian out of the Kingdom of Heaven, and that things necessary to be known for the atainment of salvation are very few and easie: and finally, that those, who pass amongst us under the name of Hereticks are notwithstanding to be tolerated.* London. 1653.

Braddock(s), John. *The doctrine of the Fathers and Schools considered: concerning the Article of a Trinity of Divine Persons.* London, 1695

Bull, George. *Brevis animadversions in tractatum Gilberti Clerke.* 1713.

Burnet, Gilbert. *Four discourses delivered to the clergy of . . . London.* Chiswell, 1694.

Bury, Arthur. *The Naked Gospel.* London 1690.

Cassaubon, M. *A discourse concerning Christ.* London, 1646.

Chewney, Nicholas. *Anti-Socinianism or a Brief Explication of some places of holy Scripture for the confutation of certain gross Errours and Socinian Heresies, lately published by William Pynchion, Gentleman, in a dialogue of his, called the Meritorious Price of our Redemption.* 1656.

Cheynel, Francis. *Theios, Divine Beares of Glorious Light; which expell the fogges of error, touching the Deity, Faith and Christian Ordinances. With a Cordial to heal the corasives which the ill potion prepared by Mr. John Fry hath engendered.* n.p., 1650.

_____. *Chillingworth novissima.* London, 1644.

Chillingworth, Wm. *Historical and Critical Account of the Life of Wm. Chillingworth.* n.p., 1725.

_____. *The Religion of Protestants.* n.p., n.d.

Clapham, Henoch. *Errour on the Right Hand.* n.p., 1608.

Clerke, Gilbert. *Ante-Nicenismus, sive testimonia patrum, qui scripserunt ante concilium Nicenum, unde colligi potest sensus ecclesiae catholicae, quoad articulum de Trinitate.* n.p., 1694.

Cloppenburg, Johannes. *Anti-Smalcius de divinitate Christi.* n.p., 1652.

Cotton, John. *Christ the Fountain of Life: or, Sundry choyce sermons on part of the fifth chapter of the first epistle of St. John.* Published according to order. London, Printed by Robert Ibbitson. 1561. New York: Arno Press, 1972.

Crell, Christopher. *Initium Evangellii S. Joannis Apostoli ex antiquitate ecclesiastica restitutum.* n.p., 1726.

Crell, Johannes. *Catechesis Ecclesiarum polonicarum.* n.p., n.d.

Crisp, Tobias. *Christ Alone Exalted.* London, 1643.

Cudworth, Ralph. *The True Intellectual System of the Universe, etc.: with A Treatise Concerning Eternal and Immutable Morality.* Edited by John Harrison. London, 1845.

Davenant, John. *Dissertationes Duae; Prima, de Morte Christi; Altera, de Praedestinatione et Electione. . . .* Cambridge, 1650.

_____. *An Exposition of the Epistle of St. Paul to the Colossians.* Translated by Josiah Allport, 2 volumes. London, 1831.

_____. *The Judgment of Bishop Davenant on the Controversy Among the*

French Divines of the Reformed Church concerning the Gracious and Saving will of God Towards Sinful Men. Cambridge, 1650.

Downame, John. *The Summe of Sacred Divinitie.* London: 1630

Du Moulin, Pierre. *A Treatise of the Knowledge of God.* London: 1634.

Eaton, Samuel. *The Mystery of God Incarnate.* n.p., 1650.

_____. *A Vindication or futher Confirmation of some other Scriptures produced to prove the divinity of Jesus Christ, distorted and miserably wrested and abused by Mr. John Knowles.* n.p., 1651.

Edwards, John. *The Socinian Creed.* n.p., 1697.

_____. *Socinianism Unmasked.* n.p., 1696.

Edwards, Jonathan. "Observations Concerning the Trinity and the Covenant of Redemption." In *Treatise On Grace & Other Writings.* Edited by Paul Helm. Cambridge: James Clarke & Co. Ltd., 1971.

Edwards, Thomas. *Gangreana.* n.p., n.d.

Episcopius, Simon. *Institutiones theologicae.* Lib.IV. Cap XXIII.

_____. "De generatione divina, quae est fundamentum subordinationis inter Patrem et Filium." *Opera.* Amsterdam: 1650.

Ferguson, Robert. *Justification only upon a Satisfaction or the Necessity & Verity of the Satisfaction of Christ as the alone ground of remission of sins, asserted and opened against the Socinians.* n.p., 1668.

Firmin, Giles. *The Real Christian.* London, 1670.

Fisher, Edward. *The Marrow of Modern Divinity.* n.p., originally published in 1644; reprint of a later edition, Swengel: Reiner Publications, 1978.

Fowler, Edward. *Principles and Practices of certain Moderate Divines of the Church of England abusively called Latitudinarians, &c., in a Free Discourse between two Intimate Friends.* n.p., 1670.

_____. *Certain propositions, by which the doctrine of the Holy Trinity is explained... as to speak it not contrary to natural reason.* n.p., 1694.

Fullwood, Grancis. *The Socinian contraversie touching the Son of God, reduced.* London. 1693.

Gailhard, Jean. *The blasphemous Socinian heresie disproved and confuted... with animadversions upon a late book called Christianity not mysterious humbly dedicated to both houses of Parliament.* London, 1655.

Gilbert, Thomas. *Vindiciae supremi Dei Dominii, cum Deo, initae sive Thesis aliquot... oppositae superae Doct. Audoeiu (John Owen). Diatribe. De justitia pecati.* London, 1655.

Gilpin, John. *The Quakers Shaken: or a Fire-brand snached out of the Fire &c.* n.p., 1653.

Gomarus, Franciscus. *Opera Theologica Omnia.* Amsterdam, 1664.

Goodwin, John. *Impedit Ira Animum or Animadversions upon some of the Looser and Fowler passages in Mr Walder's Discourse.* 1641.

_____. *Imputatio Fidei, or a Treatise on Justification.* n.p., 1642.

_____. *Redemption Redeemed.* n.p., 1651.

Gouge, Thomas. *The Principles of Christian Religion explained to the capacity of the meanest.* London, 1645.

Greenham, Richard. *The Works of the Reverend and Faithful Servant of Jesus Christ M. Richard Greenham.* Edited by Henry Holland. London: n.p., 1601.

Grigge, William. *The Quaker's Jesus.* n.p., 1658.

The Grounds and Occasions of the Controversy concerning the Unity of God, . . . By a Divine of the Church of England. n.p., 1698.

Guthrie, William. *The Christian's Great Interest.* n.p., 1658.

Hales, John. *Golden Remains of the Ever Memorable Mr. John Hales of Eton College.* London, 1659.

Hall, Joseph. *Works.* 10 vols. Edited by Philip Wynter. Oxford, 1863.

Hammond, Henry. *The Works of Henry Hammond.* (Library of Anglo-Catholic Theology). Edited by Nicholas Pocock. Oxford: John Henry Parker, 1847-1850.

Hedworth, Henry. *Controversy Ended, or the Sentence given by George Fox himself and Party in the persons of his Adversaries ratified and aggravated by W. Penn.* n.p., 1673.

_____. *The Spirit of the Quakers Tried, According to that discovery it hath made of itself in their great Prophet and Patriarch George Fox.* n.p., 1672.

Hobson, Paul. *A Discourse about the extent of Christ's death, and the nature and truth of Election.* n.p., 1655.

_____. *Fourteen Queries and ten Absurdities about the extent of Christ's Death, the powers of the creatures, the justice of God in condemning some, and saving others, presented by a Free-willer to the church of Christ at Newcastle and answered by Paul Hobson, a member of the said Church.* Durham, 1655.

Hodge, Thomas. *The Growth & Spreading of Heresie.* n.p., 1647.

Hoornbeek, Johannes. *Apparatus ad controversias Socinianas.* n.p., n.d.

Knoweles, John. *Answer to Mr. Ferguson's Book.* n.p., 1668.

_____. *The Freeness of God's Grace in the Forgiveness of Sins by Jesus Christ.* n.p., 1668.

_____. *A Friendly Debate on a Weighty Subject, or a Conference by writing betwixt Mr. Samuel Eaton and Mr. John Knowles Concerning the*

Divinity of Jesus Christ: For the beating out, and further clearing up of Truth. n.p., 1650.

Laud, William. *The Works of William Laud.* Vol. 1, 3, 6, 7. (Library of Anglo-Catholic Theology). Edited by James Bliss. Oxford: John Henry Parker, 1852-1860.

Lushington, Thomas. *The Expiation of a Sinner. In a Commentary upon the Epistle to the Hebrews.* n.p., 1646.

_____. *The Justification of a Sinner.* n.p., 1650.

Luther, Martin. *A Commentary on St. Paul's Epistle to the Galatians.* Translated by Philip S. Watson. Cambridge: James Clarke & Co. Ltd., 1953.

Maresius, Samuel. *Hydra Socinianismi expugnata.* n.p., 1651-62.

Martindale, Adam. *An Antidote against the Poyson of the Times.* n,p., 1653.

Milbourne, L. *Mysteries in Religion vindicated.* n.p., 1692.

Montague, Richard. *A Gag for the Gospel? No: a New Gagg for an Old Goose.* London, 1624.

More, Henry. "An Explanation of the Grand Mystery of Godliness," *Theological Works.* n.p., 1708.

Nayler, James. *This light within you will let you see your sinne.* n.p., n.d.

Nichols, William. *Answer to an Heretical Book Called the Naked Gospel... To Which is added a Short History of Socinianism.* n.p., 1691.

Norton, J. *A Discussion of that Great Point in Divinity, The Sufferings of Christ, &c.* n.p., 1653.

Nye, Stephen. *A Brief History of the Unitarians, commonly called Socinians.* n.p., 1691.

_____. *The Agreement of the Unitarians with the Catholick Church.* n.p., 1697.

_____. *Discourse concerning Natural and Revealed Religion.* n.p., 1696.

_____. *The Doctrine of the Holy Trinity and the Manner of our Saviour's Divinity.* n.p., n.d.

_____. *The Explication of the Articles of the Divine Unity, the Trinity, and Incarnation, commonluy received in the Catholic Church Asserted and Vindicated.* n.p., 1715.

_____. *Some Thoughts upon Dr. Sherlock's Vindication of the Doctrine of the Holy Trinity.* n.p., 1691

S. P. of Cambridge. *A Brief Account of the new Sect of Latitude–Men together with some reflections upon the New Philosophy.* n.p., 1662

Pagitt. *Heresiography.* n,p., 1645.

Pemble, William. *Vindicae Gratiae: A Plea for Grace.... wherein... the main sinews of Arminius are cut asunder.* London, 1629.

The Perfect Pharisee under Monkish Holiness opposing the Fundamental Principles of the Gospel and Scripture Practices of Gospel Worship manifesting himself in the Generation of men called Quakers. n.p., 1653.

Perkins, William. *The Workes of that Famous Minister of Christ and the University of Cambridge, Mr. William Perkins.* Cambridge, 1612-1619.

Porter, Edmund. *Theos Anthropos or God Incarnate.* n.p., 1655.

Powell, Vavasor. *Christ and Moses Excellency: Or Sin and Sinai's Glory being a triplex treatise, distinguishing and explaining the two Covenants, of the Gospel and the Law.* London, 1650

Preston, John. *The Fullness of Christ for Us.* n.p., 1640.

_____. *The Mystical Match Between Christ and the Church.* n.p., 1648.

_____. *Plentitudo fontis: or, Christ's fulness, and man's emptinesse.* London, 1645.

Pynchon, William. *A Further Discussion of that Great Point in Divinity, the Sufferings of Christ, and the Questions about his Righteousnesse, Active, Passive and the Imputation thereof.* n.p., 1655.

_____. *The Covenant of Nature made with Adam Described & Cleared from sundry great mistakes.* n.p., 1682.

_____. *The Meritorious Price of our Redemption.* n.p., 1650.

_____. *The Meritorious Price of Man's Redemption; or Christ's Satisfaction Discussed and Explained.* n.p., 1655.

Saltmarsh, John. *Sparkles of Glory, or, Some Beams of the Morning Star.* London, 1647.

Sedgwick, Obadiah. *The Nature and Danger of Heresies.* n.p., 1646.

Socinus, Faustus. *Christianismi Restitutio.* 1552.

_____. *De Jesu Christo servatore.* 1594

_____. *De officio hominis Christiani.* n.p., n.d.

Stegmann, Joachim. *Brevis disquisitio: or, A Brief Enquiry touching a Better Way than is commonly made use of, to refute Papists, and Reduce Protestants to certainty and Unity in Religion.* Translated by Biddle. London, 1653.

Taylor, Jeremy. *The Whole Works of the Right Rev. Jeremy Taylor, D.D.* 10 vols. Edited by Charles Page Eden. London: Longman, Green, Longman and Roberts, 1861.

A Third Collection of Tracts, proving the God and Father of our Lord Jesus Christ the only true God: A Reply to the Second Defence of the XXIII Propositions. n.p., 1695.

Thompson, Thomas. *The Quakers Quibbles, in three Parts.* 1675.

Tillotson, John. *Sermons Concerning the Divinity and Incarnation of our Blessed Saviour.* In *Tillotson's Works.* n.p., 1752.

Bibliography 539

Traill, Robert. *The Works of Robert Traill*. Edinburgh: T & A Constable Ltd., 1810; reprinted, Edinburgh: The Banner of Truth Trust, 1975.

Trelcatius. *A Brief Institution of the Commonplaces of Sacred Divinitie*. Translated by J. Gawen. London: 1610.

A Triumphing over Errour and Heresie. Or a relation of a Publike Disputation at Oxford in St. Maries Church, between Master Cheynell . . . and Master Erbury, the seeker & Socinian. n.p., 1647.

Turretin, Francis. *Institutio Theologiae Elencticae*. Geneva, 1688.

_____. *The Atonement of Christ*. Translated by James R. Willson. New York: Board of Publications of the Reformed Protestant Dutch Church, 1859.

Underhill, Thomas. *Hell Broke Loose: or an History of the Quakers Both Old and New*. &c. n.p., 1660.

Ussher, James. *A Body of Divinitie*. London, 1645.

Voetius, Gispertus. *Selectae Disputationes Theologicae*. Utrecht, 1648 - 1669.

Walker, G. *Socinianisme in the fundamentall point of Justification discovered and confuted*. n.p., 1641.

Watson, Thomas. *A Body of Divinity*. n.p., 1692; reprinted from 1890 edition, Edinburgh: The Banner of Truth Trust, 1958.

Whichcote, Benjamin. *Moral and Religious Aphorisms, Eight Letters of Dr. Anthony Tuckney and Dr. Benjamin Whichcote*. 1753.

Wren, Matthew. *Increpatio bar Jesus sive polemica adsertiones locorum aliquot s. scripturae ab imposturis perversiionum in catechese Racoviana, colectae hinc inde per Matthaeum Wren*. n.p. 1660.

Zanchius, H. *De Incarnatione. Lib I. Opera Theologicorum*. 8 vols. Geneva: 1617.

_____. *De Tribus Elohim*. n.p., n.d.

III. Secondary Literature: Reformation and Post-Reformation Era

Allen, Don Cameron. *The Legend of Noah: Renaissance Rationalism in Art, Science, and Letters*. Urbanna, Ill., 1949.

Baker, Herschel C. *The Wars of Truth: Studies in the Decay of Christian Humanism in the Earlier Seventeenth Century*. n.p., 1952.

Bangs, Carl. *Arminius: A Study in the Dutch Reformation*. Nashville, 1971.

Barbour, Hugh and Roberts, Arthur O. eds. *Early Quaker Writings 1650-1700*. 1973.

Barklay, R. *The Inner Life of the Religious Societies of the Commonwealth*. n.p., n.d.

Barclay, Robert. *An Apology for the True Christian Divinity, Being an*

Explanation and Vindication of the Principles and doctrines of the People Called Quakers. Philadelphia, n.d.

Beardslee, John W. III, editor. *Reformed Dogmatics.* Oxford: University Press, 1965; paperback reprint edition, Grand Rapids: Baker Book House, 1977.

Bizer, Ernst. *Fruhorthodoxie und Rationalismus.* Zurich, 1963.

Bonet-Maury, G. *Early Sources of English Unitarian Christianity.* n.p., 1884.

Braithwaite, W. C. *The Second Period of Quakerism.* n.p., 1919.

Byington, E. H. *The Puritan in England and New England.* n.p., 1896.

Clark, H. W. *History of English Non-conformity.* n.p., 1911.

Colie, Rosalie L. *Light and Enlightenment: A Study of the Cambridge Platonists and the Dutch Arminians.* Cambridge, 1957.

Cragg, G. R. *Puritanism in the Period of the Great Persecution, 1660-1688.* Cambridge: Cambridge University Press, 1957.

Dale, R. W. *History of English Congregationalism.* n.p., 1901.

De Pauley, W. C. *The Candle of the Lord: Studies in the Cambridge Platonists.* n.p., 1937.

Gardiner, Samuel R. *History of England from the Accession of James I to the Outbreak of the Civil War, 1603-1642.* London, 1895.

George, Edwin Augustus. *Seventeenth Century Men of Latitude.* New York, 1908.

Haller, William. *The Rise of Puritanism.* New York, 1938.

Harrison, A. W. *Arminianism.* London, 1937.

Harth, Philip. *Swift and Anglican Rationalism.* n.p., n.d.

Hoogland, Marvin P. *Calvin's Perspective on the Exaltation of Christ in Comparison with the Post-Reformation Doctrine of the Two States.* Kampen, 1966.

Knappen, Marshall M. *Tudor Puritanism.* Chicago, 1939.

Krogh-Tonning, Knud Karl. *Hugo Grotius und die Religioesen Bewegungen im Protestantismus seineer Zeit.* Koeln, 1904.

Lang, August. *Puritanismus und Pietismus.* Neukirchen, 1941.

Lecky, William E. H. *History of the Rise and Influence of the Spirit of Rationalism in Europe.* New York, 1873.

Lee, Umphrey. *The Historical Backgrounds of Early Methodist Enthusiasm.* n.p., 1931.

Lienhard, Marc. *Luther: Witness to Jesus Christ.* Translated by Edwin H. Robertson. Minneapolis: Augsburg Publishing House, 1982.

Marsden, J. B. *History of the Early Puritans.* n.p., 1850.

_____. *History of the Later Puritans.* n.p., 1852.

McAdoo, H. R. *The Spirit of Anglicanism.* n.p., n.d.

_____. *The Structure of Caroline Moral Theology.* n.p., 1949.

New, John F. H. *Anglican and Puritan: The Basis of Their Opposition, 1558-1640.* Stanford: Stanford University Press, 1964.

Nicole, Roger. "Moise Amyraut (1596-1644) and the Controversy on Universal Grace, First Phase (1634-1637)." Ph.D. Dissertation, Harvard University, 1966.

Niesel, Wilhelm. *The Theology of Calvin.* Translated by Harold Knight. London, Lutterworth Press, 1966; reprinted, Grand Rapids: Baker Book House, 1980.

Nobbs, Douglas. *Theocracy and Toleration; A Study of the Disputes in Dutch Calvinism from 1600-1650.* Cambridge, 1938.

Nuttall, Geoffrey F. *Studies in Christian Enthusiasm: Illustrated from Early Quakerism.* n.p., n.d.

Oberman, Heiko A. "Simul gemitus et raptus: Luther und die Mystik." In *Kirche, Mystik, Heilung und das Naturlische bei Luther. Vortrage des Dritten Internationalen Kongresses fur Lutherforschung.* Gottingen: Vandenhoeck & Ruprecht, 1967.

Orr, Robert R. *Reason and Authority: The Thought of Wm. Chillingworth.* Oxford, 1967.

Pawson, G. P. H. *The Cambridge Platonists and Their Place in Religious Thought.* London, 1930.

Raven, Charles E. *Natural Religion and Christian Theology.* Cambridge, 1953.

Ritschl, Otto. *Dogmengeschichte des Protestantismus.* Goettingen, 1926-1927.

Ryan, John Kenneth. *The Reputation of St. Thomas Aquinas among English Protestant Thinkers of the Seventeenth Century.* Washington, 1948.

Sandius, C. C. *Bibliotheca anti-trinitariorum.* n.p., 1684.

Stoughton, John. *History of Religion in England (1640-1850).* n.p., 1881.

Taylor, J. J. *A Retrospect of the Religious Life of England.* n.p., 1876.

Toon, Peter. *The Emergence of Hyper-Calvinism in English Nonconformity. 1689-1765.* London: The Olive Tree, 1967.

Wallace, R. *Antitrinitarian Biography.* n.p., 1850.

Webb, Clement C. J. *Studies in the History of Natural Theology.* Oxford, 1915.

Weber, Hans Emil. *Reformation, Orthodoxie, und Rationalismus.* 2 vols. Darmstadt, 1966.

Weber, Otto. *Foundations of Dogmatics*. 2 Vols. Translated and annotated by Darrell L. Guder. Grand Rapids: Wm. B. Eerdmans, 1983.

Westfall, Richard S. *Science and Religion in Seventeenth-Century England*. n.p., 1958.

Whiting, Charles E. *Studies in English Puritanism from the Restoration to the Revolution, 1660-1688*. n.p., 1931.

Wiley, Margaret L., *The Subtle Knot: Creative Skepticism in Seventeenth Century England*. Cambridge, Mass. 1952.

Wolf, Abraham A. *A History of Science, Technology, and Philosophy in the XVIth and XVIIth Centuries*. 2d ed. London, 1950.

V. General Works on Christology: Exegetical and Historical

Aldwincle, Russel F. *More Than Man: A Study of Christology*. Grand Rapids: Wm. B. Eerdmans, 1976.

Anderson, Norman. *The Mystery of the Incarnation*. Downers Grove: Inter-Varsity Press, 1978.

Athanasius. *Contra Gentes and De Incarnatione*. Edited and translated by Robert W. Thomson. Oxford: Clarendon Press, 1967.

Aulen, Gustav. *Christus Victor: An Historical Study of the Three Main Types of the Idea of the Atonement*. Translated by A. C. Herbert. New York: Macmillan, 1964.

Baillie, Donald M. *God Was In Christ: An Essay on Incarnation and Atonement*. 2d ed. New York: Charles Scribner's Sons, 1956.

Barth, Karl. *Church Dogmatics*. 5 vols. Edited and translated by Geoffrey W. Bromley and Thomas F. Torrance, et al. Edinburgh: T. & T. Clark, 1936-77.

Bentzen, A. *King and Messiah*. Lutterworth, 1955.

Berkouwer, G. C. *Studies in Dogmatics: The Person of Christ*. Grand Rapids: Wm. B. Eerdmans, 1954.

_____. *Studies in Dogmatics: The Work of Christ*. Grand Rapids: Wm. B. Eerdmans, 1965.

Bernard of Clairvaux. *On the Song of Songs I. The Works of Bernard Clairvaux*. Vol. 2. Shannon, Ireland: Irish University Press, 1971.

Bousset, Wilhelm. *Kyrios Christos: A History of the Belief in Christ from the Beginnings of Christianity to Irenaeus*. Translated by J. H. Steely. Nashville: Abingdon, 1970.

Bruce, Alexander B. *The Humiliation of Christ in Its Physical, Ethical and Official Aspects*. 2d ed. New York: Geroge H. Doran, 1881.

Brunner, Emil. *The Christian Doctrine of Creation and Redemption*. Translated by Olive Wyon. Philadelphia: The Westminster Press, 1952.

———. *The Mediator: a Study of the Central Doctrine of the Christian Faith.* Translated by Olive Wyon. Philadelphia: The Westminster Press, 1947.

Casey, M. *Son of Man: The Interpretation and Influence of Daniel 7.* SPCK. 1979.

Cave, Sidney. *The Doctrine of the Person of Christ.* London, 1925.

Craddock, Fred B. *The Pre-existence of Christ in the New Testament.* Nashville: n.p., 1968.

Cullman, Oscar. *The Christology of the New Testament.* 2d ed. Translated by S. C. Guthrie and C. A. M. Hall. Philadelphia: Westminster, 1980.

Dawe, Donald G. *The Form of a Servant: A Historical Analysis of the Kenotic Motif.* Philadelphia: Westminster, 1958.

Denney, James. *The Christian Doctrine of Reconciliation.* London: Hodder & Stoughton, 1917.

Dorner, Isaak A. *History of the Development of the Doctrine of the Person of Christ.* 5 vols. Translated by William L. Alexander and D. W. Simon. Edinburgh: T. & T. Clark, 1861-72.

Dunn, James D. G. *Christology in the Making: A New Testament Inquiry into the Origins of the Doctrine of the Incarnation.* Philadelphia: Westminster, 1980.

Ellison, H. L. *The Servant of Jehovah.* London, 1953.

Fairbairn, A. M. *The Place of Christ in Modern Theology.* New York: Charles Scribner's Sons, 1903.

Forsyth, P. T. *The Cruciality of the Cross.* London, 1910.

———. *The Person and Place of Jesus Christ.* 5th ed. London: Independent Press, 1946.

———. *The Work of Christ.* London, 1910.

France, R. T. *Jesus and the Old Testament: His Application of Old Testament Passages to Himself and to His Mission.* Downers Grove: Inter-Varsity Press, 1971.

Franklin, E. *Christ the Lord.* London: S.P.C.K. 1975.

Fraser, J. W. *Jesus and Paul: Paul as Interpreter of Jesus from Harnack to Kummel.* Nashville: Abingdon, 1974.

Frend, W. H. C. *The Rise of the Monophysite Movement: Chapters in the History of the Church in the Fifth and Sixth Centuries.* Cambridge: University Press, 1972.

Fuller, R. H. *The Foundations of New Testament Christology.* Collins, 1965.

Gaffin, Richard B., Jr. *The Centrality of the Resurrection: A Study in Paul's Soteriology.* Grand Rapids: Wm. B. Eerdmans, 1978.

Gasque, W. Ward, and Martin, Ralph P., eds. *Apostolic History and the Gospel*. Grand Rapids: Wm. B. Eerdmans, 1970.

Gore, Charles. *Dissertations on Subjects Connected with the Incarnation*. New York: Charles Scribner's Sons, 1895.

_____. *The Incarnation of the Son of God: Being the Bampton Lectures for the Year 1891*. New York: Charles Scribner's Sons, 1891.

Greer, Rowan A. *The Captain of Our Salvation: A Study in the Patristic Exegesis of Hebrews*. Tubingen: J. C. B. Mohr, 1973.

Green, Michael, ed. *The Truth of God Incarnate*. Grand Rapids: Wm. B. Eerdmans, 1977.

Goulder, Michael, ed. *Incarnation and Myth: The Debate Continues*. Grand Rapids: Wm. B. Eerdmans, 1979.

Grillmeier, Aloys. *Christ in Christian Tradition*. Atlanta: John Knox Press, 1975.

Gruenler, Royce Gordon. *New Approaches to Jesus and the Gospels: A Phenomenological & Exegetical Study of Synoptic Christology*. Grand Rapids: Baker Book House, 1982.

Hahn, Ferdinand. *The Titles of Jesus in Christology: Their History in Early Christianity*. Translated by H. Knight and G. Ogg. London: Lutterworth, 1969.

Hanson, Anthony T. *Grace and Truth: A Study in the Doctrine of the Incarnation*. London, 1975.

Hardy, Edward R., ed. *Christology of the Later Fathers*. Library of Christian Classics, 3. Philadelphia: Westminster, 1954.

Harner, Philip B. *The "I Am" of the Fourth Gospel*. Facet Books, Biblical Series, 26. Philadelphia: Fortress, 1970.

Hasel, Gerhard F. *New Testament Theology: Basic Issues in the Current Debate*. Grand Rapids: Wm. B. Eerdmans, 1978.

Hawthorne, Gerald F. ed. *Current Issues in Biblical and Patristic Interpretation*. Grand Rapids, Wm. B. Eerdmans, 1975.

Hay, D. M. *Glory at the Right Hand: Psalm 110 in Early Christianity*. SCM. 1970.

Hick, John, ed. *The Myth of God Incarnate*. Philadelphia: Westminster, 1977.

Hodge, Archibald Alexander. *The Atonement*. Philadelphia: Presbyterian Board of Publication, 1867.

Hoogland, Marvin P. *Calvin's Perspective on the Exaltation of Christ in Comparison with the Post-Reformation Doctrine of the Two States*. Kampen, 1966.

Hooker, Morna. *Jesus and the Servant*. London: S.P.C.K. 1979.

Bibliography 545

Hughes, Graham. *Hebrews and Hermeneutics: The Epistle of Hebrews as a New Testament Example of Biblical Interpretation.* Cambridge: Cambridge University Press, 1979.

Jeremias, Joachim. *The Central Message of the New Testament.* London: 1965.

Johnson, Dennis Edward. "Immutability and Incarnation: An Historical and Theological Study of the concepts of Christ's Divine Unchangeability and His Human Development." Fuller Theological Seminary, Ph.D. Dissertation, 1984.

Kelly, J. N. D. *Early Christian Doctrines.* San Francisco: Harper & Row, 1960.

Kingsburry, Jack Dean. *Matthew: Structure, Christology, Kingdom.* Fortress. 1975.

Knox, John. *The Humanity and Divinity of Christ: A Study of Patterns in Christology.* Cambridge: University Press, 1967.

Kramer, Werner R. *Christ, Lord, Son of God.* Translated by Brian Hardy. Studies in Biblical Theology, 50. Naperville: Alec R. Allenson, 1966.

Lawton, John S. *Conflict in Christology: A Study of British and American Christology, From 1889-1914.* London: S. P. C. K., 1947.

Lindars, Barnabas, and Smalley, Stephen S., eds. *Christ and Spirit in the New Testament: In Honour of Charles Francis Digby Moule.* Cambridge: University Press, 1973.

Little, V. A. Spence. *The Christology of the Apologists: Doctrinal.* New York: Charles Scribner's Sons, 1935.

Loofs, Friedrich. *Nestorius and His Place in the History of Christian Doctrine.* Cambridge: University Press, 1914.

Lindars, Barnabas. "The Son of Man in the Johannine Christology." *Christ and Spirit in the New Testament.* Edited by B. Lindars and S. S. Smally. Cambridge University Press. 1973.

Machen, J. Gresham. *The Virgin Birth of Christ.* New York: Harper, 1932.

Mackintosh, H. R. *The Doctrine of the Person of Jesus Christ.* 3rd ed. Edinburgh: T. & T. Clark, 1913.

Marshall, I Howard. *The Origins of New Testament Christology.* Downers Grove: Inter-Varsity, 1977.

Martin, Ralph P. *Carmen Christi: Philippians ii. 5-11 in Recent Interpretation and in the Setting of Early Christian Worship.* 2d ed. Grand Rapids: Wm. B. Eerdmans, 1983.

Mascall, E. L. *Theology and the Gospel of Christ: An Essay in Reorientation.* London: S.P.C.K., 1977.

Morris, Leon. *The Apostolic Preaching of the Cross*. Grand Rapids: Wm. B. Eerdmans, 1956.

Myendorff, John. *Christ in Eastern Thought*. Crestwood, New York: St. Vladimir's Seminary Press, 1975.

Moule, C. F. D. *The Origin of New Testament Christology*. Cambridge: University Press, 1977.

Mozley, J. K. *The Impassibility of God: A Survey of Christian Thought*. Cambridge: University Press, 1926.

Nolan, Brian M. *The Royal Son of God: The Christology of Matthew 1-2 in the Setting of the Gospel*. Vandenhoeck & Ruprecht, 1979.

Ottley, Robert L. *The Doctrine of the Incarnation*. 2 vols. London: Methsien, 1896.

Pannenberg, Wolfhart. *Jesus—God and Man*. 2d ed. Translated by L. L. Wilkins and Duane A. Priebe. Philadelphia: Westminster 1977.

Pittenger, W. Norman. *Christology Reconsidered*. London: S.C.M., 1970.

_____. *The Word Incarnate: A Study of the Doctrine of the Person of Christ*. Digswell Place: James Nisbet, 1959.

_____. *Christ for Us Today*. London, 1968.

Raven, Charles. *Apollinarianism: An Essay on the Christology of the Early Church*. Cambridge: University Press, 1923. Reprint ed., London: AMS Press, 1978.

Realton, H. Maurice. *A Study in Christology: The Problem of the Relation of the Two Natures in the Person of Christ*. London: S.P.C.K., 1934.

Ringgren, H. *The Messiah in the Old Testament*. London: S.C.M., 1956.

Robertson, O. Palmer. *The Christ of the Covenants*. Phillipsburg: Presbyterian and Reformed, 1980.

Robinson, H. Wheeler. *The Cross in the Old Testament*. London, 1955.

Rowden, Harold H., ed. *Christ the Lord: Studies in Christology Presented to Donald Guthrie*. Downers Grove: Inter-Varsity Press, 1982.

Schillebeeckx, Edward. *Jesus: An Experiment in Christology*. Translated by Hubert Hoskins. New York: Seabury, 1979.

Scroggs, Robin. *The Last Adam: A Study in Pauline Anthropology*. London: Basil Blackwell, 1966.

Sellers, Robert V. *Two Ancient Christologies: A Study in the Christological Thought of the Schools of Alexandria and Antioch in the Early Histrory of Christian Doctrine*. London: S.P.C.K., 1954.

_____. *The Council of Chalcedon: A Historical and Doctrinal Survey*. London: S. P. C. K., 1953.

Smeaton, George. *The Atonement According to Chirst and the Apostles*.

Spring, Gardiner. *The Attraction of the Cross*. Edinburgh: Banner of Truth, 1983.

Stanley, David M. *Christ's Resurrection in Pauline Soteriology*. Rome: Pontifical Biblical Institute, 1961.

Stibbs, A. M. *The Meaning of the Word 'Blood' in Scripture*. London, 1947.

Stonehouse, Ned B. *The Witness of the Synoptic Gospels to Christ: One Volume Combining the Witness of Matthew and Mark to Christ and the Witness of Luke to Christ*. Grand Rapids: Baker, 1979.

Strack, Hermann L., and Billerbeck, Paul. *Kommentar zum Neuen Testament aus Talmud und Midrasch*. 6 vols. Munich: C. H. Beck, 1922-61.

Sykes, S. W., and Clayton, J. P., eds. *Christ, Faith and History: Cambridge Studies in Christology*. Cambridge: University Press, 1972.

Taylor, Vincent. *The Person of Christ in New Testament Teaching*. London: Macmillan, 1958.

Trethowan, Illtyd. *The Absolute and the Atonement*. London: George Allen and Unwin, 1971.

Van Til, Cornelius. *Christianity and Barthianism*. Phillipsburg, N.J.: Presbyterian and Reformed, 1977.

Wagner, James B. "*Ascendit ad Coelos:* The Doctrine of the Ascension in the Reformed and Lutheran Theology of the Period of Orthodoxy." Th. D. Dissertation, University of Basel, 1960.

Warfield, Bengamin B. *The Saviour of the World*. London: Hodder & Stoughton, 1913.

_____. *Christology and Criticism*. Volume 2 of *The Works of Benjamin B. Warfield*, 10 Volumes. New York: Oxford University Press, 1929; reprinted Grand Rapids: Baker Book House, 1991.

Weber, Otto. *Foundations of Dogmatics*. 2 vols. Translated and annotated by Darrell L. Guder. Grand Rapids: Wm. B. Eerdmans, 1983.

VI. Periodical Literature

Bacon, B. W. "Hebrews 1.10-12 and the Septuagint Rendering of Ps. 102.23." *Zeitschrift fur die Neutestamentliche Wissenshaft* 3 (1902):280-85.

Brooks, W. E. "Perpetuity of Christ's Sacrifice in the Epistle to the Hebrews." *Journal of Biblical Literature* 89 (1970): 201-14.

Caird, G. B. "The Exegetical Method of the Epistle to the Hebrews." *Canadian Journal of Theology* 5 (1959): 44-51.

Campbell, J. C. "In a Son: The doctrine of Incarnation in the Epistle to the Hebrews." *Interpretation* 10 (1956):24-38.

Clarke, F. Stuart. "Christocentric developments in the Reformed doctrine of predestination." *Churchman* 98, No. 3 (1984): 229-45.

Dawe, Donald. "Christology in Contemporary Systematic Theology. *Interpretation* XXVI, No. 3 (July 1972).

DeJonge, Henk J. "Sonship, Wisdom, Infancy: Luke ii. 41-51a." *New Testament Studies* 24 (1977-78): 317-354.

Dunn, James D. G. "2 Corinthians III. 17—'The Lord Is the Spirit.'" *Journal of Theological Studies*, new series, 21 (1970):307-20.

_____. "Jesus—Flesh and Spirit: An Exposition of Romans 1.3-4." *Journal of Theological Studies*, new series, 24(1973): 40-68.

Glasson, T. F. "Plurality of Divine Persons and the Quotations in Hebrews 1, 6ff." *New Testament Studies* 12(1966):270-72.

Harvey John. "A New Look at the Christ Hymn in Philippians 2:6-11." *Expository Times* 76 (1965):337-39.

Hoekema, A. A. "Perfection of Christ in Hebrews." *Calvin Theological Journal* 9 (1974):31-37.

Hooke, S. H. "The Translation of Romans 1:4." *New Testament Studies* 9 (1962): 370-71.

Hoover, Roy W. "The Harpagmos Dilemma: A Philological Solution." *Harvard Theological Review* 64 (1971):95-119.

O'Higgins, J. "Archbishop Tillotson and the Religion of Nature." *Journal of Theological Studies* 24 (Apr. 1973): 123-42.

Reedy, Gerhard. "John Toland, and the Anglican rationalists." *Harvard Theological Review* 70, July-Oct. (1977): 285-304.

Shantz, Douglas H. "The place of the resurrected Christ in the writings of John Smyth." *Baptist Quarterly* 30, January (1984): 199-203, 247-64.

Tylenda, Joseph. "Christ the Mediator: Calvin versus Stancaro." *Calvin Theological Journal* VII (1973): 5-16, 131-37.

www.ingramcontent.com/pod-product-compliance
Lightning Source LLC
Chambersburg PA
CBHW021050080526
44587CB00010B/192